PARTY SPIRIT IN A
FRONTIER REPUBLIC

Democratic Politics in Ohio
1793–1821

Donald J. Ratcliffe

OHIO STATE UNIVERSITY PRESS • COLUMBUS

Copyright © 1998 by The Ohio State University. All rights reserved.

Library of Congress Cataloging-in-Publication Data

Ratcliffe, Donald J. (Donald John), 1942–

Party spirit in a frontier republic : democratic politics in Ohio,
1793–1821 / Donald J. Ratcliffe.

p. cm.

Includes bibliographical references and index.

ISBN 0-8142-0775-8 (cloth : alk. paper). —

ISBN 0-8142-0776-6 (pbk. : alk. paper)

1. Political parties—Ohio—History.   2. Ohio—Politics and
government—1787–1865.   I. Title.

JK2295.O3R38   1998

324.2771′009′034—dc21   98-23575

CIP

Text and jacket design by Paula Newcomb.
Type set in Adobe Minion by Keystone Typesetting, Inc.
Printed by Braun-Brumfield, Inc.

The paper used in this publication meets the minimum requirements of the
American National Standard for Information Sciences—Permanence of Paper
for Printed Library Materials.

ANSI Z39.48–1992.

9 8 7 6 5 4 3 2 1

FOR RUTH

Contents

MAPS

PREFACE

This book will be dismissed, I have no doubt, as "old-fashioned political history." On the whole I agree: it is about political contests, about electoral trends, about the ways in which electoral competition became structured in the early years of the republic. As such, it is deeply unfashionable. But "old-fashioned" implies that there is a new and no doubt superior fashion in political history—which I would deny for this period. Of course, since the 1960s the "new political history" has endeavored to use social science concepts and statistical techniques to bring a deeper understanding to the history of American politics and elections, but they are difficult to apply before the 1830s, not least because we lack appropriate data. Instead, recent historians have looked elsewhere for the key to the politics of the early republic.

The fashionable approach to the period has involved deciphering contemporary "political culture," commonly set in the context of power relationships. This body of work has undeniably produced many insights into the political outlook and social realities of the time, and I have learned much from it. But what recent historians have written is cultural and social history, not political history, not the history of how politics actually worked, and for me their writings do not answer the sort of questions I am asking in this book.[1]

Indeed, often it seems that historians of political culture assume that, once cultural attitudes are understood, it is unnecessary to investigate what actually happened in politics because behavior is the result of values, perceptions, and attitudes. Therefore political parties—in any meaningful sense of the word—cannot have existed during the Jeffersonian era simply because that generation believed that parties were evil, corrupting, and to be avoided at all costs. As Lee Benson has written, "Until the idea exists that parties are legitimate, . . . it seems to me hopelessly anachronistic to call the partisan associations anything but factions organized around temporary issues."[2] But is it anachronistic if the historical evidence shows that the actual way in which the partisan associations were structured, the way they influenced the conduct of politics, the way in which the loyalties they generated persisted over time, all fit the most rigorous definition of parties that historians of other periods have used? A close study of party development in Ohio suggests that men reluctantly began to operate in parties even as their belief systems told them that there was something improper about parties, and it was their experience of partisan behavior that induced some of them to begin erecting intellectual justifications of partisan modes of behavior. And both that behavior and the cultural adjustment began rather earlier than most historians have been wont to acknowledge.

Fundamentally this book does not attempt to contradict the understandings generated by historians of political culture. Instead it focuses on electoral process, on change and regularity in behavior, on constitutional and political structures, on grassroots support, and on the social, cultural, and economic environment within which the activists operated. It may find occasions when ideological statements look slightly different once the detailed context and momentary political realities are unlayered. It certainly suggests that the political formations of the period changed in character and outlook over time, even if the names remained the same; as a result, generalizations based on analyses of the Federalist era or even of the Jeffersonian regime cannot accurately be applied to the much-neglected but highly significant partisan formations of the 1810s. Certainly we cannot appreciate the true nature of the political contests of the early republic and the long-term significance of its political experience if we do not give more attention to the confusing contests of the Era of Good Feelings than they have customarily received.

One overwhelming danger stalks a study like this: the danger of finding scattered examples of partisan activity and piecing them together in a way that misrepresents the period. This pitfall menaces those in particular who, like me, approach this period from the Jacksonian era. However, my original intent was not to discover the origins of later partisanship but to establish what was new about Jacksonian Democracy. My aim has always been to discover differences as much as precedents and origins. In fact, what I discovered was that it is a mistake to make overly nice distinctions between the elitism of the early 1800s and the democracy of the Jacksonian period; indeed, only when the fundamental similarities in the political pressures generated by the constitutional system are appreciated does it become possible to decipher the distinctively different driving forces of each period.

Some small portions of this book have appeared in different guises in various journals. For permission to use some of that material here I am grateful to the

Society for Historians of the Early Republic for "Voter Turnout in Early Ohio," which originally appeared in the *Journal of the Early Republic* in 1987, and to the Ohio Historical Society for three pieces from *Ohio History,* entitled "Captain James Riley and Antislavery Sentiment in Ohio, 1819–1824" (1972), "The Autobiography of Benjamin Tappan" (1976), and "The Experience of Revolution and the Beginnings of Party Politics in Ohio, 1776–1816" (1976).

Any book as long in the making as this one inevitably owes much to the kindness of so many people and institutions that it is impossible to mention them all. The University of California at Berkeley gave me my first opportunity to confront real American history, and Charles Sellers played a critical role in crystallizing my interest in American political history. The American Council of Learned Societies gave me the opportunity to spend a year investigating Jacksonian politics in both Washington and Ohio repositories, during which time I first sensed that nothing could be usefully said about the subject without first clarifying the nature of Jeffersonian politics. The Department of History at Ohio State University subsequently employed me for a year as a visiting associate professor and has continued to assist me in many small ways. I am deeply grateful to successive chairmen—Harry Coles, Marvin Zahniser, Gary Reichard, Warren Van Tine, Joseph Lynch, and Michael Hogan—for their many kindnesses. The American Antiquarian Society awarded me a short-term fellowship for a somewhat different project and did not object when I found in its rich collections materials relating to Ohio which transformed my view of this subject—and delayed completion significantly. Various people and institutions have helped me build research trips around conference offerings in the United States, notably at one stage the British Association for American Studies, and I am especially grateful to Peter Onuf and Drew Cayton for inviting me to the bicentennial celebration of the Northwest Ordinance in Bloomington, Indiana, in 1987 and the associated research colloquium on the historiography of the Old Northwest. The British Academy has financed three brief research trips, while the University of Durham has given steady and (under the circumstances) generous support to my research. The University's Cartographic Unit has produced the maps, with the financial assistance of the University Publications Board, and the University Library's interlibrary loan staff have serviced without grumble one they have come to call "the Cincinnati kid."

Over the years the staffs of many libraries, in both Britain and the United States, have proved almost uniformly helpful and courteous, with some notable exceptions at the Library of Congress. The staff of the American Antiquarian Society proved a constant source of ideas and reference and friendliness, and I am especially grateful to Phillip Lampi for allowing me to study and use his growing collection of election data for this period. The staff of the Ohio Historical Society have never failed to be helpful, despite sometimes seeing too much of me for, admittedly, usually fairly brief periods, and none more so over the years than Conrad Weitzel, William Myers, Stephen Gutgesell, and especially Gary Arnold. I have benefited considerably from the assistance of the staffs of the Western Reserve Historical Society in Cleveland (especially Ann Sindelar), the Cincinnati Historical Society, the Dawes Memorial Library at Marietta College, and the local government records depositories at Wright State University at Dayton, Ohio University at Athens, and Cincinnati University. The few county historical societies I have been able to use have been unfailingly helpful and hospitable, and I am grateful to Mrs. Margaret Ford at the Geauga County Historical Society, Eric Cardinal at Lake Historical Society, and—above all— William Nolan, who made my work at the Ross County Historical Society in Chillicothe an absolute delight.

A stimulating and hospitable home for research has been provided for me in Columbus by innumerable people. Generations of editors of *Ohio History* have given generous and expert advice, as more recently have Chris Duckworth and James Richards of *Timeline*. Amos Loveday has shared his intimate knowledge of the infrastructure of Ohio history. Two former students at OSU, Marley Greiner and Stephen George, have given generous help and the advantage of their local expertise. Much encouragement and helpful comment have come from Ken Andrien, Michael Les Benedict, Mansell Blackford, Paul Bowers, John Burnham, Merton Dillon, Richard Hopkins, Austin Kerr, and Randolph Roth. The late Harry Coles was a supportive friend who made a year in Columbus possible by agreeing to a teaching exchange. Robert and Kay Bremner have been equally generous, kind in so many practical ways. Above all, I am grateful to the Bremners, to Robert and Lee Mills, to Martha Garland and Robert Davis, and especially to Austin and Rita Kerr, for providing accommodation and hospitality. There is a strong case for dedicating this book to their various children who gave up bedrooms so that a struggling British researcher could be given shelter.

I am especially grateful to William Brock and Peter Parish and W. R. Ward for their thoughtful suggestions concerning my work and to Howell John Harris for his constructive criticism, practical help, and stimulating daily conversation. Finally I must record what I owe to my wife—who has constantly forced me to explain to myself the point of it all—and to my children, who have managed to interrupt the writing of even this last sentence.

Party and Democracy in a Frontier Republic

In November 1815 the travels of Dr. John Cotton, a lineal descendant of the famous seventeenth-century Boston minister, brought him to the new town being carved out of the forest to serve as Ohio's permanent capital. The general assembly had selected the empty site on the Scioto River only three years before, yet already Columbus contained two hundred houses and seven hundred inhabitants. Inevitably, the streets were still "filled up with stumps" and the houses small and scattered. In the fastidious doctor's opinion, the settlers, "collected from every quarter," made "not very agreeable companions." Cotton was more impressed by the "elegant State House" currently being constructed of brick and finished with white marble. But, as a firm Federalist, he thought that the inscription carved on a marble slab above the west door was "truly ridiculous": the lines came from Joel Barlow's ambitious Jeffersonian poem of 1807, *The Columbiad,* and held forth "the detestable principles of the French Revolution."[1]

The contemptuous Dr. Cotton knew only half the story. After the inscription had been carved, the director of the building work, William Ludlow of Cincinnati, noticed that Barlow's lines included a reference to the "FEDERAL BAND," meaning the ties of the federal Union. As "a Democrat of the old school," Ludlow feared that some people might think this phrase a public sanctification of the much-loathed Federalist party, and so he ordered the offending word "FEDERAL" to be filled in and the word "UNION" cut over it. In later years—sometime before the statehouse was accidently burned down by excessively convivial local firemen in 1852—the filling fell out, thus restoring the "FEDERAL BAND" of Barlow's poem.[2]

Earlier on his tour, Dr. Cotton had visited Zanesville, which had itself served as the state capital for two controversial years, 1810–12. The town had grown up where the old pioneer trail called Zane's Trace—running from the

Ohio River opposite Wheeling, in western Virginia, to the Ohio River opposite Maysville, Kentucky—had crossed the Muskingum River, some eighty miles upstream from Marietta, Ohio's first town. Although Zanesville was "yet small," Cotton thought it "very flourishing" and its people "very active and busy and remarkable for enterprise." Here, too, the settlers were mixed in origin, with a goodly number of Irish and Germans. Politically, Zanesville was another center of Democratic Republicanism.

Across the Muskingum from Zanesville lay the even smaller but "pleasant" town of Springfield, which had just changed its name to Putnam. The new name honored Rufus Putnam, the Revolutionary hero who had led the first party of settlers from New England to Ohio and founded Marietta in 1788. The settlers of Springfield-Putnam were principally New Englanders and as firmly Federalist in politics as General Putnam himself or, indeed, Dr. Cotton. As such, they frequently came into conflict with their neighbors in Zanesville: gangs of boys frequently stoned each other and waged fistfights, while the rival politicians struggled for public office and even for control of the new Bank of Muskingum.[3]

The antagonism had climaxed three months before Dr. Cotton's visit. On the Fourth of July, each party had held its own celebration on the appropriate bank of the river. The Republicans in Zanesville began to fire military salutes with a cannon. But, having had too much to drink, they decided to load the cannon with rocks and fire it at the rival celebration across the river. Luckily, no one was hit. The Federalist newspaper responded by making political capital out of the incident, claiming it was the natural fulfillment of Democratic oratory, which always appealed to popular passions and encouraged irresponsible behavior, regardless of the laws and standards of a truly republican society.[4]

Such examples could be multiplied almost endlessly to demonstrate the intensity of party spirit during the presidencies of Thomas Jefferson and James Madison. The bitter fight between Federalists and Democratic Republicans that had broken out across the nation in the 1790s continued to mark political life for nigh on twenty years in many states besides Ohio, and the Jeffersonian Republicans, in particular, had begun to develop novel and effective partisan organizations. But in what sense can these formations be called "parties"? Parties such as those established by the early 1840s? Parties capable of dominating the operation of American politics? Parties capable of generating, and deriving their strength from, persisting partisan loyalties among the electorate?

In the 1960s a number of distinguished historians and political scientists, notably William Nesbit Chambers, described the national parties of the years after 1795 as distinctly modern in comparison with the factional alignments typical of the eighteenth century. David Hackett Fischer argued that, between 1805 and 1812, these parties continued to develop in organizational sophistication and campaigning techniques until they behaved remarkably like the popularly based parties of thirty years later. Out of the many works emphasizing the innovatory character of these early parties developed the concept of a "First Party System," comparable to the later systems of partisan electoral conflict that historians and political scientists have seen marking American politics since the Age of Jackson—notably, the Second Party System of 1838–52 and the Third Party System of 1856–92.[5]

Other historians, however, have been skeptical about the existence of this First Party System, believing that the concept involves "a backward projection of modern party systems" into a period to which they were alien. Like Roger Sharp, they firmly deny that "the modern two-party system can trace its origins to the 1790s."[6] They concede that great crises, like that surrounding the presidential election of 1800, prompted partisan contest in important elections, but they do not see such partisan activity as "the same as institutionalized party behavior." The most persistent critic, Ronald P. Formisano, rightly insists that, to qualify as a modern political party, a political formation has to have a life and goals of its own, must strive to perpetuate itself, and must exist in the public mind as a social organization apart from its momentary leaders. Its supporters have to maintain their commitment to the party over a period of time, its candidates have to run as the openly identified choice of a party, and its members, in office and out, have to think of themselves as rightfully members of a party that has legitimate claims to their loyalty.[7]

By these criteria, it is argued, the groupings of the Jeffersonian era have to be seen as a transitional "preparty" form of political organization. Many of their inventions in organization and campaigning technique were of great significance for the future, and they certainly learned in some states, in times of crisis, how to bring out a large vote concentrated on a single party candidate or slate of candidates. Yet at the same time, it is claimed, the politics of the period were marked by many of the features of the old-style elite politics typical of the eighteenth century: restrictions on the right to vote, *viva voce* voting with individual choices publicly recorded in a pollbook, habits of deference, general apathy broken by moments of popular excitement, and control of the government by well-heeled country gentlemen and merchants. In this political environment, early party organizations could be little more than loose collections of interest or opinion groups, exploiting an electorate that responded essentially to local issues and loyalties.[8]

Moreover, there persisted a widespread presumption that parties were a social and political evil, and the prevalence of antiparty thinking in these years has suggested to many historians that contemporaries did not pride themselves on loyalty to a party and did not identify themselves as party members. The parties of the Jeffersonian period, it is said, never developed the regularity, the persistence that came to mark the mass parties established in the Jacksonian era; they never developed the ability to survive as institutions long after the issues that originally gave them meaning had passed away. The "quest for unanimity" and the end of partisanship during the Era of Good Feelings after 1815 are taken as the most convincing evidence that the Federalists and Jeffersonian Republicans did not constitute truly modern mass parties.[9]

These criticisms have great force. No one could reasonably claim that national party organizations had been established before 1816 or that the national parties had become "institutionalized" by then; they clearly lacked the capacity and will to sustain themselves as coherent national entities after 1815. Certainly the two main parties of the Jeffersonian period did not operate in the same way as those of the "party period" from the 1830s to the 1890s. Hence it is difficult to see in Jeffersonian politics the operational features that have made the concepts of voter behavior associated with the "realignment synthesis" so fruitful for later party history: although some developments in the early period might be termed "critical elections" or "voter realignments," they cannot be seen as comparable to the phenomena that have been given these names at later periods. The rhythms and regularities and critical shifts within a stable partisan electorate that historians have detected in the later party systems simply did not exist in the same way. Originally, the attraction of the First Party System lay in the prospect of being able to create a model of American party history that would explain its operation from the 1790s to at least the mid-twentieth century. If we now find that the First Party System cannot be fitted into that broad model, there is little point in insisting that it was a "system."[10]

And yet the historiographic pendulum has swung too far. The tendency to deny that proper institutionalized parties existed before 1815 has led historians to underestimate how far the political experience of these years was structured by partisan divisions, how far these divisions penetrated into the electorate, and how significant the experiences of these years proved for subsequent party development. It has become possible to write about the period as though the party experience were the least significant development of the period, when arguably it was central to the consciousness of a highly political generation. Recent historiography has risked throwing the partisan baby out with the somewhat murky systemic bathwater.

In truth, unreasonable demands have been placed on the parties of the Jeffersonian era. Of course, they did not show "a comparable degree of maturation" to those of the Second Party System—any more than the technology of the

War for Independence could compare with that of the Civil War. Historians of the early republic have used as their criteria of "party" the characteristics of the most thorough, all-embracing, nationally penetrating party system, that from 1838 to 1852, and yet it is not clear that even the undoubted parties that operated after 1865 could satisfy that stringent definition. The fact that, before 1816, the rate of party development varied from locality to locality, or that some areas favored one party overwhelmingly, or that in some states different alignments operated in state and national elections, does not prove that national parties did not exist. These are frequently recurring characteristics of American parties throughout most of their history.[11]

Providing that the limited nature of American political parties is recognized, it is reasonable to apply the term *party* to the political formations that appeared before 1815. Admittedly, in the 1790s these formations were little more than "proto-parties," as Roger Sharp has insisted on calling them. But after 1800 they did develop, however unevenly, into formations that deserve the name party—which is what contemporaries called them. These parties were not mere "interests" or coalitions of notable-led factions; they were perceived by politicians and voters as having a real existence, as possessing recognizable symbols and leaders and even policies. In some places, certainly not everywhere or even in most places, these parties took on institutional characteristics; each behaved as an entity in its own right, with a meaning and life of its own. Some party spokesmen were willing to justify the existence of formal parties as right and valuable in a republican society, although such justifications were expressed most clearly—as in New York after 1816—only when their authority was under serious challenge.[12]

What made these parties so significant was the fact that they incidentally and unknowingly created powerful political tools and electoral forces of great importance for the future. They experimented with, and in places used extensively, organizational techniques that became the staple of the Second Party System. In particular, the practice of nominating candidates in conventions made up of delegates elected by ordinary voters in their respective localities developed rather earlier and was used more generally (at least in Ohio) than historians have commonly recognized. It is just not true, as so often claimed, that in the Jeffersonian era party nominations came from the top down rather than from the bottom up, as they often appeared to do in the Jacksonian period.[13]

More important, these parties generated much deeper loyalties than is normally believed. Even where they represented bodies of party feeling rather than institutionalized parties, the existence of those blocs of sentiment among the voters placed restrictions on the politicians' freedom of action. As at other periods, it was the stubborn adherence of ordinary voters to traditional shibboleths—to symbols and names, to memories of what defined the good cause—that prevented politicians from forming alliances and coalitions more appropriate to the problems and interests of the day. Popular commitment to the old parties remained a political force even after 1815, and significantly affected the formation of national parties in the Jacksonian era.

RECENT OBSESSIONS

The hesitation to accept the existence of parties before 1816 has been strengthened in recent decades by current historiographical fashions. The concern with studying "ideas in action" has promoted the notion that political behavior was determined by "political culture" and that ideology was the driving force of political change. The hegemony of the "republican synthesis" has made us think that proper civic behavior was the central political concern of the Federalist-Jeffersonian generation, because "republican" ideology prescribed that power could be exercised properly only by virtuous leaders devoted to the general good of the community. Assertions that parties were evil, that they contradicted the pursuit of the general welfare and therefore had no place in a republican society, are taken at face value; by definition, parties cannot have existed if men did not believe in their value. It is presumed that only when intellectual justifications for party as a permanent organization were developed could a true party system emerge. Thus, as Amy Bridges has written of party development, "The thought in some ways outpaced the deed."[14]

Yet can we safely assume that politics worked according to cultural expectations? The public expression of antiparty sentiments could equally be taken as evidence that parties did in practice exist, that partisan modes of behavior were becoming an alarmingly common feature of contemporary politics. It might even be (as so often later on) that politicians who were losing out in the struggle of parties resorted to an older but still powerful ideology in an effort to withstand the force of an all-conquering opposing party. Circumstances commonly compel those involved in politics to behave in ways that contradict their ideologies, and sometimes new modes of behavior are adopted long before a theoretical justification has been devised. Michael Wallace has argued that a full justification of permanent organized parties did not begin to gain elaborated expression until the 1820s, but he acknowledges that this justification developed *as a result* of long partisan experience. "Not until a new generation of politicians emerged—men who had been raised in parties and had grown to maturity in a world that included party competition as a fixture of political life—were Americans able to re-evaluate the ancient traditions and establish new ones that justified their political activities."[15]

Moreover, the very language of the time is open to misinterpretation if the reality of party is not appreciated. Many contemporaries understood that the labels Federalist and Republican did not accurately define the intellectual attitudes of each party. When Federalist candidates said that they were better republicans than their Republican rivals, they were not demonstrating the fluidity of party lines; they were acutely pointing out that a politician's label did not define his principles either accurately or exclusively. When Thomas Jefferson said in 1801, "We are all republicans, we are all federalists," he specifically defined "federal and republican principles" to mean no more than "attachment to union and representative government." Thus when, on the same famous occasion, he insisted that "we have called by different names brethren of the same principle," he did not mean that no significant differences of policy and priority separated the parties—as the partisanship of his presidency demonstrated. Similarly, the fact that historians have detected a pervasive, common ideology that they have labeled "republican" does not necessarily mean that when Jeffersonian politicians called on the support of "republicans" they were using the word in a broad, consensual, nonpartisan sense.[16] For the sake of clarity, this work uses a capital letter for the party name or label and lowercase for the more generalized, all-embracing, ideological, or communal meaning, except in quotations.

Historians have been equally reluctant to accept that early parties could generate mass party loyalties, insisting that mass participation did not develop until much later. The early republic is regarded as gentry-led, fundamentally aristocratic in its attitudes, and deferential in its electoral behavior; therefore, it must have lacked the grassroots involvement necessary for the generation of mass political loyalties. What popular involvement there was, it is said, concerned essentially local affairs; national politics were left to the socially superior political class. This situation changed only in the 1820s and 1830s when Jacksonian Democracy—or, in some places, Antimasonic or Workingmen's movements—aroused popular interest in politics, ending deference and encouraging mass participation.[17]

Yet studies of colonial politics have shown that the electorate was far from acquiescent in the mid-eighteenth century and that, during the course of the controversy with Britain, ordinary voters became aroused by politics as never before.[18] Indeed, the construction of a republican philosophy was partly a response to the perceived excesses of democracy—and the United States Constitution was drafted partly to mitigate the consequences of popular politics in the states following the Revolutionary War. Yet the Constitution could gain acceptance only by seeking the consent of the electorates in the individual states, and the voters in many states responded to the ratification process in a way that suggested they were neither indifferent nor deferential. The Constitution may have reduced the powers of state governments, but it otherwise did little to hamper the operation of majoritarian democracy at the state level, and it opened the way to popular involvement in national politics. As Madison acknowledged, every branch of the federal government was ultimately dependent on decisions of the popular electorates in the various states.[19]

Indeed, some historians are now beginning to emphasize that the underpinnings of an elitist and aristocratic society were already giving way in the final decades of the late eighteenth century. By 1790, according to some studies, deference as a social and political habit was already on the defensive, even in Virginia.[20] Gordon Wood has brilliantly portrayed this process of erosion in almost all its aspects, ascribing it to the impress of the forces that the Revolution released in a fluid and dynamic society. Unfortunately, Wood accepts the view that real parties did not exist before the 1830s and so he cannot give proper credit to the role of partisan political action—to the dynamism of the electoral process, to the erosive effect of partisan issues in undermining habits of deference—in furthering the very processes of democratization that he is describing. As Joyce Appleby has intimated, party action was an essential part of the emergence of liberal, individualistic, self-seeking America.[21]

Ohio History

At first sight, Ohio may seem an odd state to choose in order to investigate these possibilities. Officially, settlement did not begin until 1788, although squatters had been dribbling across the Ohio River since the late 1770s. Population growth was slow until 1795, and even in 1800 only 8,158 adult males inhabited what became the state of Ohio in 1803.[22] After 1800, however, the population grew massively, as more than 30,000 people entered the state each year; with a further acceleration after 1815, the state had become the fifth most populous— the fourth for federal purposes—in the United States by 1820.[23] The settlers inevitably found themselves preoccupied with mastering frontier conditions, and yet such was the speed of development in many places that they behaved not so much as archetypal frontiersmen and pioneers as immigrants entering a strange society and carrying their cultural presumptions and expectations with them. The men of Ohio whose private letters have come down to us retained contact with their place of origin and regarded themselves as part of the nation, as involved in national issues as Americans elsewhere, and as committed to expressing their point of view.

Their political expression has rarely been seen as conspicuously partisan. Indeed, it must seem perverse to take Ohio as an example of early partisanship, since it is commonly regarded as a prime example of a state so lightly touched by the First Party System that it did not share even the eastern seaboard's limited experience of organized partisanship before 1815. Richard P. McCormick, for example, has described Ohio politics before 1824 as following "the Tennessee model of factionalism and personalism." In this respect, he considers Ohio typical of the new states formed after 1800—"nominally Republican in allegiance, but in actuality . . . most accurately . . . described not as one-party states but as 'no-party' states." Writing of the years before 1824, Formisano insists that "at no time did a two-party system take hold" in Ohio. Most recently, Emil Pocock has claimed that "true party spirit was largely absent" from Ohio politics in the first twenty years of statehood.[24]

However, those who insist that no parties existed in Ohio before the 1820s also make concessions which should give them pause. Formisano, for example, accepts that something like partisan conflict existed at times of national crisis, as in 1800 and 1812. All historians of Ohio find it impossible to describe the statehood controversy without using party labels drawn from national politics. At other times "antiparty" historians concede that beneath many apparently personal disputes lay partisan differences, or disputes based on factional differences within a main party.[25] These concessions, put together, suggest that partisanship did exist in Ohio but that its nature, focus, implications, and range of operation fall outside the expectations of modern historians.

To play down the partisan element in early Ohio political history is to underestimate the most important driving force in politics. For example, Andrew Cayton's interesting analysis of the ideological conflicts in the frontier republic sees the statehood movement of 1801–2 as essentially a coalition of disparate local interests that inevitably fell apart after it had succeeded; by contrast, the evidence presented here will suggest that statehood was brought about by an organized protoparty with an internal dynamic that helped to keep it in being for at least another decade. After 1803, Cayton describes the ruling Republican gentry as disturbed by the contention, selfishness, and demagoguery displayed in the new state, and so he interprets the use of party mechanisms as a means of promoting harmony and ensuring the selection of the best men. It would be more accurate to say that the regular Republican leaders were committed partisans who disapproved of dissidents because they jeopardized party unity and therefore party control; in order to justify the maintenance of party mechanisms, these regular Republicans resorted to traditional arguments about the need to preserve social harmony and restrain individual ambition. Similarly, to claim that "partisan politics was a means of organizing heterogeneity" is to risk confusing effect with purpose, for if party organization operated to bind a heterogeneous society together, it succeeded only because partisanship already existed among the electorate, enabling voters to recognize the party call and respond to it.[26]

Even when historians have accepted that partisanship existed in Ohio, they have tended to treat it mainly as an indicator of social and cultural conflict. In so doing, they have sometimes shown little interest in the political process in its own right and have tended to somewhat oversimplify the party contest. In particular, cultural historians have reduced the political story to a contest of "region-based cultures"—usually between Virginians and New Englanders—or have emphasized the concern of political leaders to impose proper moral and capitalist values on the new country they inhabited. Andrew Cayton and others have exaggerated the dominance of the Virginian gentry of the Scioto Valley, when the predominance of the Republican party in Ohio was based on its appeal to a range of men of varying backgrounds and social standing. By emphasizing their concern to introduce Virginian ways into Ohio rather than their partisan commitment, Cayton makes it difficult to explain what they had in common with their non-Virginian allies.[27]

Even historians who are directly interested in the political process, such as Jeffrey P. Brown, have tended to assume that Ohio political leaders could command their local constituencies and that politics was essentially a struggle for regional advantage, with local interest reinforced by ethnocultural identity.[28] These interpretations are not wrong, but they do not explain the interaction of these various elements or adequately explain the changing role and varying power of party ties. The problem is partly, as Brown has pointed out, that the best evidence available comes from the rich manuscript collections of leading Ohio politicians, whereas the evidence of popular behavior is both scanty and difficult to handle. Voting statistics, in particular, are patchy in their coverage and, because of rapidly changing local boundaries, difficult to collate over periods longer than two or three years.[29] Yet to ignore electoral politics is to ignore the driving consideration of politicians whose first concern had to be to win votes if they wished to achieve anything at all.

In general, historians have assumed that the electorate did not matter in Ohio or elsewhere until the major political transformation normally associated with Andrew Jackson's election to the White House in 1828. It is assumed that "modern" political practices cannot have existed before 1828, regardless of appearances. Yet the fact is that what has been interpreted as novelty in the Jacksonian era is often conscious reenactment or restoration of earlier practice, and the sheer conservatism of Jacksonian Democracy has been obscured behind the assumption of populistic novelty. Even the name of Jackson's Democratic party was copied from its Jeffersonian forebear.

If it be assumed, furthermore, that democratic politics were born in the 1820s, it is easy to assume that what went before can all be described in the same breath. On this assumption historians have looked at political behavior in the

Era of Good Feelings and assumed that it can be safely read back into the years before the War of 1812. On this basis James Sterling Young calculated that there were few connections between events in Washington and voters in the constituencies and that national party ties were insignificant, even under Jefferson. Similarly, Emil Pocock has underestimated the partisan nature of elections in Ohio before 1816 by concentrating his attention on the subdued partyism of the years that immediately followed.[30]

The tendency to underestimate the dynamic changes of the Jeffersonian political world is reinforced by the simple dichotomy that historians have long accepted between premodern and modern, or preindustrial and industrial, modes of social and political behavior. They too often assume that the political developments of the nineteenth century saw a simple progression from traditional to modern forms. Thus when Kenneth Winkle, in a pathbreaking study of antebellum pollbooks, discovered that, in the 1840s and 1850s, local elites in Ohio sometimes controlled the electoral process by deciding who was and was not a member of the local community, he assumed that this represented a traditional practice that lasted until 1878, when the law at last allowed voters to choose their place of residence and voting. In fact, there is little evidence that this control of the ballot by local elites had been common in earlier decades; indeed, the historian of Ohio election practices before 1825 finds that "most judges [of election] were apparently casual in enforcing qualifications." Yet the modern assumption that Jacksonian parties were, by definition, instruments of modernization leads to the further assumption that they must have reduced vetting of voters by local leaders, when there is more reason to argue that the development of evenly balanced statewide parties actually made the practice more common. After all, only then could politicians calculate that a handful of votes in one county might determine the political balance of the state legislature, as had clearly become the case in the mid-1840s, at the period when Winkle's systematic evidence begins.[31] American democracy has not arisen in a linear progression; it has suffered periods of retraction as well as of advance since its origins in the Revolution.

Essentially this was the point of the "deferential-participant" model that Formisano proposed in 1974. Between 1760 and 1840 the United States went through a significant internal political transformation: political communities that were hierarchical, elitist, deferential, and ideally nonpartisan became democratic, demagogic, participatory, and intensely partisan. During that process there were moments of political innovation followed by periods of reversion, and at any one time both old and new methods, assumptions, and operations could be found. That is essentially the picture offered here, but with the qualification that everything was developing rather earlier, rather faster, than most recent historians have tended to say. The new world of populism and parties was becoming commonplace in some areas long before Andrew Jackson's name was put forward for the presidency.

The basic thrust of this work is, therefore, threefold. First, I demonstrate that the political system in Ohio was thoroughly democratized by the early years of the nineteenth century, as the structure of power was revolutionized by the action of energetic protoparties operating in the socially fluid conditions of the frontier. Politics in Ohio had ceased to be deferential and dominated by elites virtually from the very creation of the state. As a result, politics in the Jeffersonian period were as democratic as representative politics ever can be in an inegalitarian society.

Second, I argue that bodies of partisan sentiment, focused on national rather than local politics, existed before 1815, that politicians appealed to these party identifiers by using the symbols and rhetoric of partisanship, and that some politicians developed effective party mechanisms from which voters took their lead for quite an extensive period. Even the Federalists, so often dismissed as a body of old-fashioned gentlemen with antiquated ideas and habits, developed some features of a mass political party capable of varying its appeal to suit the demands of a far from deferential electorate.

Third, I suggest that this party experience had great significance for the future, mainly because party feeling burned deep and did not pass away easily. Even in the Jacksonian period, some people could look back on the years from 1795 to 1815 as the critical and formative political experience in their lives, and the emotional and ideological attachments created then were powerful enough to survive the Era of Good Feelings and the assault of Jacksonian Democracy.

As with the inscription over the west door of the first Ohio capitol, attempts to conceal, forget, or deny the existence of early party divisions and party loyalties are contradicted when exposure strips off the veneer of antiparty consensualism.

1

PARTISANSHIP UNDER THE ANCIEN RÉGIME, 1793–1802

Political parties have flourished in the states, not in the territories, of the United States. Historically not only could the inhabitants of a territory not participate in federal elections but proprietorial and speculative groups tended to dominate public affairs during the early phases of settlement. As a result, territorial politics have commonly expressed factional divisions based on competing local and personal interests within the territory. In time, these groupings have usually become linked with national parties outside the territory, and gradually internal conflicts have taken on the names of the national parties. Thus internal divisions have lain at the root of the national party division apparently in existence as the territory evolves into statehood.[1]

Although commonly applied to Ohio, this pattern of party development does not adequately explain the origins of national parties in the Northwest Territory of 1788–1803. Local factions did not precede the generation of party spirit. There is ample evidence that some settlers perceived the arguments taking place in the nation's capital at an early date and began to take their stands, to make personal commitments, almost as early as people on the eastern seaboard. However, politics in the future Ohio could not follow party lines, simply because the constitutional structures of the territorial regime inhibited party action and even the expression of party commitment. In time, though, partisan commitment began to influence the development of territorial politics, as much as the other way round. The struggle for statehood after 1800 became linked with the division between Federalist and Republican mainly because of the intense party spirit on national questions that had already been generated within the Northwest Territory.

FIRST SIGNS OF PARTISANSHIP

The origins of the party struggle in Ohio have traditionally been discerned in the contest between Governor Arthur St. Clair and the Chillicothe gentry. The territorial governor enjoyed extraordinary powers and secured the support of many of the leading proprietorial interests, notably the Ohio Company. Even though, down to 1798, St. Clair was absent for much of the time and left the work of government to the secretary of the territory, Winthrop Sargent, the governorship was constantly used toward a clear end: as representative of the federal government, the governor upheld the interest and outlook of the national administration in the Northwest Territory and thereby identified the Federalist interest with the continuation of the colonial regime.

The Chillicothe gentry, by contrast, were Virginian land speculators who were appropriating large areas of the Virginia Military District, between the Scioto and Little Miami Rivers. Nathaniel Massie had early begun to make surveys at great personal hazard, laying claims to the best land. According to one pioneer, Massie was selling Indian lands ceded by the Greenville Treaty of 1795 even before the ink had dried on that document! Like his fellow surveyor and partner-in-arms, Duncan McArthur, Massie built a huge personal speculative land claim in the course of the 1790s.[2] In 1796 Massie laid out the town of Chillicothe in the Scioto Valley, where he was joined by other surveyors, speculators, entrepreneurs, and professional men from Virginia, most notably the energetic and enterprising Thomas Worthington and Worthington's brother-in-law, the engaging and devout Dr. Edward Tiffin. These men were to lead the successful rebellion against the territorial regime after 1800 and so become the leading lights in the Ohio Republican party.

Yet it is a mistake to overemphasize the centrality of the Chillicothe gentry in the process of party formation. Worthington and Tiffin did not move to the future Ohio until 1798. Massie cooperated with St. Clair's administration until that year, when the governor objected to Massie's attempts to make his town of Manchester the county seat of Adams County, contrary to the governor's will and supposed prerogative. These Virginians were by no means unambiguous supporters of the Jeffersonian Republican party in the late 1790s, and in most cases it is difficult to discover evidence of clear party commitment on their part before 1800 or even 1801. By contrast, settlers in other parts of the future state had expressed their partisan commitment even before Chillicothe was founded in 1796. Moreover, these non-Virginian partisans were to play as significant a role as the Chillicothe gentry in organizing opposition to St. Clair and securing the overthrow of the territorial regime in 1802.

Land Divisions and Early Settlements in Ohio. *Source:* Bond, *Foundations of Ohio,* 276.

On the face of it, of course, there could scarcely have been much opportunity for the development of popular partisan opposition in the early 1790s. Partisan activity requires, at the very least, the opportunity for political expression, and the territorial system of government was designed to stifle any such popular involvement, at least before 1798. The first stage of government laid down by the Northwest Ordinance of 1787 thrust power firmly into the hands of officials appointed and paid by the federal government. Between 1788 and 1798 the legislature consisted solely of the governor and three territorial judges, who were responsible to Philadelphia rather than to the settlers they governed. The very object of the system was to keep power out of the hands of the unreliable,

Ohio Counties and Population Distribution in 1800. *Sources:* Downes, *Evolution of Ohio County Boundaries,* 19; and Lloyd, Falconer, and Thorne, *Agriculture of Ohio,* 37.

footloose folk who moved out to settle the frontier, and to ensure that control of affairs remained in the hands of the enlightened men of property and standing who commanded the new nation.[3]

In any case, the physical obstacles to political action within the territory were immense. Perhaps as much as 95 percent of Ohio was covered by trees—in southern and eastern Ohio mainly oak and beech, buckeyes and hickories—often huge trees, with trunks over ten feet in diameter. Beneath this canopy, so thick that sunlight rarely filtered through, roamed a rich abundance of animal life—including mountain lions, bobcats, lynx, deer, wolves, and bears—while the surface was drained by raging streams and broad rivers. Several thousand Indians still lived and hunted in this far from peaceable kingdom, and until 1795 they struggled violently to resist the beginnings of white habitation. Only after the Treaty of Greenville in that year did new settlers begin to flock into the huge area now released for settlement south and east of the treaty line.[4]

Before 1795 the tiny white population clustered in three main areas along the northern bank of the Ohio River. The first had been settled by the Ohio Company in 1788 at Marietta, at the mouth of the Muskingum, and pioneers had cautiously begun to penetrate deeper into what had been named Washington County. The second area lay 340 miles downstream, near the mouth of the Little Miami in Hamilton County, where by 1795 the "small village" of Cincinnati—with five hundred civilians, ten frame houses, ninety-four log cabins, plus five hundred or so soldiers in the adjacent Fort Washington—had begun to establish itself as an important center.[5] Third, further up the Ohio above Marietta lay Jefferson County, comprising essentially the first Seven Ranges of U.S. lands released for public sale. This area around Steubenville—founded in 1796—was the target of pioneers from the older frontiers of Pennsylvania and western Virginia, many of them Scotch-Irish in origin. In between these scattered areas of settlement, other pioneers were building their huts, often on land they had not paid for—but never, before 1795, very far from the banks of the Ohio.

Conditions of such isolation restricted the range of popular political activity. Within each concentrated settlement, as Frederick Jackson Turner perceived, primitive frontier conditions encouraged broad participation in local affairs: thus in 1788 in Cincinnati—as in Chillicothe in 1796—the first settlers held an "entirely democratic" meeting under some majestic tree to draw up bylaws. These concentrated settlements soon developed a political life focused on local issues, such as the dispute in Cincinnati over the range of Fort Washington's military jurisdiction.[6]

In most regions of the future state, settlement was more dispersed and isolated, and the pioneers could scarcely think of traveling through thick unknown forests or boating on dangerous rivers to communicate on political matters with distant neighbors. For them, more basic considerations had priority: the essentials of life, the danger from the Indians, and the need to build cabins, hunt wild animals, clear trees, and produce a crop. Under these circumstances, most pioneers of the 1790s were willing to leave political decisions to the few men among them of wealth, connection, education, and public ambition; these prominent few had the means to form relationships with other settlements and with the various governments that had been established for the territory. Thus traditional elite politics were entirely compatible with the independence of frontier life and the urge to form communities, and these were not the circumstances in which mass political involvement might be expected to appear.[7]

Consequently, the early contests surrounding the territorial government involved the conflicting interests of a small group of lawyers, landowners, and merchants able to gain access to the powers that be. They demanded office and the advantages that government favor could give to their land holdings. One consequence was the frequent squabbling among the territorial judges whenever they met, which was rare because of their prolonged absences from the territory. The most significant political conflict of the early 1790s concerned the activities of John Cleves Symmes, the proprietor of the huge Miami Purchase, stretching far into the hinterland north of Cincinnati. In selling his lands, Symmes had failed to fulfill the terms of his grant and had even sold land that did not belong to him, including the land on which Fort Washington stood! Then, in the face of St. Clair's formal protests, Symmes used his office of territorial judge to adjudicate in cases in which he had a personal interest. In opposing Symmes's far from scrupulous behavior, the governor could reasonably regard himself as the sole defender of ordinary people against the selfishness of the great proprietors.[8]

This narrow political world significantly expanded, at least in the Miami region, when William Maxwell established a printing press in Cincinnati in November 1793. St. Clair thought a newspaper would be an essential means of informing settlers of new laws, but the *Centinel of the North-Western Territory* also gave critics of the territorial regime a medium for broadcasting their views. As early as November 1793, a correspondent in the *Centinel* insisted that every self-respecting citizen should vocally object to "the oppressive hand of a legislature, in the formation or organization of which he was not consulted." The following summer the administration of Winthrop Sargent, acting as governor in St. Clair's absence, was widely condemned as tyrannical—taxing citizens without their consent, denying trial by jury, charging illegal fees. One anonymous correspondent of the *Centinel* criticized the whole system of government established by the ordinance as less "republican" even than British colonial rule, and he called for "conventions of the people" to petition Congress for its complete overthrow. These complaints diminished when St. Clair and the judges revised the laws in 1795, but the airing of grievances in the press reflected a broadening political consciousness in the Cincinnati region.[9]

These first rumblings of opposition to the territorial regime coincided with the emergence of vocal Jeffersonian opposition to the Federalist administration of the national government. By 1794 the disputes within President Washington's administration over national policy had deepened with the controversy over the United States' stance toward the war that had broken out between the great European monarchies and the French republic founded in September 1792. Should Congress have approved the controversial financial measures proposed by Alexander Hamilton in 1789–91? Should the United States assist fellow republicans in a country that had helped Americans gain their independence? How should the government react to British depredations on American shipping in the West Indies in 1793–94? Should Washington have sent an embassy to London to negotiate terms for maintaining peaceful relations? Should Congress authorize the implementation of Jay's Treaty?

Physical isolation ensured that people northwest of the Ohio River would know little of these controversies in Philadelphia or the agitation elsewhere in the new nation. In 1790 Governor St. Clair himself complained that he knew "as little as the man in the moon" of what was happening in the nation's capital, and he begged the secretary of war to forward some newspapers: "I never before thought them of any consequence—they will now be a great treat." The situation was slow to improve, because an effective postal service serving the settlements along the Ohio River was established only in 1794, and complaints about the service, especially west of Marietta, continued until the opening of Zane's Trace between Wheeling and Maysville in 1798. Even so, the western settlements—and their newspaper editors—would increasingly benefit from the cheap and unrestricted transmission of eastern newspapers made possible by the 1792 Post Office Act.[10]

William Maxwell well recognized that settlers in the western country were eager to learn more of national affairs. He hoped that the appearance of the *Centinel* would at least remove one "particular grievance, that the people have not been acquainted with the proceeding of the legislature of the union, in which they are as much interested as any part of the United States."[11] Men of such outlook regarded themselves as involved in the national political debate, despite being denied the right to participate in national elections. Even those who had settled in the territory before political attitudes began to polarize were aroused by the issues debated in the nation's capital, responding like their relations (and correspondents) in their native states.

Maxwell's newspaper not only kept his readers informed about the outside world but gave ample evidence of the growing local sympathy for the new national opposition. Although the *Centinel* ran as its masthead the motto "Open to all parties—but influenced by none," the whole thrust of the newspaper was Jeffersonian. Maxwell focused on European news and the progress of the war that threatened the new French republic, and his selection of news and comment revealed both great sympathy with European radicals and considerable doubts about the foreign policy of Washington's administration. His columns complained of the British depredations on American shipping, and objected when Congress rejected Madison's proposed discriminatory embargo against Britain. He reprinted an ode that celebrated the military success of the

French republic and promised that "Democratic Citizens, / Will by each other stand." One of his "correspondents" praised Jefferson for resigning from Washington's administration rather than "lend his name to measures which militated against his well-known principles." Significantly, the sole comments Maxwell reproduced on John Jay's mission to England in 1794 were the protests of the Democratic societies in Pennsylvania, which particularly objected to the appointment of the chief justice of the United States to a diplomatic embassy. They advocated instead the "old" principle of rotation in office, on the grounds that "the revolution in France has sufficiently proved that generals may be taken from the ranks, and ministers of state from the obscurity of the most remote village." A toast at the 1794 Independence Day celebration in Cincinnati echoed this partisan view of the outside world when it cheered on "The Sans Culottes of France and [the] cause of Liberty, triumphant."[12]

Sharpening partisanship, in the wake of the noisy public protests along the eastern seaboard over Jay's Treaty, resulted in two separate Fourth of July celebrations in Cincinnati in 1795. One was attended by both Cincinnati citizens and the soldiers of Fort Washington. "Great harmony" prevailed, and the toasts were broadly acceptable, expressing a range of sentiments. At the other celebration—deliberately not held "in the fashionable form, under a discharge of great guns"—the toasts criticized Jay's proposed settlement with Britain, praised the French republic ("our younger Sister"), and prayed for the propagation of "Republican government" around the globe, "in defiance of the . . . subtle poisonous intrigues of selfish aristocracy." Even President Washington was satirized as the "venerable . . . father who repudiated the kind nurse of his orphan children, and wished to marry the infamous strumpet that wished to poison their mother." His "illustrious reputation," it was claimed, would be "degraded by the preposterous alliance."[13]

If the opposition complained most loudly about the treaty's betrayal of the new French republic, they also criticized the thrust of Alexander Hamilton's financial policies. The toasts at the 1795 celebration advocated an end to "iniquitous distributions and establishments," "partial impositions," and "iniquitous projects of finance," which could destroy the independence of the people. Instead, they proposed a universal land tax and a fairer system of "distributing the national lands" so as to "aim a fatal blow at the vitals of speculation." Above all, they wished to see the "old harlot of aristocracy . . . speedily . . . drummed out, to the tune of Ça Ira."[14]

Moreover, the emergence of this Democratic-Republican point of view underlay many of the criticisms of the territorial regime voiced in 1793–95. In November 1793 one correspondent in the Centinel associated his ideological objections to its unrepresentative nature with the outlook of "a modern French democrat." Another cited Tom Paine to prove that the territorial government violated natural rights, and he contrasted the "aristocracy" of territorial officials with republican France, where even the title "esquire" had been abolished. The French Revolution clearly had a radicalizing effect on some settlers in the territory and made them eager to apply its doctrines, as they understood them, to their own situation.[15]

This agitation in the Cincinnati press represented an extremely prompt response to news of critical events at home and abroad, and it suggests that some men, even on the frontier, possessed high political awareness.[16] Their disposition to become involved, both ideologically and emotionally, in the new national political contest would be reinforced by future settlers who were presently undergoing a similar awakening in the eastern states or even in Europe itself. But, despite the space they received in the territory's first newspaper, it was far from clear in the 1790s that sympathizers with the Jeffersonian Republican opposition were particularly numerous in the Northwest Territory. The Federalist supporters of the national administration seemed certain to carry the day in any contest, at least for the time being.

THE FEDERALIST SUPREMACY

Jacob Burnet proved the most persistent—or long-lived—of Ohio Federalists. Later nicknamed "Cato the Censor," this strict Presbyterian of Scottish background moved from New Jersey to Cincinnati in 1796 and rapidly gained prominence as a lawyer, politician, and legislator. For the next fifty years he continued to reappear in public life at critical moments, as when he became a U.S. senator in 1829: embarrassed by the loss of two front teeth, he addressed the Senate only occasionally, but he reputedly helped Daniel Webster prepare the famous Replies to Hayne. By 1839 he was an active Whig, nominating his friend and neighbor William Henry Harrison for president at the party's national convention and then serving as one of the candidate's "conscience-keepers" during the election campaign. He saw his political course over the previous half-century as consistent, and still in the 1840s he bore the label "Federalist" with pride. In his historical accounts he defended the record of the Federalist rulers of the Northwest Territory and insisted that the people had benefited from their rule. No opposition of any consequence existed, he claimed, until after Thomas Jefferson became president and began to appeal to cynical opportunists in the territory.[17]

Throughout the controversies of the 1790s, indeed, the Northwest Territory remained a bastion of Federalist strength. Although criticisms of the Washington administration mounted in both the East and the West, the political attachments of the leading officials of the territorial government survived unshaken. As army officers in the Revolution, they were firm supporters of the new national government presided over by their old commander in chief. Arthur St. Clair himself had served with Washington, finally attaining the rank of major general. After the war, he became president of the Philadelphia Order of the Cincinnati and a prominent leader of the campaign in Pennsylvania to replace Thomas Paine's democratic state constitution of 1776 with a balanced constitution more likely to preserve order, liberty, and property. A delegate to the Continental Congress, St. Clair became president of that body in 1787 and then governor of the Northwest Territory, which Congress created during his chairmanship.

As governor, St. Clair saw his primary responsibility as saving the Northwest for the United States. Initially this duty meant defeating the Indian menace and securing land for sale and settlement. Sadly, the defeat of his expedition of 1791 against the Indians in the upper Miami Valley—the greatest single military defeat at the hands of the aboriginal population in U.S. history—destroyed his military reputation, though not his concern to ensure that the new territory became a firmly loyal part of the United States. Unsure of the patriotism of the settlers and worried by the designs of European powers, he resisted Citizen Genet's efforts in 1793 to raise an army in the West to attack the possessions of France's enemy, Spain, and he cooperated with the secretary of the treasury in enforcing the whiskey excise in both the territory and western Pennsylvania.[18] Condemning the Jeffersonians as "the d——m——d Faction that has been dragging the country to ruin," St. Clair endeavored several times to return to mainstream politics in Pennsylvania, with marked lack of success; he would finally be turned down as a congressional candidate in western Pennsylvania in 1798 because of his public identification as a "Government Man."[19] Thereafter he would strive to ensure that the territory, and any states that emerged from it, did not provide further political enemies for the cause of Federalism and good government.

Similar attitudes were to be found among the Revolutionary veterans from New England who had organized the Ohio Company of Associates and founded Marietta in 1788. Their leader, Rufus Putnam, was another of George Washington's comrades in arms as well as a business associate, and a remarkable proportion of his fellow Ohio Company settlers had served with distinction in the War for Independence and become members of the Society of the Cincinnati. The whole project for a western settlement on the Muskingum was intended partly to recompense them for their wartime services and provide them with the personal economic security due to men of their well-deserved military status. In Ohio, as Andrew Cayton has written, "the associates planned to create an orderly society based on equality and security of property, and on the institutions of school, church and government, all firmly entrenched in the purity of a natural, regular setting."[20] Their commitment to good order and social tranquility was deeply intertwined with a sense that the competing claims of local interests must be subordinated to the general good of the nation.

Accordingly, the early settlers of Marietta and neighboring communities in Washington County identified themselves with support of Washington's government and the territorial regime. Moreover, as strong Congregationalists, they reacted as forcibly as their friends in Massachusetts to the irreligion and secular radicalism displayed by the Jacobins in France in 1793–95. By 1794 the key originator of the company, the Rev. Manasseh Cutler, could see Antifederalism and the Ohio Company as natural enemies.[21] In 1797 Putnam's nephew, John Mathews, would condemn the "democratic fanitisme [sic]" of the friends of France, while Marietta's first lawyer, Paul Fearing, called the Democratic Republicans "disorganizing Partizans" who sought "the ruin of the Country or at least the subvertion [sic] of our Constitution." Such views found a welcome echo in the county's outlying settlements like Athens, where the only newspaper taken was the United States Gazette, the leading Federalist newspaper originally sponsored by Alexander Hamilton.[22]

These Washingtonians could not, however, feel confident that their views would prevail in the territory or even in their own locality. As early as the 1780s the lands northwest of the Ohio River were being settled illegally by pioneers and squatters from western Pennsylvania, western Virginia, and Kentucky. Federal troops had cleared them off in 1785, but they soon began to drift back. These frontiersmen were widely regarded as disrespectful of authority, potentially disloyal to the United States, and little more than savages. The Ohio Company settlers had trouble with disorderly, horse-stealing squatters who hailed from Pennsylvania, and they had to take firm action to protect their property. Many of these rogues were perpetual backwoodsmen, hunters, and squatters, who preferred to live on the edge of civilization and were never amenable to law and government.[23] Like the Scotch-Irish spilling over into eastern Ohio from western Pennsylvania, they sympathized with the resistance to the excise laws visible in both that state and Kentucky. Their political outlook could scarcely be less in sympathy with the Federalism of the Yankee settlers on the Ohio Company Purchase.

Similarly, farther west, in the Miami Purchase. Many of its leading settlers were New Jerseyites of Federalist outlook; John Cleves Symmes himself, although opposed to St. Clair, publicly scorned Jefferson's candidacy for the presidency in 1796.[24] Most ordinary settlers in the Purchase, however, were men of the old frontier, mainly from Kentucky, who after 1795 rapidly spilled out northwards from the river settlements and squatted indiscriminately on land belonging to Symmes or the federal government. As acting governor, Winthrop Sargent clashed repeatedly with the boisterous residents of the Cincinnati region, for they violated his New England notions of good order and good practice. By 1796 Sargent had concluded, "The people of Hamilton and Washington Counties seem not ever to have been intended to live under the same Government—the latter are like unto our Fore Fathers and the former (generally) very licentious & too great a proportion, indolent and extremely debauched." Sargent, like many easterners, mistrusted all "first Settlers" and hoped that statehood could be delayed until they had been replaced by inhabitants "of such Characters & property as may insure national Dependance & national Confidence." For the time being, he lacked "Faith in the national Attachment of the people from the Indian Line [thirty miles west of Cincinnati] quite up to the new England Settlements upon Ohio Company Lands—many of them are not the *very best* of a neighbouring State of Doubtful politics."[25]

The existence of this potentially unreliable populace committed Federalists to supporting the system of centralized control created by the Northwest Ordinance. The governor's command over the territorial executive and influence over legislation was reinforced by his command of local government. St. Clair or Sargent appointed almost all local officials, thus in theory controlling the implementation of policy, regardless of local opinion. Moreover, the governor's authority over the militia gave him an extra structure of command, at a time when all citizens appreciated the need for adequate frontier defense. These powers gave him extensive powers of patronage, which made would-be officeholders dependent on his favor. He also had some influence over the distribution of federal patronage, along with Rufus Putnam, who in 1796 was appointed surveyor general of the United States, based in Marietta. In effect, politics and government in the territory focused on the officers of the national government in a way that was welcome to every Federalist.[26]

Yet what really underwrote Federalist rule in the early and mid-1790s was not simply its command of the reins of power but public recognition that it was doing a necessary job. Despite the political unreliability of many settlers moving into Ohio before 1796, criticism of Federalist rule was distinctly muted in the territory as a whole. In the early years, the scattered settlements poised precariously on the banks of the Ohio River were involved in an Indian war that threatened their very survival and ensured their dependence on the federal authorities. In Cincinnati, the *Centinel* gave considerable attention to the preparations of General Anthony Wayne's army and its march against the Indians, and eagerly printed early news of his victory at Fallen Timbers in August 1794. Even then many felt that the troubles could be revived by British agents, and the pioneers remained dependent upon the U.S. troops concentrated in Fort Washington. Consequently, the Whiskey Rebellion of 1794 found little open support in the territory, even in the Cincinnati press; although unpopular and difficult to collect, the excise did not arouse the massive disobedience displayed in western Pennsylvania and Kentucky. Similarly, the opposition to Jay's Treaty was limited, since the treaty promised the final removal of British troops from the territory. As one of the *Centinel*'s correspondents advised, "It is admitted on all hands, that the surrender of the Western Posts will be of the utmost importance to this country [i.e., the territory] . . . it therefore behoves the inhabitants . . . to be silent" respecting the treaty. In the House of Representatives the Federalists warned that failure to implement the treaty could plunge the Northwestern frontier into savage warfare once more, and only the House's narrow vote in favor of implementation in May 1796 finally ensured the removal of the Indian threat promised by the previous year's Treaty of Greenville.[27]

Under these circumstances, there was little agitation over the presidential election of 1796. According to Jacob Burnet, "The exciting contest which agitated the States during that election was not felt in the Territory. The mass of the people who inhabited the West were calm and unmoved; and four-fifths of them were entirely reconciled to the election of Mr. Adams." Political sentiment overall supported Adams's policy in the international crisis that followed, and public meetings, notably in Cincinnati, passed resolutions "to sustain his administration against the encroachments of the French government." St. Clair himself applauded the "military spirit" and firm patriotism shown in the future Ohio in 1798, which demonstrated that "everything in the political hemisphere is as right on our side of the river as I could wish it. Although we are so near neighbors, the people on this side of the river are the very antipodes of Kentuckians."[28]

This satisfaction with the Adams administration was reflected in the new territorial assembly in December 1799. Toward the end of its first full session, Burnet drew up a complimentary address to the president, praising him for his "wisdom, justice and firmness" in the face of foreign menaces and the distractions of "party spirit." The council approved the address unanimously, and only five members of the territorial house of representatives dissented. Similarly, the presidential election of 1800 roused little controversy in the territory, which in any case had no say in the outcome: the three newspapers established by then carried little news of the contest and, as one newspaper correspondent remarked, the inhabitants were not "pestered with the clamor of party men" as the election approached. As late as 1800, Burnet remembered, "Great unanimity prevailed in the Territory on political questions, while the States were rent, and almost torn asunder, by party strife."[29]

IDEOLOGY OF OPPOSITION

Burnet exaggerated: a partisan opposition to Federalist rule did exist in the Northwest Territory in the late 1790s. It may have been a subdued and unrepresentative minority, but its emotional and ideological power should not be underestimated. Hostility to the territorial regime drew on Revolutionary objections to colonial status and the lack of responsible self-government, while the French Revolution had raised a consciousness of issues relating to the fundamental character of the polity. More important, the stirring national events of 1798–1800 roused a sense of crisis and commitment among the politically aware that invigorated their determination to oppose what they saw as an iniquitous and potentially tyrannical government. Partisan passion inspired political opposition even in the distant environment of the Northwest Territory.

In the Cincinnati area the main political agitation of 1796 and 1797 concerned the future of the territorial regime, as opponents adopted the pattern of committee organization seen earlier in the decade in Kentucky. Early in 1796, public meetings in Columbia—a few miles upstream from Cincinnati and, until recently, the more populous settlement of the two—protested the "British & princely ideas" underlying the territorial government and looked to protect "the rights of freemen." Eighteen months later, in November 1797, a series of popular meetings in Cincinnati resulted in the election of a committee of correspondence, mandated to arrange an unofficial census in Hamilton County and urge other counties to the east to do the same; the object was to prove that the eastern division of the territory—the future Ohio—already had a population sufficient to deserve statehood. This initiative failed to attract support outside Hamilton County, but St. Clair's decision in October 1798 to order an enumeration and summon a territorial assembly represented a triumph for the vociferous demand in the Cincinnati region for an elected legislature.[30]

These opposition movements did not publicly identify themselves in partisan terms, but they were prompted by a handful of prominent residents who had been among the few to openly advocate Jefferson's election in 1796.[31] Judge William McMillan, "the father of the bar," had gained local popularity by opposing the extension of military jurisdiction beyond the confines of Fort Washington. A personal friend of Jefferson, this Virginian of Scotch-Irish background "rather leaned to democracy."[32] John Smith was well known in many guises: for his feats of physical prowess (whether driving oxen, rolling logs, racing horses, or at the end of a handspike), as storekeeper, merchant, and land agent, and as an inspiring Baptist preacher who served as pastor in both Columbia and Cincinnati.[33] Major David Ziegler, from Heidelberg, had served with distinction throughout the War for Independence, and again as a U.S.

army officer against the Ohio Indians; he had subsequently settled down as a successful storekeeper in Cincinnati, where he publicly displayed his Jacobin sympathies.[34] William Goforth was an elderly merchant and local judge who had fought in the Revolution, served in the New York state legislature, and, like Smith, chaired one of the Columbia meetings of 1796; in the territorial assembly in December 1799, he was one of the five Republicans who refused to vote a laudatory address to President Adams. Goforth's son of the same name was a distinguished doctor and committed Republican who moved from Kentucky to Cincinnati in 1800.[35] By 1801, some of these men identified themselves with the radical principles of the French Revolution, referring to each other as "Citizen David Ziegler" and "Citizen Doctor Goforth," in good Jacobin style.[36]

Shadowy evidence suggests that these mainly professional gentlemen organized further informal meetings of the politically like-minded, not unlike the earlier Democratic societies elsewhere. The Columbia protest of 1796 was said by one opponent to result from the "nocturnal lucubrations" of a "club composed of philosophers, priests, bards and shoemakers." In 1800 this same handful of gentlemen joined with other residents of less than "common decency" in a small Fourth of July celebration for "real republicans" held at Ziegler's house. Their toasts focused on national politics, as they protested against Federalist policy during the quasi-war against France. They found expression in the local newspaper, *Freeman's Journal*—which was more moderate than its predecessor, Maxwell's *Centinel*—and their criticism was sufficiently forceful to prompt St. Clair to reply in the press and even publish two pamphlets supporting the Alien and Sedition Acts. By 1800 they looked to the presidential election as they toasted President Adams's "early retirement" and the triumph of "genuine republicanism" over "the pernicious seeds of aristocracy." Clearly, a party spirit focused on national politics—and buoyed by liberal draughts of a more intoxicating brand of spirit—existed in the Cincinnati area even before the statehood movement got under way.[37]

Although the evidence is scanty, these early Democratic Republicans said enough to indicate that their outlook was akin not so much to that of the leading Virginia Jeffersonians as to the more radical, democratic ideology of New York and Philadelphia, inspired by Thomas Paine and the French revolutionaries. The same was true even outside Cincinnati, if we may judge from the experience of one young man who in 1799–1800, at the age of twenty-six, found himself a lonely pioneer hard at work forming the first settlement at Ravenna on the Western Reserve. Needing to borrow a scythe from a neighbor, he walked twelve miles through the untamed forests, finding his way by marks blazed on trees by surveyors. At his neighbor's cabin a welcome package of letters and newspapers forwarded from the East awaited him. After a late dinner he set off back to Ravenna but, after five or six miles, could not resist the temptation to sit on a log and open his mail. The letters were from friends in New England, and the newspapers were several numbers of the Philadelphia *Aurora*, the leading Democratic Republican newspaper in the nation. "I soon became interested in the contest going on between Jefferson & Adams for the presidency," he later recalled, "& 'took no note of time.' The sun had set ere I was aware of it. I thought of laying down and sleeping on the ground, but about where I was I had killed a large rattlesnake on my way up & was suspicious some of his relatives might avenge his death if I put myself in their way." After wandering in the woods in the dark, "I took my road in the bed of the creek" which ran past his clearing, and "after a very labourious march or rather wade at twelve o'clock I reached my fence and was at home."[38]

The young settler was Benjamin Tappan, eldest brother of the future evangelical moral reformers and abolitionists Lewis and Arthur Tappan. Sharp, forthright, cuttingly sarcastic, Benjamin would attain distinction in rather different fields—as a man of the Enlightenment, expert on conchology and geology, patron of history and education, businessman and canal builder, lawyer and judge, but above all as a prominent politician in both state and nation. A highly partisan leader of the Jacksonian Democrats, he would be promoted in 1839, at the age of sixty-five, to the U.S. Senate, where he would exercise much influence. Regarded as "the venerable patriarch of the Ohio democracy" amidst the party excitements of 1840, Tappan would always sternly insist that he had been "a member of the democratic party from its origin"—back in the days of Hamilton and Jefferson.[39]

In an autobiographical sketch written in 1840, Tappan recalled the formative moments of his political life. He "had taken his stand on the democratic side" in 1794 when, at the age of twenty, he attended a supper to celebrate the recapture of Toulon from the British and Spanish by the French revolutionaries. The name "Democrat," he always insisted, had been taken up from the start, having been "just then adopted in France." Excited by the crisis in Europe, Tappan planned to go to France "to join the republican party," but he was persuaded not to sail because he had recently inoculated himself against small-pox and the captain feared possible complications. Instead—after a brief spell learning portrait painting under Gilbert Stuart—he became a law student in the office of Gideon Granger, leader of the opposition party in Connecticut. During his three years there, "party spirit ran very high" and partisans on both sides began to bear distinctive badges: the Federalists wore black cockades and insulted those who refused; the young Democrats, to prevent abuse, bore stiff, white hickory canes, which became their distinguishing mark. Tappan entered into the controversy over the Alien and Sedition Acts, and when President Adams called for a day of fasting during the French crisis of 1798–99, Tappan wrote a parody, based on the 148th Psalm, which was widely reprinted in "the *Aurora* and most of the Democratic papers throughout the Union." For a moment it appeared that this blasphemy might prevent his admission to the bar, "who were nine tenths Federalists," but he was admitted when—so he claimed—it became known that his alternative plan was to join the Democratic newspaper in Hartford. Not that it mattered, since he was soon striking out to the Ohio frontier to look after the family's landholdings on the newly opening Western Reserve.[40]

In 1801 Tappan delivered a Fourth of July oration at a pioneer gathering on the Western Reserve that demonstrated his understanding of what was at stake in the party contest. He warned his listeners that the sacred principles and important truths of the American Revolution were at risk, for had not other nations "burst the chains of slavery" but then failed to sustain the liberty "for which nature's god designed them"? The answer, he insisted, was to improve man by "reason, philosophy & liberty" and to make government "more simple in its operation & less pernicious in its influence." Other nations had lost their hard-won liberty because "they panted for wealth, magnificence & power": they had built fleets in order to command the channels of commerce, and "fleets and armies led by a natural gradation to foreign wars—to multiplicity of offices at home & plunder abroad—to enormous taxes & at last to despotism." The history of England in particular, he thought, demonstrated that "systems of finance & taxation" could defraud man of "that liberty which could no longer be taken by force," but the fortunately situated American colonies had been able to break free from the system. And then "France caught from us the sublime doctrines of liberty—& we have seen her goaded on to madness by surrounding despots," inflicting on Europe war, desolation, and anarchy.

The whole American people, Tappan declaimed, were interested in the French Revolution, and their disagreements over its progress lay at the root of current party divisions. Some ardent lovers of liberty mourned the excesses but looked to the ultimate emancipation of Europe; other Americans believed that not all men are capable of self-government and wanted decisions to be left to "the wisest, the best informed & wealthiest members of society." The majority of the people, he asserted, were sound republicans, but a minority devoted to aristocratic delusions had seduced part of the people by playing on their fears. They were assisted by clergymen who were "terrified at the fancied prospect of an inundation of French principles in morals and politicks," and so "changed the meekness of the gospel of peace for the intollerance [*sic*] of party zeal." These "aristocrats" had brought the management of American affairs close to the form and substance of the British constitution and so had corrupted the "forms of civil policy": the national debt had grown, expenditure and offices had been increased, a needless army raised, freedom of the press challenged, and the French Revolution opposed in league with the despots of Europe. Locally, extortionate practices had been introduced into the territorial government as part of the "aristocratic" system. Fortunately, in Tappan's view, all these evils—except the last—had been destroyed by Jefferson's election, which expressed the revival of the spirit of 1776 and underlined the lessons of history:

> To preserve liberty, the power must be in the hands of the whole people by frequent & free elections. They must consider the officers of government not as masters but as servants employed for hire or reward to transact their business. They must accustom themselves to a strict and liberal enquiry into their conduct, praising or censuring with manly freedom where praise or censure is due. And above all they must remember that economy is the key stone of popular governments—it is the test by which to try the relative advantages of any system of social order.

Although clearly drawing on traditional fears of corruption and tyranny, Tappan also looked toward a simple system of government derived from the consent and participation of a self-sufficient electorate free of hierarchical controls. But most obviously he believed a struggle between good and ill was under way, embodied in the contest between two national political parties.[41]

Tappan was far from alone in the future Ohio in identifying himself with one of the poles of the political argument raging in the eastern states. Often, as in his case, partisan identity was imported into the Old Northwest and survived even though the territory had no voice in federal elections. Those who stayed behind in the East sometimes envied the emigrants, who they believed had "removed away from all these tumults and broils into a New Country where . . . very little party Spirit arises," but then they plied these emigrants with news of party fights—sometimes fistfights—in their old homes.[42] Partisan conflict in the East seemed relevant to western settlers because, whatever the local variations, the fundamental issues were national, of concern to every politically aware American. Long-standing arguments stemming from the American Revolution about popular control of government and the nature of federal power were of particular significance in the Northwest Territory; questions of taxation and defense and foreign policy were acutely important on the frontier; while stormy events in revolutionary Europe were all-absorbing to men who remained as much a part of Atlantic civilization as did the Ohio settlers whose private letters and newspapers have come down to us. As Jefferson said, the whole future of mankind rested on the outcome of the revolution in France, and educated Americans everywhere could not help but take a stand on the fundamental issues it raised.

However, party spirit had little opportunity to express itself in practical politics in the Northwest Territory, and politicians had no incentive to press the issues upon the electorate at large in order to influence the outcome of national elections. In the eastern states the party contest of 1800 was to draw thousands of men to the polls who, though long qualified, had probably never voted before, and many of them established a Republican loyalty because short-term issues—High Federalist extremism, subservience to Britain, threats to liberty, and heavy direct taxation—ran strongly against the Federalists, as the war crisis with France receded. Nothing quite like that had happened in the Northwest Territory by the time Thomas Jefferson took power in March 1801, simply because the peculiar constitutional environment created by the Northwest Ordinance continued to prove antithetical to the development of modern-style political parties.

COURT AND COUNTRY

However many residents of the future Ohio felt involved in the national political debate and had a clear sense of party commitment, their partisanship had negligible effect on the domestic politics of the territory. Even when the territory evolved into the representative stage of government and the citizenry gained the opportunity to express themselves through the electoral system, elections were not agitated according to national party divisions. The partisan electoral conflict raging in the eastern states, and arousing Kentucky and Tennessee, was simply inappropriate to the political structure of the territory.

Even in the Cincinnati region, the elections of December 1798 for the first territorial assembly were not fought along party lines. Admittedly, four out of five of those elected in Hamilton County had been members of the pro-statehood committee of correspondence of 1797 and soon emerged as leading Republicans, but they were not nominated as a party ticket, and only a minority of voters voted for them as a ticket. The polling record shows known partisans voting for men from both parties, with Jacob Burnet, notably, gaining the votes of such Republicans as William Goforth and William Ludlow. Burnet himself recalled that "party influence was scarcely felt" in the elections, with the result that the people "in almost every instance selected the strongest and best men, in their respective counties"—although he himself lost in the race for the lower house.[43]

In consequence, the assembly's work was not marked by fixed parties of any kind. The lower house, meeting briefly in January 1799 to nominate ten men for the legislative council, chose a list containing both Federalists and moderate men with connections on the other side. St. Clair thought all of them "unexceptionable" and did not mention party identity in advising the president, who had to select five of the ten for the council. When the full legislature reassembled for its first proper session in September 1799, there were signs of moderate opposition to the territorial establishment, but it was not organized along national party lines.[44] Admittedly, some historians have pointed to the young William Henry Harrison's election as the first territorial delegate to Congress, in preference to St. Clair's son, as a Republican triumph over Federalism. However, Harrison's supporters did not describe either themselves or their candidate in partisan terms. Instead, they represented an informal grouping of interests opposed to the governor.[45] This opposition is best described as a "Country" opposition pressing for the redress of grievances rather than endeavoring to win power in the name of a clearly defined national political party.

The leadership of this opposition grouping quickly fell into the hands of the most talented spokesmen of the Chillicothe gentry, Thomas Worthington and Edward Tiffin. They made contact with the leaders of the Cincinnati opposition, including the Symmes interest as well as the proto-Republicans; the Harrisons hosted the Worthingtons during the first session of the assembly, which met in Cincinnati.[46] According to St. Clair, the Chillicotheans were especially interested in boosting the value of their property and "giving consequence to Chillicothe," by making it the capital of the territory and presumably of any future state. Hence they favored splitting the territory and creating an eastern division with boundaries like modern Ohio. To judge by their actions, they were also keen to put government on a sound, practical basis (as St. Clair had proposed) and to remove a number of general grievances that had arisen under the first stage of territorial government. Hence it seems reasonable to deduce that, in 1799, the Chillicothe gentry wished only to see the representative process enable the local electorate and its leaders to place some limits on the range of action of the territorial regime.[47]

Beyond that, it is not clear whether the Chillicothe leaders were motivated by partisan dislike of Federalist rule at this time. St. Clair himself suggested that the more politically minded Chillicothe leaders had a hidden agenda: "almost all of them are democrats, whatever they pretend to the contrary," he claimed, and they wished to create a new state and "model it as they please." Thus, according to St. Clair, the growing bitterness of their opposition arose out of partisanship as much as from antagonism to his own administration and its policies. However, their connections in Virginia were with men on both sides of the party battle, and they were not openly identified with the national opposition at this time. Indeed, in the territorial assembly in December 1799, Worthington joined with Burnet in drafting the laudatory address to John Adams.[48]

In the event, St. Clair himself ensured that the Country opposition became more extreme and more partisan by his actions at the end of that first "harmonious" legislative session of late 1799. Had he been willing to accept the reforms passed by the assembly, a political crisis within the territory would have been avoided. Instead, the governor vetoed eleven out of the thirty bills passed. Some of the vetoes prevented the removal of long-standing grievances, such as the governor's supposed right to charge fees for licenses to marry or practice law or operate ferries. Other vetoes not only injured the interests of the Virginia land speculators but raised serious constitutional issues concerning the governor's right to decide the limits of the legislature's competence. Even many of St. Clair's supporters now came to believe that the governor's powers must be cut down, and opponents such as Worthington began to argue that only statehood could end the arbitrary rule of an externally chosen chief executive.[49]

As a result, the issue of statehood began to be agitated earnestly in many parts of the territory. Men who regarded themselves as committed Republicans generally took the lead in opposition to the Federalist tyranny in the territory, and even on the Western Reserve Democrats such as Benjamin Tappan circulated propaganda in favor of statehood.[50] Certainly, greater partisan awareness was displayed in the assembly elections of October 1800, and the second session of the first assembly in late 1800 was marked, according to historian Jeffrey P. Brown, by "a growing and clearly identifiable party split." Yet this legislative conflict was still not couched in terms of national parties: some known Republicans backed the governor, while the shifting balance between the two groups showed that a clearly demarcated division had not yet been created in the legislature.[51] The peculiar constitutional climate continued to restrict the development of party action.

Even in the second stage of territorial government, the governor was absolutely supreme and beyond the reach of the local electoral process. Not only could he decide when the assembly met and for how long but he could even determine the basis of apportionment of the lower house. His veto power was unlimited, and he retained a real independence of the assembly since his salary was paid by the federal government, which alone could get rid of him. Moreover, he controlled most avenues of political preferment in the territory, and had considerable influence over the distribution of federal patronage. In effect, the governor enjoyed a position even stronger than that of most royal governors in the earlier Thirteen Colonies. In no way could local people command or capture this potentially overpowerful executive.[52]

St. Clair's preeminence over the territorial legislature was further buttressed by the restricted opportunities for popular participation. The Northwest Ordinance laid down a franchise that was more limited than in any of the states, restricting it to adult males who owned fifty acres freehold. There was only one polling station in each county, at a time when the whole area of future state was divided into only five or six counties. Under such a system, turnouts were low, rarely reaching 20 percent of the adult male population, and county seats, where polling took place, enjoyed undue influence. In 1800, at the first territorial election in Trumbull County—covering the eastern half of the Western Reserve—the sole polling place was at Warren in the southeastern corner; since there were no roads, this virtually ensured "that only a portion of the electors" would attend, and "none were present from Cleveland."[53]

The actual manner of conducting the election also inhibited the free expression of the popular will. The election law passed by the first assembly, in December 1799, probably reflected accurately what had happened in the somewhat disorganized territorial elections of 1798–99 and laid down the rules followed in the elections of 1800. The law required the poll to be held at the county courthouse, or the usual place of holding the court, which sometimes was a private house. To cast his poll, a voter had to "approach the bar in the election room, and addressing the judges of such election, in his proper person, in an audible voice, to be heard by the judges of the election, and the poll-keepers thereof, to mention by name the person or persons, to the number of representatives to which such county shall be entitled, and the poll-keepers shall enter his vote accordingly, and then he shall withdraw." As this was a slow process—allowing about thirty votes to be cast in an hour—the poll was open for two days, from between ten and eleven in the morning until five in the afternoon, and could be opened for a third day. Obviously, since ballots were cast *viva voce* in front of the candidates or their proxies, the voters were exposed to the scrutiny of those who could bestow or withhold favor. Voting behavior was therefore greatly conditioned by the presence of men of influence, often a great proprietor or his agent; according to St. Clair, the great landholders had it in their power "to influence the whole elections in the country."[54]

But St. Clair himself was well placed to influence the electoral process. The governor appointed the sheriffs, who supervised elections and made the returns. The sheriff selected two of the justices of the county court of common pleas, all of whom owed their position to the governor, to serve with him as the judges of election; together, they chose the two poll-keepers. The judges of election had the power to challenge a voter's right to vote and to interrogate him under oath. Traditionally the sheriff and these same judges could decide whether the poll should open for a third day, and on occasions this ploy could affect the result.[55]

For example, in the special election held in Cincinnati to choose two additional territorial representatives for Hamilton County in September 1799, it was clear by the end of the first day that the most popular candidate was Francis Dunlavy, from the northern part of the settled area of the county. The pollsheet suggests that Dunlavy's antagonists around Cincinnati organized overnight to ensure his defeat, for in the later stages of the poll voters concentrated disproportionately on the two candidates who had emerged, in the course of voting, as the two most popular from the area close to Cincinnati. Significantly, when these two at last got their noses in front of Dunlavy, the sheriff himself cast his vote for them and immediately declared the poll closed. Denied the opportunity to bring in outlying voters on the third day, Dunlavy challenged the result of this "very warm election," but the assembly turned down his appeal. However, the first election law passed that December gave candidates the right to insist that the election continue into a third day.[56]

If the authorities had their means of influencing elections directly, St. Clair also enjoyed more indirect means of influence. He cooperated with the major proprietorial interests of eastern Ohio, including the two great land companies that were organizing the settlement of Washington and Trumbull Counties; in 1800 he allowed the Connecticut Land Company to name the governmental officers for the Western Reserve.[57] He could use his monopoly of official patronage to attract the support of local notables everywhere, including the socially dominant elite in the towns where elections were held. In Cincinnati, for example, the "officers of the colonial government were the monied men" who used their wealth and influence to discriminate against the professional interests of their political opponents. Lesser men could not always resist their pressure.[58] As in eighteenth-century England, a restricted electorate made executive influence over the legislature easier to attain.

In such a system there was little mileage in formal political opposition within the territory. The executive would generally have sizable support in the legislature, and the legislature had no means of extending its control over the executive. As a consequence, even men who were sympathetic to the Republican party found it expedient to subdue their Jeffersonianism in order to secure advantages and advancement from the Federalist regime. This process led to many notable Republicans later being accused of having been Federalists at this period, when in fact they had merely been accommodating to the realities of territorial political life.[59]

The most notable example was William Henry Harrison, who had served with distinction in the army of the northwest since 1791 and had earned General Wayne's praises as his aide-de-camp and right-hand man at the battle of Fallen Timbers. Harrison openly advocated Jefferson's election in 1796, at least according to later evidence.[60] But in 1798, after he resigned from the army, Harrison secured the key post of territorial secretary by playing the faithful servant of the Federalist administration; he carefully exploited all the connections, including George Washington himself, that he had made through his distinguished Virginia family and his father's reputation as a signer of the Declaration of Independence. Although he had married John Cleves Symmes's daughter—not entirely to Symmes's satisfaction, but without any serious breach—Harrison was regarded as a sound man, tested by military service and trusted by his predecessor, Winthrop Sargent himself. Even St. Clair approved his appointment as secretary, although he would have preferred his own son. Only thereafter did Harrison draw close to the Chillicothe leaders, becoming the Country party's successful candidate for territorial delegate. Harrison continued to be trusted by Federalists in Philadelphia, as he persuaded Congress in 1800 to pass the land law requested by the territory's Country leaders and to create the Indiana Territory. It was entirely in keeping with his ambiguous course that President Adams should appoint him governor of Indiana in 1800—and that President Jefferson should keep him on.[61]

Other Republican sympathizers, too, hovered between the parties for the sake of office and advancement. Harrison's friend, James Findlay—who consorted with the St. Clairs in Cincinnati, was raised to the legislative council in 1799, and gained appointment as receiver of the Cincinnati Land Office in 1800—inevitably subdued his sympathy with the political views of his father and brothers, who were prominent leaders of Pennsylvania Republicanism.[62] For all his Virginia connections, Thomas Worthington also carefully maintained business and personal relations with leading Federalists; he and his friends clearly recognized the key role that the governor and Rufus Putnam could play in securing their promotion. Worthington himself was later accused of "playing the courtier" in Philadelphia in 1800 to secure appointment as register at the Chillicothe Land Office from President Adams.[63]

The pull of patronage in weakening partisan opposition was most obvious in the case of George Tod, a young Republican lawyer from Connecticut, who became St. Clair's private secretary and so intimately involved in his schemes. He spelled out to Republicans on the Western Reserve the attractions of the governor's plans, and conjured up visions of future eminence before the eyes of his ambitious friend Samuel Huntington, another Republican freshly arrived from Connecticut. So fully was Tod associated with St. Clair's regime that former party associates back home frankly told Tod of their "fears . . . that your office from the Governor will damp your ardour in support of Democracy." In such ways the appointive character of the territory's government inhibited the development of party action along national party lines.[64]

Equally important were the regional tensions within the territory, which St. Clair exploited to his own advantage. In effect, sectional rivalries cut across the potential national political alignment and allowed St. Clair to attract extra support for his "Court" party. The major centers of settlement—Marietta, Chillicothe, and Cincinnati—appreciated the advantages that would flow from becoming the capital of a new state and realized that the choice of capital would depend on the boundaries specified for each state. The Northwest Ordinance had envisaged the division of the territory into reasonably large states, with the most eastern one defined by a western boundary like that of modern Ohio—a line drawn due north from the mouth of the Great Miami. Cincinnati and Marietta would be on the margin of such a state, and the Virginians' town of Chillicothe would occupy the most convenient situation for a state capital. St. Clair's scheme to create smaller territories involved boundary changes that favored Cincinnati and Marietta, to the detriment of Chillicothe.

The first, quite viable, version of this scheme was defeated in January 1800, when Congress established the Indiana Territory and confirmed the ordinance's boundary between Indiana and Ohio. St. Clair's second proposal subdivided the modern state along the line of the Scioto, thus completely destroying the prospects of Chillicothe. Like its predecessor, this project appealed powerfully to Cincinnati, and some of the town's leading politicians—known Republicans, formerly enemies of the governor—shifted to his support. Although still sympathetic to early statehood, the prominent Cincinnatian William McMillan privately recognized that "both interest and policy require that the eastern and western Counties should unite" to bring about the proposed boundary changes.[65]

Accordingly, in the legislative session of late 1800, a Cincinnati-Marietta combination appeared that supported St. Clair on many measures. It markedly triumphed in electing the next territorial delegates to Congress—McMillan himself to complete the balance of Harrison's term, and the Marietta lawyer, Paul Fearing, to take over in the new Congress due to meet in December 1801. By that time the second territorial assembly was in session, and the same sectional combination pushed through a Division Act requesting Congress to modify the boundaries proposed in the ordinance. So powerful were considerations of local interest that Republicans felt compelled to cooperate with Federalists in the region of Cincinnati and Marietta, while in the interior even Federalists such as Philemon Beecher of Lancaster supported the Chillicothe interest. Thus the central issue of territorial politics cut across the emerging national party alignments, and a powerful Court could exploit the situation to its own advantage.[66]

As was to remain true throughout the nineteenth century, the territorial

system encouraged the persistence of Court vs. Country politics within each
territory. In every case, the presence of a powerful executive independent of
local control effectively prevented the development of a two-party system such
as operated in the existing states.[67] Statehood was therefore the first essential
step toward the development of a modern party contest. This emancipation
would give the state not only a voice in national elections and a government
responsible to the local electorate, but also the opportunity to determine for
itself the structure of that electorate. Statehood would also bring what the
United States as a whole had gained in 1789 through the new Constitution—a
center of power which could be captured through the electoral process—and
that inevitably spelled the end of Court vs. Country politics. In practice, this all-
important constitutional revolution came more quickly than might have been
anticipated, mainly as a result of the political changes that were already transforming national politics.

A CHANGE OF DYNASTY

Ohio achieved statehood by March 1, 1803—the official date for celebrations—
because Thomas Jefferson and his party triumphed in the nationwide elections
of 1800–1801. The Court of King Arthur, which seemed to hold such arbitrary
sway over the territory, was always dependent on higher authority, and that
superior power would not necessarily always support the governor's pretensions. Not only did his opponents in the territory have access to that higher
Court but, unlike the territorial executive, the federal government was open to
capture by the opposition. The colonial government was, therefore, always
vulnerable to something akin to a change of dynasty at the imperial court,
which encouraged the discontented in the colony to cluster round the rever-
sionary interest. Of course, statehood and internal responsible government
were inevitable sooner or later, but it was critical for the future that, as it
happened, they came in 1802 as a gift from above.

What was at stake in the struggle was the political character of the new state,
which might prove decisive in future close national elections. Contemporary
politicians were well aware that the different groups settling in different parts of
the Northwest Territory had established partisan propensities, and they recognized that party success in the new state would be influenced by how the
boundaries of the new state were drawn. In 1800, for example, Federalists in
Congress had agreed that the federal government should take over Connecticut's claim to jurisdiction over the Western Reserve, and confirm the title of the
Connecticut Land Company, only after receiving assurances that there was no
truth in the rumor that "the Settlement of the Reserve is to be a Democratic

one." A similar concern for the political composition of future states underlay a significant provision in the act creating the Indiana Territory in 1800: it decreed that Wayne County, the area around Detroit, which was known to be strongly Federalist, should be part of the slimmed-down Northwest Territory and then of any state created out of it (i.e., Ohio) until special arrangement had been made for the future Michigan Territory. But when Ohio was finally granted permission to become a state in 1802, the majority in Congress had changed and Wayne County was deliberately excluded from the constitutional convention and therefore from the future state, much to the chagrin of Federalists like Burnet.[68]

Similarly, St. Clair's division schemes were designed to ensure the political soundness of any new state. The governor repeatedly warned fellow Federalists that the Virginians of the Scioto Valley who would "take the lead" in an undivided state of Ohio possessed political "prejudices" hostile to Federalism. His partition plan, in both its versions, aimed to gerrymander a state in the eastern division that would be "surely Federal," because of the sound allegiance of both the Ohio Company settlers and the major proprietorial interests in eastern Ohio. At the same time the Virginians and other unreliable elements would be placed in a western division so lightly populated as to be ineligible for statehood for years to come.[69] Yet each version of this scheme was voted down by Congress, even by the overwhelmingly Federalist Congress of 1800, with members of both parties voting together. Fundamentally, the proposal was unacceptably radical, since many Federalists regarded the Northwest Ordinance's description of future state boundaries as a compact with the settlers, a charter possessing prescriptive and binding force.[70]

This critical failure resulted partly from St. Clair's lack of prestige within his own party. In January 1798 some New England Federalists at Philadelphia had opposed his reappointment as governor because of his "nonattendance in the government, infirmity of health, predisposition toward the gout, and Sinecure Appointments." They wanted a more effective proconsul in the Northwest. Again, three years later much of the opposition to his further reappointment came from within the Federalist majority in Congress, whereas some Republicans voted for him for fear of "exchanging an old and feeble tyrant for one more active and wicked."[71]

Moreover, the governor had no monopoly on access to the federal government, and the ambiguity of territorial politics allowed his opponents to gain influence and advantages that weakened St. Clair's position. Thus in 1799–1800 territorial delegate Harrison gained great influence at Philadelphia, voicing the views of the Country party and frustrating St. Clair's first division scheme. Partly through Harrison's influence, President Adams at that time made some territorial appointments unwelcome to St. Clair, notably that of the well-born Virginian, Charles Willing Byrd, who was Nathaniel Massie's brother-in-law and a committed Republican. Byrd's appointment as territorial secretary in December 1799 meant that in St. Clair's absences—admittedly now not so frequent—the executive power in the territory fell into the hands of a man sympathetic to the opposition.[72] This lack of support at the center became absolute, of course, when the friends of St. Clair's opponents in the territory captured the federal government.

With Jefferson's accession to power in March 1801, the central authority could no longer be expected to reinforce St. Clair's Courtly power, and the change of dynasty guaranteed a major shift of power and advantage within the territorial establishment sooner rather than later. The vital influence on the distribution of federal patronage shifted from St. Clair and Rufus Putnam to Thomas Worthington, in whom the new administration, according to Albert Gallatin, had "a more perfect confidence than in any other person . . . in the North West Territory."[73] Covert Republicans now emerged in their true colors in Chillicothe, Cincinnati, and Marietta. Some Federalist self-seekers in the territory changed to the stronger side, as did John Cleves Symmes, who was anxious to retrieve his fortunes and popularity. So too did his ambitious nephew, Daniel Symmes, the clerk to the general court of Hamilton County, who had repeatedly drunk "damnation" or "confusion to democracy." With cabinet members by August 1801 asking Worthington's advice on new appointments in the territory, office seekers had every reason to demonstrate their political soundness.[74]

Under these circumstances the achievement of statehood might reasonably be seen as simply transferring power from a Federalist establishment reinforced by territorial rules to a Republican hegemony operating within the more decentralized structures of statehood. A change in command of patronage, in other words, simply shifted officeholding from King Arthur's knights to the Virginia gentry and their allies. The ambitious Federalists who turned their coats were therefore doing no more than the Republicans who earlier had accommodated to the territorial regime. Yet, however tempting and fashionable this interpretation, by itself it gives a fundamentally misleading view of the political transformations surrounding Ohio's achievement of statehood.[75]

To start with, the new president did not use his patronage to help the statehood cause in 1801–2. He did appoint Republicans to one or two new offices and filled some vacancies. Otherwise, in his first eighteen months in office, Jefferson dismissed almost no federal officeholders in the territory, with the significant exception of the Marietta postmaster. Jefferson was widely expected to fire St. Clair and appoint a Democrat in his place, especially when the territory's Republican leaders pressed charges against "Arthur the First" in January 1802. But the president refused to act, pointing out that early statehood could provide a better remedy soon enough.[76] Only after the statehood forces had triumphed did the president begin to dismiss Federalist officeholders, with Rufus Putnam, for example, continuing to hold the influential office of surveyor general until September 1803.

In practice, the statehood leaders targeted not so much the new president as the Republican majority in Congress. Worthington, in particular, cultivated his contacts in both houses and spelled out to them the partisan motives behind St. Clair's division schemes. As he told a Georgia senator in 1801, "All good federalists . . . fear that our state will give three republican votes at the next election for president—send you two republican senators and a Republican representative in Congress."[77] St. Clair and his allies believed it essential to counteract such arguments by emphasizing the bipartisan nature of the support for the territorial assembly's Division Act of December 1801, which proposed dividing the territory at the Scioto. Unfortunately, the territorial delegate was no longer William McMillan, who had worked closely with Republicans in Congress in the early months of 1801, but Federalist Paul Fearing. St. Clair saw the need to reinforce him by sending some Republican from Cincinnati, preferably McMillan, plus another from the Western Reserve, ideally George Tod: the latter's "political principles would, in the present case, render him more useful than some other, or than he otherwise could be."[78] Fearing himself warned that "unless some one from the Territory should be here who enters fully into the politics of the majority," the agents sent from Chillicothe to lobby against the Division Act "will try to make a party question of it." Fearing accurately predicted that the agents—Thomas Worthington and Michael Baldwin—"will make the Democrats think that the object is a fatal stab to Democracy in the territory, and denying it will be but a confirmation; but if we had some one here in their Politicks, he could do these ideas all away." In fact, however, the St. Clair men failed at this critical moment to persuade any one that it was worth the trouble and expense actually to go as a special agent to Jefferson's Washington.[79]

In any case, St. Clair's scheme was lost. "The whole of the reigning majority" in Congress united in voting the Division Act down, and then, at the prompting of the president, William B. Giles of Virginia brought forward a bill "enabling" the territory to call a constitutional convention and apply for statehood. With "the Democratic members" influenced "very strongly in their cause," the Chillicothe proponents of statehood were "able to carry any thing"—and in April Congress passed the Enabling Act on a strict party vote in both houses.[80] Under the terms of this act, a constitutional convention was to be elected that must decide whether to apply for statehood and could then draft a constitution for the new state.

Yet this critical election, to be held in October, would see St. Clair and his allies still in command of all the advantages and electoral influence that office could bring. In March, James Pritchard, the leading Republican in Jefferson County, had declared St. Clair's replacement before the election absolutely vital: "As his pets are Chiefly in office it will give them a greater weight and should a majority of them be elected to a Convention perhaps our situation will not be much mended." Pritchard believed that, if St. Clair could be removed, "a small Revolution in this County will be necessary," notably the removal of the sheriff and the postmaster. In June, John C. Symmes still thought the Republicans would "never have fair play while Arthur and his knights of the round-table sit at the head." Worthington complained that Jefferson's failure to dismiss St. Clair amounted to permitting "a tyrant by his acts and intrigue to destroy the prospects and thwart the wishes of the people" at the moment when they were at last allowed "to form for themselves a government of their own choice." Worthington calculated that the governor controlled seven hundred patronage positions that he could use to obstruct Republican election victories.[81]

In practice, with typical neglect, St. Clair was absent for several months during the spring, thus allowing Secretary Byrd to exercise the governor's powers of patronage. Byrd accordingly made nearly forty major militia and judicial appointments to offset the influence of local Federalist officials. On his return in July, St. Clair promptly revoked many of the commissions and reestablished the predominance of the "governor's party." When he departed again in October, he took the public seal of the territory with him so that Byrd could not again upset the Court's electoral machine.[82] Some Federalists thought that St. Clair remained so powerful that he could win a seat in the convention and thereafter be elected governor "under the new order of things."[83]

It was largely this apprehension of St. Clair's continuing influence that drove the statehood men on to secure their goal as quickly as possible. Given an excuse, the governor might conceivably reconvene the second territorial assembly, while the third one was in any case scheduled to meet on November 22. If either met, with unreliable house and unrepresentative council, St. Clair might yet manipulate a division of the territory that could delay statehood or even produce a Federalist state (called "Erie") east of the Scioto. The Enabling Act offered a means of outflanking the governor, and Byrd accordingly refused Federalist requests to reconvene the second assembly. For the same reason the Republican majority in the constitutional convention refused to risk referring the constitution to the people, since that would delay its submission to Congress until after the scheduled meeting of the third assembly.[84]

By that time, however, St. Clair had ruined himself. He had tried, "*1st Consul like,*" to take command of the convention, only to be outfaced by Worthington "with a manly intrepidity." All St. Clair gained was the right to address the convention on the third day, and his remarks were so critical of Congress and the Enabling Act that they led to his dismissal by Jefferson in December 1802.[85] Most Ohio Republicans now confidently expected that "his old train of Sycophants will soon forsake the poor old man's cause as they find the loaves and fishes are no longer at his disposal," but some still feared that his old electoral influence might yet prove embarrassing in the first state elections of January 1803.[86]

In fact, however, the January elections confirmed the original triumph of the statehood forces in the convention elections of October 1802. Together, these victories revealed the electorate's overwhelming desire for an end to colonial status, for a government responsible to the people of Ohio, and for full membership of the Union. But the October elections had also demonstrated that the character of politics had changed: the political system no longer operated under the old rules; the *ancien régime* of influence and deference was giving way to more democratic and even populistic ways of determining who should control the advantages and responsibilities of government. And that change opened the way further for the development of more modern-style party politics.

The Democratic Revolution of 1802

The coming of statehood in Ohio bore some extraordinary resemblances to the American Revolution. Ohioans commonly saw the territorial regime as a "colonial system," akin to that of Britain earlier, and viewed the governor as "a British nabob." Throughout the controversy of 1800–1802, proponents of statehood made rhetorical appeal to the memory of the Revolution. In the end, the territory became an "independent state" without recourse to violent protest, simply because Ohioans benefited from exactly the kind of revolution in the metropolis that colonial radical leaders had hoped for in vain in the early 1770s. Moreover, as with independence, the achievement of statehood was associated with something of an internal revolution. The statehood men appealed to the public at large, including those formally excluded from politics; they resorted to extralegal action sanctioned by public opinion, and adopted extraconstitutional organizational devices—such as committees of correspondence—previously used in the struggle against Britain; and the contest resulted in increased public participation in political decision making and a highly democratic state constitution enshrining the best Revolutionary principles. In the long run, both on the eastern seaboard and in Ohio, revolution and constitution prepared the way for a new kind of partisan politics.[1]

This view runs counter to the long tradition of seeing Ohio's statehood as the work of the self-interested Virginia gentry centered on Chillicothe and their fellow speculators elsewhere. Influential as they were, these leading opponents of St. Clair's regime found it necessary to rouse the support of other social elements in the territory, and the elections of October 1802 virtually became a plebiscite on the question of statehood. This broadening of the political universe amounted to a permanent shift in the character of politics and opened the way for modern-style mass parties in the new state. But this result was possible only because of the democratic revolution that Ohio had been undergoing since before statehood.

DEMOCRATIC IMPULSES

An *ancien régime* of influence and deference could not survive long in the social and ideological conditions of the Northwest Territory. From the beginning the process of settling frontier Ohio was not conducive to erecting systems of elite leadership and voter deference. It was obviously difficult to erect traditional social relationships in a new country, but the weakness of elite control resulted less from the democratizing effect of the frontier than from the pace of develop-ment. Admittedly, in some places where a consolidated settlement was made by people of the same ethnocultural background, as in the early years at Waterford or Gallipolis or Dayton, there was every chance that community feeling would establish recognized leaders, "natural aristocrats" who were accepted as magis-trates and spokesmen for the community.[2] Such closed communities, however, lasted only as long as frontier isolation protected them. Those such as Marietta that were always accessible to the passing world attracted a more diverse popu-lation fairly quickly and so took on the variegated and conflictual character typical of the river towns that were the main early centers of population.[3]

More common in territorial Ohio were isolated settlements in the forest clearings, where individual pioneers of varied background established their homesteads and only slowly began to create communities. Even on the Western Reserve, destined to become a transplantation of New England, the scattered nature of the shareholders' properties meant that early settlers such as Ben-jamin Tappan found themselves starting up their would-be settlements in isola-tion, many miles away from their nearest neighbors. In such situations a sense of communal solidarity developed only slowly, and any acquiescence in the rule of the rich and the well-born derived not from a cultural acceptance of the social and political propriety of deference but from economic dependence.[4]

Yet even the economic foundations of deferential behavior were shaky. The land companies of southeastern and northeastern Ohio might have retained a political dominance akin to that of the Holland Land Company in western New York, but the Ohio Company, though initially constructive and beneficial, divided up its lands among its members and dissolved itself in 1796, and the Connecticut Land Company was to do little for its settlers.[5] Throughout the Northwest Territory many wealthy individual proprietors and land speculators possessed extensive lands, but their object was to sell their lands as prices rose. This route to riches and social preeminence disappointed because of the slow

rate of settlement before 1795, the scarcity of cash, the landowners' own indebt-
edness, and the pressure of frontiersmen and squatters who settled where they
willed. Moreover, the opening of lands available at public sales—not just federal
lands but also the Virginia Military District—persuaded most large proprietors
and land speculators to sell more cheaply than they wished. In particular, they
could only sell on terms comparable with those offered by the federal government, which became especially competitive after the passage of William Henry
Harrison's Land Act of 1800: "Congress lands" could now be bought in smaller
lots than before (with a minimum of 320 acres), the minimum price was halved
to two dollars an acre, generous credit spread over five years, and the title was
indisputably freehold. Jacob Burnet saw this "most beneficent act" as in direct
"opposition to the interests of speculators who were, and wished to be, the
retailers of land to the poorer class of the community. . . . It put it in the power
of every industrious man, however poor, to become a freeholder."[6]

As a result, by 1810 landowning in Ohio would be "widespread and substantial," according to Lee Soltow. His study of the tax records for that year shows
that half the males over the age of twenty-six owned land outright and paid
taxes on it in their own names. Only 1–2 percent of landowners owned fewer
than 40 acres, and the median landholding was 150 acres, a "bountiful or
munificent" allotment by any standards. Of course, a relatively small number of
men possessed some huge landholdings, mainly for speculative purposes, but
this inequality must not obscure the fact that a substantial class of independent
smaller owners existed. Eighty-two percent of landholders held only one property and were almost certainly working farmers. This broad distribution was
the result of a process of unloading land during the previous fifteen years, as
may be seen in the shrinkage of holdings in the older settled counties of the state
compared with the more recent. The largest holdings remained on the slowly
settling Western Reserve.[7] Landholding was probably even more widespread
than these figures suggest, since it seems probable that many others were buying
land on credit from private owners but cannot be discerned in the tax records
because the responsibility for paying the tax lay with the original owner.[8]

These middle-class farmers were not necessarily grateful to those from
whom they had bought or borrowed. Notoriously, John C. Symmes had possessed a mighty domain, but he handled it so irresponsibly that he was deeply
unpopular with the settlers of his huge Miami Purchase in southwestern Ohio.
More responsible and respected speculators, such as Bezaleel Wells in eastern
Ohio, found that they could promote settlement only by making generous
concessions which encouraged—indeed, required—the creation of alternative
sources of political power and the participation of smaller men interested in
boosting the settlement. In other words, the great proprietors quickly dis-

covered that even partial sale of their speculative holdings prompted the emergence of a class of independent men who were not always inclined to follow the lead of their benefactor. As Stanley Elkins and Eric McKitrick have written, although "much has been made of large engrossments of land by speculators in the Northwest Territory, yet before the admission of Ohio in 1803, . . . it was apparent to all that the day of the great land magnate was at an end."[9]

This development was not unacceptable to those who dominated the territory's political life. The territorial legislature itself contributed to the process, for it facilitated the breakup of large estates by passing a law for the partition of real estate held jointly (for example, by speculative partnerships and companies), and it taxed unimproved lands owned by nonresidents in order to encourage them to sell to actual settlers. The assembly was sympathetic, on the whole, to those who had paid Symmes for lands he had no right to sell them. When Congress in 1799 granted to these unfortunates the right of preemption, the territorial assembly protested that those who had already paid once for their land deserved something more than just the right to make a second payment to the United States for the same piece of land. This sympathy is not surprising, since it fulfilled the original ideal of a new country filled with independent yeoman farmers capable of sustaining a true republic in the Northwest.[10]

The political leaders of the territory also shared the ideological commitments generated by the Revolution and accepted the rightfulness of popular participation in the political process. In the Ross County election of 1800, all spokesmen agreed that the representative must not only serve the interests of his constituents but be accountable to them. From the start, the territorial legislature published its proceedings, and the votes on particular measures, at the request of any member, were recorded; the assembly even published addresses to the people on important questions.[11] The practice of "instructing"—too often regarded as a Jacksonian innovation—was widely accepted, for the assembly repeatedly sent instructions to the territorial delegate in Congress, while on occasion members openly accepted their constituents' dictates. On the question of where the assembly should meet in 1801, one member from Hamilton County "informed several members of the house, that if he had voted according to his sentiments, he would have given his vote for Chillicothe; but his constituents had instructed him to vote as he had done." According to Jacob Burnet, this respect for public opinion ensured that the territorial assembly would never allow the introduction of slavery in any shape or form, in view of the "universal" hostility of the people.[12]

These highly "republican" and "democratic" sentiments resulted in significant political reforms, as even the rulers of the territory tried to broaden the basis of the regime. In 1795 St. Clair and the three territorial judges passed a law providing for tax assessors to be elected by ballot by the "free male inhabitants" of each township, although all other local officers were appointed by the governor. The territorial assembly further reformed the system of local government in January 1802 by allowing local taxpayers to elect (again by ballot) most of the township officers, though not the justices of the general court of quarter sessions, who ran the county government. With regard to territorial elections, St. Clair himself decreed that the Northwest Ordinance's suffrage rule should be construed so as to give the vote to holders of town-lots comparable in value to the land qualification, a view with which Congress concurred. In December 1800, the assembly (at the governor's recommendation) introduced voting by ballot in elections for the house, which made possible the reduction of the election to a single day. It also drastically extended the practical opportunity to vote by increasing not only the number of counties from six to ten but also the number of polling places in each county, so that voters could vote in their own township and no longer had to travel to the county seat. Finally, the assembly extended the suffrage by declaring that the ordinance's freehold franchise included all taxpayers who held legal preemption of the United States for fifty acres or more, and it petitioned Congress to amend the ordinance so as to allow all adult male taxpayers to vote in territorial elections, just as they already could in local elections.[13]

These changes in election rules inevitably began to transform the way in which politicians and voters approached each other. When elections were conducted *viva voce,* as before 1801, they lasted more than one day and the progress of the vote was known; hence it was common to adjust tactics once voting was under way, as voters began to concentrate on those candidates whom the early voting showed stood the best chance. Once secret ballots were deposited in locked iron boxes and polling was confined to one day, those hoping to produce particular outcomes had to organize candidacies and argue their case publicly well in advance of election day. This pressure confirmed the habit, already apparent in the territorial election of 1800, of candidates announcing their intentions in the press and reassuring voters of their commitment to the local community.[14]

Of all the measures passed, the increase in the number of polling places was of most immediate consequence. In Hamilton County, for example, which then embraced practically the whole of the Miami country, an area of some 4,000 square miles, voters no longer had to travel to Cincinnati, since there were now eight voting places distributed throughout the region. This enfranchisement of backcountry voters effectively threatened Cincinnati's political dominance in the county, for the settlers of interior townships had little interest in supporting

Cincinnati's pretensions. In the county's elections for the third assembly, held under the new rules, a ticket devoted to immediate statehood for the territory with its present boundaries triumphed, even though that meant a state capital on the Scioto. The victory of the statehood forces in 1802 throughout the territory ensured that the third assembly would never meet. But, if it had, the new rules were expected to ensure that the overall political complexion of the lower house would have been far more hostile to the territorial regime than had earlier assemblies.[15]

Even as the *ancien régime* was undermined and the way opened to a larger degree of popular control, the statehood movement began to broaden the political forum. In view of St. Clair's command, leading Republicans had to look beyond the established sources of power in the territory. They appealed to the public at large, including those excluded from voting in assembly elections, and used extraconstitutional expressions of public opinion to put pressure on key decision makers. In 1800–1801, in some places, they arranged public meetings to instruct their representatives in the assembly to support statehood. In Trumbull County, for example, the sense of the district was taken at the military elections of September 1801, and the organizers formally forwarded the result—a 53–6 victory for statehood—to their territorial representative "for his instruction." When the assembly instead passed the Division Act of December 1801, the Chillicothe leaders launched a great petition campaign requesting Congress not to approve the redrawing of the territory's boundaries.[16] To their gratification—and the shock of their opponents—they discovered, in many counties, a great popular demand for early statehood that resulted in the amendment of the petitions. In Adams County, where Nathaniel Massie—"by far the most wealthy [man] in the County"—counseled caution and delay, the county's petitions advocated statehood. As Joseph Darlinton explained, the people were unanimous in their eagerness to "shake off the iron fetters of the tory party in this territory."[17]

This demonstration of the popular will decisively influenced events. As more than one politician observed, local notables with an eye to future election quickly changed their attitude. According to David Vance, had even the second territorial assembly—which had passed the Division Act—been reconvened in 1802, in all probability "a large Majority . . . would be in favour" of statehood. As Burnet remarked disapprovingly, "Popularity is the governing motive of many of the Members of the House."[18] Congress, too, was impressed by the evidence of popular feeling: one of the key arguments against the Division Act was that some members of the assembly who voted for it had been "positively instructed by their constituents to use their best exertions in obtaining an independent government." Hence Congress could regard itself as fulfilling the popular will when it rejected division and gave Ohioans an opportunity to vote on statehood under the terms of the Enabling Act.[19]

This response went beyond what many of the statehood leaders had hoped for. Many landholders, notably Massie, feared the burden of taxation that statehood would bring, since the tiny population of the new state would now have to pay for its own government. Furthermore, the Enabling Act placed conditions on Ohio's admission such as no other state had suffered, and although Worthington worked hard to have them eased, unwelcome financial conditions remained. In particular, Congress insisted that federal lands in the new state were to remain untaxed until five years after sale, which would considerably reduce the value and "injure the sales" of lands in private hands, including the lands of proprietors in the Virginia Military District. Thus, as was pointed out at the time, "the Great landholders" among the Chillicothe leaders suffered financially from the terms upon which statehood was secured—but they were pushed on by the popular pressure they had aroused.[20]

Some Republican leaders had anticipated such problems and recognized that their opponents would make great capital out of them. The Federalists had already argued forcefully in the public presses that a scanty population, scattered and still struggling with the wilderness, could not afford to take on board the costs of government at present paid for by the federal authorities. Moreover, the Enabling Act was a political gamble, since by it Congress was interfering in the internal affairs of the territory, over which it had had no legal control since the beginning of the representative stage. This, some suspected, would be resented by the people, who clearly prized self-government above all. Why not be patient and wait a short time for the population to grow to sixty thousand? For then, within two years at most, the territorial assembly could itself call a convention and the new state apply for admission as a matter of right under the ordinance, without being penalized by heavy conditions.[21]

The decision on this issue was quite deliberately given to the people, as never before. At Worthington's suggestion, the Enabling Act authorized the election of the constitutional convention on the more liberal franchise proposed by the territorial assembly for regular elections, but not yet officially adopted. Confusion reigned over which election law should apply in the election—a confusion that does not reflect well on Worthington—but in the end it was agreed that Congress must have intended the recent territorial law to apply, which stipulated ensuring voting by ballot in townships.[22] The statehood men found themselves pushed on to ever more democratic positions by the logic of the popular forces they themselves had unleashed.

This extension of the political universe, it should be emphasized, had not been opposed by the territorial regime. All the measures of reform were approved by a council that had been appointed by President Adams, with St. Clair's approval, and the governor himself signed them into law. Even Governor St. Clair was less reactionary in his political views than historians have traditionally maintained: although he feared that "a multitude of indigent and ignorant people are but ill-qualified to form a constitution and government for themselves," he accepted that the people were the true source of political power and, on occasions, he was guided in his appointments by nominations made at public meetings. Federalists as well as Republicans accepted the rightfulness of popular participation as an essential feature of the republic, and both were caught up in a cultural shift that increasingly valued individual autonomy more than the communal will.[23]

THE BOISTEROUS SEA OF REVOLUTIONARY POLITICS

Changes in electoral rules and the extension of the franchise made possible the creation of a broad-based, participating, questioning, demanding, nondeferential electorate—made it possible, not inevitable. What forced on the transformation of electoral politics in 1802 was the intervention of men willing to bring pertinent issues to the voters' attention and so win popular support. Committed Republicans in the territory strove to exploit the printing press, to campaign, to coordinate, to persuade voters how important it was to elect men devoted to securing an end to the colonial system and creating a new state based on true "republican" principles. As a consequence, they intruded into communities formerly regarded as harmonious and deferential, and they undermined the influence of the traditional representatives of those communities. What was more, they discovered that, even in their own areas of strength, the electorate could no longer be taken for granted but expected candidates to justify themselves.

Of course, competition and appeals to the electorate had marked earlier territorial elections. Ross County, for example, had a long record of electoral struggles between would-be leaders. In the territorial election of 1798, Worthington was said to have succeeded only because Tiffin had persuaded the sheriff to close the polls at sunset on the second day when Worthington was just three votes ahead of his nearest rival, William Patten. In 1800, the local newspaper published statements from most of the candidates in the form of advertisements, all pledging themselves to serve the interests of the community. Tiffin and Worthington had a proven record in this regard. Elias Langham, by contrast, was implicated in St. Clair's schemes to promote Cincinnati, but Langham argued that anyone who "cast an eye to the little property I possess in the town & neighbourhood" could see that he could not be inimical to local interests. Skeptics said that he subsequently took great care how he voted in the assembly because he appreciated the danger of "tarring and feathering" when he returned home. By February 1802, Langham had become "a great advocate for state government." According to Edward Tiffin, "a new election, which is approaching, has made him a convert."[24]

This concern to conciliate public opinion became even more important when the Enabling Act of 1802 expanded the electorate and increased the rewards of winning support among the previously disfranchised. In Ross County, by April, the various candidates for the constitutional convention had "begun to break ground in the electioneering field." According to Michael Baldwin, one candidate, presumably Tiffin, had "begun to preach, which is generally a sympton [sic] of an election not being far off." Articles about the election filled the local newspaper, the Chillicothe Scioto Gazette, and by October Chillicothe was "glutted with handbills and long tavern harangues."[25]

In these circumstances, five Republicans issued a handbill, republished in the Gazette, calling upon the various candidates in Ross County to answer precise questions relating to statehood, slavery, and the Republican party. The speed with which Tiffin and Worthington replied suggested to some that they were privy to this effort to force candidates to reveal their political standpoint. Most candidates obliged—including all the successful ones. The only two respondents who openly favored the introduction of slavery found themselves denounced as "negro feds" and received only 50 and 87 votes, compared with the 621 received by the least popular of the successful candidates. As Jonathan Mills Thornton has written of Jacksonian Alabama, when candidates have to explain their views to the voters, deference is dead and elections belong to the electorate.[26]

Similarly, the dominant proprietorial interests of eastern Ohio found that even their apparently impregnable position depended on publicly satisfying voter concern. The wealthy Bezaleel Wells—a firm Federalist ever since he witnessed the disorders of the Whiskey Rebellion—had bought 15,700 acres in eastern Ohio in 1796 and laid out the town of Steubenville. As county clerk, he headed a Federalist establishment in Jefferson County that was reinforced after 1800 by control of the newly opened Steubenville Land Office. In March 1802 James Pritchard, the county's leading Republican, insisted that this political establishment could not be defeated at the polls unless President Jefferson first carried out a "small revolution" among the officeholders. Even without such external assistance, however, the Republicans elected three of the county's five delegates to the 1802 convention, and two of their Federalist opponents succeeded only by asserting their conversion to statehood and their support for a "Republican" constitution.[27]

Ohio Counties in 1802. *Source:* Downes, *Evolution of Ohio County Boundaries,* 22.

Afterwards Pritchard described how Wells—so often considered a prime example of the "old-style" elitist Federalist—won election to the convention:

> Bazaleel [*sic*] Wells he changed sides and made profession in a handbill he put out that if he was Elected he would endeavour to procure a Constitution like that of Pennsylvania. he out runs me 15 voices. his Private interest is Great having a great Number indebted to him for Lands sold to them in small Quantities and for Town Lots. he has always before this been a Great Stickler for a Territorial Government and an alteration for States bounds in the Territory &c. that I am not without hopes if he sees the Republican Party the strongest he will fall into all their views to acquire Popularity at home, but will be from Principle and interest I think a strong advocate for a Federal Governor as he has long basked in the sunshine of Power— . . . The adverse Party to me . . . Represented

me as a friend to slavery. their Peace [*sic*] came out at a late time and I had not
an opportunity publicly to Repel the assertion. I believe with the Ignorant and
uninformed it did me some injury.

Clearly, even old-style political leaders now had to orient their words and deeds
less to each other and more toward the voter.[28]

The most obvious example of agitation and electioneering challenging an
entrenched political establishment came in Washington County. The Revolutionary officers and their kin who dominated the county had benefited from
the support of territorial and national governments, on one hand, and the
Federalist sentiments of their neighbors, on the other. Marietta's attraction
toward St. Clair's schemes for dividing the territory further reinforced this local
consensus. The first Marietta newspaper—the *Ohio Gazette and the Territorial
and Virginia Herald*—was founded in December 1801 by Wyllys Silliman, a well-
connected New Englander who had published a Federalist paper in western
Virginia. The new paper's politics were "evidently Federal," as it preached the
need to avoid "a spirit of discord," supported the Division Act, and reprinted
material critical of the "Democrats." Even those local politicians who had
openly begun to display Republican sympathies felt obliged to participate in the
various public meetings that were called in the county in 1801 to protest against
statehood, and so a specially summoned delegate convention in June resolved
against statehood unanimously.[29] So powerful did this sentiment appear that
when the two Return Jonathan Meigses—the father a Revolutionary veteran,
the son a territorial judge—began privately to express some sympathy for early
statehood, the Chillicothe leaders regarded them as untrustworthy because of
their "connection with our determined enemies" in Marietta.[30]

By August 1802, however, the county's "political horizon" had changed.
First, the new federal government had introduced an agent of subversion by
dismissing David Putnam as postmaster at Marietta and conferring the post on
an enterprising early settler from Rhode Island, Griffin Greene. Previously a
moderate Federalist, Greene had "lately tur'd a rank Democrat." Then the
younger Meigs had gone to Washington "to pay adulation at the shrine of the
democratic Idol" and, according to local Federalists, to secure a plum office.
Although unsuccessful, "the frequent conversations with the president refresh'd
his republican Soul," and Meigs returned "in high spirits" with "a plan to
systematize a Jacobin party here." Meigs and Greene "aroused all the energy of
the party," sent "letters and runners . . . to every corner of the county" with
"secret whispers," and campaigned vigorously in Marietta, treating generously,
keeping "open house," and encouraging "riot and drunkenness." When a

Federalist-dominated county convention nominated three well-known Ohio Company settlers—a Putnam, a Gilman, and a Cutler—plus the leading man of Zanesville, John McIntyre, as candidates for the constitutional convention, the Republicans became "almost crazy . . . , endeavoring to pull us down who are in nomination." The "public mind" was disturbed as never before and all pretense of consensus destroyed, as the Republicans uncovered elements of discontent in the county. In the October election, the Federalists managed to carry their ticket by a 2:1 margin, but their supremacy now depended on persuading the local electorate. As Ephraim Cutler had reported to his father in August, "From being one of the most harmonious communities, we have been forced on to a most tremendous, boisterous sea of revolutionary politics."[31]

Similarly, in Hamilton County the statehood campaign had to confront a vested local interest opposed to the Enabling Act. Cincinnati had served as unofficial territorial capital for much of the time before the creation of the Indiana Territory, and most of the 750 inhabitants of this strategically located village wished to secure the advantages of a state capital. This ambition persuaded some of the future city's best-known Republican critics of the territorial regime—notably William McMillan and John Smith—to join in St. Clair's logroll and so cooperate with local Federalists. However, the county at the time embraced a backcountry that spread northwards to the Greenville Treaty line, and the newly growing areas, especially around Lebanon, Hamilton, and Xenia, resented the political dominance of the officeholders, merchants, and professional men residing in and near Cincinnati. These tensions had ensured that territorial elections had normally been characterized as contests between "the gentlemen in Cincinnati" and "the Rabble in the country," in which partisan identity played no role.[32] However, the activities of the dissident minority in Cincinnati, led by David Ziegler, the two William Goforths, and Daniel Symmes, soon destroyed the internal unity generated on each side of this sectional divide.

Early in 1801, this dissident element in Cincinnati launched a "paper War" against those Republicans who were flirting with St. Clair's logroll and so "set [the county] by the ears." Finding allies in the outlying parts of the county, these committed party men then organized petitions to Congress against the Division Act—and secured a great number of signatories "from their zeal in the cause and the unusual degree of Party spirit that prevails in that County at present on this subject."[33] With the passage of the Enabling Act, "the parties" were soon "at it pelmel [sic] in Cincinnati," according to Daniel Symmes. By August, the old settler Jacob White detected "grate devitions . . . at present I can scarcely name a man in this County whoes Election I can think any how shure [*sic*]." By the eve of the election, Nathaniel Massie feared that, with "the parties in that county . . . exerting themselves to the utmost, . . . the dividing party are gaining ground."[34]

The burden of the contest was undertaken on the statehood side by the Republican Corresponding Society of Cincinnati. Akin to the Democratic societies founded in other states after 1793, this society probably derived from the committee of correspondence set up in 1797 to promote statehood, although its date of organization is uncertain. By March 1802, similar Republican societies were appearing in the outlying townships of Hamilton County, until there were nineteen, all devoted to discussing and propagating "the leading principles of genuine republicanism." As in some parts of late eighteenth-century England, such clubs and societies offered a means for men of small and middling means to exercise political influence in the face of men of wealth, consequence, and power.[35]

Delighted by the opportunity offered by the Enabling Act "to lay the axe to the root of all our little territorial aristocracies," the societies operated as a means of organizing the statehood campaign in the county. In their own view, the societies provided "a good means of collecting the sense of the people," and so they took it upon themselves to produce an electoral ticket that could claim to have the widespread support of men of sound Republican principle. Hence seventeen Republican societies elected delegates to attend a county convention in August, which duly nominated a slate of candidates for both the constitutional convention and the third territorial legislature. As Emil Pocock has written of the Jacksonian period, such tickets "undermined the informal control the standing order exerted over elections by offering voters a clear choice" between the old regime and its critics.[36]

The societies themselves came under great criticism from the "governor's party" and those unwilling to follow their lead. The societies' nominees countered these mutterings by answering in the press questions concerning statehood, slavery, suffrage, and popular control of officeholders. Other candidates followed suit, displaying their respect for public opinion; one of the societies' candidates, Stephen Wood, even stated that, while he sincerely believed the ideas he put forward in reply to the request for a public statement, he would happily change any views that the people disapproved of! According to Francis Dunlavy, statehood now became the "universal cry," and the electors preferred those most clearly committed to deliver it. In the event, the societies' ticket overthrew the "governor's party" and the Cincinnati-Marietta logroll: the societies carried seven of the nine places at the constitutional convention and were to become the arbiters of county politics for the next decade.[37]

The passions stirred by the vigorous statehood campaign prompted the voters in every county to turn out at the elections in unprecedented numbers. The proportion of the adult white male population voting doubled and even trebled. In Hamilton County, for example, about 52 percent voted compared with about 22 percent, at best, in earlier elections; in Ross County over 64 percent voted compared with about 17 percent in 1800. In two sparsely populated townships in Washington County, the proportion of adult males voting increased from under one-third in a special legislative election in 1801 to over two-thirds in 1802.[38]

This response partly reflected the removal of the restrictions imposed by the Northwest Ordinance. The impact of rule changes can be measured because the election for a third territorial assembly was held at the same time as the election for the constitutional convention. The figures for Hamilton County are uncertain, but between 1,180 and 1,790 voted for the assembly, while between 2,045 and 2,401 voted for the convention. Thus, in this instance, it appears that the increase in the number voting for the convention compared with previous years was made up equally of two elements: about half the proportionate increase since 1800 was due to those qualified to vote in territorial elections who had not bothered to do so, but were now attracted by the excitements of the day and the greater accessibility of polling places; and half was due to those who, whether previously interested or not, had been disfranchised under the territorial regime. That participation had been artificially held down under the old regime is strongly suggested by the fact that, even after the excitements of 1802 had passed away, turnout levels would never fall back to the levels typical of territorial elections.[39]

Undoubtedly, the increase in popular involvement reflected the overwhelming popular demand for emancipation from colonial status. The statehood men's appeal to traditional Revolutionary values, to the virtues of self-government and the evils of aristocracy, proved almost irresistible. As Burnet later conceded, "Impressions were made on the popular mind that a plan had been formed to perpetuate the colonial system, with a view of continuing the influence of a few individuals in the councils of the general government, and in the management of the affairs of the Territory." The result, as in Belmont County, was "a great reformation wrought in the minds of some of the people,"[40] enabling the Republicans to carry, overall, three-quarters of the seats in the constitutional convention. Even members of the St. Clair party, although armed with strong arguments against submitting to Congress's interference, recognized the popularity of statehood and shifted to its support during the campaign. In effect, they had admitted the growing importance of public opinion in Ohio politics and acknowledged that the election amounted to a plebiscite determining Ohio's immediate constitutional future.[41]

A TRIUMPH OF PARTY SPIRIT

The peculiar dynamic behind Ohio's revolution was essentially partisan: competition among the elite politicized the lower orders and made their participation the decisive element in the electoral system. Throughout the nation, the bitter polarization of political opinion forced on by events in France and Europe in the 1790s divided the elite and persuaded the opposition to appeal to the lesser members of society for the support necessary to defeat their opponents at the polls. But that appeal downwards depended for its success upon making politics more understandable to the less politicized members of society, rousing their enthusiasm, and giving them some means of identifying their own team in the political game. That meant teaching the electorate to see the world in partisan terms—to categorize politics into Republican and Federalist, black and white, good and evil—and then to act on that basis. To succeed in that task, politicians had to create something akin to a mass party—if they could.

Certainly the agitation of Ohio's political waters in 1802 owed everything to the frenetic action of partisan politicians. The struggles within the territory were now expressed in terms of Federalists and Republicans, and the critical elections of 1802–3 were regarded as a contest for party supremacy. This development arose partly from the statehood movement's need to win the support of the new Democratic Republican majority in Congress, but it also reflected the growing partisan consciousness among the inhabitants of the future Ohio. Committed Republicans, such as Benjamin Tappan, were the first to start arguing for statehood on the Western Reserve, while in Cincinnati those who refused to accept St. Clair's logroll were ideologically committed partisans who objected to the territorial regime on grounds of principle. Looking back on the statehood campaign from the vantage point of the 1840s, Jacob Burnet thought "party spirit" had been "carried to unusual lengths" in 1802, comparable to "the spirit displayed in the political strife of the present day."[42]

During 1802, some newspaper correspondents argued that national party divisions were irrelevant to the issues facing Ohioans. "What . . . has federal and anti federal, republican and anti republican tickets to do with the ensuing elections?" asked one Federalist. The Republicans responded that more than just statehood was at stake, for the voters must also decide which set of politicians to trust with the new state's future. It was not, therefore, sufficient for Federalists to declare their conversion to statehood, since their close association with the territorial regime and the discredited former national administration made them fundamentally suspect. The much respected Samuel Finley of Chillicothe had resisted St. Clair's pretensions and supported the town's interests throughout the statehood struggle, but his openly avowed Federalism made him a less trustworthy candidate for the convention than some undistinguished farmer of ordinary means, such as the Pennsylvanian James Grubb, who happened to be a self-proclaimed Republican. Thus the Republican leaders gave the campaign for the constitutional convention a clear partisan character, and the public questioning of candidates in Hamilton and Ross Counties always included inquiries about their party preferences. By the end of the year, according to that ambiguous politician Samuel Huntington, "Though it might not be expected that general politics would have found their way across the Allegany [sic], yet the line that divides parties in the States is as distinctly drawn here as there."[43]

The belief that the election of Federalists would be disastrous, at this critical moment for the new state, made many Republican worthies subordinate their own personal ambitions for the greater good. As John Cleves Symmes said, "We shall have much to dread if republicans do not harmonize like clock-work. Jealousies ought to be banished from republicans, or we fail altogether." In Ross County, Duncan McArthur overlooked his personal differences with Thomas Worthington in order to ensure that Republicans pulled together, because he feared that a multiplicity of statehood candidates might allow their enemies to sneak into the constitutional convention.[44]

Thus, from the commencement of the crisis, Republicans adopted partisan techniques to coordinate political action and mobilize support. The decision to send Worthington and Michael Baldwin to Washington to fight the Division Act in December 1801 had been made by a "general meeting" of Chillicothe citizens and Republican legislators; the meeting had also appointed a committee to devise their instructions and orchestrate the petition campaign which, in the end, brought about the Enabling Act.[45] Faced next by the need to defeat their opponents at the October election, the Republicans organized correspondence and vigilance committees at the various county seats, similar to those already used by party colleagues in the seaboard states. The Ohio Republicans even called county nominating conventions, mainly in the few counties where the Federalists seemed strong, to concentrate support on the appropriate number of candidates. These conventions, made up of delegates elected in the townships, were among the first in the nation, with only Pennsylvania and New Jersey for certain adopting this device before Ohio. Republicans also commonly demanded that candidates state their attitude to the Republican party. As Emil Pocock has pointed out for the 1820s, such a demand served to impose a party identity on candidates and a subsequent party obligation.[46]

The adoption of partisan exclusivity and coordination marked a perceptible weakening of the traditional hostility to "party" and all its evil works. Men on both sides disapproved the excesses that partisanship was introducing into national politics, but then duly threw themselves behind one party or another. Benjamin Van Cleve, a pioneer settler near Dayton, was always "averse to every man who is warm or violent of any party," but at this time was "induced . . . to rank among the Federalists." Worthington had complained in January 1801 of the "Jarring in congress" and the "unharmonious (if it deserves so gentle a name) proceedings of the H of Rep of the US but what will not party spirit do when indulged—I fear if we do not harmonize in future all will be confusion." Yet sixteenth months later he had become convinced that the party fight was all-embracing, that everything must be sacrificed to achieving Republican victory. Every good man, he urged sympathizers, "must take his stand firmly, that no middle ground could now be tenable."[47]

Since great issues of national import were at stake in the Ohio struggle, Republicans saw their partisanship as neither selfish nor partial nor "interested." There was no hypocrisy involved in Worthington's complaint to Jefferson that St. Clair "has created and endeavored to attach to himself a party, and in conjunction with them has made attempts, and in some measure succeeded, to destroy the harmony and divide the interests of the people, affecting to promote the local interests of certain places, thereby enlisting partisans to support his views." The Republicans saw themselves as acting for the general good in a way that St. Clair's gerrymandering and logrolling coalitions, in their opinion, had not.[48]

Republicans could persuade themselves that their partisan techniques were fully justified, but ideological justification did not in itself ensure that partisan modes of behavior would triumph in Ohio. Traditional antiparty attitudes remained powerful and could be used to mobilize arguments against sacrificing all considerations of communal and local interest to the broader but divisive issues emphasized by the Republican committees. Federalists were especially eager to deny the propriety of party calls—at least outside Washington County, which they were confident of winning.

In Hamilton County, the Federalists combined informally with those Republicans who objected to the efforts of the Republican societies to control the election. St. Clair himself, in a speech that was reprinted in the press, complained that the "design" of the societies was "to keep people that are not Republicans out of the convention" and to reserve to themselves the right to decide which candidates were to be considered true Republicans. An anonymous article in the Cincinnati newspaper, almost certainly written by St. Clair, complained that the meetings of the Republican societies were restricted exclusively to members: "The rules . . . are that persons wishing to become members should be proposed by members, and admitted or rejected by a vote, constituting themselves, as it were, a court of Inquisition." These self-appointed judges of political purity then raised "odious distinctions among the citizens, and set them at variance with each other." Their nominees were not "the wisest, the ablest, and the best informed men," and they did not, in many cases, have a "real interest in the property of this particular part of the country," which contained more than one-third of the population of the proposed state. Furthermore, St. Clair asserted, the Republican societies were probably the agents of Ross County, the leaders of which had constantly imposed on Hamilton County, to its considerable detriment. In these ways the Republican societies were branded as hostile not only to traditional republican respect for the general welfare of society but also to the best interests of the local community.[49]

Such attitudes ensured that the societies' nomination of a party ticket would not deter other Republicans from running in the Hamilton County election. Many rival nominations were made, both by township meetings and by anonymous individuals. One meeting, in Mad River Township, virtually confirmed the Republican society nomination, but the others all named more or less the same rival set of candidates. The most powerful attempt to break the Republican ticket was made by a "respectable" meeting in Cincinnati which produced a compromise ticket that included, among its fifteen names, just eight of those nominated by the Republican convention. But, in spite of arousing disappointed ambition and local pride, the Republican party leaders still confidently asserted that the official ticket "will be supported by a very large majority of Republicans" in the county.[50]

The election scarcely revealed a general respect for party nominations. Ninety-nine men ran for Hamilton County's ten seats in the convention and 116 ran for its seven seats in the third territorial assembly. Only twenty-six of the former and twenty-seven of the latter gained more than fifty votes; those with fewer votes, the local newspaper generously supposed, "could not have been generally considered as candidates." The official Republican candidates for the constitutional convention won between 791 and 1,635 votes, whereas even those who gained three or four other nominations for the convention received only between 458 and 964 votes. The official Republican nomination was obviously the decisive advantage a candidate could have, although the irregularity of ticket voting meant that the Republicans failed to win two of the ten convention seats.[51]

The weakest of the society candidates were overtaken by the strongest Federalist, John Reily, who enjoyed a strong local standing in what became Butler County, and by the dissident Cincinnati Republican, John Smith. "A successful merchant, an adroit politician, a sagacious legislator, and an able divine," blessed with a fine appearance and magnificent voice, Smith stood high in public regard. St. Clair himself claimed the previous December that anything

"Mr. Smith enters into . . . will go down almost universally in Hamilton County."[52] However, Smith had alienated "the Democratic Societies of Hamilton" by his brief flirtation with St. Clair's logroll and his initial criticism of the Enabling Act, although he recanted before the election. Without the official nomination, Smith trailed well behind most of the society ticket, but managed to scrape into ninth place in the poll for ten delegates. Despite their disappointment at the success of Smith and Reily, the Republicans could reasonably regard the outcome as a great triumph, since their nominees had swept the concurrent assembly election and all those elected to the constitutional convention had recently declared in favor of statehood.[53]

In Ross County, by contrast, Republican attempts at party coordination proved abortive. Admittedly, there was little doubt that the majority of the community favored the statehood and Republican cause, but party leaders still wished to ensure that the voters knew clearly who were the party's preferred men. McArthur and four Republican colleagues issued a handbill proposing that voters should assemble in their election districts to choose two representatives to meet in a county convention that would nominate a county ticket. The convention never met, not so much because of the public protests against the procedure, but because of the shortness of the notice before the primary elections would have to be held. When it was clear that no formal nominations could be made by a delegate process, McArthur urged that some of the Republican candidates should voluntarily withdraw, but apparently with no effect. In any case, the publication of statements by candidates—as requested in the same handbill—and the subsequent controversy in newspaper and broadside ensured that those known as Federalists or suspected of conniving with St. Clair were clearly earmarked, and the Ross County electorate plumped strongly for the best-known Republican leaders of the statehood cause.[54]

In other counties, too, the party was not so well organized, nor was its authority sufficiently accepted, for the 1802 election to be described simply in party terms. In every county where delegate conventions met, official nominations did not deter other members of the party from running, and everywhere there were many privately nominated candidates. On the Western Reserve, at least three Republicans ran for the two vacancies, without any sense of contradicting the best interests of the party. In Fairfield County, ten candidates competed for the two places open, and they all received very different numbers of votes.[55] Yet, in almost every case, it seems clear that the party identity of the candidates was widely known, and leading politicians quickly worked out the partisan implication of the election results. Overall, as a writer in the *Marietta Gazette* complained, Worthington and his friends had succeeded in their efforts "to stir up a party spirit." They had taught the people that "two parties do exist, by the names of Federalists and Republicans, and that one party is their friends and the other is their implacable enemies."[56]

THE FEDERALIST RESPONSE

Modern historians have tended to caricature the Federalist party. It has often been treated as primarily a social and cultural group committed to a single body of ideas, as an "ism" rather than a party. As a result, the Federalists have been seen as old-fashioned gentlemen, outdated in outlook and habit, and incapable of competing against the highly partisan and demagogic Jeffersonians. Yet, as Andrew Cayton has argued, they were a dynamic and creative force in the Northwest Territory in the 1790s,[57] and the record shows that they were by no means opposed to popular participation and contributed largely to the broadening of the political universe before 1802. Moreover, as a party, they faced the changing political environment in Ohio with realism and adjusted—admittedly, with some hesitation and ambivalence—to the demands of party conflict.

Undoubtedly, most Federalists continued to express more aversion than the Republicans to laying aside traditional antiparty attitudes. They persisted in believing that society ought to be an organic whole, its individual members concerned only with securing the general good; political organization by a part of society was at best a conspiracy against the rest and at worst a threat to the integrity and very survival of society. Hence they particularly valued and trusted established organs of government as means of expounding political news and views and organizing political action expressive of the communal viewpoint. When obliged to gather the sense of the people, as in Washington County in 1801 and 1802, they turned naturally to county delegate conventions, which they saw as expressing the will of the whole community rather than only a section. Federalists took great pride in reflecting accurately the undoubted will of their constituents, as when Ephraim Cutler insistently stood alone to vote against statehood in the constitutional convention.[58] Antipartyism seemed particularly attractive to men who felt that they expressed the true sentiments of the local community and who believed that their opponents were unscrupulous partisans who deliberately agitated popular passions irrelevant to the best interests of the country. In expressing this outlook, they were appealing to a traditional cultural attitude of persisting power.

Yet Federalists, young and old, also believed that Republican partisanship represented a deleterious influence in national life that must be resisted at all costs. They were, therefore, as responsible as the Republicans for the embitterment of political relations during 1801–2, as national events increasingly horrified them. In January 1801 the elder Return Jonathan Meigs attributed

Federalist animosity in Washington County to "the spirit of the times roused by the event of the late election" for president. In his son's opinion, many Federalists in Marietta opposed statehood mainly because they feared that in the next presidential election "the present administration may receive three votes from our then state." For a time, local Federalists were appeased by the inaugural address of March 1801 and hoped to "see Mr. Jefferson unite the candid Republicans & Federalists throughout the United States." But then, according to Benjamin Ives Gilman, "what a sad falling off." The presidential messages that followed were partisan, the behavior of the Democratic majority in Congress malicious, and the president's patronage policy despicable, since it meant "foreign minions, who deserve the Gallows, enjoying Posts of profit and revolutionary characters neglected." For Federalists, Jefferson had become "the head of a party: and the patron of men who are despised by all good citizens."[59]

As a result, the Federalists themselves played a large role in heightening party passions in 1801 and 1802. In Washington County, in particular, the Federalists made it very difficult for Republicans to cooperate with them in supporting St. Clair's schemes. When the citizens of Marietta met in January 1801 to protest against statehood, a "large majority" approved the inclusion in the address of comments on national affairs that local Republicans present— and even some moderate Federalists—found offensively "illiberal & dangerous." The events of early 1802—especially Jefferson's dismissal of the Marietta postmaster and Congress's rejection of the Division Act—further stoked "the fire of Federalism," and the younger Meigs could report that "Federalism has raged here this Spring with intolerant Fury." Even Manasseh Cutler, father of the Ohio Company and currently a Federalist congressman from Massachusetts, felt that the people of Washington County "carried Federalism to too great lengths."[60]

Federalist antagonism to the impending Republican ascendancy in Ohio arose primarily from their awareness of external events. They became concerned about the constitutional character of the future state because Napoleon's rise to power in France since 1799 demonstrated how easily republican liberty could be overthrown if proper constitutional safeguards were not maintained. The Republicans, they feared, were demagogues who might too easily slip into encouraging an undisciplined populace to exercise unrestrained power. Thus Ohio Federalists saw huge menace in the new Jefferson administration's assault on the federal judiciary.

Benjamin Ives Gilman, for example, regarded himself as "a moderate in politics," but was horrified in 1802 by the repeal of the Judiciary Act of 1801, "one of the vilest acts of party malice." In February, territorial delegate Paul Fearing warned Ephraim Cutler that congressional assaults on the independence of the judiciary threatened that "barrier of the constitution . . . , which so much controls the liberties of our public concerns."

> When once the Democratic enthusiasts shall disregard the constitution of our country, I think we have reason to fear, that . . . a greater than a Republican would appear. Some favorite Democrat who has sacrificed the faith, the honor, and the interests of his country to his own popularity will rise up (Bonaparte like) and proclaim equality to all the citizens of his country with the fraternal extension thereof to his neighbors. Then will the free citizen of the republic of his own choice be at liberty to annul the laws and be duly taxed in such a manner as this great favourite of the people shall dictate.

Fearing believed that if "our judges have no right to judge a law unconstitutional," then "our constitution is at an end, and a French convention can do no more than an American Congress."[61]

In these circumstances, Federalists proved willing to compete electorally with the Republicans for command of the nascent state. They had always been willing to exploit the advantages they gained from their control of official organs of government. In 1798, for example, Rufus Putnam had used the post offices to circulate materials justifying the government's position in the growing crisis with France. The ability to use the government machine removed some of the pressure to create extraconstitutional forms of organization and propaganda, at least until the tables were turned in 1801. Thereafter, the Federalists could still exploit St. Clair's electoral machine and their command of the printing press, outside Chillicothe. In 1802 there were only three newspapers in the territory: in addition to the irredeemably Republican *Scioto Gazette* and the avowedly Federalist *Ohio Gazette* in Marietta, the *Western Spy* in Cincinnati claimed to be politically neutral but devoted to the interests of the town. By June, the statehood men in Cincinnati were complaining that "the printers there do not give the republicans a fair chance; print every thing for aristocrats, and only now & then a piece for Democrats."[62]

Throughout the statehood contest, the Federalists were perfectly willing to organize and to appeal to the voters. Their leaders fully saw the need to develop "some general system, so that we may act together." In Washington County, they called two delegate conventions, the first of which met before any Republican convention in the territory had been called.[63] In Chillicothe, Republican activists were "astonished to find the pains taken by the few federalists in this place to send federal representatives to the [constitutional] convention." They showed every willingness to canvass for support, as they had in 1800 when one of St. Clair's supporters, John S. Gano, "visited every family in Cincinnati and its vicinity, except two, and . . . found them well-disposed" toward signing a petition for St. Clair's reappointment. Admittedly, Rufus Putnam complained that such a petition drive served "no purpose but to create prejudice and a party spirit among the people," but no such inhibition prevented the Hamilton County Federalists from taking the initiative in organizing a similar mass petition in favor of the Division Act late in 1801.[64] If Federalists in other parts of the state subsequently hesitated to follow suit, it was principally because they saw that they could not outbid the Republicans in their locality in an appeal to the people on the statehood issue.[65]

In the campaign for the constitutional convention, the Federalists showed little reluctance to play politics unscrupulously. In Ross County, for example, they knew that they had little chance of winning in their own right, but recognized that some Republican voters in the county were disappointed when local Republican leaders publicly opposed the introduction of slavery. Federalist candidates in Ross, accordingly, announced that they favored slavery, thereby hoping to win over some valuable Republican votes.[66] Elsewhere the Federalists took the opposite line, insisting that the Democrats were rushing the territory into statehood in order to escape the ordinance's prohibition on slavery, and Republicans felt obliged to refute this charge publicly and repeatedly. In Athens Township, Washington County, there were "hot times about slavery and Republicanism," as the Republicans denounced this "federal villainy." As a local Republican said of the Federalists, "The party is weak here, but d——d saucy."[67] The establishment party more than contributed to whipping up the boisterous sea of 1802, as the actions of competing partisans effectively democratized politics.

Moreover, the Federalists had little difficulty in accepting statehood. They were not absolutely committed to maintaining an overarching hierarchical authority that would keep the people under control. Accepting the popular origins of government, as they had in the U.S. Constitution, the Federalists were, in theory, perfectly willing to accept statehood as soon as they were convinced that the people of Ohio were loyal Americans. If they had stubbornly defended territorial status, it was because they were not so convinced—and because, as partisans, they still controlled the territory whereas they were less confident of controlling the state. Their pragmatism had been fully demonstrated in February 1802 when they contemplated taking up the statehood cry themselves, if Jefferson dismissed Governor St. Clair and replaced him with a Republican. Hence during the 1802 electoral campaign, many followed the same route as Bezaleel Wells and declared for statehood in their attempt to win election to the constitutional convention. Similarly, at the beginning of the constitutional convention, the Federalist leaders recognized that they "had better all vote" for immediate statehood if they were to "obtain a greater influence in the future proceedings."[68]

This decision was a deliberate concession to "popular motives" that Jacob Burnet found "painful" forty years later. By contrast, the Federalists present in the 1802 convention had little trouble in deferring to the popular will. The only one to refuse to vote for statehood, Ephraim Cutler, did so explicitly because he felt obliged to represent the opinion of his constituents. Moreover, all the Federalists present would vote to refer the new constitution to the people for their approval—while all twenty-eight Republicans voted against—although this was probably a matter of tactics rather than high principle.[69] As the process of constitution making was to demonstrate, Ohio's Federalists had no ideological difficulty in adjusting to a new world of popular politics.

CONSTITUTIONAL AGREEMENT

Contemporaries commonly assumed that fundamental differences of opinion divided Republicans and Federalists on constitutional issues. Federalists were branded by their enemies as monarchists, hostile to republican forms and devoted to central controls; Republicans were caricatured as Jacobins, determined to give all power to unrestrained popular majorities elected in the localities. Hence the victory of the Democratic Republican forces in the Ohio election of October 1802 has widely been interpreted as allowing them to impose a constitution reflecting their partisan view. In David Massie's words, the Ohio constitutional convention was the first fruit of Republican victory, and the new constitution represented "the full and complete triumph of Democracy."[70]

The term is, of course, deeply ambiguous. Massie was accepting the original identification of the party ("the Democracy") with the principle ("democracy"), without asking whether the two coincided, and he failed to consider whether the principle of democracy merely meant the rule of the majority or included protections for individual liberty that necessarily involved limitations on majority rule. Debates in the convention revealed that the differences between the parties on such issues were not so great or marked as to prevent agreement on a constitution. In the end, the constitution preserved traditional protections for liberty while placing the new state government on a widely extended elective base, without solving the tensions between the two ideas.

The proceedings in the constitutional convention are not well documented, especially as many critical discussions occurred in committee and were not recorded in the official journal. It appears from Ephraim Cutler's recollections, written long afterward in his old age, that initially a group of Virginia Republicans endeavored to control the convention, relying on the partisan support of the Republican majority to impose something akin to the Tennessee constitution, which had extended democracy while maintaining some conservative restraints. At first, leading Republicans attacked the more prominent Federalists in debate, and the seven undoubted Federalists voted together on eight of the first ten roll calls. However, serious divisions among the Republicans emerged which prevented them from acting together and so enabled the Federalist minority to gain some influence on decisions. Showing far more unity than their opponents, the undoubted Federalists voted with the majority on more than half the recorded ballots. Not for the last time, they helped to determine which side of the argument in the Republican party would triumph.[71]

The achievement of a bipartisan consensus was indicated when every member of the convention signed the new constitution—a feat not achieved by the Founding Fathers in 1787. Overall, Cutler recalled, "Party divisions, as respects Federalists and Democrats, were not prominent" in the convention, and shortly afterwards Samuel Huntington, a delegate from the Western Reserve newly revealed as a Republican, reported that "those politics but seldom were brought up in debates and never disturbed the calm discussion of any question." He thought that, in its final version, "our frame of government is not such as to suit any one member of the Convention," but, considering how varied the habits, prejudices, and opinions of the delegates, he found it remarkable that "they should unite with so much cordiality" on the principles and forms it embodied. Republican societies in Hamilton County "highly" approved of the constitution. On the other hand, according to Cutler, no member of the convention was, "at the conclusion, better, if so well pleased, with the result of our labors" than the Federalist leaders Rufus Putnam, Benjamin Ives Gilman, and Bezaleel Wells.[72]

The delegates attained consensus largely because they recognized the basic demands of public opinion. These had been outlined throughout the summer in the learned articles and candidates' statements printed in the territory's three newspapers. All agreed that governments derived their legitimate powers from the sovereignty of the people. All agreed on the desirability of a broad franchise. All agreed that the power and patronage of the chief executive must be reduced and control of public officers by the electorate increased.

On many other issues, significant disagreements were obvious in many of the statements in the press prior to the elections, but there had been little direct argument or grappling with the implications of the various assertions. The disagreements can be defined as lying between two ideological extremes, "democratic" and "federalist." A similar analysis was apparently adopted by Cutler early in the convention. He detected four groups among the thirty-five members:

> Ready to go all lengths, about twelve or fourteen.
> Something more moderate, six.
> Federal & rational, ten.
> Moderate and inclining to rational principles [3 or 5].[73]

On such an analysis, "federalism" was not identical to support for the Federalist party, while the Republican party scarcely had an agreed position.

The "federal & rational" pole of the argument followed the U.S. Constitution in advocating restraints on excessive popular power. Not that most Ohio Federalists had shown any difficulty before the convention in accepting the principle of popular sovereignty and democratic control: candidates such as Samuel Finley of Chillicothe and Ephraim Cutler not only accepted "the people as the legitimate source of all authority and power" but declared that "the voice of the people . . . is the voice of god in a republican government." But while a Federalist writer in the Marietta paper could argue for frequent elections and rotation in office, he also wanted a council elected by the legislature to make all appointments, including local law-enforcement officers—"for it would be dangerous to let the people elect them." As Burnet later commented, "There was an honest apprehension that the popular election of officers who, by a faithful discharge of their duty, must incur the displeasure of those on whom their re-election depended, might be productive of injurious consequences."[74]

But this desire for institutional safeguards against popular irresponsibility was not unique to Federalists. Most notably, many Republicans agreed with them in wanting a powerful and independent judiciary, appointed for life but subject to good behavior, and capable of defending the constitution and bill of rights by determining the constitutionality of laws passed by the legislature. Otherwise, according to Charles Willing Byrd, leader of the Virginia group in the convention, "the whim of the moment would be the law of the land, and there would be no security for the enjoyment of life, liberty or property."[75]

At the opposite pole stood the more radical democrats, who objected to limitations on the operation of the popular will on government. There were large implications behind the assertion of the young Chillicothe lawyer, Michael Baldwin, that "the people are fully competent to govern themselves; that they are the best and only proper judges of their own interests and their own concerns; that in forming governments and constitutions, the people ought to part with as little power as possible." Another writer in the *Scioto Gazette* asserted that "the people ought to delegate their officers" so that only laws acceptable to the people are passed, while an anonymous letter from "Some of the People" of outlying parts of Ross County told Worthington they wanted "frequent elections and a general suffrage to elect, making all officers responsible to the people."[76]

But the most sustained expression of a democratic viewpoint of the campaign came in a widely reprinted manifesto published by the "committee" of New Market Township in Ross County. The three signatories were farmers and middling landowners in this isolated, backward, "high and elevated" township, then still a "dense wilderness," which was to become Highland County in 1805. Constantly stressing the need to protect the rights of "laboring men" and farmers, they wanted a government that would not maintain a large establishment of officeholders at taxpayers' expense. Demanding safeguards against exploitation of the disadvantaged by a selfish ruling class, their address demanded a constitution "that will annually leave it in the power of the electors to continue in office or discontinue them that fill the various departments of government." Beyond that, they demanded genuine equality before the law: "We want a constitution that will set the natural rights of the meanest African and the most abject beggar upon an equal footing with those citizens of the greatest wealth and equipage."[77]

These radical democrats gave allegiance to the Republican party, and their views were supported most consistently in the constitutional convention by six of the eight members elected in Hamilton County on the Republican society ticket. Francis Dunlavy, for example, "advocated the most liberal civil, religious and political privileges for all citizens of whatever name, country, color or religion." The two members from Clermont County—recently carved from Hamilton—also voted in the spirit of a local petition "praying that those privileges which are the absolute right of all men, may be secured to them." On some questions of popular rights, however, the democrats found their best allies in the convention among the Federalists, who wished to offset the future power of the Chillicothe gentry by giving the constitution "a strong democratic tendency."[78]

The most notable incident occurred late in the convention as the Republican leaders worked to create a centralized judicial system modeled on that of Virginia. The Federalists argued that this would penalize the less wealthy who could not afford to pursue cases at a distance from their home; they preferred a peripatetic system like that of Pennsylvania, which might bring justice "as near every man's door as was practicable; to the poor man equally with the rich." After a late-night cabal, a Republican group centered on the Hamilton County delegation changed sides on the third reading and allied with the Federalists to outvote the Virginia party in the committee of the whole. Thereafter the Federalist leaders enjoyed "respectful attention by those who had before manifested something close bordering upon contempt."[79]

More complex alliances arose on the emotive questions concerning slavery and black rights, which, according to Burnet, generated enough "warmth of feeling" to jeopardize the whole constitution. President Jefferson, so it was claimed, had privately made known his wish that the new state should allow slaves to be held up to the age of thirty-five for men, twenty-five for women, in the belief that the diffusion of slavery would hasten its abolition nationally. The proposal was put forward in the constitutional convention by a loyal Cincinnati Democrat, John W. Browne—who had earlier publicly pledged himself to oppose the introduction of slavery into the new state—and received support from some men of sound antislavery credentials, but it was crushed by determined opposition from both Federalists and the Ross County Virginians. Many of the latter, including Worthington and Tiffin, had left Virginia and Kentucky specifically to escape an institution they hated and had promised in the Chillicothe press not to admit slavery "in any shape whatever."[80]

The delegates then gave serious thought to allowing some civil rights to those blacks already in Ohio. Initially they were given the right to vote, but a motion questioning that decision resulted in a tie vote, 17–17, which was broken to the disadvantage of blacks by the president of the convention, the English-born Edward Tiffin. The main support for black rights came from southwestern Ohio, especially from those nominated by the Republican societies, and from the Federalist members, but faced fierce opposition from representatives of constituencies with southern and Scotch-Irish populations who were afraid of encouraging black immigration.[81]

On the question of white political rights, the radicals found broad (but far from unanimous) support within the Republican party. The Hamilton County delegation voted almost unanimously for extending the suffrage as widely as possible and tended to support provisions strengthening the electorate's hold over the government. While some Virginians such as Nathaniel Massie showed by their votes that they suspected unrestrained democracy, most others agreed with the democrats on this point. Interestingly, Thomas Worthington—who has sometimes been characterized as an elitist republican—privately proposed extending the franchise for the convention elections to "all actual residents," and in the convention he voted consistently for the broadest possible distribution of power and for giving the vote to nontaxpayers. As Samuel Huntington said soon after attending the convention, "Many men of talents & information who emigrated here early from Virginia, Maryland and Pennsylvania have acquired immense property & had a seat in the Convention—those men were among the most zealous to secure inviolably the equal rights of the people & to bar the door forever against the admission of slavery."[82]

The critical test was the definition of the political class, of those with a right to express their will at the polls and so determine the public good. Before the convention, candidates had almost universally agreed that the suffrage should be on a taxpaying rather than a property basis. Tiffin had wished to extend it also to members of the militia, while the more radical insisted that all adult male citizens should be allowed to vote.[83] In the end, the constitutional convention adopted a taxpaying qualification, but also gave the franchise to all adult

white males "who are compelled to labor on the roads" and had lived in the
state for at least twelve months. Since territorial laws already made all males
between the ages of eighteen and fifty-five liable for up to two days' work on the
roads each year, the provision amounted to creating a universal white manhood
suffrage, embracing tenants, squatters, and nontaxpayers who met the residence requirements. The Federalists found little difficulty in accepting the taxpaying idea, but voted against interpreting physical labor on the roads as, in
itself, giving a man a sufficient "stake in society" to warrant the suffrage.[84]

Moreover, the constitution ensured that the right to vote was going to have
real meaning. All voting was by ballot, and bribery and treating were prohibited. The electors chose the governor and the senate biennially and the house of
representatives annually. Every vote counted equally, because a quadrennial
census would ensure that the apportionment of both houses of the legislature
reflected accurately the distribution of the adult white male population; as a
consequence, voters were to vote only in the county in which they resided. The
voters would have a free choice of representatives, because to sit in the house a
man had only to be a U.S. citizen, at least twenty-five years old, a resident of the
county for one year, and a state or county taxpayer. Poor men could afford to sit
in the assembly, since its members could be paid both per diem compensation
and traveling expenses. Above all, the electorate would know what was going on
in the legislature because its proceedings were to be open to the public; anyone
who wished to comment on its work must not be denied access to the printing
press; and the journals of both houses were to be published, including the
record of the "yeas and nays" on any vote upon which any two members asked
for the names to be taken. To complete a remarkably "Jacksonian" set of provisions over which there seems to have been little argument, the constitution also
recognized that "the people have a right . . . to instruct their representatives."
Clearly, in Ohio the critical change from "the old conception of the elected
representative as a sort of quasi-magistrate" to "the idea that the representative
was the servant of the people and owed humble obedience to them," which
according to Michael Heale marked the acceptance of a democratic polity, had
already occurred.[85]

Scarcely more disagreement arose over the distribution of power in the
future state capital. As in the original states in the 1770s, the colonial experience
of an authoritative executive ensured that the governor of the new state would
be, as Thomas Corwin later said, "a mere dummy." His discretionary powers
were restricted to command of the militia and the granting of pardons; otherwise, in Tiffin's phrase, he was "charged with the execution of the laws alone."
Powers of appointment were handed over to the legislature, with the governor
filling vacancies that occurred during recesses only on a temporary basis until

the assembly had time to act. Moreover, the memory of St. Clair ensured that the new constitution "put to sleep, forever, the Governor's negative upon the acts of the Legislature." Joseph Darlinton later recalled that "but one member . . . was willing to give the Governor a qualified negative upon the acts of the Legislature"—and Cutler claimed that one member was the radical Democrat Jeremiah Morrow.[86]

Federalists would have preferred a less feeble executive. St. Clair had always advocated "a very accurate distribution of executive and legislative power" in order to prevent tyranny, but his particular fear had been an unrestrained, omnipotent single-chamber legislature. At least the Republicans in the convention appreciated the advantages of a second chamber elected in larger districts than the house, and they agreed to insulate the senate from popular passions somewhat by providing that only half its members would be elected at each annual election. Otherwise, the qualifications for senators differed from those of representatives only in minor respects of age and length of residence, while both houses were to be elected on the same franchise. There was apparently not a heated demand, as there had been in Kentucky, that the senate have a clearly differentiated representative basis from the house.[87]

Equally, Federalists would have liked more power to be left in the hands of government. Most of them objected to the prohibition on poll taxes, passed by a vote of 26–7, and to the radical democrats' insistence that the pay of state officials be strictly restricted until 1808 and the erection of "public buildings for the accommodation of the legislature" be prohibited before 1809. The Federalists outside the constitutional convention complained that the document legislated too much and should have allowed later legislatures to adjust detailed implementation instead of tying their hands.[88]

Potentially the greatest area of disagreement arose over the position of the judiciary. Before the convention, most correspondents wanted the judges to be independent of popular and political pressures, since only then could they defend the liberties enshrined in the Bill of Rights. However, influential Republicans of democratic tendency, such as Edward Tiffin, had wanted some "constitutional check to prevent the assumption of the attribute of omnipotence" by the judges. As a result, the justices of the supreme court, the president judges of the district circuits, and the associate judges of the county's court of common pleas were all to be elected by the assembly for a specific term of seven years, rather than during good behavior as preferred by most correspondents. On the face of it, those who wanted the legislature to be omnipotent had their way in the convention, but time would soon reveal the strength of the feeling that judges ought to be able to call the legislature to account.[89]

Fundamentally, however, the Federalists accepted a constitution that removed most of the existing obstacles to popular rule. Outside the convention, the Chillicothe Federalist Levin Belt may have grumbled that "few Constitutions were ever so bepeopled as it is throughout," but he restricted his criticisms to the judiciary article. In practice, Federalists could accept the democratization of politics, and in several seaboard states they played an active role in broadening the suffrage and popular access to politics. In adopting what John P. Foote would later call "an ultra Democratic Constitution," Ohio had opened the way to mass participation in politics.[90]

This loosening of the political structure was not necessarily a consequence of the frontier environment. Many areas in eastern states that were experiencing rapid development and social diversification were undergoing a similar process of democratization. The Anglo-American political tradition also had a distinctive impact: most settlers in Ohio prized self-government and popular participation, especially in the generation following the Revolution; French settlers in the Old Northwest, by contrast, preferred territoriality to statehood, because it cost less. In more slowly settling and homogeneous regions of the West, older traditions of communal solidarity persisted, and constitutional change proved less dramatic: in the open-country settlement of Sugar Creek in Illinois, for example, the continuance of *viva voce* voting allowed a more deferential structure to persist well into the nineteenth century.[91] The persistence there of more old-fashioned constitutional structures may be ascribed to differences in timing: Illinois was the creation of the Era of Good Feelings, whereas Ohio was generated amid the popular passions released by the French Revolution.

3

THE MERIDIAN HEIGHT OF PARTY,
1803–1804

Despite the apparent harmony achieved by the end of the constitutional convention, Ohio's party men continued to mistrust each other on national issues. If anything, partisan differences intensified with the growing crisis over Louisiana, as Napoleon's American ambitions became clear in the last months of 1802. Ohio Republicans insisted they would "never submit for the navigation [of the Mississippi] to be stopped," but stressed the need for a diplomatic solution. They disapproved of Federalists in Congress who advocated seizing New Orleans by force—but then Federalists, they said, always want "to increase the army and get into a war." In reply, Ohio's Federalists cursed Jefferson for his feebleness in the face of the Napoleonic threat. As the younger Meigs reported from Marietta in January 1803, "The Federalists here have grown (if possible) more bitter than ever. They fulminate their anathemas against the administration with unprecedented malice."[1]

Such extreme antipathy ensured that the two parties would continue to battle for control of the new state through the crucial elections of 1803 and 1804. In the process, the Republican party took on some characteristics of a modern mass party, and the electorate showed signs of aligning itself between two sides that it clearly identified. Inevitably that division reflected some basic cleavages within Ohio society, but in a less straightforward way than most historians have assumed. Before the Republicans could be certain of their continuing control, however, they would first discover that the electorate set strict limits on the degree of central party control they would tolerate.

THE LIMITS OF DEMOCRACY

Under the political circumstances in which Ohio was born, leading Republicans recognized the need to secure their control of the state in the elections in

January 1803. For the first time, the key office of governor—the symbol of control, if no longer the center of power—was to be decided by a statewide popular election. Republicans therefore had to agree on a single gubernatorial candidate; otherwise, the Federalists might win on a plurality of the vote. But any nomination would test the strength of party allegiance, because voters in the various districts must take on trust the political soundness of a nominee personally unknown in their locality. Accordingly, toward the close of the constitutional convention, the Republican members met to agree on a candidate. Their choice, Edward Tiffin, was given a clear run by Ohio Republicans, and he won handsomely with at least 90 percent of the vote.[2]

This triumph of partisanship was achieved only in the face of strong regional tensions. In particular, the residents of Hamilton County believed that the first governor ought to be taken from among their own ranks, as the most populous county in the state. Accordingly, the St. Clair party in Cincinnati took "great pains to influence the people of Hamilton," damning Tiffin as the Chillicothe candidate. The Federalists called a public meeting to choose a proper gubernatorial candidate, and they fixed on John Paul, an elderly Cincinnati Republican who had been elected to the constitutional convention on the ticket named by the Republican societies. This "compromise" nomination was unanimously rejected by the societies because they wished to ensure statewide success and so accepted the lead of the Chillicothe caucus. The Federalists and their allies promptly put forward a full ticket including some sound Republican names and endeavored to exploit local resentments. The Republican societies countered by calling a delegate convention, which chose a strict party ticket headed by Tiffin, and then worked hard to coordinate support throughout the county. As in 1802 in Hamilton County, large numbers ran for each post—twenty-two for governor alone—and, once again, there was considerable ticket splitting. Yet the candidates of the "society party" swept the board, winning all the representative positions. Tiffin secured 1,387 votes compared with the 241 won in Hamilton County by his nearest rival, the Federalist candidate Benjamin Ives Gilman of Marietta.[3]

Submission to a central nomination for governor did not necessarily guarantee that sound Republicans would win the various county elections for the general assembly. Tiffin himself doubted that the party's statewide advantage would automatically bring command of the assembly: "There will be more federalists in the Legislature than we supposed, owing to the great division existing in the several Counties on Local questions, such as dividing Counties, fixing Seats of Justice, &c." However, within two weeks of the election Tiffin could calculate that Republican victories in most counties had given the party easy control of the first legislature.[4]

A further test for the party came in June when the state's sole congressman was to be chosen in a special election, thus creating the need for statewide party coordination for the second time in six months. In March, toward the close of the first assembly, the Republican caucus met again to choose its congressional candidate. It selected Jeremiah Morrow, the relatively radical Democrat from Lebanon, but the session broke up amid some confusion and much doubt as to whether he was the accepted nominee. Other Republicans came forward as candidates, notably in Cincinnati, where local Democrats pressed hard for the elder William Goforth to be nominated. Worthington and the Chillicothe leaders mounted a correspondence blitz, emphasizing to colleagues the need for united support of the caucus nomination, because "a division of republican interest" would result in "the election of a federalist." The Cincinnati Federalists tried once more to exploit local feeling, this time by nominating William McMillan. In the event, McMillan won 169 of the 252 votes cast in Cincinnati, while Goforth ran as well as Morrow both there and in his home town of Columbia. But in the rest of the old Hamilton County Morrow won 449 out of 537 votes, to McMillan's 84 and Goforth's 3.[5] Across the state, Morrow won 48.19 percent of the vote, compared with 11.74 percent for his nearest Republican rival and 26.6 percent for the Federalist nominee.[6]

Behind these decisive party triumphs of 1803 lay some significant local victories that confirmed the overthrow of the old Federalist establishment. Even in the Federalist stronghold of Washington County, the Republicans triumphed, partly because the arrival of statehood deprived the Federalists of a key electoral asset—the promise to make Marietta a state capital. They also suffered some significant desertions, notably by Wyllys Silliman, who after the constitutional convention changed the allegiance of his newspaper, the Marietta *Ohio Gazette,* and so gave the Republicans command of the most important means of communication in southeastern Ohio.[7] "Knowing that they could not carry a Federalist governor" in a statewide contest, the Washington Federalists boycotted the gubernatorial election in January, but even in the county election for assemblymen and local offices—for which they did vote— the Federalist ticket was thoroughly defeated by an average margin of 14 percent. So, too, the Federalist ticket failed to carry Jefferson County for the first time: they elected only two out of six representatives in a January election that saw much ticket voting.[8]

These election successes enabled the Virginian leaders of the Republican party and their allies to seize control of the machinery of state government and secure the levers of state and federal patronage. When the first assembly met in special session in March 1803, Nathaniel Massie and Michael Baldwin were elected to preside over state senate and house. Massie's son-in-law, William

Creighton Jr., became secretary of state, and Thomas Gibson of Hamilton County was appointed state auditor. The assembly chose Thomas Worthington and John Smith to represent Ohio in the Senate, and federal patronage duly flowed to those they favored. The president appointed another of Massie's in-laws, Charles Willing Byrd, judge of the U.S. district court, and made David Ziegler of Cincinnati marshal.[9]

Besides deciding who should hold the great offices, the first assembly had to make more than seventy key appointments throughout the state. The members, on joint ballot, had to name the majors general and quartermasters general who commanded the militia, although lower officers were elected by those under their command. In addition, the assembly appointed the judiciary, including three judges of the state supreme court and the three president judges whose task would be to preside over the county courts of common pleas within their respective districts. Each of these county courts also employed three associate judges, usually laymen, who were to sit with the president judge. This power of patronage was likely to disappoint as many aspirants as it satisfied, even as it put Republican sympathizers in strategic positions.[10]

Moreover, the first assembly could do much to determine how far the democratic revolution associated with statehood was actually put into practice. A new election law definitively confirmed the election district as the township and instituted a mechanism enabling local officials to create new townships. This measure, together with the creation of eight new counties, effectively brought polling stations ever closer to the voter. The election law also protected the secret ballot by ensuring privacy at the polls and facilitated party organization by insisting that each voter include all his votes for the different offices at stake on a single slip of paper, "written or printed." But with regard to county government, the ruling groups in the legislature now chose to create a centralized system of local control that would presumably serve to strengthen their command of the state.[11]

The constitution had been remarkably silent about the structure of county government. It had, it is true, maintained the territorial reform of local government below the county level by allowing the people to elect annually all town and township officers. But its sole provision concerning county government was the requirement that the sheriff and the coroner be popularly elected, with the sheriff—traditionally a post of great influence—restricted to serving four years in any six. The first assembly decided to maintain the old system of government by county courts: it simply transferred most of the governmental powers of the old territorial courts of quarter session to the three associate judges of the court of common pleas. The assembly gave these appointees the power, among other things, to create townships, build and maintain roads and bridges, and even to list land for tax purposes, which had previously been the task of specially appointed commissioners. In addition, the associates were to appoint the other county officers, including the key post of county treasurer as well as the surveyor, recorder, and clerk of the common pleas court.[12]

Thus the first assembly put local government largely under the control of men whom it itself named. In theory at least, this situation opened the way for an elective despotism exercised by the leaders of a legislature elected in counties run by their own appointees. In practice, however, there was little evidence of central management or coordination in the assembly, and most observers saw the first legislature's proceedings as marked mainly by "logrolling," an expression used now perhaps for the first time: "I do not well understand the Term," said the Federalist Levin Belt, "but I believe it means bargaining with each other for the little loaves and fishes of the State." Members not only favored their friends but even appointed each other to governmental posts, in defiance of the spirit of the new constitution.[13]

The appointment of patronage-rich associate judges in March 1803 should have helped the state leadership to consolidate its control in the counties. Indeed, the motives behind the measure may have been primarily partisan—to assist the party in the forthcoming elections. Yet, as it turned out, the seizure of the patronage machine at state and county levels jeopardized the Republicans' hold on the very center of power, the assembly itself. Immediately, dissatisfied politicians criticized the distribution of offices as excessively self-seeking and tantamount to creating a new aristocracy. Newspaper correspondents attacked all "electioneering or logrolling partizan[s]," especially those members who had gained appointive office in defiance of the new constitution and were running for reelection in the fall elections.[14]

The Federalists saw the issue clearly as an opportunity to break down the Republican ascendancy. In "the old county of Hamilton," they placed "some popular republicans on their ticket," including those assemblymen who had returned from Chillicothe without offices. The county's Republican voters failed to turn out in the numbers typical during the previous year, and the Republican societies managed to elect only one candidate contrary to Federalist wishes. Stunningly, "*old Hamilton . . .* progressed backwards" by electing two "federal" senators. In Fairfield County, likewise, divisions among the local Republicans resulted in the election of a "rank Federalist," Philemon Beecher. Throughout the state, there was a drastic turnover in the fall elections: only three members who had served in the Ohio house in March were reelected.[15]

As a consequence, the assembly that met in December 1803 was firmly in the hands of dissidents, malcontents, and Federalists. Partisan imperatives failed to prevent a coalition of Federalists and dissident Republicans from commanding the house of representatives, where they elected Beecher speaker pro tem and then replaced him with Worthington's old enemy, Elias Langham. According to David Abbot, an unreliable Republican from the Western Reserve, nearly half the Republicans objected to "a party who are for forcing everything down our throats by the lump; if we object, they say 'you ought to unite.'" In rebellious mood, many new members in the house declared its predecessor's appointments "unconstitutional and therefore void" and appeared "to have a wish to invert the whole order of things." Only the "men of business" in the state senate, where only half the seats had been up for reelection, prevented the rebels from overturning the appointments made in the previous session.[16]

Under the circumstances, the established leaders of the state had to accept— not necessarily with much pain—a series of measures that pressed even further the state's democratic revolution. Central control of county affairs ended when the governmental functions given in April to the associate judges were handed over to three county commissioners, who were to be popularly elected each year, in rotation, for three-year terms. The commissioners, in turn, were to appoint the county treasurer, although the associate judges retained the power to appoint the other officers, who were, in a sense, servants of the court of common pleas. In effect, the electoral processes set up by the constitution—in particular, annual elections for the legislature—had proved sufficient to prevent legislative chiefs from reinforcing their power by giving their allies control at the county level.[17] Not for the last time, Ohio voters proved reluctant to accept rule by a small group of men, whether aristocratic, partisan, or both.

Yet even this dissident legislature proved vulnerable to the dictates of popular partisanship, for party differences divided the rebel coalition. During the session the regular leadership proposed a set of resolutions commending the Louisiana Purchase. Determined to condemn Jefferson's government and all its works, the Federalists in the house protested formally and were joined by some of their dissident Republican allies. The regular Republicans immediately recognized the unintended "salutary effect" of the protest, which had "fixed on those who signed it such a mark as to enable not only the majority of the present legislature but the constituents of those persons to distinguish between professional and practical [i.e., professing and practicing] republicans. It has in fact had the effect of arranging the majority decidedly and almost uniformly against anything which originates with any member of the minority." Several dissidents still supported the Federalists on other matters, but now "a fear of their truly republican constituents . . . keeps them in some bounds." The fear of offending party loyalties of the voters at large gave the Republican leadership its best means of maintaining a degree of party discipline among legislators.[18]

Similarly, persisting partisanship ensured that the Republican majority would pull together in preparation for the forthcoming national elections. Some anxiety had been felt that this unreliable assembly might make unsuitable arrangements for the first presidential election, which federal law required to be held later than the regular October general election. The Federalists themselves wanted a popular election in districts, hoping through "great exertions" to win one of Ohio's three electors. Tiffin had been willing to consider keeping the election in the hands of the legislature if that was the only way of ensuring complete Republican victory, but he recognized that this solution was impractical in this assembly. No politician dare oppose giving the election to the electorate at large, as Wyllys Silliman acknowledged, for any other proposal would be made "use of by our enemies, as an evidence of an encroachment on the privileges of the people." Instead, the Republican majority adopted a democratic scheme that would minimize Federalist chances: Ohio's branch of the electoral college was to be elected by the people on a general-ticket system, in a statewide election to be held in November.[19]

The consequence was that, by mid-1804, the new state possessed a constitutional climate highly conducive to the existence of mass parties. The constitution itself had opened all state offices to control through the electoral process, either directly or indirectly, and the recent legislature had increased the number of local offices elected directly by the people. Elections were frequent and the franchise had been opened, in effect, to all adult white males. Voting districts were small and were to shrink as the number of counties multiplied. Elections for governor, congressman, state representatives, and county offices were all consolidated on one day in October, although township elections were to be held in April and presidential elections usually in November. Statewide popular elections were now required for governor, for the state's single congressman, and for electors in the electoral college. These conditions closely approximate those which Richard P. McCormick has suggested made possible the new party system of the 1830s: in Ohio at least, "the rules under which the political game was to be played" scarcely changed between 1803 and 1850, and were throughout conducive to the creation and survival of mass parties.[20]

PARTY CLIMAX

Not surprisingly, under these political and constitutional circumstances, the party conflict in Ohio came to a head with the national elections of 1804. The overriding need to reelect Thomas Jefferson and return a Republican Congress compelled Republican politicians to coordinate their efforts more successfully than before, and in the process they gained the chance to restore party control in Ohio. In February, a legislative caucus nominated Morrow for reelection to Congress, together with three electoral college candidates "unequivocally" committed to vote for Jefferson's reelection. The task of appointing a corresponding committee to produce united support across the state, however, was left to the Republican Society of Ross County. More essential was the restoration of party unity in the counties after the disaster of the previous fall. In the months that followed, regular Republicans everywhere worked to ensure that the "next election will bring about a different order of things." In Fairfield County, the Republicans had been determined for the past year to "fall upon some plan or other to inform each other and unite the republican interest closer than it has been heretofore in this County."[21]

In Hamilton County, the energetic Federalist party in Cincinnati endeavored to play the same old game again. They called a public meeting and nominated a ticket that once more included dissident Republicans. The Republican societies insisted that only a full turnout and strict loyalty to their own party ticket would frustrate such intrigue, since the Federalists "to a man turn out at elections." As the *Western Spy* pointed out, "The township of Cincinnati appears to keep to its own compliment [*sic*] of federalists, two to one, but in every other part of the county the republicans on an average carry five to one." So it turned out in the election: "Both parties tried their strength," and the "republican ticket . . . obtained universally, except in the instance of sheriff, . . . an immense majority."[22]

Across the state as a whole, Morrow was triumphantly reelected congressman in a strictly two-way election. In the assembly elections, Federalist-backed candidates went down to defeat almost everywhere and a new legislature was elected "composed of almost entirely new Members." During the year the governor had filled a vacancy for president judge with a well-qualified Federalist, Levin Belt; the new assembly refused to confirm the appointment, preferring a Republican, who proceeded to neglect his duties. So powerful was party feeling among this fresh majority that they even considered changing the names of the counties of Ross, Adams, and Hamilton. As Tiffin acknowledged, this surely was "republicanism . . . run mad."[23]

To ensure statewide unity in the November presidential election, the legislative caucus had named a ticket for the electoral college. Yet again, Hamilton County Republicans were reluctant to accept guidance emanating from Chillicothe, and they claimed the right to name one of the three electoral college candidates themselves. Generously, they promised to support the two named elsewhere—as long as Republicans in other parts "by some means procure the sense of the people that we may be united on the day of Election throughout the State." The need for party unity was clearly paramount, and although confusion reigned when one of the caucus's nominees moved to Indiana in September,

Ohio Republicans did finally focus their support on the two remaining electoral college candidates named by the caucus and on a third nominated by the Chillicothe corresponding committee. In Hamilton County, the Republican societies developed "a new plan of organization" specially for the presidential election, and urged their supporters to "draw together more closely than ever the ties of your affiliation." The outcome was obvious, and in a much-reduced turnout, the Jeffersonian ticket romped home in Ohio by a 7:1 margin.[24]

In these first two years of statehood when "party spirit" visibly approached its "meridian hight [sic],"[25] Republican politicians were building an electoral structure that came reasonably close to satisfying the strictest definition of "party." At the state level, legislative caucuses identified the official Republican statewide candidate in November 1802, March 1803, and February 1804, and the participants took home both the message and enthusiasm for the fight. Subsequent coordination depended, however, entirely on personal correspondence and newspapers, which also served to promote activity in the localities. In elections for state and county office, most candidates made their partisan identity known and gave the label they adopted an exclusive meaning, distinguishing them from the hated partisan enemy. Although there were many private nominations, most candidates were named by some sort of public meeting, which commonly identified itself in partisan terms. The newspapers did not usually have an avowedly partisan editorial line, but the articles and correspondence they printed commonly interpreted politics as a contest between Republican and Federalist, good and evil, with appropriate references to party symbols, leaders, and binding memories. What is more, the behavior of the voters in many counties suggests that this party consciousness pervaded the electorate.

Surviving returns for the elections of these early years in Washington County certainly demonstrate a high level of partisan awareness. The township returns for the October 1803 election, when over 63 percent of adult white males voted, show amazing consistency, as table 3.1 demonstrates. Rare evidence of individual voting—from Adams Township—shows that, in three elections held in 1804 and 1805, only 14 out of 143 ballots failed to vote a strict party ticket, and most of those 14 voters did not split their tickets but simply failed to vote for one or two candidates on the ticket. In the county as a whole, voters showed some partisan consistency between elections: the distribution of votes by township in the election for congressman in October 1804 closely reflected that in the election for state senator a year earlier.[26]

Washington County may have been unusually partisan, but similar high levels of ticket voting were apparent elsewhere—even in the elections of October 1803, when Republican discipline partially collapsed and returned the

Table 4.1
Distribution of Votes in Washington County, October 1803

	State Senator (two-year term)		State Senator (one-year term)		State Representatives (three to be elected)					
	Backus (R)	Gilman (F)	Buel (R)	Fearing (F)	Mills (R)	Fulton (R)	Jackson (R)	Cushing (F)	Higley (F)	Deming (F)
Adams	10	25	8	26	10	10	10	26	26	26
Kugger	24	5	24	5	24	24	24	5	4	5
Newtown	51	24	51	24	51	51	51	24	24	24
Salem	15	22	—	22	15	15	14	22	22	22
Gallipolis	37	3	37	4	38	36	36	3	3	3
Waterford	49	37	45	40	49	51	50	43	39	45
Marietta	98	63	103	63	103	102	102	61	60	63
Ames	—	25	—	25	7	7	6	26	26	26
Letort	16	—	16	—	16	16	16	—	—	—
Belpre	—	56	—	56	—	—	—	56	56	56
Tuskarawa	40	—	36	—	36	39	36	4	4	—
Middletown	105	9	105	10	116	114	115	10	6	10
Hockhocking	—	12	—	12	6	6	5	12	6	12
Newport	15	6	15	6	15	15	15	6	6	6
Grandview	8	1	9	—	9	8	9	—	—	—
Total	468	263	449	267	495	494	489	297	288	298

Source: Abstract of Votes, October 1803, Washington County Courthouse, Marietta.

Note: R = Republican, F = Federalist.

troublesome house of 1803–4. In Cincinnati, on that occasion, the Federalist-backed candidates gained 123, 123, 122, 122, 120, 119, 119, and 117 votes; the regular Republicans gained 51, 52, 53, 57, 57, 58, and 62—while the two men named on both tickets received 174 and 178, or the sum of the two parties' votes. The brief returns extant for counties as different as Jefferson and Montgomery—at opposite ends of the state—suggest a similarly high degree of ticket voting elsewhere in 1803. A year later, the voting for the state and federal legislatures in Hamilton County as a whole saw the Republican candidates securing 540, 533, 525, 522, and 516, compared with the Federalists' 183, 184, 199, 205, and 208 votes. A month later, in the presidential election, the county gave the three Republican candidates for the electoral college 503, 501, and 500 votes. In Ross County's Scioto Township, which contained Chillicothe, they gained 118, 116, and 108, compared with 29, 23, and 23 for the Federalist ticket.[27]

Such results came about largely because politicians drew up slates of candidates and distributed tickets before and during polling. Sometimes these tickets were handwritten, as at Franklinton in 1803, sometimes specially printed; they could always be clipped out of newspapers. In Ross County in October 1804, every Republican was urged to come to the polls "prepared with the 'Ticket' he means to support; if not, carefully to examine such as may be handed to him, previous to his putting it in the box." It was not unknown for an individual—as in Hamilton County in 1806—to "go to the expense of having one thousand tickets printed" repeating the official nomination, but inserting his own name for one of the offices.[28]

Such deceptions make consistent levels of ticket voting impressive, although there was a tendency for them not to carry over to the minor county offices on the ticket. Since the number of votes for these offices was often slightly lower, it is possible that voters sometimes deleted names they knew and disliked rather than write in an alternative or hand in a split ticket of their own devising. There was likely to be less partisan feeling over county offices, and the indications are that there was usually no partisanship involved in the April township or municipal elections, elections of justices, or even special elections for county offices. In Greene County in 1803, for example, at the first election for sheriff, "The words Federal or Republican were never heard throughout the day."[29] Such a pattern suggests a degree of discrimination on the part of the voters, and it emphasizes the extent to which they perceived national politics and legislative control in essentially partisan terms.

Yet, however partisan the electorate in 1802–4, it is difficult to describe the politics of these years as constituting a "party system"—simply because the Federalists did not provide an effective opposition. They had made "great exertion" in the first congressional election and focused their votes behind one candidate more effectively that the Republicans, but they lacked an institutional means of coordination to ensure agreement on a candidate in those first critical statewide elections.[30] In January 1803, the Federalists of Fairfield County "united all their force" behind a candidate for governor who was not the candidate in Hamilton or Ross, while in Washington they boycotted the election.[31] In effect, they simply adopted the course or supported the candidacy which might best strengthen their local ticket, recognizing that they could not win a statewide election.

By 1804 the signs of demoralization and even disintegration were already apparent. In the congressional election, the Federalists did not put up a candidate to oppose Morrow's reelection, but allowed Elias Langham to provide a focus of opposition for all malcontents. Langham found support in centers of Federalism, although in Washington County Rufus Putnam also received twenty-three votes. In the presidential election, the Chillicothe Federalists passed off their nomination meeting as "a respectable meeting of Republicans," and named an unpledged ticket somewhat different from that advertised in other counties. In some other places, as Charles Willing Byrd reported from Adams County after the 1804 elections, "The Opposition Party have dwindled to a number so inconsiderable that they are altogether silent on Politics."[32] The sad truth was not so much that the Federalists were antiquated, outmoded, or unwilling to adopt partisan measures; they simply lacked the numbers to challenge the emerging Jeffersonian majority in the new state.

ETHNOCULTURAL SOURCES OF PARTISANSHIP

Whatever the virtues of the Federalist creed, whatever its appeal to nationalism and a desire for stability, it conspicuously failed to attract the people of frontier Ohio. Traditionally this preference for Democratic Republicanism has been explained in simple ethnic terms: Federalism appealed to New Englanders, who were outnumbered by emigrants from Virginia and Kentucky who favored Jefferson's party. Leadership in the new state fell into the hands of southerners, who imposed their outlook on the new state. In other words, the undoubted cultural clash between two different streams of migration into the Old Northwest explains the party division in early Ohio.[33]

In recent years Andrew Cayton has elevated this interpretation to a higher level of cultural understanding. Recognizing that nationalist concerns were central to the Federalist outlook, he points to the translocal experiences of the various groups that supported that party. By contrast, the Republicans represented a coalition of disparate groups eager for a local autonomy that would allow various groups to develop in their own way. This coalition accepted the leadership of leading Virginians of the Scioto Valley, whose social and cultural expectations most committed them to this point of view: they wished to establish a position of economic independence and social preeminence that would bring them honor and respect. Thus, for Cayton as earlier for John D. Barnhart, the Virginians are to be seen as the focal and defining group of the party, in contrast to the New Englanders who settled near Marietta.[34]

Undoubtedly, an ethnocultural conflict of this kind underlay the party conflict in Washington County. The most persistent support for Federalism came from the New England pioneers on Ohio Company lands in the western two-thirds of the modern county. The banner township, almost uniformly Federalist, was Belpre, "a rich handsome place," with well-managed farms stretching along the Ohio River—and a "greater proportion of Revolutionary Officers" even than Marietta.[35] By contrast, the county's Republicans preponderated in the townships not settled by New Englanders, including the areas of French settlement. In general, the distribution of partisan support in Washington County closely followed the distinction, frequently remarked upon by travelers, between the "ignorant, lazy and poor . . . rough and savage . . . Back settlers" from Virginia and the more orderly settlers from New England, "the Region of Industry, Economy and Steady Habits."[36]

It is a mistake, however, to extrapolate Washington County to the whole state. Undoubtedly, there was an ethnocultural aspect to the party division in Ohio, but it was slightly more complicated and less all-embracing than most historians have supposed. The Republican party represented a coalition of many groups that did not easily accept the leadership of southerners, as the constitutional convention had demonstrated.[37] Furthermore, southerners were somewhat less numerous in early Ohio than has often been assumed: settlers from Pennsylvania outnumbered them, and even upland southerners sometimes represented a stream of migration from Pennsylvania that had turned south before crossing the Ohio River. This explains the speed with which people from Virginia and Kentucky were blending with those from the middle states and creating, in the Miami Valley in particular, the peculiar midwestern culture that came to mark such areas as central Indiana after 1815.[38]

Moreover, even those ethnocultural groups in Ohio that remained most distinctive were by no means homogeneous in their political outlook. Most notably, the New Englanders who began to settle the Western Reserve after 1799—such as Benjamin Tappan—were far less prone to Federalism than earlier migrants from the northeastern states or, indeed, those who stayed at home. One Connecticut Republican remarked, "Most people of much enterprise move away." Some found their opportunities restricted at home because of their Republican associations. For example, Elijah Wadsworth, "a very respectable man and unshaken Republican, . . . was an inhabitant of Litchfield, the strong-hold of Aristocracy in Connecticut, and was induced to leave that state from the political and religious intolerance affected and supported by his Townsmen . . . (whose strong and persevering efforts left him little room to hope for better times)." Samuel Huntington Jr. had also been an active Republican campaigner at home, but he had found the "atmosphere of Connecticut is infectuous [sic]" and decided to "get out of it as soon as I can." Like many others, he had seen opportunities in the West acting as an agent for eastern holders of Western Reserve land.[39]

The same selective process of migration even affected the political situation in Washington County. As a local Republican from Marietta told Jefferson late in 1801, "These days there is not an Emigrant from Connecticut within this county, but what is really a friend to your honor and a true Republican." This new wave of importations from the East explains, perhaps, the younger Meigs's confidence, by May 1802, in the ultimate triumph of Republicanism in this presumed stronghold of Federalism.[40]

Similarly, in Jefferson County, the Republicans owed their success by June 1803 to the western Pennsylvanians, predominantly Scotch-Irish in origin, who had been crossing the river in large numbers since the late 1790s. Among these people, according to one contemporary Pennsylvanian, "The seeds of party had been early sown, and had taken deep root in the western counties." They had opposed the U.S. Constitution in 1788 and "felt the most lively interest in the French revolution," forming Democratic societies to support its principles. In-spired by "the wild spirit of liberty," they decided to resist the whiskey excise—"a direct tax on the products of labor" which seemed "but the commencement of a system of taxation as odious and oppressive as that of the British govern-ment." If many of them had actively participated in the Whiskey Rebellion, even more remembered with bitterness the crushing of the insurrection—the thir-teen thousand militiamen who marched from the eastern seaboard, the "star chamber" proceedings of Alexander Hamilton's inquisitorial court. For the inhabitants of eastern Ohio, as a local newspaper correspondent remarked in 1806, the Whiskey Rebellion was the event that had created true Republicans.[41]

Recent European immigrants, too, were commonly thought to have brought radical attachments with them to Ohio. Federalists complained about the political influence of foreigners, especially Irishmen, in the Cincinnati Democratic Society in 1802, and protested when they thought noncitizens had voted, as in Gallipolis in 1803.[42] After 1802, settlement by emigrants from Ire-land and Germany increased, although many of them may previously have lived in Pennsylvania. In 1806 the German Lutheran missionary Paul Henkel found German settlers in many parts of southern Ohio, but they were giving up their

distinctive language and religion in an effort to assimilate into somewhat suspicious local communities. In Montgomery County, however, though not in
Dayton itself, he found a large and coherent German community loyal to the
ancient ways; in elections the German townships never voted Federalist.[43]

Germans had also moved into Fairfield County and the county seat, New
Lancaster, while eastern Ohio was coming to be regarded as an extension of the
"Europe-American" settlements of Pennsylvania, made up principally of emigrants from Germany and Ireland. The Irish must have been mainly Protestant,
since there were only fifty Catholic families in Ohio by 1811. The more recent
arrivals from Ireland, especially refugees from the abortive 1798 uprising, were
intensely patriotic and commonly refused to alienate their nationality by becoming U.S. citizens.[44] Still, by 1807 the Steubenville *Western Herald* made a
point of appealing to Irish patriotism and linking it with Democratic commitment. In general, the Republicans benefited from the reputation for nativism
that undoubtedly stained the Federalist party.[45]

The consequence of the Republican party's success in attracting support
from such different ethnic groups was that it subsumed within itself many of
the ethnic tensions within society, notably the widely perceived tension between Virginians and New Englanders. Benjamin Tappan, firmly Republican
but New England bred, responded with "disgust and loathing" to the state of
society he found in Chillicothe in 1803–4. As he told his wife, "There is one
marked distinction between the New England & the Southern gentlemen. None
of the latter have what we call delicacy of sentiment, none have any regard to
chastity or think it other than a useless incumbrance to a Gentleman—they are
open, frank & liberal, but personal purity they leave wholly to the women. The
consequences of this you can better imagine than I can describe. It is no more
disgraceful here to —— with a Negro wench than it is in the West Indies."
Virginian Ohioans returned the compliment, commonly criticizing the "Yankees" for their sharp business practices, and they took pride in their own
cultural characteristics. As one Virginian said in 1806 when the younger Meigs
seemed prepared to challenge the leadership of Tiffin and Worthington, "If two
Virginians suffer a single Yank to oust them, horseracing must cease & we may
hang up the fiddle." Yet such differences did not prevent Yankees and southerners from supporting the Ohio Republican party.[46]

Party lines did not coincide with ethnic divisions, simply because the electorate was divided by other social determinants, some of which reinforced
ethnic identity while others cut across it. New Englanders, most notably, were
divided by religious tensions, for the later stream of Yankee emigrants were
generally hostile to the "Standing Order," the traditional religious establishment back home. These (commonly) younger men were frequently dissidents,

often freethinkers; many were also involved in Freemasonry, which in Connecticut was identified with liberal opposition to the establishment.[47]

A major source of Benjamin Tappan's Democratic Republicanism, for example, lay in his rebellion against the traditional religious values of his family. Objecting to indoctrination, the young Tappan reacted against the Calvinism of his distant relation, Jonathan Edwards, and the evangelical piety of his mother; he found in Voltaire and David Hume a skeptical attitude that he preferred to what he saw as the bigotry and narrow-mindedness of religious enthusiasm. In the 1790s he bitterly opposed the close connection of the "Standing Order" with the established Congregational Church in Connecticut, and supported the dissenting sects in defeating plans to give the proceeds of Connecticut's western lands to the Congregational Church. His views were echoed by his fellow student and future political rival, Calvin Pease, who corresponded with him after his departure from "the nursery of saints." Pease grieved that, in Connecticut, "Priestcraft" still rode "triumphant on the necks and consciences of the People," and he reflected that Religion, Hypocrisy, and Tyranny "shall endure so long as ignorance lends its friendly aid." He and Tappan could rejoice at the small local triumphs of the Democrats in Connecticut, which taught the representatives of the "Standing Order" that "vox populi was superior to vox dei." Little wonder that Tappan's highly partisan Fourth of July oration at Hudson in 1801 should be condemned by the renowned missionary Joseph Badger for its "many grossly illiberal remarks against Christians and Christianity."[48]

Certainly the first settlers of the Western Reserve were not noted for their devotion to religion, whatever the later reputation of the Reserve. As the most perceptive of the Reserve's nineteenth-century historians remarked, out of "the early settled townships, . . . not a fifth had a germ of the church of the parent states. . . . Deism, Unitarianism, in at least two forms, Universalism and Universal Restoration, were largely prevalent"—and settlers from Massachusetts he thought even more heterodox than those from Connecticut. By contrast, older settlers on the Ohio Company lands were more likely to be orthodox Congregationalists, although some among the Marietta upper crust indulged in liberal deviations and some among the populace at large in millennial heresies.[49]

In other words, the political cleavage among Yankees in Ohio tended to reflect the basic religious cleavage in New England between the established Congregationalist Church and its opponents. The difference can be symbolized by two hard-pressed New England agricultural communities that by 1803 were planning their removal to the West virtually en masse. Granville in Massachusetts, which was Congregationalist, transferred not only itself (and its name) to central Ohio in 1805 but also its Federalism. By contrast, the people of Granby, Connecticut, were Episcopalians, outside the ranks of the establishment; accordingly, when they moved in 1803 to their episcopal haven of Worthington, ten miles north of the future Columbus, they established an undoubted center of Republicanism.[50]

Apart from Yankee Episcopalians, however, the denominations associated with settled, homogeneous communities mainly gravitated toward Federalism. The Quakers who were entering the state—4,000 of them by 1803, mainly from North Carolina—formed close communities where they could pursue their religion as "a peculiar people," most notably at Mount Pleasant in Jefferson County. The people of that county elected a Quaker minister, Nathan Updegraff, to the constitutional convention as a moderate Federalist, although their choice possibly owed something to the slavery issue conjured up in the course of that election campaign. Thereafter, little doubt remained about their preference for Federalism, except when they supported Republican efforts to maintain peace with Britain.[51]

The Congregationalists, too, maintained a strong position in transplanted communities already committed to their church, as in Marietta, Belpre, and Waterford. Sometimes, as in the case of Granville in 1805, these frontier churches had been organized back in New England long in advance of the migration. Unequipped to undertake missionary enterprise, the Congregationalists had to rely on the assistance of the more aggressive Presbyterians, with whom they agreed on the Plan of Union in 1801 to facilitate religious provision, especially on the Western Reserve. The Presbyterians had early established a preeminence in the Ohio River valley, especially in southwestern Ohio, but they tended to concentrate on reaching those who were already "Presbygationalist" in allegiance rather than on making converts among the pioneers. In effect, the denomination's emphasis on the need for a settled ministry, well qualified educationally, ensured that, in time, its influence was confined to the larger villages such as Dayton and Cincinnati.[52] Except for the Scotch-Irish Presbyterians from Pennsylvania, who had their own reasons for preferring the Republican side, a happy consonance of outlook existed between the more conservative sects and Federalism, both wishing to preserve established structures and traditional forms in their immediate communities.

By contrast, Republicans tended to do well among those pioneers transformed by evangelical enthusiasm. Many settlers in southern Ohio hailed originally from the Virginia backcountry where the religious revival of the eighteenth century had undermined traditional structures of social authority and bred a spirit of thrusting individualism. The Word was broadcast further by the Great Revival, which spread from Kentucky in 1801 and influenced southern Ohio in particular, encouraging doctrines that emphasized individual choice, human capacity, and the unacceptability of many of the restraints and

monopolies of the older churches. The presbyteries of southwestern Ohio suffered directly from the New Light revival, which introduced doctrines of free
will, simple church government, the equality of all believers, and the abolition
of hierarchy and church discipline. Within a year or two of statehood, every
Presbyterian church in southwestern Ohio, except for three in or near Cincinnati and Dayton, had been swept into this New Light organization—only to be
promptly swept up yet again after 1805 by Shakerism.[53] By that date the Great
Revival had passed its peak. Although open-air camp meetings remained common, revivals now became sporadic and local rather than general. At this point
the more evangelical churches made great strides in absorbing the newly awak-
ened into their communions, at the same time as large numbers of church
members from seaboard states settled throughout southern Ohio.

    The evangelical sects included an unusual proportion of Republican lead-
ers—and virtually no Federalists—among their most prominent members.
Many of the "Chillicothe Junto" were active Methodists, including Massie and
Worthington, while Tiffin had been ordained in 1792 and was organizing Meth-
odist societies in the Scioto Valley even before the circuit riders reached there.
Thomas Scott, as a young preacher in Virginia, had converted both Tiffin and
Worthington; he was now a lawyer in Chillicothe and an active Republican, and
he served as secretary of the constitutional convention.[54]

    In southwestern Ohio, the highly popular John Smith was the first pastor in
Baptist Columbia, and he preached widely in the Miami Valley. He and three
other active Baptists were elected to the convention from Hamilton County—
Judge Goforth, Francis Dunlavy, and Matthias Corwin, Tom's father.[55] Two
other ministers associated with the more dynamic sects were elected to the constitutional convention as Republicans, besides Smith and Tiffin. The successful Methodist revivalist preacher, Philip Gatch, sometimes called the "Prince
of Zion," represented highly Democratic Clermont County, while John W.
Browne, an active Independent preacher from Hamilton County, nearly got
thumped by the upright Ephraim Cutler, on his way to the convention, for
calling St. Clair an infidel and a Socinian and mocking George Washington
along similar lines![56]

    The sects that did well after 1801 were those traditionally regarded as socially
subversive because they gathered believers into voluntary churches rather than
working within a formal parochial system. The Baptists were unusually numerous among the western Pennsylvanians who in 1788 had settled in Columbia, which from an early date had been a center of political dissidence; and
Baptism expanded further, as the settlers who had originally huddled for protection in Columbia took up lands in the interior, creating by 1802 twenty-one
Baptist churches in the Miami Valley alone. By 1812 the Baptists would be the

second largest church in Ohio, with sixty churches and 2,400 baptized members. With their emphasis on the separation of church and state, local self-government, and the responsibility of the individual to God, the Baptists had no difficulty in accepting the principles of Jeffersonian rule.[57]

Methodism had taken hold even earlier among the squatters of the early 1780s, and regular Methodist circuits had been established in Ohio by 1798. In 1804 the denomination had only 1,215 members, but after statehood it increased its number of preaching circuits from the three of 1803 to twenty-one in 1810, when the church had 8,781 members. The Methodists were Arminian whereas the Baptists were Calvinist, but they shared a flexibility in adapting to frontier conditions, creating new congregations, and employing ill-educated preachers where necessary. They were particularly successful in bringing religion to the scattered and isolated cabins of the backwoods. As the famed circuit rider James B. Finley later wrote, Methodism was "admirably adapted in its economy to the early settlements of the country." Universally regarded as predominantly Republican, the Methodists' evangelicalism not only reinforced their antihierarchical political beliefs but also, as Andrew Cayton has suggested, "provided them with a model for organizing relatively powerless groups, disciplining them, and creating a sense of collective identity that cut across social and economic distinctions."[58]

This connection between religion and politics indicates how the evangelical sects both fed on and fostered attitudes that appreciated the advantages of a more liberal and democratic political system and a government that imposed fewer constraints on a self-sufficient people. Of course, church members constituted only a minority of the population and probably a smaller proportion still of voters.[59] Revival meetings were frequently disturbed by rowdy opposition, and Universalism, Deism, and skepticism were stronger than is sometimes acknowledged, but these liberal and irreligious attitudes too were often associated with a Jeffersonian outlook.

In practice, however, the religious differences associated with the party division did not affect questions of government policy. Throughout the first years of statehood, the general assembly passed and strengthened a series of "Blue Laws" that forbade gambling, profanity, cockfighting, horse racing, drunkenness, and Sabbath breaking. This strict code was not, however, the work of corporatist Puritans or moralistic Federalists, as some would have us believe, but of a general moral consensus. These laws largely maintained legislation passed by the territorial judges as early as 1794–95, and they were fully supported by the main evangelical sects associated with Republicanism. The Methodists and Baptists, in particular, maintained a strict moral discipline over their congregations and displayed a militant concern over the moral behavior of other people. The Methodists went further, condemning also "superfluous dressing," dancing, and the consumption of alcohol, but they had no hope of imposing their standards on these matters through the law.[60] The Republicans were as divided over drink as they were over theology, and such matters never became a source of party difference.

Religious issues could lead to fierce public controversy and at times occupy the attention of a neighborhood more fully than politics. But while religious outlook may have affected the language and rhetoric of politics, religious questions and allegiances were never raised in public political argument, at least not before 1810. The political press commonly refused to print articles on religious controversies, no doubt hesitating to alienate any part of their clientele. Like the Republican newspaper in Marietta in 1808, most editors refused to allow their columns to be used as "the channels for disseminating Deistical opinions or advice; nor the religious opinions of any sect:—a discussion of religious topics cannot be had in this paper."[61] Politicians and publicists looked instead toward more material issues arising from local experience to provide the legitimate subject of political argument.

ARISTOCRACY AND SOCIAL TENSION

The ease with which the epithet "aristocracy" was attached to the Federalist party suggests that its support lay primarily among officeholders, professional men, militia officers, merchants, lawyers, and those who had established their reputation during the American Revolution. The Republicans, by contrast, found it easy to identify themselves with the "democracy." The distinction was symbolized in dress and fashion: the Chillicothe Federalist Levin Belt long persisted in wearing a queue, knee breeches, and silver-buckled shoes; the Cincinnati Democrat David Ziegler in the 1790s gave up the aristocratic habit of wearing his hair in a long queue, adopting—like Republicans in New York—the short, cropped style of the French Revolution.[62] This simple distinction between aristocrats and democrats may be seen as a rhetorical device rather than as an objective description of the social origins of the parties' support, yet it has a core of truth.

The Federalist party undoubtedly attracted some genuinely popular support, especially in the small urban centers, such as they were. In Cincinnati, most noticeably, the Federalists could not have continued to win the majorities they did, even after 1802, without some support from among the "mechanics" who made up the bulk of the population. Coming from "the other middle, and eastern states," these skilled craftsmen must have included—like their peers in New York City—many who cherished the party of nationalism, of effective economic action, and of vigorous commercial exchange on a cosmopolitan scale. Like the founders of Marietta and the territorial hierarchy, these Federalists were marked by nationalizing experiences that made them look beyond the immediate horizons of their locality.[63]

The urban centers may have been disproportionately Federalist, but they also produced some enthusiastic Democrats. As in Tom Paine's Philadelphia and Aaron Burr's New York, active leadership often came from some of the artisans and professional men, as well as from educated, often younger, men trying to establish or advance a career, and these energetic politicos usually managed to flush out supporters from quarters not traditionally involved in politics. In Cincinnati a handful of respectable men—doctors, lawyers, and traders as well as men who wished to preserve their offices under Jefferson—were regarded as leading a local party not otherwise marked by social respectability. So too, in Chillicothe, the anti-Federalist "Blood Hounds" led by lawyer Michael Baldwin were drawn from the "rabble," according to Herman Blennerhasset.[64]

Even Marietta contained similar unruly elements that could be agitated by dissidents among the political elite. Incorporated in 1800, by 1802 the town contained more than two hundred houses, some of them two or three stories high and "somewhat elegantly built" in brick. Although still "principally" inhabited by New Englanders, it had already taken on some characteristics of a typical river town, attracting a variegated population including some rougher, rowdier elements who clustered at the Point—at the confluence of the Ohio and the Muskingum—rather than at Campus Martius, where the original settlers had fortified themselves.[65] Ephraim Cutler had no doubt that the Democrats in Marietta appealed to "every dirty scoundrel that could be met with on the street." He thought Meigs had been elected a delegate to the 1802 county convention "by men who do not possess five per cent of the property of Marietta, taking into account his own and Judge Green's also, and if we were to take into calculation character and abilities, they would be found to possess a still less share." When this municipal election was over, the Republicans formed a procession that Cutler thought worthy the attention of a Hogarth:

> To behold a judge of our Supreme Court [Meigs], the honourable G Green Esquire [the new postmaster] & little tailor B. Preceding about fifty dirty, drunken newly imported Irishmen, scape gallows and jail birds, part of whom were quareling [sic], and part of them singing the praises of their leaders, must have been an interesting group for a painter. The procession proceeded to the Academy, where his Honor, Judge Meigs, delivered an oration, which was as well understood by his audience as Greek would be by as many Delaware Indians.

By mobilizing such marginal men and lower-class elements, including what one local Federalist called "the dregs of Foreign Nations," the Republicans were able to turn even Marietta into a Democratic stronghold.[66]

In both town and country, the Republicans benefited from the expansion in popular interest that they had helped to stimulate in 1802. In January, the Marietta Federalist Dudley Woodbridge had prophesied that the petitions against the Division Act would gain numerous signatures in the territory: "Few, however, will be freeholders or who have any fixed residence, they are made up of that Class principally that are vulgarly called Squatters." The Enabling Act deliberately gave the vote to precisely such men because, according to one Mariettan, "it was well known that the great mass of those people without property, . . . would favour the measures of the present administration. In proof of the fact . . . I refer you . . . to the evidence of your own eyes!"[67]

More convincing evidence derives from the fact that the election for the constitutional convention on the new franchise was held at the same time, and in the same places, as the election on the old franchise for the third territorial assembly. In Newport Township, Washington County, thirty-one men voted for the convention but only thirteen for the assembly, presumably because the other eighteen were excluded by the ordinance's property qualification. The thirteen better-off all voted Federalist in the more closed election. If these men voted the same way for the convention—and the returns suggest a high level of ticket voting—virtually all the poorer voters who qualified only for the convention election must have voted Republican, since the Republican candidates carried the township by an average vote of 18:13. A similar calculation for Adams Township suggests that 85 percent of the wealthier voters were Federalist, and 84 percent of the poorer voters were Republican. The uncertain figures for Hamilton County indicate that the average vote for the official Republican ticket increased from 44 percent ($\pm$ 6%) for the assembly to 57 percent ($\pm$ 5%) for the convention. If those who voted in both elections did not cross over, then in this key county, at least 72 percent of those disfranchised under territorial rules voted the Republican ticket for the convention.[68] Such evidence hints powerfully at a significant difference in the socioeconomic complexion of the two parties in 1802.

In winning the allegiance of the new voters in the countryside, the Republicans were able to exploit social grievances that were easily directed against officeholders and the legal profession. For over a decade, people had complained about the inconvenience and expense involved in traveling to the county court, often for cases involving relatively small sums of money; the obvious solution was to extend the jurisdiction of local justices, acting without a jury and often untrained, to cases involving larger sums and larger property values. As a result, their civil jurisdiction was gradually extended from five dollars to twelve in 1795, to eighteen in 1799, and then to twenty in 1800, but many still demanded that it be raised to fifty dollars—a demand not satisfied until the malcontent assembly of 1804. This persistent controversy was just one aspect of a widespread feeling that lawyers and judges dominated the lawmaking process in order to ensure that the legal system continued to provide fat fees for the privileged few. In 1802, the opposition pushed through the territorial house of representatives many measures making admission to the bar easier, reducing the fees and allowances of judges, officeholders, and attorneys ("to nothing," some complained), and also lowering the county rate while increasing the land tax and appropriating a part of it to county purposes. Burnet described these measures as "framed on popular principles, and intended to entrap the Council," with a view to "weakening the public confidence in the Governor and Council." The upper house felt obliged to accept some measures with amendments, reject some, and pass others "on such principles as will excuse their loss between the House[s]." As a consequence, some popular grievances remained in 1802 that the Republicans were able to redress, at least partially, in the first years of self-government.[69]

Such grievances commonly led to the argument that those who benefited from government expenditure, or were friendly to judges and lawyers, should not be elected to legislative positions. In the territorial election of 1800, newspaper correspondents had complained that lawyers and judges sitting in the legislature had refused to pass laws regulating their own fees, and they advocated the reelection of only those "good republicans" who had supported frugal government. In 1802 some Republicans urged the voters to elect only fellow farmers who worked alongside them, in place of officeholders who lived on the labor of the people, while others insisted that the object of popular and republican government was to provide "protection to the poor from the avarice and oppression of the rich—to the weak from the grasp of the mighty."[70] Social resentment against the petty aristocracies created by executive favor under the territorial regime helped boost the demand for a system of government more open to genuinely popular control, such as the Republicans delivered after 1802.

But it was not only in territorial or state affairs that the Republicans appeared more likely to rule in the popular interest. Ohio's attraction toward Jeffersonianism was, after all, but part of a shift affecting all parts of the nation between 1800 and 1804. In the critical years when previously uninvolved voters everywhere were being drawn into politics, short-term issues had made the Republicans the more attractive party. "High Federalist" extremism in national affairs between 1798 and 1800 had identified the party with illiberal and militaristic measures and, more disastrously, with high direct taxation. Such policies turned most farming communities outside New England toward the Republicans, who in 1801 and 1802 had reversed these policies and established a government devoted to economy. In Cincinnati, Republicans formally celebrated the "death of the Alien, Sedition, Stamp, and Excise Laws." At Chillicothe, the paper containing the hated acts was publicly burned, and orators condemned Federalist policy for maintaining "a standing army, navy, and a host of sycophants, dependents and drones." All present at this celebration in 1802 cheered "the present economical administration." As Jared Mansfield observed in 1804, "The economy and frugality practised are very congenial to the feelings of the hardy countryman" so common in Ohio and other uncommercialized or rapidly expanding agricultural areas.[71]

This preference in Ohio for weak, frugal, laissez-faire government at federal and state levels cannot usefully be seen as the consequence of the spread of commercial farming. Despite the enterprise of some individuals in the Marietta, Chillicothe, and Cincinnati areas, Ohio farmers by 1802 had scarcely begun to be involved in market operations; in that year, the traveler François Michaux noticed that the settlers on the very banks of the Ohio River "share but very feebly in the commerce that is carried on through the channel of the Mississippi." Thomas Worthington, who was making a fortune through speculation and beginning to organize the sale of agricultural produce downriver, believed that "federal or expensive measures may do in new england where nearly all the money collected from the people of the union is expended in ship building, etc., but it will not suit the people of this country who must live by the sweat of their brow—Money must be scarce among us and thanks to my God it will make us more virtuous." Even in Ohio, the sense of republican virtue, of needing to preserve the values and fulfill the promises of the Revolution, was powerful enough to motivate political choices, and in that frontier community, beyond the direct reach of Atlantic commerce and British hegemony, social environment as well as inherited prejudice pulled most men toward the Jeffersonian side of the national argument.[72]

THE PROCESS OF DIVISION

In effect, politics in the new state had come by 1804 to be dominated by a deep-rooted sense of political polarization, which divided politicians and voters into two camps. This cleavage had developed over the previous decade, both outside and within Ohio, as the nation's political elite struggled for control of America's future. Since control could be won only through the electoral process, each side appealed for additional support from the people, especially from among those who had not previously participated in politics or elections. In broadening their appeal, the politicians created a new electorate at a moment of national and local crisis, and the new voters were deeply impressed by their perceptions of what each party offered them at that crucial time.

Undoubtedly, in Ohio the contest for statehood had a mighty effect on the new electorate. At least in the short run, the appeal of St. Clair's division schemes to the local interests of Cincinnati and Marietta had some influence on partisan identifications. For example, William McMillan, an early Democratic Republican who had associated himself with St. Clair's logroll, found himself cast by 1803 as an "independent American," unstained by "the least tincture of the baleful and pernicious mania of democracy."[73] Overall, there can be no doubt that the Republicans gained most from the crisis, by standing out as the party opposed to a territorial regime that became increasingly unpopular after 1799. By 1802 the people of Ohio were persuaded that they were going through the struggles of the Revolution once more, overthrowing the constraints of colonial status and establishing government on a proper republican basis. Ironically, in doing so, they were rejecting the local leadership of the patriots who had fought most prominently in the American Revolution—St. Clair and the Ohio Company Associates—and accepting the leadership of a younger generation of politicians. These adherents of the Jeffersonian Republican party could, in the future, claim to be the state's own revolutionary heroes, who had rescued the people of Ohio from colonial subservience and given them all the advantages of statehood. However, such claims quickly diminished in political importance, as the rapid increase in population brought in large numbers of people who remembered nothing of Ohio's struggle for independence. For them, what mattered was the fact that they could identify the Ohio Republican party with the Republican party in their state of origin, an identification easily made because of the essentially national focus of the party conflict.

Throughout the formative years, Ohioans themselves were well aware of the national and even international overtones of their local political struggles. As a former colony of the United States, they had better reason than most Americans for seeing the federal government as giving tone, character, and direction to the country. The very political parties they were dividing into derived their names and principles from national rather than local politics; and the electorate showed its interest in national affairs when a record proportion of the adult white male population participated in the first congressional election in June 1803, producing the largest statewide turnout (50.15%) before the 1820s.[74] In the years that followed, Republican politicians called up memories of this formative period to reactivate political prejudices established at this time, and what they recalled was not so much the struggle for statehood as the Federalist "tyranny" of 1798–1800 in the nation as a whole.[75]

The events of these years remained memorable because of the depth of passion they aroused. The establishment of the iconoclastic, messianic French republic in 1792 raised issues that broke apart the consensus achieved by the

"Revolutionary Center," as the governing groups of the late eighteenth century have been termed,[76] and aroused enthusiasm among many who were customarily apathetic about politics. Some wished to embrace the "democratic" crusade, whereas others feared that blind egalitarian enthusiasm would undermine the delicate republican balance that held the country together. The Whiskey Rebellion was attributed by one observer to "the political violence which had broken out in France, and was sweeping over Europe like a sea of lava, threatening to overwhelm in its fury all forms of government." Ephraim Cutler believed that the partisan conflicts that were troubling the Northwest Territory by 1802 had arisen because "our Country has been so deeply engaged in the political warfare of Europe." The sense, on each side, that the rival party was the creature of a foreign power raised fundamental suspicions about its loyalty to the American experiment. The Republican press in Ohio clearly identified the Federalists with "British influence," and one of the very few articles on the presidential election of 1800 in the *Scioto Gazette* made it clear that, however wrong-headed the "Simple Federalists," the real danger came from the "Anglo-Federalists," who were capable of reversing the gains of the Revolution.[77]

In doubting whether partisan opponents could be trusted to accept the fundamental principles upon which the independence and republicanism of the United States were based, Ohioans were identifying their own "party" as the repository of patriotic virtue. In so doing, they were creating a loyalty upon which a mass party as a continuing and stable political structure could be created. It matters little that the parties were still loosely organized and ill-disciplined or that the voters had had little opportunity to demonstrate whether their partisan attachments would persist over the years. Undeniably, each party in Ohio by 1804 had a recognized name, a set of principles, an array of well-known leaders, and something less easily defined but even more important—in Hendrik Booraem's words, "a shared set of symbols, a sort of charter myth for the people who composed the party, something that could provide an emotional basis . . . for cooperative effort."[78] It may be that each of these political formations was less a party than a state of mind, but that party consciousness would prove capable of dictating political behavior in the future.

4

THE STRUCTURE OF POLITICS AFTER THE ACCESSION TO STATEHOOD

Originally much of Ohio's early history was written by Federalists who thought that Ohio statehood had amounted to a seizure of power by selfish Republican landowners and politicians.[1] In recent years adherents of the "republican synthesis" have seen the early republic—and the frontier state—as expressing the worldview of educated gentlemen who held predemocratic and prepartisan notions of how society and government should operate.[2] Both schools of thought have, therefore, assumed that Ohio was a patrician state republic in its early years until more democratic notions triumphed twenty-five years later. On this view, the revolution of 1802–3 had simply replaced one elite with another of more localist political outlook; traditional patterns of deference and gentry leadership still operated, but with different beneficiaries.

This view comports with the assumption that voters turned to the support of particular national parties out of deference to regional leaders and social superiors. After all, particular groups of voters may have overwhelmingly favored a particular party not so much because of popular preference but because of some leadership decision. According to Richard Buel, "During the formative stage of the first party system, the disposition of the regional leadership was often more critical than anything else in determining the political complexion of an area."[3] In the case of particular ethnocultural groups the distinction is not entirely clear, since elite leadership tends to thrive where an ethnic group can clearly identify with a particular leader. In other cases, the proposition is more dubious. Not only does this view depend upon assumptions about the nature of society and politics in frontier Ohio that are not wholly justified, but the political class itself was not necessarily marked by a sense of commitment to party organization. Left to themselves, many politicians would have broken out of party constraints and made the maintenance of party after 1804 virtually impossible.

WHO GOVERNS?

Arthur St. Clair had predicted that the new state would be "democratic in its form and oligarchic in its execution," thus neatly suggesting a contradiction between the forms of government and the social reality determining who took charge of the new instruments of government.[4] The question at issue, however, is not whether men of wealth, education, and social prominence tended to dominate government but whether they ruled in their own interest or depended on the support and participation of relatively ordinary people. To approach that question, we need to understand both the nature of the elite and how government operated, especially in the localities.

Certainly frontier Ohio possessed a landholding upper class capable of dominating public life. Lee Soltow has shown that, in 1810, some men owned extraordinary amounts of land: the top 1 percent of all Ohio landowners owned 23 percent of the land, while the top 10 percent owned half of the land. These great men can be regarded as a social and economic elite, although they were not cut off from the rest of a landowning class that included half the adult males in the state. There were no marked discontinuities or class demarcations in the distribution of landed wealth in that top half of the population; each wealth range fitted smoothly between the ranges above or below it, in a straight-line distribution.[5]

Moreover, those who enjoyed the greatest wealth were often parvenus, and the characteristics of an old patrician class ought not to be ascribed to them too readily. Nathaniel Massie and Thomas Worthington were scions of the Virginia gentry establishing themselves in the position of social eminence they considered theirs by right, but they owed the vastness of fortunes and estates to the sordid business of speculation in a land market that had become accessible to men of moderate means and much initiative. Some associates, equally successful in speculation, were men of more humble background. The hugely wealthy Duncan McArthur, for instance, was the son of destitute Scottish Highlander immigrants. He never went to school, and began in the territory as "a poor backwoods boy, with nothing but a hunter's dress and rifle." When old Arthur St. Clair referred to the Chillicothe leaders as "gentry," he was undoubtedly being somewhat sarcastic.[6]

There were other sources of elite privilege. Younger sons of old families in the East often came west with pockets full of useful introductions and, like Samuel Huntington, had little difficulty in gaining acceptance in polite society. But, by definition almost, they had little ready money and had come west in search of their fortunes. Their access to good society—possibly through church or lodge—gave them advantages such as a sound credit rating or favorable consideration for appointive office, but they were not in themselves men capable of carrying great influence with their poorer neighbors, unless they could persuade those neighbors that they were the best qualified men to serve in local office or to represent them in court or in the legislature. If they won elections, it was not necessarily because of their established position or economic superiority.[7]

Lawyers also formed an elite group but did not belong to an exclusive or aristocratic profession. Law was the main route of upward mobility, and many bright young men without means looked to it as the best hope of breaking away from a future of farm labor. Young men of intelligence persuaded local lawyers to take them on and allow them to study their law books. Then they took the far from strenuous test before the bar—and sometimes at a bar! As a consequence, the profession was soon to become crowded with poorly qualified young men who found it difficult to build up a practice and looked to public office of some sort as a valuable boost to their careers.[8] The more successful lawyers, who were soon entering the state assembly in numbers, could be regarded as spokesmen for the landowners and merchants who were their best customers, but entry into politics meant looking to a broader electorate. In any case, it was often criminal lawyers with a good jury manner who succeeded in Ohio politics.

The presence of landowners, businessmen, and, above all, lawyers ensured that men of above average property tended to preponderate in representative bodies. Lee Soltow reveals that "the first several [United States] senators . . . had acreage usually two or three times the average of 271 acres in 1810." The twenty-nine members of the state constitutional convention for whom there are figures owned landed property, in 1810, with a median value of "1,537 acres, a value more than ten times that of property owners in general." The early general assemblies also saw the presence of some very wealthy men, including usually the most influential men in the assembly.[9]

Yet it is a mistake to conclude with Soltow that "a dozen great landowners . . . held many of the reins of political power . . . in the new state." The men he mentions did not hold significant office—certainly not before 1812—and some were Federalists already cast out into the political wilderness. Nor were those who held power all notably wealthy. The first congressman, Jeremiah Morrow—who served from 1803 to 1813—was a substantial farmer, but his 383 acres in 1810 did not constitute an unusually large holding and, to the amazement of foreign visitors, when at home he customarily worked in the fields with his hands. In the constitutional convention, as Soltow acknowledges, "there was a strange mixture in the sizes of the holdings of the various delegates." The high average landholding of the delegates reflected the considerably greater wealth of six delegates (three of them Federalist) who owned more than 5,000 acres each, and they were balanced by at least two delegates who owned much less than the median for all the state's landowners. Landed wealth was more significant in some parts of the state, since seventeen of the nineteen delegates who owned more than 800 acres came from either the Virginia Military District or the eastern counties of Trumbull, Jefferson, and Washington. The situation was different elsewhere: the two Belmont County members owned 476 and 320 acres, while seven members of Hamilton County's ten-man delegation averaged 297 acres (those seven were all elected on the society ticket, the other three being the Virginian Byrd, the dissident Smith, and the Federalist Paul). These were substantial holdings, but typical of the large parcels in which land was distributed among a wide section of the community. The first state assemblies displayed a similarly varied pattern, with some men of relatively few acres gaining election.[10] Local political situations determined what sort of people gained public office, although the socially prominent were more likely to run.

In the few incorporated urban centers, merchants, businessmen, and professional men dominated local government, although some artisans and mechanics also gained election. In Cincinnati, municipal government was already falling into the hands of a closely knit economic elite—a group that even the anti-egalitarian Englishman Thomas Ashe admitted in 1806 "would be respected in the first circles of Europe." This oligarchical situation was encouraged by the restricted franchise that operated in municipal elections. Cincinnati, Marietta, and Chillicothe had been incorporated under the territory, and in each case the suffrage was restricted to freeholders plus either householders or taxpayers. This restriction ensured that only local residents and taxpayers could levy municipal taxation, but in Marietta, reciprocally, only voters could be taxed. There were further restrictions on who could hold office, while the mayor, recorder, and other officeholders were usually elected by the council. Similar restrictions tended to apply to charters granted during the first decade of Ohio statehood; Dayton's charter of 1805, for example, gave the election of the town council to adult male householders and freeholders who had paid the town tax. In spite of these provisions, however, elite rule depended on a degree of popular support. In Dayton, trustees were elected and taxation had to be approved by ballot in a town meeting. Under this charter the town's politics were marked for a decade by personal conflicts, no single group established control, and town government was ineffective.[11]

Local affairs in rural areas also tended to be dominated by prominent men. At the township level, local worthies usually acted as justices of the peace and were dignified with the title "squire," even after they gave up their posts. Governmental duties were the responsibility of township trustees and various in-

ferior officers, who were elected each April in public meetings of voters qualified to vote in state elections. Until the system changed in 1820, township
government was presumably open to control by small groups, especially as the
election meetings were often held in the homes of prominent men. One old
pioneer later recalled that whoever owned the house where the election was
held usually won—since it would "have been rude indeed, even for that free
time, . . . [to] go into a neighbor's house for a social election and vote against
him for justice of the peace." Yet, to be valid, at least fifteen men had to attend
the meeting and vote by ballot, while the dissident assembly of 1803–4 limited
the powers of trustees by providing that township taxation had to be approved
by a majority of the electors in a township.[12]

County government, too, was open to popular control. Had the scheme of
government adopted by the first general assembly in 1803 been maintained,
things could have been very different. For if judicial, administrative, and appointive powers had been concentrated in the hands of the associate judges of
the county courts of common pleas, then Ohio would have retained, and
strengthened, a system of all-powerful county courts akin to both that of Virginia, where it had long underwritten the influence of the local gentry, and that
reimposed in 1799 on Kentucky. There would have been a critical difference in
Ohio, in that the judges were not co-opted but appointed by the legislature;
however, the system could have developed to give significant power and patronage to local notables. The reduction of the county courts to their judicial
and constitutionally specified duties in 1804 still left them with some appointive
powers, which they tended to use in socially conservative ways. In Republican
Butler County, for example, the moderate Federalist John Reily was appointed
recorder and county clerk on its creation in 1803, and he held those offices for
eight years and twenty-seven years, respectively. Thus the transfer of governmental powers to locally elected county commissioners in 1804 was important
in ensuring that local electorates in the countryside would have the final say in
determining their immediate governors, at county as well as township levels.[13]

Whether their say had any real effect depended, as Kenneth Winkle has
pointed out, on how the informal polling place operated. However democratic
the suffrage, in reality the voter's influence depended on those who had the
right to accept or reject his ballot. Under the election law of 1803, the three
judges of election in each township, and their two clerks, were selected by
the voters present at the commencement of polling. This method of choosing judges of election derived from the traditional assumption that elections
were essentially meetings of the community: although appropriate for township meetings, the fall county elections had ceased to be meetings even before

statehood. Until revised in 1809, this anachronistic system undoubtedly gave an opportunity for those who commanded the polling station to seize control of the election at the start of the day.[14]

The evidence for the mid-nineteenth century suggests that judges of election were, disproportionately, older men of wealth, usually merchants, professional men, or farmers long resident in the township. There is every reason to think that before 1809, too, local notables served as judges of election and that judges would accept votes from established settlers more readily than from newcomers or transients. Yet we have surprisingly little evidence of complaints about the way in which judges of election exercised their power. Votes were indeed disputed and the cases carried to the general assembly, but objectors most commonly complained that due form had not been observed in the election or the return. Otherwise, complaints arose more because judges had allowed men of doubtful qualification to vote rather than because they had disqualified men who claimed to be eligible. In such cases the complaint rarely arose on the grounds that a voter had not paid a tax or worked on the roads; as later, the complaint was more likely to be that unnaturalized aliens had been allowed to vote. Hence the reform of election law in 1809 also clarified an ambiguity in the state constitution by restricting the suffrage to citizens of the United States. Otherwise, command of the polls does not appear—at least, according to evidence currently available—to have been used to protect the political interests of those in charge, as occasionally happened in the 1840s and 1850s.[15]

Local government could not be exclusive, in either town or country, for the simple reason that its operation required the participation of too many people. Each county government required ten officers, each township twelve more, and each incorporated town another twelve. With most counties therefore needing about one hundred civil officers and the number of counties gradually increasing to thirty-six by 1810, about one in ten adult white males had to serve at any one time. The rate of turnover in such offices was high, since the financial reward was negligible and the inconvenience considerable. Elected justice of the peace in 1804, Benjamin Tappan later recalled how "very troublesome" the office proved: "I lived about a mile from any other person &, when I held a justice's court, I entertained all parties & witnesses, because they could not well do without food for themselves & horses. This, & my never charging any fees, made the office rather burthensome & I was glad to be rid of it."[16] Men of wealth did not always wish to devote time and effort to the work of government if the rewards were few, and those who ran local government had to conduct themselves in ways acceptable to those upon whose cooperation they were dependent. Such grassroots realities also limited the freedom of action of the better-off even in county elections for the general assembly.

The Myth of Gentry Control

Ohio's senior politicians would have been amused to learn that they controlled an "aristocratic state republic" where followers followed wherever leaders led. The old Federalist governing class in Washington County already had learned that they could not control the representation or local government of a county once the majority of voters associated them with an unpopular political party. Arriving in Marietta in 1803 to take over from Rufus Putnam as Jefferson's U.S. surveyor general, Jared Mansfield found himself facing the antagonism of those neighbors who had "always considered themselves as a kind of Noblesse" but who now found themselves out of power in local as well as state and national affairs. As one former Revolutionary army officer told British traveler Thomas Ashe in 1806, "We majors, colonels, and generals . . . are so cheap and common here that people don't mind us, *no more than nothing.*" The new electoral politics could turn the elite's world upside down.[17]

Undoubtedly contemporaries thought that the electorate could be influenced by men of social and economic influence. Local Republicans explained some local defeats in 1803 as resulting from the influence of Federalist officeholders, who exercised their patronage in ways that militated against the Republicans. On the other hand, this explanation was not entirely disinterested, and Federalist officeholders who held on to their offices—until 1808, in the case of the receiver at the Steubenville land office—did so because they showed some discretion. Similarly, Republicans sometimes blamed a defeat on the influence of the local Federalist notable—and "all he could do." Republicans could themselves exercise a similar influence in the townships where they owned large lands, but their broader success arose mainly from their use of the issues of the moment to rouse voters even in areas commanded by their opponents.[18]

Basically, the Republican gentry retained their influence because their political sympathies were acceptable to the electorate, but they quickly found that their authority depended on not defying the voters' basic prejudices and interests. In Adams County, for example, two of the three Republican delegates to the constitutional convention—both significant landowners and friends of the local magnate, Nathaniel Massie—failed to secure election to the first state assembly because some of their votes on the constitution had created popular dissatisfaction. One of them, who failed election by seven votes, and a colleague in Ross County who was also defeated had "lost much credit by their negro vote" in favor of extending civil rights to blacks. Could this possibly mean that even the "Chillicothe Junto," so beloved by historians of early Ohio, could not exercise effective control over the voters in their own locality?[19]

Ross County is traditionally seen as a transplant of Virginia's political traditions of gentry leadership and popular deference. At its center lay Chilli-cothe, county seat and state capital, a settlement that was rapidly growing from the twenty cabins of 1796 to the prosperous town of 1807, when it was to have "14 stores, 6 hotels, . . . a Presbyterian and a Methodist church, both brick buildings, . . . and 202 dwelling-houses." At this period, proximity to Chillicothe was not considered an advantage by settlers, as it did not provide a particularly good market, and settlements were developing within Ross County at some distance from the town, especially on the west side of the Scioto, in the Virginia Military District. These outlying settlers were sometimes described as scruffy and unkempt, immoral and irreligious; they included many Virginians, although most came from Kentucky. Veterans of an older frontier, they were not used to behaving deferentially.[20]

Admittedly, Edward Tiffin had established a great personal popularity in the county, both as a readily accessible doctor and as an itinerant Methodist preacher. He carried Ross with negligible opposition in the elections for repre-sentative of 1798, 1800, and 1802 and as candidate for governor in 1803 and 1805. Thomas Worthington's firm advocacy of the interests of Chillicothe and the statehood cause made him almost as unassailable by 1802. They were closely as-sociated in politics with two other men of wealth and local influence, Nathaniel Massie and Duncan McArthur, as well as with the lawyer William Creighton Jr. McArthur had not always been a friend of Worthington, but in 1802 he saw the political dangers of division and threw his considerable personal influence behind the Republican effort. But this powerful combination, although trium-phant in 1802, found itself incapable thereafter of commanding the county in the face of quite disreputable rivals within the Republican ranks.[21]

Elias Langham was a Revolutionary soldier from Virginia who had been on bad terms with Worthington ever since 1799. Although a Republican, Langham had drawn close to St. Clair as political ally, officeholder, and drinking partner. One mutual acquaintance in Virginia thought Langham more likely than Wor-thington to succeed in an electoral contest, because "he could take a drink of grog and smoke a pipe and 'kick up a fight' and make it up again." In 1802 Lang-ham raised charges of corruption and abuse against Worthington over his man-agement of the Chillicothe land office, and accused him of being a secret Feder-alist who had shifted to the Republicans only on hearing the results of the 1800 presidential election. Worthington's allies gave as good as they got, branding Langham a coward, cheat, drunk, debtor, speculator, and—for good measure—a turncoat during the War of Independence. In the end, his support for state-hood was not sufficient to overcome the stigma of association with St. Clair, and Langham failed in his bid for a seat in the constitutional convention.[22]

Michael Baldwin occupied a more ambiguous position in Ross County politics. A young, well-connected, Yale-educated New Englander of "pleasant and . . . unassuming" manners, Baldwin was a lawyer of respected ability who had developed a lucrative practice since his arrival in Chillicothe in 1799. In 1801, thanks largely to his brother, who was a senator from Georgia, he gained appointment as U.S. district attorney for Ohio. But he also spent much time in the taverns of Chillicothe drinking with his Blood Hounds—"an organization of the roughs and fighting men of that day, which . . . did his electioneering and fighting for him." Despised and feared by "the law-abiding element of Chillicothe," efforts were made by the young Republican justice of the peace, Thomas Scott, to "break up the company," but they continued to trouble the peace and influence the conduct of public affairs in Chillicothe. Baldwin had cooperated with Worthington over statehood in 1802, won election to the constitutional convention, and contributed constructively to the drafting of the constitution; according to local tradition, he wrote most of it in a Chillicothe barroom, using "a wine-keg for his seat and the head of a whiskey barrel for a writing table." But there remained strong tensions between him and Worthington, dating back at least to the moment during the Christmas of 1801 when Worthington had protected St. Clair at gunpoint against the physical menaces of Baldwin's thugs. Many objected to Baldwin's "violence in politicks" and considered him "like the wind," since he "beats round to every point of the compass in as short a period." But he still gained election to the first assembly, where he served "with éclat" as speaker of the house.[23]

In that first assembly, Baldwin opposed Worthington's promotion to the U.S. Senate on the grounds that he was not a true Republican. Thereafter Baldwin and Langham drew together—through, it was said, sharing a whiskey bottle. In the special election of June 1803, both came out as candidates for Congress in opposition to the official Republican candidate preferred by the Chillicothe leaders—and Langham carried the county.[24] In the fall elections Baldwin produced a ticket that elected only one of its candidates—Langham—although those actually elected were no more satisfactory to the Chillicothe leaders. Langham became speaker of the dissident house of representatives in December 1803 and, backed by the influence Baldwin exercised "out-of-doors" in the state capital, almost got himself elected major general of the district's militia in place of Massie. Only one member of the Ross delegation voted for Massie.[25]

Again, in the fall of 1804, Langham carried Ross in the congressional race, in the face of the official candidate favored by Worthington and Tiffin. The representatives elected in 1804, 1805, and 1806 were no friends of the great men, and in January 1807 almost the whole Ross delegation opposed Tiffin's election to the U.S. Senate. In 1806 Ross and the two counties spawned from it in 1803 and

Ohio Counties in 1806. *Sources:* Downes, *Evolution of Ohio County Boundaries,* 31; and Utter, *Frontier State,* 29.

1805—Franklin and Highland—were the only counties in the state to give a majority to the renegade congressional candidate from eastern Ohio. According to Tiffin, any representative from Ross County who dared to vote for Massie in 1804 was likely to draw upon himself "the vengeance of the Junto."[26] The fact that Tiffin and Worthington thought of their opponents as the county's "Junto" suggests how far historians have overestimated the local influence of these two worthies.

Until 1806, it must be emphasized, the great men of the county stood together. The support that the two reprobates received they gained essentially by their appeal to politically independent men of lower status. In Chillicothe,

Baldwin's Blood Hounds continued to drum up support, despite the attempts of law officers to crush them; as late as November 1807, Herman Blennerhasset thought Baldwin remained "a giant of influence" because of his popularity with these "blackguards," as Aaron Burr termed them.[27] More notably, the independent pioneers in the wilds of what became Highland County in 1805 continued to give majorities to those who stood in opposition to the great men. No doubt these backcountry voters appreciated a rhetoric directed against "aristocrats" and "family arrangements," in the spirit of the extreme democratic manifesto produced in the locality in 1802.[28] Certainly the renegade congressional candidate of 1806, James Pritchard, loudly denounced Jeremiah Morrow, his incumbent opponent, as the "disgraceful" representative of "federalists, land jobbers and speculators," and the positive response of voters particularly in the Virginia Military District suggests the deep social resentment that underlay the persisting local opposition to the Chillicothe gentry.[29]

The opposition forces had strengthened by the beginning of 1806 when a now discontented Nathaniel Massie and two prominent lawyers, Henry Brush and Massie's son-in-law, William Creighton Jr., drew close to Langham and Baldwin. They gained the support of a new opposition paper in Chillicothe, the *Ohio Herald,* which made "violent efforts to destroy the reputation of the Bourbons," as it called Tiffin and Worthington. However, "a violent discharge of filth proved fatal," for the assembly refused to transfer the public printing from the *Scioto Gazette* to this "Oracle of Billingsgate," and the paper collapsed. Support in the general assembly was reinforced by influence at Washington, where Worthington and Tiffin persuaded the president to dismiss Baldwin from his important federal office as U.S. marshal. Worthington and Tiffin clearly owed their position in Ohio more to their statewide and national standing than to any automatic control of the county in which the state government sat.[30]

The limited power of large landowners such as the Chillicothe gentry resulted in a state tax policy unfavorable to their interests. From the start, government raised its money from taxes on the value of land. The assessment system inherited from the territorial legislature and adopted by the state in April 1803 valued land crudely, according to its quality as potential farmland rather than according to its state of improvement or its present commercial value. Such a system deliberately penalized those, like the great landowners, who were holding large chunks of land off the market in the hope of future capital gains. Furthermore, the exemption of federal land in Ohio from taxation for five years after sale reduced the state's tax basis and threw the onus of taxation on private landholders, especially the great speculators. As a result, by 1805 landowners were grumbling with William Rufus Putnam, Rufus's son and a large owner of

Ohio Company lands in his own right, that "the new system of Government adopted by our state is not quite so cheap as was pretended—the taxes have risen 25 per cent yearly since the adoption of our constitution."[31]

The dissident assembly of 1803–4 tried to make sure that the burden fell on speculative interests. It ordered a more complete listing of land for tax purposes and adopted a harsh policy toward nonresident landowners. On both the Western Reserve and in the Ohio Company Purchase, much of the land was owned by nonresidents who were either shareholders in the company or who had bought from them as a speculation; many lived in Connecticut and Massachusetts. The tax law of 1804 encouraged the breakup and sale of such estates, in particular by making them liable to full taxation regardless of their state of improvement. The law required payment in each township in which lands were held, and compulsorily confiscated 60 percent of the land if taxes were not paid. This burden fell heavily on all land speculators who had no exemption from taxation, including the Chillicothe gentry and other investors in the Virginia Military District. But the burden fell especially heavily on the Western Reserve, where the slowness of sales prevented landowners from paying their tax bills by cashing in some of their holdings. By 1804–5 the Reserve was said to be paying one-fourth of the state's land tax, with the members of the Connecticut Land Company, both resident and nonresident, contributing three-quarters of the Reserve's share.[32]

Not unnaturally, the Western Reserve's great proprietors, including the "Company interest," exercised whatever political influence they could muster and tried, as they had successfully in territorial days, to ease the tax burden. However, those settlers who had bought land, often on credit, from the company and its legatees showed themselves not deferential, as St. Clair had feared in 1800, but politically hostile to the landlord interest. Local residents favored taxation of nonresidents because half the land tax was paid into the county treasury, which meant that nonresidents were subsidizing local government, to the benefit of the inhabitants. After the 1803–4 assembly, one representative "circulated a tale" that Benjamin Tappan, as state senator, had been opposed to taxing nonresidents, and this "falsehood," according to Tappan, "had the effect to prevent my election [in fall 1804], or indeed to prevent my being taken up as a candidate again."[33]

After the 1805 election, Tappan complained that the men elected paid little tax and so, although they might deserve to be in the legislature for other reasons, "they cannot represent the property of the county." He insisted the legislature should consider the "good" of "this company interest," which had opened up the Reserve to settlement and still paid "more money into the state treasury than *any other* equal number of men." While this argument helped to secure a change in the tax law in 1806 so that nonresidents did not have to pay their taxes separately in every township in which they owned lands, it could not prevent the legislature from satisfying local opinion by dividing Trumbull County against the wishes of the Company interest. After such experiences, the large landowners decided in 1808 that it was necessary to appoint a lobbyist to attend the assembly on their behalf, since the Reserve's elected representatives would not risk unpopularity on these issues.[34]

As in the Virginia Military District, the opposition to the great landholders on the Western Reserve suggested severe tensions bred of social, even class, conflict. Much resentment had long existed against the "pack of land specula-tors" who were making great fortunes out of the state's development, and this hostility had been exploited earlier by the Republicans wherever the speculators were Federalist. But in some areas the speculators were Republican and con-tinued to exercise much political influence after 1802, and popular resentments fueled opposition to them, regardless of their political coloration. Thus wealthy men could never assume that the electorate would do their bidding, and they even discovered that social and economic prominence could be disqualification for electoral success. In 1805, Simon Perkins found it an electoral liability to be a major landowner on the Reserve and the most important of the proprietorial agents. As he complained, "We have a singular kind of Republicanism in this County, i.e. that no man whose property is above mediocrity (and if so much it is very dangerous) is safe to be trusted." He and his friends lost the election.[35]

PATRONAGE AND AMBITION

As in Namier's England, so in Ohio ambitious men looked to government to provide them with what they thought was their due. In an unsophisticated society that provided few opportunities for men who considered themselves above manual labor, public office could confer honor, distinction, recognition, influence, and even a source of profit. The effort to secure these advantages provided a basic drive behind the political activity of many ambitious individ-uals. That drive existed regardless of how electoral politics were structured, and although it could prompt energy and enthusiasm to invigorate party efforts, it could also operate to destroy formal party discipline.

Ambition and the desire for office were critical in attracting support to the Republican party in Ohio. King Arthur's Court had provided many jobs, but those who were not within the narrow circle of favor had no alternative paths to pursue. Jefferson's victory had caused many to jump ship in the hope of gaining favor either from the federal government or from a more open and many-layered dispensation under the state government that now seemed inevitable.

The appointments available from the state government provided an important means of reinforcing the Republican party, but the opening of more offices to popular election also allowed the dissatisfied to seek promotion by running for election in defiance of party dictates. Ambition was a force that the party needed to harness and had to strive to control.

Potentially, the greatest rewards lay in the hands of the federal government. Charles Willing Byrd found distinction and a decent salary as U.S. district judge from 1803 to 1828, and many ambitious lawyers coveted the prestigious offices of U.S. district attorney and U.S. marshal that Michael Baldwin held in turn. Perhaps the most lucrative posts were those in the federal land offices, which carried the fairest salaries in the state, ranging from one to three thousand dollars per annum, according to the extent of business done. Jefferson's triumph, in theory, opened up eight highly desirable posts in the land offices at Marietta, Cincinnati, Chillicothe, and Steubenville in 1801, but three of the current receivers and registers were Republicans, and Jefferson was in no hurry to fire even Federalists who performed their tasks satisfactorily and did not dabble in elections. But ambitious Republicans such as Daniel Symmes in Cincinnati pressed hard for the office, and Jefferson appointed sound Republicans to the new offices opened up in Zanesville and Canton during his presidency.[36]

The consolidation of Republican power in 1803 owed much to the attractions of office. In Washington County, for example, the Republicans' acquisition of the local newspaper, the Marietta *Ohio Gazette*, greatly facilitated the party's eventual triumph in the January elections, and that coup resulted from Wyllys Silliman's decision to change sides late in 1802. Silliman turned up in Chillicothe at the first session of the assembly looking for office. He gained appointment as president judge, only to resign the next year when he received the splendid prize of receiver at the new Zanesville land office. He was soon followed by his brother-in-law, the young Lewis Cass, who rejected his father's "Hamiltonian Federalism" and proceeded to become one of the Republican party's more successful office seekers. After working energetically for the cause and assiduously cultivating Worthington, Cass became U.S. marshal in 1807 and governor of the Michigan Territory in 1813.[37]

Once appointed, these officeholders provided a ready-made network of political supporters for a ruling party, especially those associated with the sale of federal lands. The surveyor general and his staff, based in Marietta until 1805 and in Cincinnati thereafter, had many jobs to hand out, especially to surveyors. As late as 1803, politicians in Fairfield County blamed their defeat in the fall elections on Putnam's appointment of Federalist surveyors who, "to a man, exert themselves against the republicans"—and Jefferson soon removed the cause of complaint. Especially important were the officials of the land offices in the six counties fortunate enough to possess one by 1808—fortunate because a land office could bring "considerable appearance of activity" and business to a county seat. In the two new land offices created after statehood, Jefferson appointed Republican political activists, and their eminence—and relative permanence—made them leading figures in local party circles. The first and only receiver in the Canton land office, created in 1808, was John Sloane, who became the central figure in Stark County's early politics. By 1809 he was the county's first recorder and a colonel in the county militia, eminent on every public occasion. In the Zanesville office, the key officers were Receiver Isaac Van Horne and Register Wyllys Silliman, both of whom enjoyed important contacts with Republicans in other counties. They and their minions energetically organized the local party, "caucussing, electioneering, and voting adulatory addresses to the President."[38]

The key federal position in most counties, however, was the post master, of whom there were eighteen or nineteen in 1803, rising to ninety by 1810. A post office could boost the business of any professional man or merchant who secured the position, since the public had to attend the business premises of the holder to collect their mail. The postmaster could be the local fount of information: he could distribute (or not) the official reports, broadsides, circulars, and newspapers that came his way, and his franking privilege provided a means of free correspondence. Could any committee of correspondence function effectively without the close involvement of the local post office?[39]

The state government, by contrast, had few centrally appointed officials who worked in the localities. Obviously legislators returning home could convey news of decisions made at the state capital, whether of a governmental or party character, but the judicial network proved equally critical. Each president judge traveled a circuit of several county courts, where he acted in conjunction with the associate judges in each county; inevitably, he developed strong political connections with local notables and the rapidly expanding number of lawyers on his circuit. On the western circuit, for example, Francis Dunlavy—who had no legal training—was to act for nearly fifteen years, 1803–17, as a force for party regularity. Similarly, supreme court judges became a significant means of gathering and distributing information of political significance, since they had to hold court in every county annually. At a time when lawyers were already deeply involved in politics and government and usually rode the circuit together, the meetings of federal, state, and county courts were critical opportunities for the advancement of both political and professional interests. For years, at court time in Butler County, for example, judges, lawyers, and "the elite of the country" regularly gathered in the evenings to talk in the office of the most prominent local officeholder.[40]

In this situation the influence and standing of Worthington and Tiffin at the state level derived above all from their influence in the awarding of federal patronage. Quite apart from their standing within the Ohio Republican party as the fathers of statehood, they clearly possessed powerful voices in advising the federal government. Worthington in particular was regarded as the greatest "general influence" over the president's distribution of patronage, and that gave him a prestige and standing that other Ohio politicians were bound to respect— and perhaps resent.[41]

For, if ambition satisfied or hopeful could reinforce the authority of those in command at Chillicothe, ambition unrequited could operate to break it down. The demand was simply greater than the supply. Arriving from Connecticut in 1803, Jared Mansfield was astonished by the "perpetual competition for office" he found in Ohio. For every office, he reported in 1806, there seemed to be ten candidates, and people applied without considering whether they were qualified: "In this part of the country no other qualifications, except perhaps a little Law knowledge, are deemed necessary for filling any office, under the State, or even the General Government. . . . Those who obtain places are considered only as more fortunate, not more meritorious than others of the *Corps.*" This "barefaced and ruthless . . . Office hunting" Mansfield ascribed to "the composition of the people of these parts, except the industrious yeoman and mechanics." There were too many "fortune hunters" from the seaboard states: "Landed speculation, Surveying, Jobbing, Pettyfogging, Fakery, Electioneering for public places, and everything except labor and industry are the means in operation. Hence the feuds and disorders in Louisiana and Indiana Territory and in this state."[42] Even officeholders of higher principle acknowledged the attractions of an office which, even if not lucrative, would not interfere with their regular professional practice. Indeed, for the growing number of lawyers in Ohio, public office of some sort could be a valuable boost to their career.[43] And if they could not secure office by conciliation of the men in power, then they had to seek the road of factional opposition.

Such motivations were involved even in the contests over the highest offices of state, the posts of eminence and distinction enjoyed by the "Chillicothe Junto." Tiffin and Worthington knew they had many rivals eager to win distinction, and they blamed the trouble in the assembly of 1803–4 on such unrequited ambitions. In December 1804 they feared a logroll uniting the members from Hamilton and Trumbull in an attempt to win the major offices for the great men of those counties, with the help of dissidents from Ross. Accordingly, the Chillicothe leaders paid great attention to Trumbull County and its leaders, making the influential Samuel Huntington chief justice and pressing his claims to become governor of the new Michigan Territory. In general, they seem to

have seen great virtue in promoting rival Republican leaders to the state supreme court or in securing them federal office outside Ohio! As Tiffin remarked to Worthington in December 1806, Ohio was "fruitful in producing
Men who is [*sic*] self-accomplished for every public station" and think "themselves equal and perhaps superior to either of us."[44]

Of course, Tiffin and Worthington's determination to remain in command
of Republican Ohio was itself an expression of personal ambition. While perfectly legitimate, it served to frustrate the equally legitimate claims of their
rivals. In 1806, the supporters of the dissident congressional candidate, James
Pritchard, insisted that Ohio's leaders must be taught that public office was not
their "exclusive inheritance," for "no such degree of entailed aristocracy exists
in the state of Ohio." After successfully rejecting this criticism, Governor Tiffin
created much personal bitterness by attempting to engineer an exchange of
offices with Worthington as the latter's Senate term came to an end in 1807. In
effect, the scheme obstructed every other claimant to either the governorship or
the Senate seat, and could legitimately be condemned as an example of "family
arrangements" by men in power.[45] Tiffin quickly found that he had "many
enemies who were waiting to rejoice at my miscarriage" during the sudden
crisis that broke early in December 1806, when Aaron Burr's military preparations on the upper Ohio River were revealed. His prompt measures "happily
disappointed" them, and he won the election handily, despite the intrigues of
his opponents. But then a degree of personal bitterness found expression in
press criticisms from Cincinnati and Lancaster that bespoke the hostility of
disappointed rivals.[46] This antagonism at the highest level merely replicated the
tensions that rival ambitions created throughout the state at the local level.

ROOTS OF SCHISM

Behind personal ambition often lay social pressures. Discontented politicians
were often expressing—or could claim they were representing—the interests of
their constituents. The ruling Republicans had gained power by representing a
combination of groups and interests, and it was almost impossible to satisfy
them all. Regional interests, for example, far from fusing with partisanship, as
some recent historians claim, served rather—like personal loyalties—to undermine it. Rather than expressing the major regional and social tensions that
divided Ohio, the structure of party conflict in the first decade of statehood
existed in defiance of them.[47]

The Chillicothe leadership of the state party always had to remember that
their power rested on a coalition of different regional majorities. As a consequence, the distribution of state assistance around the counties required careful

handling. In the dissident assembly of 1803–4, members argued over the distribution of the 3 percent fund, Ohio's share of public land sales, which was earmarked for road building within the state under the compact made with the federal government at the time of statehood. To the anger of many, most of the money initially went to build roads radiating from Chillicothe, to the great benefit of Ross County. Creighton feared that Langham and his friends were giving too much to Ross County, thus breeding a resentment that would embarrass the Republican party in the future. Subsequently the benefits were spread around more evenly—and therefore more thinly—thus ensuring that by 1820 there would still not be a decent road in the state.[48]

Sectional tensions further ensured that, in the competition for state or congressional office, ambitious individuals frequently pressed themselves forward as the candidates of a neglected region. Cincinnati, Marietta, and Chillicothe still competed for political preeminence, and the "upper end of the State"—above Marietta—complained of neglect in the distribution of office and patronage. In 1806, opposition to Morrow's reelection to Congress justified itself on the grounds that the southwestern counties had too great a say in national politics, with one of the two senators as well as the sole congressman, although in the end Morrow would carry the supposedly discontented eastern counties.[49] Again, in 1807 the gubernatorial election would be marked to some extent by a contest for power between Marietta and Chillicothe—between the younger Meigs and Nathaniel Massie—reminiscent of territorial days.

At the county level, too, contests between different sections of the county could override larger issues. In particular, questions concerning county boundaries and the location of county seats, which could only be decided by the general assembly, constantly produced contests that cut across party lines. In Jefferson County, for example, the official Republican nomination was challenged in 1806 by local Republicans who feared an attempt to move the county seat from Steubenville; the dissidents succeeded in electing the representatives to the general assembly, apparently with the help of the Federalist minority.[50]

Such rivalries were most acute on the Western Reserve, where the system of distributing the land had caused the Reserve's relatively few settlers to be widely scattered in innumerable isolated settlements. Yet the region was still organized as a single county, and settlers with official business had to travel long distances to the county seat at Warren, at a time when control of the county's offices could give significant advantage to particular sections of the Reserve. In the first state elections, the Reserve divided sectionally between the Lake Shore and the southern districts: the more heavily populated inland district usually predominated, except when Samuel Huntington deceived some southern voters as to the date of the election.[51] In 1806 the Lake Shore area was set off as Geauga County, but by then "a terrible conflict" had arisen respecting the division of the remainder of Trumbull County. In particular, Youngstown had ambitions to become a county seat, to the detriment of Warren. Various rival schemes of partition were drawn up, each creating a different set of county seats, and the proposed schemes were modified annually to attract a winning coalition of voters. According to Leonard Case, then a justice of the peace in the locality, this contest "was extremely bitter while it lasted—some five years—whole townships giving their vote on one side or another without a dissenting voice."[52] So too, on many occasions thereafter, struggles over the location of county seats would prevent local elections on the Reserve from being fought along party lines—until at last Youngstown became a county seat in 1876!

Regional tensions and rivalries came in time to be underwritten by the ethnocultural differences that increasingly distinguished particular parts of Ohio. In eastern Ohio by 1807, a marked increase of settlement from Pennsylvania, notably by people of Irish and German origin, distressed many earlier settlers. In Coshocton County, according to the first settler, a Virginian, "Wee was the hapest pepel in the world when ontill our Countery was fild with ireash and yankes other spoklen davels thay got between the pepel." New Englanders at large—be it Ephraim Cutler driving cattle east from Washington County in 1809, or Margaret Dwight traveling west to New Connecticut in 1810—voiced their disapproval of the sloth and profanity of the "dissolute vicious . . . wretches" moving in from Pennsylvania, especially the Germans.[53] Tensions were particularly marked between the Yankees and the Irish who were settling along the southern edge of the Western Reserve, notably in the Youngstown area, and these tensions embittered local struggles over county seats. So, too, the efforts to divide Muskingum County had to reckon with the Germans who "flock in from the Eastward" to settle in the northern part of the county; they were attracted by a scheme to create a county they could dominate, preferably named "Moravia." The assembly obliged in March 1808, although the new county was actually named for the Tuscarawas River upon which it stood.[54]

In such contests, some men voted who were not naturalized citizens. The state constitution did not clearly state whether only U.S. citizens could vote, although many people assumed that such was its intention. As a result, unsuccessful candidates, including Republicans, often challenged the votes of unnaturalized citizens. When the assembly revised the law regulating elections in February 1809, it clarified the ambiguity by ordering judges of election to check that each voter was a citizen of the United States. Only then was the contest between Warren and Youngstown stilled for the moment, for the judges sternly put an end to voting by aliens, "mostly Irishmen," who naturally resented this assault on their liberties. The Republican party had gained its supremacy by uniting people of many different kinds, but these ethnocultural differences provoked tensions that made it difficult to hold the party together after 1804.[55]

There are also signs that religious differences were becoming more acute after 1805, as the various denominations strengthened their hold in the more advanced communities. In particular, hostility to religious revivals evidently increased, as crowds of youths—often smartly dressed—turned up to disrupt camp meetings and even regular services. In 1808 the *Liberty Hall* reported that the Methodists in Cincinnati "for a long time past, have experienced much serious inconvenience in their devotions from the unjust and outrageous conduct of an infuriated mob." Rioters were taken to court, but that did not prevent the society from being "again assailed . . . during divine service." In Marietta, the Methodists seldom met to worship in the years after 1805 "without being assaulted by a lawless mob, who stoned the house, broke the windows, fired squibs, and drove them from the house of God." Much opposition also came from "Predestinarians"—Congregationalists, Presbyterians, and some Baptists—who, at the height of public excitement in 1808, organized a public debate on points of doctrinal difference. The "men of high standing" involved in such disputations were often accused of being behind the assaults by "lewd fellows of the baser sort." The famous preachers of the day later recalled the "many fierce and fiery trials" ministers had to face at this period, as interdenominational rivalry increased. Although almost never referred to in election campaigns, such religious antagonisms—often between members of the same party—would make it increasingly difficult to hold any sort of political coalition together.[56]

Twenty years later William Woodbridge would compare the state of society in territorial Michigan with what he remembered of Ohio on the eve of statehood: "Amongst people collected from the four winds of Heaven, there is but poor chance for unity of sentiment—for congeniality of feeling—& there can be no political amalgamation of the elements of which this society is composed until a complicated chemical process shall have been completed—until 'the fire shall have passed over us.' "[57] Early Ohio was marked by deep internal divisions that cried out for expression in politics, and it was almost impossible for any one political party to contain them. All in all, the social situation in early Ohio was not one that made it easy for a major political party to survive, since it must endeavor to transcend powerful forces in the state. Of course, some men may have seen party as a means of providing a common bond of union among different peoples—although the evidence is scanty—but a major party could survive only if it could draw on popular partisan loyalties that rivaled those of regional, ethnic, and religious attachment.

5

THE REPUBLICAN ASCENDANCY, 1805–1809

At first sight, the infant Ohio is the last state to fit any model of continuing two-party conflict. The gubernatorial elections after 1804 did not reflect a party struggle: all the candidates were Republicans, their motivation apparently personal ambition, and it is difficult to make much sense of—or see much consistency in—the voting returns. Studies of early Ohio politics are almost universally impressed by its personal quality, the importance of wealth, connection, and patronage, and the apathetic character of the electorate. The very existence of any effective sense of party seems dubious.

In reality, however, political life remained intensely partisan, especially at the county level, but the imbalance in the structure of party loyalties gave Ohio the characteristics of what has been called "a modified one-party system." In many respects, early Buckeye politics are reminiscent of those in states on the western "periphery" during the Third Party System of the late nineteenth century.[1] The lack of close competition made it difficult to maintain party unity and discipline; schisms and factions became prevalent; and considerable resentment gained expression against the dominant party. Despite all internal disagreements, the Republican party maintained its dominance, not least because the minority party persisted in active opposition, and did so at a time when events in America and Europe made it seem that the survival of the Republic depended on keeping the government in the hands of those whom the people had learned they could trust. Although by no means displaying the organizational discipline and voter commitment of the Second Party System, these years demonstrated that the party spirit created by 1802 could persist, could to some extent structure the political life of the new state, and could even gain intellectual legitimacy in the eyes of some activists.

THE MEASURE OF PARTY

Political parties can be too popular for their own good. In all one-party situations, the dominant party finds it difficult to maintain its unity without the pressure of an effective opposition. As in the post-Reconstruction South, so politics in Jeffersonian Ohio became the story of conflict within the ruling party rather than between two parties. Factionalism was rife, personalities obtrusive, and local antagonisms acute. State politics did not express a two-party conflict—at least not at the state level.

Until 1808, there was little reason for the people of Ohio to regret their overwhelming loyalty to Jefferson's administration. Republican rule had brought peace and lower taxation. The Louisiana Purchase had removed the main Franco-Spanish threat from the Mississippi River valley and opened the great artery that led to outside markets. Southern Ohio enjoyed a boom as the downriver trade expanded between 1803 and 1806 and demand in Europe for the pioneers' agricultural surplus increased. The population expanded; the frontier of settlement moved forward; land values rose; residents began to build frame and even brick houses as well as schools and churches; and parts of southwestern Ohio took on the air of long-settled countryside.[2] In the years of Jeffersonian prosperity, Ohio's party orientation could remain almost unthinkingly Republican.

Under the circumstances, the Federalists gave up formal organized opposition in Ohio. After the electoral disasters of 1804, as one of their newspapers later reported, they could no longer even think of mounting "any general effort against their enemy." Some, deprived of public office, withdrew from active politics, including "old" Rufus Putnam and "young" Ephraim Cutler. Others, "more luke-warm," according to the same Federalist paper, "have, in hopes of *patronage* being extended to them, become strenuous advocates and servile adulators" of Republicanism. Only a few, such as Philemon Beecher of Lancaster, had enough personal standing in their localities to win a seat in the assembly in 1805 or 1806.[3]

By 1806 the firm Republican John Sloane could claim, "There has for the last two years been no party who dared to make head against the republicans." The general assembly of that year had "one of the most agreeable sessions ever experienced in this or any other State, as there was not the least appearance of anything like party during the whole time." The dissident Republican and Federalist leaders who had caused such strife and difficulty in 1803–4 now "find themselves in quite a different situation . . . as their influence does not extend much beyond their own votes, especially on political questions or those that have a bearing that way." In the next session, 1806–7, the emergency created by the Burr Conspiracy ensured that, as Creighton reported at the beginning of the session, "great unanimity prevails in our Legislature, parties are lost in the consideration of our common safety."[4] Tiffin's reelection as governor in October 1805 had been almost entirely uncontested; the secretary of state, state treasurer, and state auditor were all reappointed by the assembly for three years in January 1806; and the Federalists did not formally oppose Morrow's reelection as congressman in October 1806.[5]

In this situation the conduct of politics and government in the state capital bore few signs of party management or party coherence. The general assembly apparently had little discipline and less structure. The members did not caucus in order to agree on policy or legislation but only where high office was concerned. The executive, with limited powers of patronage, lacked the influence to push any policy through or secure agreement on measures. The speaker had some authority in each chamber and named all the committees, but no one before 1810 built up any experience in the post. The frequent roll-call votes show that voting alignments constantly shifted, as members devoted themselves to essentially local issues, especially laying out roads, creating new counties, and distributing minor offices. Logrolling became notorious at Chillicothe, lobbyists abounded, and wealthy Federalists such as Bezaleel Wells could informally gain much influence on issues that affected their local or business interests. There was a high rate of turnover among the members; Jefferson County, for example, had eighteen representatives in twelve years, with only one serving as long as four years.[6] Perhaps because of the lack of controversy over state policy before 1807—beyond the struggle for personal and local advantage—Ohio politics were not defined by state legislative parties in the early years.

Even the rudimentary caucus techniques used in 1803 and 1804 to coordinate Republican support in statewide elections now broke down. In 1806, for example, many legislators wanted Morrow replaced by a candidate from "the upper part of the state." However, the Republican legislators could not agree on which of the three possible candidates from the eastern counties was sufficiently "capable & firm in politics," and no caucus decision was made. Under these circumstances most leading Republicans favored the reelection of the incumbent, but one eastern candidate, James Pritchard, the earlier statehood leader from Jefferson County, insisted on running against him.[7] Worthington had his doubts about Morrow's qualifications to be the state's sole congressman, but valued his integrity and good sense—and thought him far preferable to the unreliable Pritchard. In a contest marked by "the spirit of electioneering," much personal abuse was hurled at Morrow in some newspapers, but he finally triumphed with 74 percent of the popular vote, carrying even Pritchard's own county.[8]

The worrying feature of this division, from the point of view of the regular leadership, was the willingness of discontented Republicans, at all levels, to cooperate with Federalists in their search for political office. As in New York and Pennsylvania, these malcontents were already coming to be known as "Tertium Quids," a third force in politics. Pritchard, for example, was called a "Quid" in his own county, even before he declared his intention of running against Morrow in 1806.[9] So, too, the opposition in the assembly to Tiffin's promotion to the Senate, in January 1807, came from Federalists and Republicans whose "intrigues, caucuses, etc., were carried to a length which beggars all description." According to Tiffin himself, "After trying what could be done for five or six different persons, the opposition were finally obliged to settle down" on the most prominent Federalist, Philemon Beecher, who won twelve votes to Tiffin's twenty-five, with six scattering.[10]

Such personal rancor made it unlikely that the party would agree on a candidate for the 1807 gubernatorial election, even had the party leadership decided to hold a legislative caucus, as on previous occasions. Initially Tiffin had planned to have Worthington succeed him as governor, but Worthington proved unwilling to run. Hoping to change his mind, Tiffin's friends prevented the caucus from meeting, and the resulting election became a highly confused contest between Return Jonathan Meigs Jr. and Nathaniel Massie. Even the result proved uncertain, for the assembly threw out nearly half the votes cast in the state for technical reasons (in a turnout of over 36 percent), but without overturning Meigs's statewide victory. Then, at Worthington's prompting, Massie contested the result on the grounds that Meigs did not meet the residence requirement for governor. Although successful in his challenge, Massie refused to take the office himself, and left the government in the hands of Thomas Kirker, who as speaker of the state senate had been serving as acting governor since March, when Tiffin resigned to take up his seat in the U.S. Senate.[11]

In 1808, once more, the caucus failed to name a candidate, and two Democratic Republicans ran for governor who had each initially said he would not run if the other did. Similarly, no nomination was made for Congress, while the accounts of what had been decided about presidential electors were so varied that the most extraordinary confusion and intrigue resulted. Under these circumstances, much depended on personal correspondence to discover whom party members in other parts of the state were intending to back. As Philemon Beecher, Morrow's sole challenger for Congress, explained, "The state composing but one district it is impossible to be personally acquainted in every neighbourhood. Therefore a candidate must . . . be under obligations to friends to make known his pretentions in the several sections or Counties within the state." Such a situation operated strongly to the advantage of incumbents and helps to explain Morrow's continuance as congressman for the whole decade, 1803–13, during which the state comprised a single congressional district.[12]

Amid this comparative chaos, voters could scarcely have shown any partisan consistency in the way in which they cast their ballots in gubernatorial and congressional elections. Since elections were rarely between a proclaimed Federalist and a single Republican candidate, it is impossible to see a consistent party division in the aggregate distribution of votes. In any case, the rapid increase in population required the creation of new counties and townships, and so frequent boundary changes make it impossible to trace most voting districts through these years. The fact that turnout fell slightly from the heights of 1802–3 suggests a decline in voter commitment—although some evidence of individual turnout suggests that voters did not stop voting entirely but simply failed to vote regularly, at a time when voting could require giving up a whole day. Thus the inconsistency in mass voting behavior from one statewide election to the next arose, in part, because a somewhat different set of people were voting on each occasion.[13]

In a situation of such irregularities, Ohio politics at the state level cannot be seen in terms of the classical two-party model, and historians of these years have naturally seen the major conflicts as essentially personal, the contest of ambitious men and jarring personalities. Yet if the focus is shifted away from the center, it becomes clear that, even during these years when party competition declined, politics in much of the state remained structured along party lines at the county level.

The heart of the Ohio Republican party beat not in Chillicothe but in the numerous county seats where effective party control was exercised. In Hamilton County, most notably, the Republican societies continued to manage the nominating process. Usually in July a notice appeared in the press announcing the date of the "delegate convention." Each township society then gave public notice of its own meeting, which appointed two delegates to attend the county meeting and sometimes gave instructions as to whom to support for the nominations. At the convention, delegates had to present credentials from their parent societies before they could participate in the work of nominating candidates and selecting a committee to manage the election. Once the slate had been chosen, the rule of the societies bound delegates and members to support the nomination. One critic protested in 1805 that the county meeting was not representative, since "not more than from four to six met in any one township to appoint their delegates." But one of the delegates for that year responded that the certificates produced at the county meeting revealed that some delegates had been elected by majorities in excess of forty or fifty. In any case, he added, all Republicans were invited, by advance notice, to attend the township meetings and participate in the process. Whatever the realities in practice, there can be little doubt that this procedure was meant to operate from the bottom up, ostensibly allowing the grassroots to determine the choice of candidates.[14]

Similar conventions were commonly called in many parts of eastern Ohio, notably in Jefferson and Muskingum Counties. As the young Lewis Cass reminded Worthington from his home near Zanesville in 1807, "In our part of the country the election business is generally managed by Committees from the several Townships chosen to meet for that purpose." Whereas conventions in the Cincinnati area nominally represented the Republican societies and their members, in eastern Ohio these "committees" or "caucuses" or "conventions" (as they were indiscriminately called) were made up of delegates who had been popularly elected by those local Republicans who cared to vote. A typical convention was called in Jefferson County in August 1806: a party meeting in Steubenville resolved that Republican voters be invited to meet in their respective townships and choose three delegates to attend a general meeting; these delegates were to be instructed whom to support for the county nominations, which would be decided at the "General Committee," as this county convention was dubbed. At the same time the Steubenville meeting formed a small committee to discuss with delegates from neighboring Columbiana County the nomination of a candidate for the state senatorship which the two counties shared for the time being; this technique was commonly resorted to in order to mitigate rivalries between neighboring counties that were linked for a senate seat. In every case, the aim was to concentrate the Republican vote behind a single set of candidates; Federalists were excluded from the election of convention delegates to ensure that only sound Republicans were nominated.[15]

The extent of society control and the convention system should not be exaggerated. In many counties where Federalism had never been a threat locally, party nominating procedures were less formalized, and certainly less authoritative, than in the extremes of Hamilton and Jefferson Counties. In Ross, for example, nominations were usually made informally by various party gatherings, by grand juries, and by interested individuals through newspaper announcements, but even there efforts were made to introduce a more formalized convention system—and a convention was held in 1809. Similarly, bodies calling themselves Republican corresponding societies operated at times in one or two counties, including Ross, but they were not as institutionalized or as authoritative in making nominations as the Hamilton County prototype.[16]

Where county conventions were held, they played a critical role in statewide elections, especially when the legislative caucus had failed to make a nomination. In the 1806 congressional election, for example, Morrow's identification as the regular candidate owed much to his nomination by every county delegate convention that met, including the one held in his opponent's own county, Jefferson. The Hamilton County Republicans always tried to exert statewide leadership by having reports of their own convention's choice for Congress published in newspapers in other parts of the state. Their committee of correspondence played a crucial role in 1806, communicating their preference for Morrow to "republicans throughout the state, requesting their concurrence therein."[17] Such information was valued elsewhere as giving reassurance that the local party's votes were not going to be wasted on a no-hoper. Thus, in September 1806, newspapers in both Marietta and Cincinnati eagerly published news from Chillicothe that the delegates from all the townships in Muskingum County had met in Zanesville and determined unanimously to support Morrow's reelection to Congress. Often, of course, these convention decisions were themselves a result of prior private consultation. In July 1808, for example, a committee of correspondence was elected in Zanesville to find out, in advance of the county convention, whom leading Republicans elsewhere were going to support in the forthcoming statewide elections, "so as to enable us to write in a general republican ticket at the ensuing election."[18] As in the Revolution, correspondence among activists and publicity through the local press remained the key means of ensuring coordinated action.

Michael Heale has written of the Jacksonian period that "it was the convention system which gave shape and discipline to a party." In Jeffersonian Ohio, as in some other states at the time, notably New Jersey, that discipline was exercised not at the state level or by a legislative body but at the county level by whichever party members dominated the local nominating machinery.[19] It was because such a clearly identified spokesman for the will of the local party existed—and was accepted as such by many voters—that the Republican party preserved an institutional existence throughout the many schisms and internal tensions that troubled it after 1804.

THE CONVENTION SYSTEM IN ACTION

The significance of county delegate conventions in maintaining the sense of party cohesion, direction, and discipline is most powerfully illustrated by Hamilton County during these confusing years. By 1808 the original county of 1801 had been reduced by the creation of eight new counties from its limits, but it remained the most important part of southwestern Ohio. By 1810 the county would have 15,204 inhabitants, which represented 7 percent of the state population and more than the population of the original county fifteen years before. British traveler Thomas Ashe was generally critical of America, but he developed the highest opinion of the Miami country and its metropolis, as he saw them in the summer of 1806. Cincinnati's backcountry he considered to contain land that was "among the richest on the continent of America" and already "considerably settled." Along the stretch of the Ohio from Cincinnati to North Bend, he saw how "improved farms, villages, seats . . . decorate the banks of the finest piece of water in the world." The town had "three hundred houses, frame and log," housing a population of about 950. Although E. D. Mansfield thought it still "a small and dirty county town," Ashe saw Cincinnati as already becoming a great emporium, where "the keepers of thirty stores" were growing rich exchanging imported goods for the agricultural produce of the locality. Socially, the town was heterogeneous in character, with many European immigrants, but the population in general was "orderly, decent, sociable, liberal and unassuming." Its tone was set by the officers of the disbanded western army who had settled there: "They and their offspring are known by certain aristocratic traits, a distinction in living, and a generous hospitality." Ashe himself, if compelled to live in the West, would have chosen Cincinnati—that is, if he had not been so eager to purloin from Cincinnati's savant, Dr. William Goforth, the great fossil bones of the mastodon Goforth had excavated in Big Bone Lick in Kentucky.[20]

By 1805, Hamilton County was firmly in the grip of the regular Republicans of the county's Republican corresponding societies, led by the influential Daniel Symmes. The longer-established Cincinnati newspaper, Joseph Carpenter's *Western Spy*, had become essentially the propaganda sheet of the societies. Its more critical rival, the *Liberty Hall*, founded in 1804, was edited by the firm Democratic Republican John W. Browne, who had chaired the county's nominating convention in 1802 and served in the constitutional convention.[21] In 1804, the societies' ticket had completed a clean sweep of the county offices and representative positions, thanks to consistent ticket voting by the electors. In 1805, the Federalists and their former coalition partners tried yet again to "divide the *republican* interest" by setting up a number of tickets including some of their opponents' candidates, but once more the entire regular Republican slate swept the county. The power of the societies manifested itself even more completely the following spring, when the town society—in an unprecedented move—named a full ticket for the election of *township* officers in April and elected twenty-three of its twenty-five candidates. In the general election of October 1806, the ticket nominated by the delegate convention triumphed by a 2:1 margin, except for one highly unpopular candidate for the assembly, Joseph Kitchel, who ran between 220 and 230 votes behind the rest of the ticket and was narrowly beaten by a last-minute Federalist candidate, Ethan Stone.[22]

In general, the authority of the societies' convention was decisive. In the spring of 1806, several candidates had offered themselves for nomination as sheriff, a post that was considered "pretty lucrative, and occasions more strife and contention than all the other offices." Challenged in the press to demonstrate that he was "a decided, not a wavering Republican," each candidate had to declare whether he was a member of one of the societies or had uniformly in the past supported the Republican ticket agreed on by the convention. At the same time, the Cincinnati society proposed one of its own members as a suitable congressional candidate instead of Morrow. The delegate convention in July settled both matters, ending the argument over the shrievalty and committing local Republicans to support Morrow's reelection. Admittedly, some Republicans afterwards objected to Kitchel's renomination for the assembly, but they were answered by the strong point that he was a faithful member of his local society and had always acquiesced in the convention nomination. By contrast, the dissident candidate put forward by his opponents had himself been a delegate at that year's county convention and so ought to have been "bound, by the strongest ties of honor, to support that ticket." Disloyalty to the party's nominating process was a sin, and Kitchel's Republican opponents garnered relatively few votes.[23]

However impressive the command that the societies enjoyed over the county's politics, in Cincinnati itself their authority and popular support were less certain. In municipal elections, following incorporation in 1802, they did not contest control and the town was ruled by a nonpartisan coalition of eminent figures who did not always see eye-to-eye with the local party. In 1806, two separate Independence Day celebrations were held, one partisan, organized by the local Republican society, and the other communal, organized by the town council. The regulars' position further weakened when the *Western Spy* changed hands and adopted a more trimming editorial policy less sympathetic to the societies. By the turn of the year, crisis was overwhelming the Cincinnati society: as Edward Tiffin reported in February 1807, "At Cincinnati all is confusion and worse than confusion . . . relative to John Smith and the state of parties there—horrid business indeed."[24]

John Smith had long had a personal following in Cincinnati, but he was viewed with distrust by many devotees of the Republican society. They had opposed his election to the constitutional convention and objected to his elevation to the Senate. They blamed him for preventing the appointment of Daniel Symmes as register of the Cincinnati land office in 1804, and accused him of cooperating with Federalists in local elections.[25] In 1805 Smith had given hospitality to Aaron Burr on his trips to the West, although he almost certainly was not privy to Burr's plans. When the conspiracy was arrested in December 1806, there was widespread indignation at Smith's supposed involvement, and the general assembly requested him to resign.

Public meetings in Cincinnati approved Smith's refusal to obey, claiming that he had been "maliciously traduced" and urging the assembly to withdraw its demand. Some firm Democrats, including David Ziegler, John W. Browne, and John Bradford, supported these demonstrations of public opinion, but others, notably Daniel Symmes and Elijah Glover, refused to back Smith. Insisting that he must be suspect because of his past political unreliability, they held their own breakaway meeting—attended by about fifty men—to uphold the assembly's request. Accused of attempting "to annul the general sentiments of the people," this "private caucus" was assaulted by a crowd of Smith's supporters, a "banditti" of about one hundred men, "boatmen, draymen, mulattoes and negroes," armed with "staves, bludgeons and dirks." Although accounts of this violent episode differ, clearly the society did not find its firmest support among the town's lumpenproletariat. The dispute—which dragged on until April 1808, when Smith resigned following proceedings in the U.S. Senate— further embittered the society's relationships with other Republican groups in the county, notably in Cincinnati and in Smith's home township of Columbia.[26]

In spite of these difficulties, the county's Republican corresponding societies still managed to hold off challenges to their authority. The delegate county convention continued to meet, observing all the forms of township election, credentials, and instructions. In 1807, a minority rejected the nomination of John C. Symmes for the assembly and held a rival meeting that drew up an "independent" ticket, "the primary object of which is to disappoint John C. Symmes and his partizans." Symmes remained deeply unpopular not only for his dubious land sales but also because he had failed to donate a township for the foundation of a college within the Miami Purchase, as required by the terms of his grant. Although they exploited the issue, the independents were easily brushed aside, and the whole regular ticket was elected, including Symmes. Even in Cincinnati, the convention candidates all received between 225 and 231 votes, compared with between 70 and 76 for their opponents.[27]

More worrying to some Democrats than such electoral challenges were doubts about the integrity of their own nominating process. They feared that men who were not true Republicans were gaining control of one or two township societies and getting themselves elected to the delegate convention, even though they had no intention of accepting its nominations if they disliked them. The most notorious of these men, Joseph Kitchel of Whitewater and John Jones of Columbia, had both been nominated in the past by the county convention, but then objected when they were dropped from the ticket the following year. To forestall infiltration of the county convention in 1808 from these two sources, the regulars set up alternative societies in Whitewater and

Columbia Townships, with the result that two delegations arrived from each township. When the convention refused to accept the credentials of the delegates from the suspect societies, they seceded, held a rival meeting, and produced an alternative ticket to run against the convention nomination.

These dissidents laid the blame for the dispute at the door of "a few juggling politicians in Cincinnati," who dominated the town's society. The meetings, normally attended by fifteen to twenty men, took place under a rule of secrecy, unless the proceedings were ordered to be published. They were supposedly dominated by Elijah Glover and Daniel Symmes, who now enjoyed great influence through his recent appointment as register of the land office. This "junto," the malcontents claimed, manipulated the county convention and so could "dictate for the county of Hamilton." The confusion these arguments caused in 1808 resulted in a close-run contest: the state senator was elected by only two votes, and the representative positions were shared by candidates from each ticket. The township returns show a distinct pattern of ticket voting, with the successful candidates breaking the pattern by their strong local appeal to particular townships. That apart, the regulars maintained their predominance in five of the eight rural townships. As they had also elected their candidate for Congress, the society men claimed the result as yet another "triumph of Republicanism in this county."[28]

The Republican corresponding societies owed their power in Hamilton County to one single asset: they were regarded as trustworthy supporters of the national administration, sound interpreters of true Republicanism. Every organized challenge to the convention nomination was embarrassed by its obvious dependence on Federalist support at the polls; in 1807 the dissident ticket included a well-known Federalist as a candidate for the state senate, and the regular Republicans knew exactly what advantage to take of that indiscretion.[29] In 1809 a newly organized protest movement in Columbia Township—entitled the Society of United Citizens of Columbia for Information—demanded that the nominating meetings be opened up to *all* citizens, as in New England town meetings. The Republican societies, however, insisted that Federalists must be prevented from infiltrating a nominating process that had served the county well since 1802. As one supporter wrote, no good would result from the reform proposed: "The chasm is too wide to close—every man has attached himself to one or another of the contesting parties; and as soon would fire and water unite, as principles so variant as democracy and aristocracy." The only hope, therefore, was to keep the Federalists out of office. The societies, whatever their faults, had at least "secured to us republican representatives, and they will continue to do so, while they are properly supported, and remain pure." The societies had institutionalized party action in Hamilton County and would continue to do so as long as the voters remained willing to follow their lead—as they still were, by overwhelming margins, in October 1809.[30]

ISSUES OF DIVISION

The Hamilton County elections of these years reveal the range of personal, local, and social tensions that could disrupt the Ohio Republican party. In general, however, these divergences cut across each other and varied from time to time; they could not, therefore, provide a fixed line of division within the party. But increasingly one issue of principle was appearing that concerned the very nature of the party. Republicans were divided between those who were committed to maintaining its unity and those who thought that party was developing into an illegitimate device to deny them the opportunity to pursue their legitimate personal or local ambitions. In the course of their disputation, antiparty arguments would be refined and justifications of party developed. What was to deepen that cleavage—and enable it, in future years, to structure state politics—was the emergence of a further issue of high principle, relating to state affairs, that split the Republican party from top to bottom and raised further serious questions about the value of party organization.

The evidence from Hamilton County clearly demonstrates that, by 1806, at least some Jeffersonian Republicans in Ohio detected an inherent virtue in the organizational strength of the party. They wished to perpetuate the party, recognizing that the party nomination possessed considerable power to direct the ballots of its supporters. As in parts of eastern Ohio, this commitment to a party organization based on the delegate convention was cherished mainly by the more radically minded, by those devoted to "the genuine principles of Democracy, the rights of the people," by those who most feared the "aristoc-racy" of the Federalists. Like the Steubenville *Western Herald,* these Democrats insisted that the United States was a true "democracy" in which the popular will must always be respected. They therefore defended their party as an instrument for respecting and preserving that principle, and justified their strictly orga-nized local nominating procedures as a means to "procure the sense of the people," as Daniel Symmes put it. Admittedly, Republicans who had voted for delegates might disapprove of the nomination that emerged from the conven-tion, but as "A Republican Elector" remarked in the *Liberty Hall,* the delegates were able to "choose for me . . . much better than I could myself, from a general view of conflicting pretension and interests that there presented," and out of respect for the delegates' honest effort and integrity, he felt bound to sup-port the Republican ticket. "Should I do otherwise I furnish my enemies with strength to destroy my dearest and best interests. United, republicans can do, politically, whatever their happiness and good governing may require: but scattered and divided they become an easy prey to their enemies, and prepare the way for their returning to power."[31]

This conspicuously partisan creed was commonly buttressed by an appeal to community solidarity and nostalgia for a less contentious form of politics. Because the party claimed to represent everyone except the "well-born," its spokesmen could on occasion portray it as endeavoring to express the will of the whole community. The convention, by providing a forum for the representatives of the people, made possible the public assessment of the claims of possible candidates and the requirements of the public welfare. Thus the convention helped to prevent candidates from running under false colors, imposing on the people, or forming secret combinations to secure the election of themselves and their friends. Moreover, a delegate nomination reduced the evil of public disputation during the election campaign, since the best candidates had already been decided upon. To dispute that selection, so "An Old Farmer" claimed in the Cincinnati press in 1806, was to sow the "seeds of discord" and to introduce an unwholesome "party spirit" into the election! In theory, at least, conventions and caucuses made up of elective representatives gave a candidate all the recommendation he needed; a delegate nomination obviated all need for personal canvassing, whereas an office seeker who came forward "on his own bottom"—like Pritchard in the 1806 congressional election—had to indulge in "the wretched practice of self-trumpeting." On these arguments, party organization was not a contradiction of traditional republican ideals but rather a means of fulfilling the ideal of proper behavior and disinterested concern for general interest, even though part of the community was excluded from its deliberations.[32]

Moreover, party nominations could serve to reveal the natural aristocrats among ordinary people. Delegate nominees did not have to be great men or incumbents known to the electorate in their own right; they could be humble or unobvious men, picked out for their appropriateness at a particular time, and so conventions could be valuable means of ensuring "rotation in office," that "grand feature in republican institutions." Indeed, hostility to a delegate nomination was often blamed on the reluctance of incumbents to recognize that they had served their turn and must "make way for some one else to come forward."[33]

Such justifications of strict party organization and discipline roused the opposition not merely of Federalists but of all who found party dictation incompatible with republican liberty. Antipartyism was indeed widespread, and even a good Jeffersonian newspaper such as the Cincinnati *Liberty Hall* could assert in 1804 that its Republican editor "dares to judge for himself; and . . . will never become the dupe of any party." Many objected that "the rage of party spirit . . . excited by the leader partizans" roused popular passions and prejudices, disrupted social harmony, and led the people into praising or cursing particular groups of men without thinking out the rights and wrongs for themselves. In particular, convention nominations were denounced because they reduced the number of candidates, and therefore the voter's freedom of choice, in the election proper. In Steubenville in 1807, a supporter of a dissident Republican ticket denounced the right of any caucus or convention to dictate to the people and deprive them of the right of suffrage by telling them whom to elect.[34]

Such partisan control was considered inherently wrong because it gave power to the few—and so to whatever interests they represented—and that amounted to "aristocracy." In Washington County, in 1808, a newspaper correspondent attacked the Republicans' growing reliance on convention nominations "to collect and concentrate the sense of the people," because it allowed "one or two in our state or county to be our dictators." Similarly, in Cincinnati during the controversy over John Smith's role in the Burr Conspiracy, leaders of the Republican society were denounced as men who had "for too long presided over our councils, and deprived us of the privilege of thinking for ourselves." Soon critics were claiming that, however democratic the convention process might appear, the proceedings were directed to produce the result the leadership wanted, and even the election of the delegates to the convention might be manipulated. And how could the voters be sure that the men behind the scenes, controlling the election process through their command of party machinery, were themselves "purely republican"?[35]

Thus as early as 1807 political conflict in Ohio had begun to focus on what would remain a central concern of politics for the next decade and a half. What right had a party to choose a candidate for an election, when the act of nomination virtually guaranteed his victory? Could supporters of that party vote for a different candidate and yet remain true supporters at heart? On one side of the argument stood those who objected to party control and party loyalty and, for whatever purpose, emphasized the virtues of independence. Their antiparty creed provided ample justification for cooperation with the Federalists, whenever the "best interests" of the country demanded it. On the other side stood those who valued strict Republican partisanship and the more democratic purposes of the party. Whatever the outlook of the Jeffersonian national leadership,[36] these local Republicans took pride in their party and sought its perpetuation, and in many Ohio counties they developed a local nominating process based on delegate conventions that served to focus the votes of the most partisanly inclined Republican voters. It was their nominating process, however uneven and flawed by later standards, which helped to hold the local parties together through the tensions and schisms that marked the years of Republican ascendancy.

These arguments over the proper role of party were given further edge at this time by fundamental differences over the power of the judiciary in a republican society. In Ohio as in many other states, much popular hostility endured against lawyers and a legal system that seemed designed to boost professional fees rather than to secure justice and individual rights. The popular demand for cheap justice in civil cases in territorial days had been met, at long last, by the rebellious state legislature of 1803–4, which had extended the power of justices of the peace to hear cases for the recovery of debts by raising their jurisdiction to fifty dollars. But the justices' decisions were made without a jury, and the United States Constitution, ever conscious of the need to safeguard property, had forbidden trials without jury in cases involving debts greater than twenty dollars. Accordingly, in 1806 an Ohio state judge, Calvin Pease, declared the fifty-dollar law unconstitutional and, in so doing, asserted a right of judicial review identical to John Marshall's innovative claim in the famous *Marbury v. Madison* decision in the Supreme Court in 1803.[37]

Such an assertion offended many of those Republicans who referred to themselves as "Democrats" and to their constituency as "the Democracy." Believing in the political supremacy of the people, they thought the people's representatives were the supreme power in the state and therefore the only possible interpreters of a constitution established through popular sovereignty. Hence Democrats were unwilling to accept that decisions of the judiciary, that "dictatorial court of infallibility," were "paramount to [the] voice of the great mass of the people and their constituent sages."[38]

Not all Republicans agreed, however. A number of them believed that Pease's nullifying of "a favorite law of many" was erroneous as a decision but legitimate as an exercise of judicial power; others thought him fully justified in every respect. The house of representatives in 1807 divided evenly on the question of whether the judiciary had absolute discretion in declaring laws unconstitutional, and the dispute had some bearing on the elections that fall. Then the state supreme court itself nullified the fifty-dollar law and so brought forth a newspaper controversy and a stream of popular protests from the "upper and middle" parts of the state. In the assembly that followed in 1807–8, "the question relative to the unwarrantable conduct of the Judges was one that was more warmly contested than any that has ever come before the legislature." The more radical pressed impeachment through the house, but the senate disagreed.[39]

The controversy entered the gubernatorial election of 1808, especially in counties where the "high Court party . . . and their sycophantic gentry" were determined "to prevent the impeachment of the Judges." And in some county elections—for example, in Ross—there was "a very great political struggle this fall: 'Law or no Law,' 'Lawyer or no lawyer.' "[40] This dispute sharpened differences among Republicans, embittering relations, for example, between Worthington and Tiffin, who both remained firm Democrats, and their former associates in Ross County, Nathaniel Massie, William Creighton Jr., and Henry Brush. In a short while, when the judicial issue became thoroughly politicized and voters began to identify with one of the competing factions, it would overwhelm and subsume all other cleavages.

The combination of disagreement over party discipline and disputation on the judiciary question potentially threatened the very existence of the Republican party. The judiciary question provided, for the first time, a divisive issue of long-term significance that arose out of affairs internal to the state—an issue powerful enough, in that republican society, to polarize the politically conscious and provide a new principle of organization. The conservative supporters of the judiciary were capable, by 1807, of systematically cooperating with Federalists, in defiance of the prescriptions of excessively partisan Democrats. In doing so, they threatened, as in other states, to lay the foundations for a new, overriding political division. Some historians have seen in this cleavage the origins of the Second Party System,[41] but whether such a realignment could come about at this period depended on developments in the broader political universe of which Ohio was but a small part.

THE FEDERALIST REVIVAL

The Republican party survived the tensions and disagreements within its ranks because, at this critical period, the old party imperatives still operated. Men had not forgotten the battles of earlier years, and the old enemy, if less openly combative, was still active, still to be feared. Supporters of the national administration noted that Aaron Burr's associates in 1806 were usually men of dubious political reputation, and the assistance that he had gained from old Federalists in Steubenville, Marietta, and Cincinnati did not go unnoticed.[42] So hostile were the Federalists to Mr. Jefferson that Republicans thought them willing to disrupt the Union—as a few of their colleagues in eastern states undoubtedly were. The survival of such irreconcilable opponents made many Republicans conscious of the need to hold together at crucial moments to prevent defeat, and this feeling was heightened in the course of 1807 and 1808 by the signs of a Federalist revival at a time of severe national crisis. Indeed, Ohio historians have commonly underestimated the extent to which the supposedly personal struggles of those years involved elements of national party conflict; even in Ohio, there was a Federalist revival after 1807 akin to that discovered by David Hackett Fischer in the New England and Middle Atlantic states.[43]

Many Republicans had never lost their fear that a malignant and persevering Federalism survived, even if its votaries had ceased to act openly. They knew personally of irreconcilable Federalists who, like the young Marietta editor James B. Gardiner, claimed to be "*too proud* to pay homage to a rabble because they are more *numerous* than the friends of order and good government." These uncompromising opponents could not be discounted, because they still possessed wealth, business connections, social influence, and even official positions that they could exercise to political effect. For example, in Hamilton County in 1806 the Federalists were able to exploit Republican divisions over the nomination of Joseph Kitchel because they held high office in the militia. According to John Cleves Symmes, these Federalist "generals of militia" ordered four general musters for the week before the election, and "with considerable address" withheld until the last minute the fact that they were intending to run a Federalist candidate to challenge Kitchel. At the musters, "grand dinners were given, and Mr. [Ethan] Stone, the federal candidate, made the hero of each day, and the burden of their toasts." With the county's Republicans divided and unprepared, this "management was crowned with success," and Stone just beat Kitchel, the least popular of the official Republican candidates, for the third assembly seat.[44]

The Federalists may have been adept on occasions at exploiting Republican differences, but their intervention often played into the hands of the more radical, more partisan Democrats. In 1806, Pritchard's race for Congress was damned in his own county by evidence that his campaign was encouraging local Federalists. Early in 1807, Federalists in Cincinnati sprang to the defense of John Smith, but that only strengthened Elijah Glover's claim that Smith was politically unreliable.[45] In the assembly's senatorial election of January 1807, Federalists persuaded the opposition to Tiffin to take up Philemon Beecher as the sole rival candidate. But, as Lewis Cass wrote, "a more improper selection could not have been made," because dissident Republicans opposed to Tiffin found it difficult to justify voting for an open opponent of Jefferson. As Silliman said, Republican representatives would "give to the State a federal Senator" only if they "forget or disregard the wishes of their constituents." Again, in the fall of 1807, spokesmen for the Hamilton County corresponding societies could damn their opponents for their past and present associations and insist, to great effect, that the dissident ticket was designed "to strengthen the federal interest in the Senate." As a Federalist was to comment in a Marietta paper a year later, whenever the "Junto" that controlled a county saw its supremacy challenged, it had merely to shout "Federalism!" to retain its position.[46]

What operated most strongly against Federalism was the upsurge of popular anger at everything associated with Britain following the *Chesapeake* outrage of June 1807. All over Ohio, Republicans of every shade united in public meetings that demanded strong measures of retaliation and pledged support for the seaboard areas in protecting the rights of American sailors.[47] But, besides their inopportune liking for Britain, Ohio Federalists recognized that their main political disadvantage lay in popular prejudice against their party name and the memories it evoked of the supposed "Reign of Terror" of 1799–1800. They therefore increasingly resorted to other labels—occasionally adopting the name "American," but in Ohio preferring to call themselves "Federal Republicans" in order to highlight their commitment to the liberal republicanism of the U.S. Constitution. In emphasizing the political consensus that underlay the republican fabric, Federalists blamed the growing international difficulties of the country upon the narrow "partyism" of the administration, its miserly reluctance to spend money on national defense, and its adulation of France. In particular, they blasted the unthinking partisanship of local Republicans and, by denouncing party discipline as unrepublican, eased the way for dissident Republicans to cooperate with them. The fear that behind the Quids lay the specter of Federalism persuaded many Republicans to approach the apparently personal and regional contests of 1807–8 with an acute consciousness of the need to hold the old party together.

Even in the gubernatorial election of 1807, too glibly dismissed as "the epitome of personal and local rivalry,"[48] party feeling was evident, despite the lack of party coordination and firm leadership. In January, two opponents of the state leadership, U.S. Marshal Michael Baldwin and his deputy, William Creighton Jr., made "a federal mongrel selection" of members for two juries and used them as the basis of a public meeting in Chillicothe. After speeches by leading Federalists from Cincinnati, including Jacob Burnet, the meeting nominated for governor the increasingly dissident Nathaniel Massie, who happened to be Creighton's father-in-law. According to Tiffin, the members of the assembly had not been told of the meeting, and "not a friend to any but Massie suffered to be present." When the result was made known, "several of the members were highly disgusted" and pressed for a single regular candidate to oppose Massie. However, Tiffin's determination to persuade the reluctant Worthington to enter the race effectively stymied efforts to call a legislative caucus.[49]

From the Chillicothe regulars' point of view, the problem was that Return Jonathan Meigs Jr. had for some time made clear his intention of running, and it was generally presumed that he would inevitably carry the counties in Marietta's range of influence—Washington, Gallia, Athens, and Muskingum. Unfortunately, the leading Scioto Republicans regarded Meigs as opportunistic and unreliable. Since 1804 they had secured for him, in rapid succession, a colonelcy in the army in Missouri, a federal judgeship in the Louisiana Territory, and nomination to another judgeship in the Michigan Territory, but he had neglected his duties quite grossly, provoking investigation and later rejection by the Senate for the Michigan job. In all, he had drawn over $5,000 in pay for less than nine months of actual service![50] At first the Chillicothe regular leaders hoped to persuade him to withdraw from the governor's race in favor of Worthington, especially as, "by securing Meigs, we can have the Marietta press." When Meigs refused, Worthington's claims continued to be pressed, especially by the regular Chillicothe paper, the *Scioto Gazette,* although for several months the man himself would not confirm or deny his candidacy. When he at last withdrew, the Chillicothe regulars did not leap on Massie's local bandwagon, as often assumed: Worthington made at least one public statement friendly to Meigs, while Tiffin used his influence among the Methodists to prevent the "dissipated" Massie from sweeping Ross County.[51] Worthington, however, decided to run for the assembly and so became more sympathetic to the local preference, and after the election he supported the challenge to Meigs's eligibility as governor—ironically, on the ground that Meigs's tenure of federal office outside Ohio must have prevented him from residing in the state for nearly three years![52]

Although regional rivalries affected popular judgment, many Republicans saw this election in clear partisan terms. Regular party newspapers such as the Cincinnati *Liberty Hall* and the Steubenville *Western Herald* came out for Meigs, and he received nominations from apparently every delegate convention that met. In Hamilton County, the societies never hesitated in their advocacy of Meigs, and they sent out circulars stressing his claims to Republicans in other counties. In its address, the Cincinnati society emphasized the need for Republicans to unite in resistance to subversives and Burrites, and approved Meigs because "his politics have ever been republican, and strictly uniform," while Worthington was much criticized for dictatorial ways and a supposed softness on Federalism.[53] Elsewhere, notably in eastern Ohio, the judicial question was thought by some to be at stake in the contest, since Massie had been one of the first to protest against unconstitutional legislation. John Sloane, one of the first Democrats to go on record against the right of judges to set aside the laws, believed Meigs must be elected, for otherwise "it will fall out ill for democracy, as the majesty of the people is about to be dethroned and prostrated at the feet of our Judges."[54] Historians have erred in reading the situation of 1810 back into this election and have failed to appreciate Meigs's identification in 1807 with the more Democratic and regular wing of the party.[55]

As partisan Republicans outside the Scioto Valley backed Meigs, so Federalists turned to Massie. Some, especially in Chillicothe, had preferred other candidates initially, but soon important Federalist groups, like those in Zanesville, rallied to his support. Although Meigs gained almost solid support in his own county of Washington, the hard-line Federalists of Belpre refused to vote for him. In Fairfield County, too, Meigs "had a universal suffrage, except at Granville," the home of Federalism in the county.[56] Massie also attracted Quid support, as in Jefferson County, where Pritchard led a powerful resistance to the delegate convention's nominations and prevented Meigs from gaining a clear majority.[57] Otherwise, Meigs won most strongly in counties with a tradition of Republican regularity, whereas Massie carried only nine counties, all in the Virginia Military District or upper Miami Valley. Although the assembly upheld the challenge to Meigs's governorship, his standing with his party was still high enough for him to be elected an additional justice on the supreme court by the same assembly. This, and his promotion the following session to the Senate, owed little or nothing to Federalist support.[58]

The increasing Federalist activity in the election was most conspicuous in Cincinnati, Zanesville, and Marietta. In the last city, "an association of federal gentlemen" established a party newspaper in September 1807. Under its editor, James B. Gardiner, it quickly gained a reputation for "violence and personal vituperation" until a more sober editor was appointed in 1808.[59] Statewide, the Federalists even made some gains in the 1807 county elections: the Ohio house elected then contained, according to Sloane, "ten decided feds" out of a total of twenty-eight members, which with "two or three quids" put them close to a majority. In the state senate, only half elected in 1807, there were three "feds" and three Quids out of sixteen members. Thus there was "a firm & decided majority of republicans in the legislature, but as the members were mostly new it was sometime before they could properly understand each other and this produced the election of Beecher [as speaker of the house]." In this nice situation a Federalist candidate, Ethan Stone, with a united party behind him, could reasonably hope for election to the state supreme court, and the Republicans were obliged to call a caucus to find a compromise candidate that all factions in the party could unite on. Although successful in this instance—electing William Sprigg, a Chillicothe lawyer who had already served from 1803 to 1806—the regular Republicans could not prevent the election of that old Federalist, Levin Belt, as president judge of one of the state's three common pleas circuits. Some members thought there were "more Federals in the legislature than there are republicans," if all were fully revealed.[60]

Federalist vigor became even more threatening in the course of 1808. As in the eastern states, the opposition to the Jeffersonians grew in confidence and assertiveness, as it began to glimpse the possibility of a revival in its electoral fortunes. New opposition newspapers appeared in Dayton and Chillicothe, the latter an avowedly Federalist state newspaper, with a system of agents covering the whole of Ohio. First published in October 1808, the *Supporter* announced from the start its devotion to Washington's principles and its determination "to break through [the] state of apathy and venality" that had crippled Federalism in Ohio. "Such has been the prevalence of party," it claimed, "such its bitter acrimonious effects, and such the powerful influence attached to the present administration of the general government of the United States, that many in these NEW REGIONS whose political opinions are in opposition have been deterred from stemming the torrent." That it could be stemmed was demonstrated by the recent Federalist gains of sixteen out of the thirty-six seats at stake in the congressional elections in Rhode Island, New Hampshire, New York, and North Carolina.[61]

The vitality of the Federalists in 1808 was undeniably a result of the embargo that Congress had imposed on all foreign trade in December 1807 as a result of the war crisis with Britain. Republicans in Ohio rallied to the support of the administration: even in Cincinnati where "exportation is become totally stagnant," according to John W. Browne, "we seldom hear a murmur . . . because the people have such a confidence in the wisdom and integrity of our government." The Republican press ardently supported the government's policy, assuring the seaboard states of Ohio's eagerness to support sailors' rights against foreign oppression, and it called on Federalists to unite with them in this time of national emergency.[62]

However, the embargo also produced widespread economic suffering and a shift in public opinion against the ruling party. Republican politicians were soon bemoaning that present-day Americans, unlike their fathers, were unwilling to undergo the material deprivations necessary in order to preserve the country's independence of foreign tyrants, preferring to listen instead to the blandishments of those who were mere tools of Britain.[63] From an alternative point of view, if the strength of Republicanism is supposed to have derived in part from the expansion of a grain-growing economy, exporting its product to the markets of Europe, then the embargo was effectively destroying a main buttress of the party's popular support. Undeniably, the collapse of farm prices injured all those in southern Ohio who had bought land on credit and depended on the sale of surplus crops to pay off their debt.[64]

The full impact of the new policy was most dramatically felt in Washington County. Since 1801 Marietta had been building seagoing ships, the first

appropriately named the *St. Clair*. These ships carried local farm produce down
the Mississippi and on to the West Indies. The ships themselves were often sold
in seaboard ports to merchants eager to use them in Atlantic and even Mediter-
ranean commerce. The industry had expanded, stimulating the local economy,
and by 1806 Marietta was even building gunboats for the United States government. The town by that year had "about one hundred and sixty houses, frame
and brick of the neatest workmanship," and a population almost as large as
Cincinnati. Thomas Ashe described how in 1806, from the high hill across the
Muskingum, he saw Marietta, "her gardens, poplar trees, ship yards, public
buildings, and her highly cultivated plains, extending in a narrow breadth along
the Ohio many interesting miles."[65] But then, according to distinguished local
Republican and historian Samuel Prescott Hildreth, the restrictions on over-
seas commerce after 1807 ended shipbuilding, rope walks, and hemp growing.
"Town property, as well as farms, sunk in value; a stop was put to improvements
in building and Marietta . . . retrograded as fast as it had ever advanced."[66] This
retraction inevitably hit local farmers as well, and by May 1808, according to
William Rufus Putnam, land could not be sold in southeastern Ohio "on account of the scarcity of money and the stopage [*sic*] of business." To make
matters worse for Ohio Company landowners, the state legislature in 1808
increased the land tax by a mere 44 percent.[67]

Naturally, local Federalists exploited the discontentment arising from these
hardships. They bombarded both local papers with savage criticisms of the
administration's policy, including some memorable doggerel:

> Our ships all in motion
> Once whitened the Ocean,
> They sailed and returned with a cargo;
> Now doomed to decay
> They have fallen a prey
> To Jefferson, worms, and embargo.

In September, the Federalists called a nominating meeting that was chaired by
the venerable Rufus Putnam and made up "of all the real Federal-Republicans
in Marietta and in the vicinity, together with all other well-disposed citizens
who are sensible of the necessity of a reformation in our State and General
Government." The editor of the local Marietta Republican newspaper argued,
to the contrary, that the real choice was "embargo or submitting to vassalage,"
and he called for local prejudices to be given up by all who were "True Americans at bottom." In October, Washington County gave a small majority to the
Federalist ticket and for the first time elected a Federalist delegation to the
general assembly. Local Republicans might console themselves that such results

were "obtained by local prejudices and the inactivity of the Republicans, and not that the sentiments of a majority of the citizens of Washington are federal"—but that could not prevent the Federalists from carrying the county in the presidential election, too.[68] But could Federalism mount a similar challenge in the state as a whole?

THE APPARENT CHANGE OF 1808

Philemon Beecher stood out as the most effective Federalist politician in Ohio, and in 1808 he gave his fellow partisans "great hopes of success" in a statewide contest. Encouraged by "the rappid [sic] strides of federalism in the different parts of the Union (in Massachusetts and Pennsylvania for instance)," Federalists ran candidates in every congressional seat north of the Potomac in 1808— and by July Beecher had emerged as the Federalist candidate for Congress in Ohio. Born in Litchfield, Connecticut, in 1775, Beecher was apparently a half-brother of Lyman Beecher but had little contact with him, as they were brought up in different households. Settling at New Lancaster in central Ohio in 1801, Philemon opposed St. Clair's division schemes, despite the pronounced Federalism he shared with his father and half-brother. Taking advantage of divisions among Fairfield County Republicans, Beecher won election to the state house of representatives annually from 1803 through 1807 (except in 1804), and came to be regarded as leader of the opposition in the assembly. "A man of fine address and presence," Beecher was widely respected as a lawyer of "fine intellect, though of irregular and limited education. Naturally eloquent . . . and impassioned," his addresses to juries were "seldom excelled" in their "strength and pungency."[69]

Leading Ohio Republicans appreciated the seriousness of the challenge—in an election season when every major office was up for grabs. John Sloane feared that Beecher "in the Middle part of the state . . . will get many more votes than he merits," but he trusted that Republicans would remain firm behind Morrow not merely in the western part but also "in the upper part of the State," where "Great exertions will be made by the feds and Quids." Sloane anticipated that "Beecher no doubt will attempt to pass for a moderate republican or, as they call it in New York, will be one of the american ticket," but he trusted that the electorate would see things in their true partisan colors: "As soon will the Ethiopian change his colour as that Philemon will be brought to respect the right of the people."[70]

Sloane also reported that Beecher was to run "in company with Little Sammy for governor, birds of a feather, &c." Samuel Huntington, although a Republican, had long been mistrusted as a "political thistle (i.e., a Burr)," an ambitious office seeker, eager for public status commensurate with his growing wealth. In the course of the year Tiffin and Worthington tried to buy his loyalty with a land-office job and then with promises of support for the Senate, and they endeavored to divide him from Beecher.[71] However, Huntington had long been in communication with Worthington's enemies in Ross County as well as the Cincinnati Federalists, and he implicitly appealed to all who were conservative on the question of judicial review, since he himself was chief of the offending supreme court judges. In Trumbull County, he was nominated by a meeting made up of Feds and Quids, by what one Republican called the "high Court party . . . and their sycophantic gentry." As was later generally acknowledged, the judicial dispute ensured that Federalists in Ohio would vote for Huntington, and certainly the Federalist nominating meeting in Washington County named him for governor.[72]

Huntington's campaign undeniably benefited from a division among his opponents. The legislature of 1808 had made no caucus nomination, but when Worthington announced his candidacy, some regulars felt "obliged" to support him. "There is no other chance," Sloane argued; "if we divide Huntington is elected and federalism will triumph." However, Acting Governor Thomas Kirker also decided to run, presumably encouraged by those Republicans opposed to the Scioto's claims to preeminence and upset by Worthington's uncertain course in the previous year's election. Kirker was nominated by party conventions, and ran most successfully, in many of the counties that had backed Meigs as the regular candidate in 1807—especially counties on the western edge of the state and those in the area of Marietta's influence. In Cincinnati, there was some resentment at the legislature's exclusion of Meigs the previous year; as a toast at the Republicans' and Mechanics' Fourth of July celebration prophesied concerning the coming October election, "The People of Ohio having been once duped, will then be cautious to whom they delegate the power to deprive them of a Governor whom they have chosen, and the placing of a six years Legislator in the Senate of the Union." The regulars' convention named Kirker for governor. The dissidents preferred Huntington, who carried the county with open backing from the Cincinnati Federalists, and Worthington was ignored.[73]

Elsewhere, however, Worthington's candidacy appealed not only to his own Ross County but also in the regular Republican counties of eastern Ohio, where his leadership in the legislative attack on the judges was much approved. Once he had won the support of the Jefferson County delegate convention, it was certain that Worthington would carry Jefferson and the neighboring counties. In general, Worthington and Kirker were regarded as being on the same side, opposed to Huntington, and both never did well in the same county. In Columbiana County, Worthington and Morrow were seen as the ticket opposed to

Huntington and Beecher, while in some townships in Hamilton County the votes for Huntington or Kirker were related to ticket voting for the county offices and, to a lesser extent, for congressman.[74]

Huntington's victory, with virtually 45 percent of the votes cast, was widely interpreted as a revolution in Ohio politics. Outside Ohio, reports described Huntington as the Federalist candidate for governor, even as far afield as Raleigh, North Carolina, and Tiffin saw newspapers in Washington that dubbed Huntington "a Federal Republican," as did the Chillicothe Federalist newspaper. But the most acute observer of the election, John Sloane, knew that it was not Federalism as such that had won:

> It appears that republicanism is on the wane, and for no other reason than that her votaries believe her invulnerable. At least, this in connection with the exertions of a few men who are endeavouring to climb into office at the sacrafice [sic] of all principle, men who although they make a general profession of republicanism . . . are ready at all times to Join the federalists in opposing those who have been continually engaged in advocating the rights of the people. It is this class of men who have produced the apparent Change in the Politicks of this State.[75]

Despite the dissident triumph in state affairs, events soon revealed that Ohio and its newly elected rulers would continue to support the national administration. The state legislature remained in Republican hands and promptly elected Meigs to the Senate as a sound Democrat. The new governor, too, even while flirting with Federalists, privately numbered himself "among those who approve the measures (particularly the late measures) of the General Government." His first official message expressed firm support for Jefferson's administration and its foreign policy. In Washington, the delighted Senator Tiffin had an extract published in the *National Intelligencer,* the official Republican mouthpiece, to counteract claims that Huntington was a Federalist—a slander which, Tiffin thought, the message had "effectually wiped away." When Tiffin resigned from the Senate to devote more time to his new bride, he felt able to ask Huntington to appoint Worthington as his interim replacement. Rejecting his former opponent, Huntington appointed instead a newcomer to Ohio, Stanley Griswold, a Connecticut Republican who had served as secretary of the Michigan Territory but who proved so quarrelsome that Jefferson had fired him. Ohioans on both sides claimed that Griswold was a "Federal Republican" friendly to the "British party," but Huntington knew him to be a firm supporter of the administration's foreign policy. Although much criticized in Ohio, the appointment of a Republican was generally appreciated in Washington, whatever Griswold's personal shortcomings.[76]

The 1808 presidential election had in any case confirmed that there was no political mileage in any other course. Early in the year factional disagreements among Ohio Republicans—the desire of each side to gain credit from the election—had prevented "a nomination of electors . . . whilst the representatives of the people were together," although all seemed to favor Madison. The members agreed to correspond, and the Cincinnati Corresponding Society confirmed which of the Hamilton County candidates it preferred and agreed to support those chosen elsewhere, even when "not altogether satisfied, . . . for the sake of unanimity."[77] Some dissident Republicans and Quids favored George Clinton's claims to the presidency, and Gideon Granger, from within the cabinet, exerted his influence among the politicians of the Western Reserve against Madison. The confusion over the third electoral college candidate opened the way for further names to be put forward in northeastern Ohio, with much doubt as to whom these candidates would support; this seemed a perfect opportunity for mischief, with a multiplicity of candidates possibly allowing an unreliable Republican or Quid or even Federalist to sneak in as an elector.

The full potentiality for disaster became clear when the Federalists in other states took up the New York Republican George Clinton as their candidate. In Ohio, various Federalist electoral college tickets were proposed, without mentioning the ultimate candidate's name, and in the end the ticket named by the Federalists of Washington County was generally accepted by that party. In Columbiana and Jefferson Counties, the Federalists said nothing publicly but apparently "their friends in the several settlements had their instructions, the republicans not expecting any opposition were careless, and the consequence was that in this county [Columbiana] only fifteen votes of a majority was given for the Republican ticket. In Jefferson the votes will be nearly equal."[78]

Yet the statewide result was never in doubt. Huntington himself had always known that "it is the general wish, with very few exceptions, to have Mr. Madison for our next President" in order to continue Jefferson's policies, and he recognized that Republican politicians who supported Clinton would be damned by the fact that, even in Ohio, "Clinton is openly supported by the Federalists." The Quids who opposed Madison and tried to exploit the confusion over electoral college candidates soon came to the same conclusion: "Mr. Pritchard himself was first in favour of Monroe and secondly for Clinton, but now he finds what the public sentiment is he is very noisy for Madison."[79] The low turnout in the election (about 14 percent) showed there was little popular doubt as to the result, and the Madisonian electors duly received more than three-quarters of all the votes cast.

In spite of the low turnout, in spite of the failure of central nominating procedures, and in spite of the confusion surrounding the various electoral tickets offered, popular voting in the presidential election still bore some hallmarks of consistent partisanship. There was not, as Noble E. Cunningham has claimed, "a considerable scattering of votes" across the state. Admittedly, there was more than one ticket in the field on behalf of each candidate, but most voters identified the official ticket correctly and the alternatives attracted only a couple of hundred votes each. Overall, the leading Republican candidates gained 3,645, 3,331, and 3,307 votes and the leading Federalists received 1,174, 1,057 and 1,031. In each case, the leading candidate ran ahead because his name alone appeared on all the tickets published for his party. In Cincinnati the votes were distributed 152, 149, 149 and 65, 64, 63, and in Marietta 130, 130, 130 and 89, 89, 88, respectively.[80]

If ticket voting was common, a lack of evidence—and rapidly changing boundaries—make it difficult to compare the voting behavior of 1808 with that of 1804, the most recent occasion when national party division dominated the fall elections. But it is noticeable that Marietta remained about 60 percent Republican and that Cincinnati remained the one place where Federalism maintained a substantial presence in Hamilton County. In the congressional election, Dayton showed itself still the stronghold of Federalism in Montgomery County and German Township was still almost unanimously Republican, whereas in Hamilton County the areas outside the townships of Cincinnati and Columbia were 82.2 percent Republican compared with 84.36 percent in the partisan congressional election five years earlier.[81] The scanty evidence at least reconciles with the view that, when election choices were presented in terms of the national party conflict, established loyalties to a party were strong enough to be a major determinant of voting behavior.

Although the Federalists tried to put a bright face on the result, there could be no doubt that when national issues were at stake, especially those involving the great international confrontation between Georgian Britain and Napoleonic France, Ohio Republicans overlooked their differences and closed ranks against Federalism. Most of them agreed with their president's belief, expressed to William Henry Harrison in 1805, that Federalists were incorrigible: "Even the honest among them are so imbued with party prejudice, so habituated to condemn every measure of the public functionaries, that they are incapable of weighing candidly the pro and the con of any proposition coming from them, and only seek in it the grounds of opposition." Faced with such fixed partisan prejudices, the minority party quickly found that their prospects for a political revival were strictly limited. The columns of the Chillicothe *Supporter* show the high hopes of 1808 quickly receding and being replaced by a determination to lie low, agitate less, and maintain neutrality in elections.[82] Then, and only then, might the Republicans reasonably be expected to indulge more fully in the internecine warfare for which they had already shown such a cheering appetite.

6

THE LIMITS OF PARTISANSHIP, 1809–1814

After 1809 the Republican party in Ohio faced major crises that raised questions about its very existence. The first of these crises arose out of the dispute over the judiciary, when some radical Democrats attempted to impose stricter tests on the party's candidates in order to ensure their political soundness. In doing so, the radicals provoked a popular rebellion by those who felt that the Republican party existed to support sound national government and should not impose opinions on matters of state policy. This contest soon developed some features of what Richard P. McCormick has called a "dual party system," with a different cleavage coming to operate in state politics from that which dictated the behavior of the state's electorate and politicians in national affairs.[1]

The second crisis arose from the international situation and affected basic national partisan identifications. Faced with foreign menaces, the outbreak of war against Britain, and the invasion of the state by enemy hostiles, party divisions seemed meaningless to those caught close to the front. The effect of both crises was to suggest to many Ohioans that their old loyalty to the Republican party and their antagonism toward local Federalists were irrelevant to the pressing needs of the moment.

A MILITANT TENDENCY

In later years John W. Campbell became a Jacksonian Democrat of some public distinction. In December 1825 he stood as the Jacksonian candidate for Speaker of the federal House of Representatives, and in 1828 he ran for governor. Unsuccessful in both bids, he was appointed U.S. district judge for Ohio in 1829 and confirmed unanimously by the Senate. Never an ardent partisan, he disapproved of factiousness and party violence and condemned unprincipled demagoguery. Shortly before his death in 1833, he publicly objected to the growing management of the Jacksonian party by a small group of insiders who "decide what is to be done, dictate politics, interfere with elections, and say who are to be elected." This system of manipulation he denounced as "Tammanyism," and he warned that the evil consequences of such a system had been demonstrated a quarter of a century earlier when the council fires of St. Tammany had burned across Ohio. Through the efforts of that dangerous fraternity to extend party power, he remembered, "the civil institutions were reduced to anarchy, from which a recovery was effected with difficulty."[2]

Other Ohio politicians of his generation could recall those years equally clearly but not always with the same conclusion. Caleb Atwater was another Jacksonian of the 1820s who by the mid-1830s was warning that tightly organized parties could encroach on the rights and liberties of the individual citizen. In preparing his *History of Ohio,* published in 1838, Atwater talked to all the surviving actors in that "stormy period" of state politics from 1809 to 1812 and came to the conclusion that the proceedings of the radicals at that time had been "highhanded, unconstitutional [and] flagrant," the product of unprincipled political selfishness. By contrast, Benjamin Tappan, whose own partisanship was reawakened in the 1830s, believed that the "Democratic" politicians of the time had been in the right and that their views were subsequently misrepresented and stigmatized only because of "Federalist" influence.[3]

The origins of this domestic crisis which so lingered in the memory lay in the dispute aroused by the state supreme court's audacity in overturning a law passed by the people's legislative representatives. Throughout the upper and middle parts of the state an outcry arose against the judges' decisions of 1806 and 1807 prohibiting local justices from hearing cases involving debts over twenty dollars, and the controversy unleashed popular resentment against the fat fees that the legal profession secured from the complexities of the more formal branches of the judicial system. The elections of 1808 gave the Democratic faction in the Republican party a majority in the legislature, but their subsequent effort to impeach the offending judges narrowly failed to gain the necessary two-thirds vote in the state senate. However, the radicals did elect two of their number to supreme court seats vacated by the promotion of Huntington and Meigs, and they further flaunted the supremacy of the legislature by extending the justices' jurisdiction to seventy dollars. These proceedings, according to the Marietta Federalist William Woodbridge, were marked by much warmth, animosity, and agitation: "You can hardly form an adequate idea of the degree of fervour and irritability which has unfortunately pervaded the minds of Members . . . this year." As a consequence, the state senate Republicans who voted against impeachment found themselves facing "the odium of being called Federalists—for it has become a party question."[4]

This controversy again entered the fall campaign in 1809, with several newspapers violently assaulting the would-be "judge-murderers." The results, according to the newly arrived Democrat John Hamm, put "the advocates of
Judiciary infallibility . . . all in the suds," for the next legislature was to have "the
strongest Democratic majority ever known in this state."[5] Even so, the radicals
still lacked a two-thirds majority in the senate. In their frustration, the Democratic leaders persuaded themselves, at Tappan's suggestion, that the state constitution had intended all offices to be filled for a full term of seven years and
that any vacancies arising in that period should have been filled, not for seven
years, but for the balance of the original term. As one of them said on the floor
of the house, "In a short time it would be seven years since the constitution
went into operation and certainly all civil officers ought to go out of office every
seven years, and so have the field entirely cleared off for new aspirants to office."
The advantage of this application of the old republican principle of "rotation in
office" was that a simple majority of the legislature, declaring the true meaning
of the constitution, could dismiss the offending judges and appoint new ones
who had a proper sense of their own subservience to the will of the people.
"Thus, by a mere resolution," Atwater commented, "the general assembly swept
off out of office every civil officer in the state!"[6]

This "Sweeping Resolution" of January 1810 gave the Democratic faction its
opportunity to establish a firm hold on the state machine. They must now elect
not only new supreme court judges, a new secretary of state, state auditor, and
state treasurer, but also new president judges for the three common pleas districts and new associate judges for all thirty organized counties. This opportunity was of considerable political importance not merely because of the patronage it offered but also because of the key influence exercised by judges as a
coordinating force across the state. The assembly elected nearly all the men the
Democrats wanted, reelecting incumbents they trusted and getting rid of Federalist president judges like Levin Belt in the Chillicothe district. As John Hamm
proclaimed privately, "Our friends deserve immortal gratitude for their reno-
vated exertions in the common cause on which we are embarked. Thanks to a
good destiny! The Democracy of Ohio is yet triumphant—the insidiousness of
quiddism and the wickedness of federalism to the contrary notwithstanding!"[7]

The resolution, however, had consequences that roused public awareness
and turned people against the "sweepers." The supreme court judges who had
been fired protested publicly and challenged the validity of all judicial business
under the new dispensation. Furthermore, according to Atwater, "Many of the
counties had not been organized one half seven years, and the judges, in not a
few instances, had not served two years. In some such cases, both sets of judges
attempted to act officially. The whole state was thrown into utter confusion for

Ohio Counties in 1812 and Congressional Districts of 1812–1822. *Source:* Downes, *Evolution of Ohio County Boundaries, 48.*

a time, but finally, one and all became convinced that the 'sweeping resolution' was all wrong."[8] In Scioto County, the new judge and the "resolutional" party threw into jail an old-order judge (and future Jacksonian governor) named Robert Lucas who had insisted on exercising his office. From his cell Lucas called out the militia company he commanded to "rescue your constitutional officers" and so threatened a major disturbance in Portsmouth.[9]

A year later a similar incident occurred in Greene County. The new president judge ordered the sheriff to remove from the court a recalcitrant associate judge who refused to be swept away, but the sheriff would not recognize the court order. The coroner was then ordered to imprison the sheriff and remove the offending judge by force, which he did "after much violent exertion."

Thereupon one of the associate judges, the young John McLean, the future long-serving U.S. Supreme Court justice, resigned in protest. As a result, "then there not being a constitutional court," all business had to be held over to the next term.[10] In other parts of the state, too, new judges such as John Thompson of Chillicothe strove to "weigh down all opposition," but recognized that "every exertion will be used to produce a change in the sentiment of representations next session."[11]

This electoral challenge to the "new order of things" disturbed the Democratic leadership of the state not merely in its own right but also because of the context in which it arose. At this very moment, some Republicans seemed to be suggesting that the Democratic Republican party should give up its separate organization and identity and harmonize with its opponents, for the sake of national unity in a time of international crisis. Such Republicans as James Findlay in Cincinnati, Benjamin Ruggles in Marietta, and John W. Campbell in Adams County expressed this view in Fourth of July orations. Newspapers devoted to assuaging party passions were founded in 1809 in Chillicothe and St. Clairsville, and yet more were planned.[12]

Another worrying development was the growing discontent of poor farmers who found it difficult to keep up payments for land they were buying on credit. This distress led to the formation of the Society of True Americans in Pennsylvania, which formed an active branch in Champaign County, Ohio, in 1810 and organized a "flying petition" in favor of what would later be called a homestead law. Menacingly for Democrats, the society declared that, in its quest for reform, "henceforward we will no more be Federalists nor Democrats, but True Americans, governed by the principles of equity."[13]

Such antiparty movements seemed to threaten Republican predominance and were therefore especially menacing to Democratic politicians who retained—like Benjamin Tappan—a profound sense of the ideological menace of "that old monster Federalism," which might yet sneak back into power. Danger arose, above all, from weak-principled Republicans who wormed their way into office and then did deals with their supposed Federalist opponents.[14] It was to obstruct such fellow travelers that the Democratic leadership decided to introduce a means of tighter, centralized control to keep the party on the right lines.

In March 1810, a Tammany Society was founded in Chillicothe, on the pattern of the New York and Philadelphia societies, with a dispensation from the latter. The seventy-seven men who joined this "No. 1 Tribe of Ohio" included Edward Tiffin, Thomas Worthington, and other prominent Chillicothe politicians, Daniel Symmes and Elijah Glover from Cincinnati, and several of the new judges. Proceedings were secret, but membership was not; as in New York, every member, when processing in public, was to "wear a buck's tail in his hat." The object of the society was to provide a close bond of fraternity and cooperation for "citizens of known attachment to the political rights of human nature, and the liberties of this country." It further revealed its sympathy with the secularizing principles of the French Revolution by adopting a non-Christian calendar, with years dated from the "year of discovery," i.e., 1492. Great care was taken in admitting new members, who had to be approved by nine-tenths of existing members. As all branches were constantly advised, "Better have twenty members Good as fifty bad." With membership restricted to sound Democrats, the society's real object, according to Campbell, was "to make nominations and control elections. The elements of their doings were secrecy and concert; and to insure the fidelity of members, the obligations of an oath were imposed."[15]

Quickly, in 1810, St. Tammany flexed its political muscles at the state capital. The regulars had called a "grand caucus" to nominate a gubernatorial candidate: although seventy-two legislators had attended, half of them abstained, allowing Worthington to win the nomination with only eighteen votes! The Tammany Society now worked for his election, with the *Scioto Gazette* as its mouthpiece. This "Tammany Gazette most vehemently attacked" lawyers in general and judges who wished to make themselves kings(!), and it vilified Return Jonathan Meigs Jr., who had been prevailed upon to become the candidate of "the ex-judge party." In reply, the Chillicothe opposition press damned Worthington as the "Idol of Tammany," bitterly attacked that secret and conspiring society, and warned of the dangers of unrestrained legislative supremacy. The anti-Tammany men portrayed Meigs not as a friend of the judges nor as an opponent of the seventy-dollar law but as a Republican willing to resist the dictation of Worthington and Tiffin and their conspiring friends. As one newspaper correspondent wrote, Meigs "employs no runners to carry the resolutions of your state controlling society into the different counties." So definite was the Tammany and anti-Tammany alignment in Ross County in 1810 that even the minor county officers were classified on that basis, and the county's returns show considerable ticket voting.[16]

The influence of St. Tammany was not yet an issue in other counties, but in many places the embittered feeling over the Sweeping Resolution resulted in an intraparty struggle for command of local nominating machinery. Most conspicuously, in Cincinnati, where the newspapers had been arguing over the judicial issue since 1809, the town radicals found their control of the county Republican party slipping. In several townships, delegates to the 1810 county convention were chosen not by the societies but by the voters at large at special open meetings; thus, in those townships, the convention was ceasing to be a partisan device and becoming instead a means of gauging the sense of the entire

community. The county convention then named a full ticket that satisfied every
township delegation except the Cincinnati society. This keeper of partisan recti-
tude denounced the nominations as an "infamous federal ticket," both because
of the irregular manner in which the "delegate meeting" had been constituted
and because it had nominated men "of wavering and doubtful politics," including Meigs. The Cincinnati society named a rival ticket headed by Worthington and was rightly criticized for its inconsistency in opposing the very
county nominating "engine" it had justified in previous years. In protest against
the narrow interpretation that the town society was placing upon Republican
purity of principle, a breakaway Republican Association of Cincinnati was
founded, which supported the delegate convention's nomination. Meigs and
every other candidate on that ticket (except Joseph Kitchel) carried the county
easily, and three of the four representatives elected duly associated themselves in
the next general assembly with the opposition to the Sweeping Resolution.[17]

So too, in many counties, the more conservative, pro-Court faction won
control of the nominating machinery in 1810. According to the Chillicothe
Independent Republican, delegate conventions backed Meigs in eight counties,
including Washington, Jefferson, and Muskingum; only in Belmont did a properly convened delegate convention nominate Worthington. On occasions, the
more radical rebelled successfully, as in Warren County: there an official Republican meeting nominated Meigs and a Quid ticket, but the minority, "not
feeling themselves bound by the nomination (which was stated as a condition at
the time)," held a second meeting that unanimously decided to support Worthington. He duly carried the county, with the support of the local newspaper,
edited by John McLean. In Worthington's main areas of strength, notably the
Virginia Military District, it was the conservatives who turned against party and
preached the virtues of independence, but in effect they appeared in the field
like an organized opposition, under the name "Independent Republicans."[18]
Outside of Ross County, however, there is little sign of fixed "state parties"
among the voters in 1810, and ticket voting was the exception rather than
the rule.

The cleavage between Democratic and Independent Republicans represented something more than a continuation of the earlier factionalism that had
troubled the party. Some prominent politicians distinctly changed sides: for example, the Marietta *Ohio Gazette,* once known as "a violent democratic organ,"
by 1809 was attacking the "judge-murderers." Conversely, in Ross County, the
editor of the *Scioto Gazette,* who in 1807 had supported Massie as governor, in
1809 opposed his election to the assembly because he was "an ardent advocate
of the rights of the Judiciary."[19]

The broader pattern is complex and confusing, although apparently most lawyers supported the court faction while poor debtors supported the radicals. More striking are the ethnocultural preferences discernible in the strife, for ethnic tensions seemed to be sharpening by 1809. New England constituencies tended to be conservative, even where most solidly Republican, as did the French of Gallipolis, whereas the eastern counties, where there was "much of the Democracy of Pennsylvania"—a state experiencing similar contests—provided much support for the "Judge Killers." In Montgomery County, the more radical candidates tended to do well—although not consistently so—in the German townships, and the more conservative found most support in the traditional Federalist townships.[20]

The attitude of the Federalists was, in fact, critical. Since their disappointments of 1808, they had adopted a low profile, claiming to "have no interest in the present rupture between the two parties styling themselves *Republicans.*" But in 1810 their editors urged them to intervene in order to defend the power of judicial review, for "without this power in the judiciary, a written constitution is of no real or essential value." Since Worthington's supporters were opposed to this "vital" principle—and made "the destruction of federalism . . . the whole burden of their song"—they must be opposed; indeed, the Democratic radicals were making the same mistake as in 1808, when they had placed "the controversy upon such grounds as left [the Federalists] no alternative but to oppose them." Admittedly, Meigs was no Federalist and his views on policy were not clear, but at least he was opposed to those "ambitious disorganizing demagogues" who appealed to established prejudices in order to maintain party distinctions and their own power. Federalist support was probably decisive in 1810, as two years earlier, in electing the more conservative, less partisan of the Republican candidates.[21]

THE REVOLT AGAINST TAMMANY

In this struggle for the soul—and control—of the Republican party, the central focus of state politics shifted away from Chillicothe and Ross County. Internal sectional rivalry had become more acute as the "upper counties"—the counties of eastern Ohio, including the Western Reserve—complained about the political dominance of the "middle" and "western" districts focused on Chillicothe and Cincinnati. By 1810 some were arguing that in the future a balance should be maintained between eastern and western Ohio in elections to the U.S. Senate. Such tensions affected the 1810 gubernatorial election, for although the antijudicial party found much support among the small settlers and debtors of the eastern counties, Worthington did not run as well there as expected. As Tappan later explained, Worthington had many friends in Jefferson County, but in 1810 they had voted for Meigs from "motives of policy" concerned with regional advantage.[22] The easterners' sense of grievance also prompted the legislature's decision, in January 1810, to remove the seat of government from Chillicothe to Zanesville for the time being, although rumor had it that some members from other parts of the state had supported the move in return for election to offices vacated by the Sweeping Resolution.[23]

This relocation brought Muskingum County to the forefront of state politics, together with its political leaders. In 1807 the county seat, Zanesville, was still a village in the woods, but it had begun to grow rapidly and by 1812 contained nearly 300 houses and a thousand inhabitants. Surrounded by iron ore and coal in abundance in the encroaching hills, it was already seen as potentially "the greatest manufacturing town in the western country." The county was settled mainly by Pennsylvanians, with some Virginians and a few Germans, and had always been Republican in politics; there were, however, many Federalists in Zanesville itself and especially across the Muskingum River in the New England–settled town of Springfield, soon to be renamed Putnam. Although the voting strength of the Republicans came from the rural areas, the local party was dominated by what Federalists called "the nest of public officers at Zanesville."[24]

The most important of this "set of . . . restless jacobins" was Isaac Van Horne, receiver of the public moneys in the U.S. land office. Connected with him were a number of young lawyers, including the recorder, Wyllys Silliman, Samuel Herrick (who became U.S. district attorney in 1810), and Silliman's brother-in-law, Lewis Cass, since 1807 the state's U.S. marshal. These men dominated the county Republican convention, ensuring that Federalists were excluded, and with some difficulty maintained the Republican supremacy. In November 1809, they began a party newspaper, the *Muskingum Messenger,* and in July 1810, they established the second Tammany wigwam in the state. In August or September, they were joined by Dr. John Hamm, a former pupil of Benjamin Rush in Philadelphia, who had attained political prominence in his one year's residence in Chillicothe, where he had introduced St. Tammany to the state. Hamm soon married Van Horne's daughter and established a political influence that for over twenty years would be constantly directed toward tightening party organization and pursuing Democratic policies. Under the editorship of David Chambers, the *Messenger* increasingly became the mouthpiece of the radical faction, and the group as a whole quickly became an important partisan influence on the general assembly when it first met in Zanesville in December 1810.[25]

Too often in the past, the Democrats believed, new representatives had been misled in the early days of a session by "pretended Republicans." Now the

Zanesville Tammany Society operated as a means of influencing legislators elected in 1810 in those counties where the Sweeping Resolution had not been an issue. The division in the party was fully displayed when a caucus, called to secure party unity in the election of a U.S. senator, "ended in a farce," because the Court faction wished to nominate Huntington, the retiring governor, whereas "the Anti-Judicial party" had determined that "politically [Huntington] shall die." The "late governor and his party exerted themselves with uncommon ardur [*sic*]," but their radical opponents took up Worthington and elected him, in spite of claims that the eastern counties should have the senatorship on this occasion.[26] Although a majority of the house probably favored a repeal of the Sweeping Resolution, "in the Senate it is safe enough," and the Court faction, led by Henry Brush and William Creighton Jr., found it "impossible to subvert the present order of things."[27]

In the course of the session, Tammany influence spread, as representatives who showed themselves good Democrats were admitted to it. Apparently "no less than SEVENTEEN MEMBERS OF BOTH HOUSES joined this nefarious association in one night." These members then introduced the "council fire" to their own counties, and at least six more "wigwams" were established in the early months of 1811. These societies influenced nominations, issued circulars, used runners, employed heelers at the polls, maintained a system of "espionage," and conducted an extensive correspondence—all designed to ensure Democratic success. In addition, the Tammany leaders at Zanesville, on behalf of the state caucus, wrote to supporters "of this state as now administered," proposing the establishment of a state newspaper to inculcate "a union of sentiment among Republicans throughout the State" and "GIVE A TONE TO OTHER REPUBLICAN PAPERS." The object clearly was to impose and maintain a view of party policy that only a militant tendency within the party believed in.[28]

As a consequence, Tammany itself now became the central issue. By March 1811, Tammany communications were referring to "the storm of calumny and persecution which hovers over our wigwams." The Cincinnati press began to carry bitter attacks on the order, which it blamed for the survival of the Sweeping Resolution in defiance of the popular will, and stories were reported of how Tammany men had offered public office in return for votes to preserve the new judiciary. In Columbia Township, the new society founded in 1809—the United Citizens of Columbia for Information—produced a damning report on Tammany influence that echoed across Hamilton County; there, and elsewhere, public meetings resolved not to support Tammany members for elective office. In Greene County, attempts to organize a wigwam in Xenia faced "strong and formadable . . . oposition [*sic*]," which threatened to "tar and feather all of us at our next meeting."[29] Indeed, St. Tammany replaced the judicial question as the leading political issue of 1811. As Creighton reported in June,

> The middle and western part of the State is in an uproar in opposition to the Tammany Society. The establishment of this institution has produced more warmth and division than anything that has occurred since the organization of the State Government. The fears of the people have been justly excited against this Infernal institution. . . . The Tammany scenes that were acted last winter have been laid open to the people and justly exposed. Many good men that have been drawn into the institution are abandoning it. . . . The only names of distinction now used are "Tammany & Anti Tammany."[30]

Tammany men responded to these "persecuting storms" by emphasizing their own political righteousness. James Heaton, a legislator from Butler County who had joined Tammany while at Zanesville, justified it as "a friendly political school, in which the nature of our government is explained" and men "of known attachment to the political rights of human nature" are encouraged. Its prime objective was "to prevent counterfeits" from securing election as Democratic Republicans, when in reality they were hostile to the genuinely democratic principles on which the republic was based. Such *"wolves in sheep's clothing,"* emphasized the *Muskingum Messenger,* "dread nothing more than a test, whereby the consistency of their principles might be estimated." St. Tammany was a safeguard of popular interests: as the *Scioto Gazette* warned, "The opposition to the Tammany Society originates from a concealed plan to pull down the leading Democratic Republicans, and with their seventy dollar law to rescind the [sweeping] resolution, and give judges the unlimited right to set aside law." Anyone who supported such measures, according to the Cincinnati radical Thomas Henderson, had joined the "federal Phalanx," whatever label they gave themselves.[31]

To all intents and purposes, the Tammanyites were trying to impose their own interpretation of party policy on their colleagues and followers. They were insisting that they alone understood the true nature of the Republican church; anyone who disagreed was a heretic, to be read out of the party. But, in so doing, they were making party attachments apply to areas of internal state policy that many Republicans thought had no relevance to the party contest; it appeared, quite reasonably, that the radicals were trying to gain factional advantage on a local issue by controlling a party that gained its existence from national issues. This degree of party dictation by an unrepresentative few was widely condemned as "aristocracy," and Independent Republicans proclaimed the virtue of allowing the people a free choice without "the few Dictating to the many."[32] Such antiparty arguments encouraged resistance against those who wished to make the Republican party stand for something more than the original purposes which many of its supporters had detected in it.

In reality, the radicals' attempt to use St. Tammany to help defend "the new order of things"[33] was a confession that their electoral position was weak. As writers in the Cincinnati press pointed out, radically minded Democratic leaders had been looking for some means of restoring their political control in Hamilton County. For this reason, it was claimed, "almost all the *remaining* members of the old corresponding society had joined the TAMMANY ORDER," when Council Fire no. 3 was established in Cincinnati in January 1811. These Tammanyites included the county's sole pro-Resolution representative, Samuel McHenry, such stalwarts as Elijah Glover and John Cleves Symmes, a promising young lawyer from New England named Ethan Allen Brown, and the land register, Daniel Symmes. These Democrats now called upon the township Republican societies to elect delegates in the old exclusive fashion, and delegates from five or six townships came together in convention and named what was known as the "Tammany Ticket." The recently formed, consensual Republican Association, by contrast, invited citizens (not necessarily Republicans) to meet in open town meetings to choose delegates to a rival convention, and in some townships the meeting's first business was to decide which convention to support. In Sycamore Township, the vote was 40–6 in favor of the association's "Township Delegate Meeting"—upon which the minority seceded and chose delegates for the societies' convention. The association's broader county meeting named the incumbent conservative representatives as part of the "Anti-Tammany ticket," which duly won four-fifths of the popular vote in an election that saw marked ticket voting in most townships.[34]

In other parts of western and central Ohio, too, the popular rebellions against Tammany control met with remarkable success. In Ross County, the conservatives swept the field, and Tiffin concluded, "It would be best to dissolve that Society—it won't suit the meridian of Chillicothe—by artful designing men it has divided the Democratic Republicans, & thrown them for a while (at least) in the background." Over the state as a whole, however, John Hamm thought that the 1811 elections had resulted in "a small but firm majority of Democrats in both houses, determined upon supporting the present state of things in this state," and his view seemed confirmed when Samuel Huntington, now a representative, was rejected as speaker.[35]

The meeting of the assembly soon disabused Hamm. "In early part of the Session . . . , the watchword was beware of Ta—y—, and the members from [Ross] County & Ci[nci]nnati took a lead in the *hue and cry.*" Huntington, in particular, was "unusually bitter against every thing that looks like Tammany." With support from the members from the New England–settled counties, the opposition leaders turned upon the Sweeping Resolution, used their superiority in debating skill to embarrass the Democrats in the house, and brought impeachments against the overly assertive "Resolution Judge," John Thompson. Threatening not to participate in any elections that came up under the terms of the Resolution, but agreeing to treat as valid all appointments already made under it, they pushed through the house "by a considerable majority" the repeal of the law establishing that all offices were commissioned for a full seven years. They then put considerable pressure on the large Democratic majority in the state senate, and enough Democrats caved in to approve this virtual repeal of the Sweeping Resolution.[36] In effect, tight partisan control had collapsed before public opinion, and many Republicans had shown they would cooperate with Federalists rather than accept Tammany leadership.

According to Isaac Van Horne, "the Feds" viewed the repeal "as a great triumph" and hoped that "this Majority was by sympathy of feeling &c. to be kept together, for all important measures." The decision to elect the state's hugely increased congressional delegation by districts rather than on a general ticket was "carried by the same influence," while, in the elections to judgeships and state offices at the end of the session, "none were to be elected but disciples of the *new school*," sympathetic to judicial prerogatives. As it turned out, however, "throughout the counties where Judges were elected, the result has been near an equal division as to parties."[37]

Similar considerations influenced the decision to establish the permanent seat of government across the Scioto River from Franklinton, at what was to be called Columbus. Duncan McArthur thought "the exertions of the Tammany society here [in Zanesville] to prevent the repeal of the commissioning law will be a means of removing the seat of government from this place," while the exertions in the assembly of Colonel James Dunlap, a leading Chillicothe Tammanyite, would prevent it from returning there on more than a temporary basis. Since those "who are insulted at the conduct of the Colo. and [of the] Tammany men chiefly reside to the west," their triumph guaranteed a permanent state capital on the Scioto, but not at Chillicothe. Even the outcome of regional conflicts was determined by the bitter factional disputes generated by the arrogance of the Tammanyites.[38]

Moreover, the crisis over St. Tammany had distinctive polarizing effects on different groups of politicians and voters. In eastern Ohio, heavily influenced by the Democrats of Pennsylvania, debtors and democrats learned to trust the leadership of those most rigidly attached to the principle of a Democratic Republican party defined by devotion to an unrestrained popular will. Elsewhere in Ohio, however, lessons had been taught about the dangers of following party wherever it led. On the Western Reserve and in central Ohio, especially in the

Scioto Valley, many Republicans had preached the virtues of independence and worked informally with old Federalists. Even in those parts of southwestern Ohio where the forms of party machinery remained intact, the delegate machinery had in places been opened to all citizens, and Federalists had been allowed to participate in choosing delegates. In general, the anti-Tammany crusade had emphasized the irrelevance of national party divisions to the great state issue of the moment—and had demonstrated that local party leaders could not lead the majority of the electorate in directions it did not wish to go.

POPULISM TRIUMPHS

Some historians have seen the dramatic events of the years between 1809 and 1812 as showing the persistence of an older style of politics in Ohio—of politics as the duty or business of gentlemen, of patterns of deference and communal solidarity, of personal loyalty as more important than impersonal party ties.[39] Yet the evidence presented here suggests a different picture: a picture of a political system in which men of birth, wealth, and education continued to rule only if they behaved in ways that satisfied their constituents; and an impression of constituents viewing politics not only in terms of ethnocultural prejudice, regional interest, or personal loyalty but also in terms of partisan allegiance. That allegiance, however, was restricted by a sense of the proper limits of party loyalty, and the destruction of St. Tammany was essentially a triumph for antiparty sentiment.

Certainly, Ohio politicians of the time would have been surprised to discover that the decisive considerations in their political careers were "friendship," spheres of personal influence, or neofeudal clientage systems—or that "personal loyalties remained more important than impersonal party ties."[40] In Chillicothe, Levin Belt, although a Federalist, was regarded by many Republicans as "our very good friend," partly because he had supported statehood. But that did not stop his dismissal as president judge of the Chillicothe circuit when the party feeling of Chillicothe Democrats such as Worthington sharpened in 1810. Duncan McArthur had been regarded as a friend of Worthington and Tiffin since 1802, but that did not stop him from rebelling over the Sweeping Resolution and leading the fight against Tammany in 1810–12. And what are we to make of well-known Federalists such as William Woodbridge of Marietta and Ebenezer Buckingham of Zanesville, who betrayed both personal and party loyalties in 1811–12 when they turned their coats? Like earlier apostates, they were rapidly rewarded by the Republicans once they had demonstrated their strict loyalty to the new party.[41]

In fact, party loyalty as well as personal connections were necessary for political advancement, since office and patronage were usually reserved for active partisans. Several legislators deserted former friends in 1810 to support the Sweeping Resolution; like the formerly conservative David Abbot, they chose to "follow the majority" and hoped that party gratitude would provide them with one of the offices now swept open. In 1811 Tiffin was reluctant to advance a friend for federal office, simply because "he has never done or suffered for the Republican cause."[42] National office was almost entirely reserved for active partisans, and President Madison would show some skill in maintaining a balance among factional groupings within the party, as when he gave significant promotions to Tiffin, Cass, Hamm, and Meigs between 1812 and 1814.[43]

Nor can it be claimed that politics were commanded by the great office-holders, although they undoubtedly exercised considerable influence locally. That influence derived from more than just the social influence and patronage that their positions gave them. The important consideration was that appointment by Jefferson marked them as sound Republicans of proven service to the cause, and therefore their advice and guidance could be trusted by party loyalists. Even before his elevation to the receivership of the Canton Land Office in 1808, John Sloane had won three consecutive elections to the Ohio house from Jefferson County, served as speaker in 1805–6, and had gained public notice as a defender of Democratic principles and persecutor of arrogant judges. What gave such a man local political influence was the fact that the party he could claim to speak for had the support of the overwhelming majority of local voters. As one Federalist said of Muskingum County in 1808, "The nest of public officers at Zanesville . . . [could] contrive to keep the balance of power in their own hands" because they were "aided by the rabble in the country."[44]

Certainly, Ohio's senior politicians recognized the need to cultivate lesser men on whose support they depended. In 1807, after arresting the Burr affair, Governor Tiffin stood high in public regard, but he still had to canvass the members of the assembly personally before the Senate election; significantly, Tiffin reminded the legislators to think of their constituents before deciding how to vote. Ohio's representatives in Washington thought their colleagues there were equally concerned about opinion back home: Tiffin found the House of Representatives in December 1808 "still manufacturing speeches . . . to fill the papers for their constituents," and by 1810 Morrow believed this "lust for speechifying" obstructed the course of business. At the end of his brief wartime term as U.S. senator, Joseph Kerr would complain that political leaders had to spend too much time conciliating "the sovereigns," who were never happy with what their representatives did on their behalf. His own votes were "not all popular now," and that meant the end of his political career: "I had some Idea of the hard pullings of the popular string on a small scale [in the general assembly], but was . . . unacquainted with it on the extended plan." As the Federalist Charles Hammond was to say in 1816, a representative in Washington often had to neglect public duty and do whatever was "requited in the article of popularity."[45]

Similarly, it is by no means clear that "county-based political juntas" could necessarily command the votes of their constituencies.[46] Rival candidates rapidly seized on any evidence that nominations, whether private or delegate, reflected "the unnatural influence of family influence and arrangement," while one of the favorite forms of mockery was to call a candidate or a rival "Squire."[47] In practice, large landowners, especially on the Western Reserve, could exercise great influence, but if overt, it could backfire on them. Benjamin Tappan was the leading proprietor in the new Western Reserve county of Portage, centered on his property at Ravenna. His "friends in the assembly" named his preferences as the county's associate judges in 1808, but the new appointees were cold toward him—apparently because they had been told that he regarded himself as "the God that made them." Even in Ravenna his authority was challenged by "rough fellows" among the early settlers. County elections for three years were dominated by a struggle over whether to have Ravenna as the county seat, and Tappan's attempts to influence local Republican voters in statewide elections were almost completely ineffective at this time. On the whole, politicians who relied on wealth and connection met with little success: Samuel Huntington achieved the political eminence he sought only after he had become associated with a broader cause, the defense of the judiciary.[48]

In any case, control of county politics by local notables was made more difficult at this time. Before 1809 the judges of election had been elected at the start of the day's polling by those present at the polling station, and this system, in theory at least, gave control of the election to those who owned or commanded the polling station. In 1809 this provision was amended to make the township trustees the judges of election; the clerk of the county's court of common pleas would be one election clerk, and the other was to be elected by the trustees. Only if any of the ex officio judges were themselves candidates would the older system of ad hoc election be used. This change meant that control of the county election in the fall would depend on township officials who were locally elected each April and could be held responsible by the electorate for their conduct of the polls. As before 1809, there would be few complaints in the next twenty years about judges of election excluding citizens from the polls.[49]

The creation of St. Tammany in 1810–11 has recently been described as a deliberate attempt to restrict true decision making to small groups of gentlemen who knew and trusted each other.[50] If so, that in itself implies they felt that the popular voice was gaining too great an influence in elections and could not be relied upon to follow its natural leaders. Yet the membership lists of the various Tammany wigwams show that membership was not confined to gentlemen, large landowners, merchants, and lawyers. Artisans and small farmers who were of the right political outlook were equally able to join and participate in the secret cabals of the wigwam. Indeed, a common complaint against the Tammany Society was that "its members are generally composed of the poorer class of the community."[51] These Democrats advocated rotation in office, and several of the local politicians who turned against them were incumbents who had been told to step down in favor of lesser men.

In no way did St. Tammany try to restrict the power of the electorate. Rather, it encouraged candidates to make promises to voters, and it defended the right of voters to instruct their representatives. As one official Tammany declaration asked, "Is the creature above the creator? Neither is a public officer above the people, who breathed into him the spirit of political life." These radical Democrats even advocated the right of state legislatures to recall U.S. senators who transgressed, such as John Smith in 1806–7 and, ironically, Thomas Worthington in 1812, when he disregarded public opinion by voting against the declaration of war. The whole logic of their philosophy was to extend the power of popular majorities, and their belief that the popular will could not be limited by constitutional restraints—since the constitution was nothing more than the popular will—represented a more radical view of democracy than was ever put forward by the Jacksonian Democratic party.[52]

The exaggerated democratic faith of the Tammanyites received a jolt when the people preferred those who favored the right of judges to declare statute law invalid. The Democrats had to accept the repeal of the Sweeping Resolution, since they could scarcely appeal to the courts! But, at the same time, conservative Republicans mouthed Democratic platitudes, asserting "the truth of the maxim that the people may err mistakenly, but seldom intentionally." Republicans of all kinds continued to advocate the principle of instruction: like William Henry Harrison, they thought a congressman properly the agent of his constituents and under a "moral obligation to execute their will." Even those who advocated the power of judges to enforce the fundamental rules of a written constitution accepted the omnipotence of the popular will within its legitimate fields of action.[53]

The disputes over the Sweeping Resolution and St. Tammany provide the most significant demonstration of popular power in Madisonian Ohio. Initially it prompted a number of legislators to break away from earlier personal and factional alignments to vote for the resolution. The malcontent irregular James

Pritchard, for example, followed the clearly expressed wishes of his county in supporting the antijudicial cause backed by his old enemies in Chillicothe. Thomas Morris at first approved the resolution but then turned against it, probably because of his disappointment at not being reelected to the supreme court; in doing so, he jeopardized his standing in his home county. But then the popular reaction set in, and even some supporters of the resolution began to fear for their reputations. In the state senate of 1811–12, Speaker Thomas Kirker, although counted a Democratic leader, "felt bound to vote contrary to his Judgement to satisfy public opinion," while those who had their eyes on one of Ohio's extra seats in Congress decided to vote "on the strong side in stid [*sic*] of the more right side."[54] Public opinion, in effect, decided the outcome of the factional struggle within the Republican party, and Democratic leaders had to accept that their Tammany maneuvers had provoked an irresistible outswelling of prejudice, hysteria, and paranoia. Indeed, the campaign against St. Tammany bore many resemblances to the Antimasonic crusade of twenty years later, which so many modern historians have emphasized as the novel democratizing experience of the late 1820s and early 1830s.[55]

As with Freemasonry later, the Tammany Society aroused popular passions in 1810–12 partly because it had alarming religious implications for those born again in an evangelical revival. Admittedly, most commentators mocked Tammany ritual, with its Sachems and loincloths and bearskins and "mid-night wigwams." Poking fun, one reported rumors that "it is a new religion, made to fetch about the Malenium [*sic*]; and that all mankind will become Indians." But others questioned the drinking of "spiritous liquors" at its meetings, and asked whether it is "consistent with the spirit of Christianity to unite with or countenance cabalistical associations?"[56]

Some evangelical Methodists had already begun to wonder whether partisan activism was compatible with true spirituality, and in 1809 the Hockhocking Circuit resolved that "the attending of barbecues and Drinking of toasts on the 4 of July is contrary to the Sperit [*sic*] of Christianity." As a result, several Methodist politicians in Ross County were expelled from the church, even though their offending toast to Liberty had been drunk in cold water.[57] Given this attitude, it is not surprising that those Chillicothe Methodists who joined the Tammany Society were also expelled from the church, including Edward Tiffin; despite his long service as a Methodist preacher, Tiffin was suspended from all ministerial functions—on charges of idolatry, of worshiping an Indian saint! Those expelled were soon reinstated by the Quarterly Conference, which acknowledged that "a large majority of [Methodists] are firm democratic republicans"; the church, it insisted, had "nothing to do with the political opinions of its members." However, the incident persuaded some Tammanyites, notably the Methodist minister who ran the *Scioto Gazette,* to abjure the new political society. But typical of the paranoia Tammany induced was the popular suspicion that their renunciation was not sincere, that the secret oath which members had taken retained its compelling power for sinister purposes.[58]

Similarly, the Tammany lodges conjured up the same political fears and resentments that Freemasonry was later to arouse. Men warned of the consequences of suffering themselves "to be governed by the machinations of *Secret Societies*—by men who shroud their actions in *mid-night* gloom, and their orgies in the darkness of the night." It was, above all, the secrecy surrounding Tammany's proceedings that made men suspicious of the society's objectives, for if the first principle of Republicanism was that "every measure ought to stand the test of public opinion," then the votaries of St. Tammany must be plotting "Treason, . . . Aristocracy, Monarchy, or Tyranny, when they please." As one correspondent warned, "Except we nip them in the bud, I have no doubt we shall in a few years, from these Tammany Societies, have a Nobility with hereditary titles and estates descending to their offsprings." Less extravagantly, it was reported that the Tammanyites in the assembly had worked out the disposition of all future state offices and even the future districting of the state's congressional representation, naming one of their own confederates for each vacancy. If their power spread into each county, they could control elections by their "secret selection and invisible support of candidates," and they needed only a few more recruits to form a clear majority in the assembly. Understandably, ninety-nine out of a hundred Republicans in the Miami Country were said to be as opposed to Tammany as they would be "to any other *secret political engine* for filling offices without the consent of the people."[59]

These were exactly the sort of arguments to be used twenty years later, and they reflected identical impulses behind both countersubversive movements: the anti-Enlightenment thrust of a populistic religious revival, and the anti-aristocratic fears of a liberal democracy under threat. Popular concern directed itself in 1810–11 against St. Tammany rather than Freemasonry because the latter was not perceived at that time as advancing an exclusive set of men. Admittedly, Masonry provided a means of contact and consultation and recruitment, but the leading Masons—notably those involved in founding the Grand Lodge of Ohio in 1808—came from all political groupings in the state. Significantly, when the Masonic lodge at Zanesville refused in 1811 to admit John Hamm because of his Tammany ties, the state's grand master rebuked the action on the grounds that Freemasonry "had nothing to do with politics." If anything, Masonry was a unifying force bridging partisan and sectarian differences, although incapable of mitigating them.[60]

Unlike Antimasonry later, the anti-Tammany crusade never generated an independent political party. The need did not arise because the condemnation of the society in 1810–11 was more widespread, more universal, than the essentially limited protest against Freemasonry in 1826–33, and the wigwams collapsed far more quickly than the lodges. But the fact that a popular social movement could impress itself on the polity and gain legislative satisfaction so promptly demonstrates that the processes of politics in Ohio were not much different under Madison from those of Jacksonian America. A similar demonstration soon came from the success of another impassioned popular demand of 1812—for war against Great Britain.

THE EXPERIENCE OF INVASION

Throughout the first decade of statehood, Ohio's domestic politics were quite overshadowed by the repeated international crises that threatened the republic as a whole. The wars in Europe dominated newspaper columns and even the private correspondence of politicians, especially at moments when it appeared that the United States could scarcely expect to avoid involvement in the general bloodletting. From 1806 onwards, Ohio politicians repeatedly stated that local opinion favored war, if only the country could decide whether it preferred to fight France or Britain, and by 1811 many agreed with John Hamm that only war could rescue the United States from "our present degraded condition."[61] But when war finally came in 1812, it proved more deadly than most Ohioans had imagined, for the settlers faced an invasion of redskins and redcoats that threatened to roll back the process of settlement and even to diminish the territorial boundaries of the state. This disturbing, if rousing, experience was to have prolonged political consequences.

Before 1812, Ohio's representatives displayed a remarkable unanimity on questions of foreign policy. After briefly hoping for improved relations following the repeal of the embargo, the state's Republican activists became increasingly eager to stop Britain from imposing its own rules on the conduct of neutral commerce, a practice they saw as a challenge to the United States' rights as an independent nation. Each year the toasts given at Republican Fourth of July celebrations expressed a determination to fight, if necessary, to protect "our national dignity." As a toast at Cincinnati in 1811 put it, "War is preferable to a sacrifice of rights." Economic considerations played little part in this sentiment, despite the prevailing depression; Ohio was not sufficiently involved in external commerce for the decline in commodity prices at New Orleans to seriously affect more than a section of her population.[62] Indeed, it was common to blame the timidity of the seaboard upon its closer involvement in the profits of trade with Britain. According to the Marietta Republican, Levi Barber, "the public mind" in Ohio was prepared for war simply because it was not "cankered with mercantile cupidity." In this spirit, a growing number of Ohioans favored the development of domestic manufacturing, and hoped that a greater degree of financial and economic self-sufficiency would help the country maintain its rights more effectively against its neocolonial mistress.[63]

Certainly, maritime issues fired the overt expressions of hostility toward Britain. Far from inspiring demands for war, the Indian threat operated to deter militant action, for many settlers feared the incursions of malicious savages. There may have been only 2,000 Indians residing in Ohio by 1812, but tiny settlements such as Worthington, Franklinton, and Urbana were strongly aware that Indian villages lay close at hand. Greenville, the center of the Shawnee Prophet's resistance movement from 1805 to 1808, lay only forty miles from Dayton. The Indian villages in Indiana were scarcely fifty miles from Cincinnati, and even Indian hostility on the far side of the Wabash appeared potentially menacing to the Ohio settlements. In 1807 and 1809, the Ohio militia was put on alert because of reported breaches with the Indians on the western frontier, and the state's representatives parleyed in Chillicothe with Tecumseh and the Shawnee Prophet for their neutrality in the event of a British war. The growing assertiveness of the Indians after 1808 was inevitably blamed on British agents, and undeniably British traders were active among the Indians even in Ohio, notably at Sandusky.[64]

Anxieties arose about the gathering of two or three thousand warriors at Prophetstown in the Indiana Territory in 1811, and Harrison's supposed victory at Tippecanoe did little to settle the unease. Senator Worthington feared that this "unfortunate occurence" would excite "the greatest alarm on the frontiers of Ohio." He and the state's other two representatives in Washington persuaded the president that the Northwest frontier was inadequately defended and needed further protection to ward off the "coming storm." Madison ordered companies of volunteer militia to be armed as frontier rangers, and he appointed three commissioners to try to settle the Indians' grievances "without bloodshed."[65] When early in 1812 some settlers in western Ohio were murdered in minor Indian attacks, some newspapers advocated strong action against "those treacherous and perfidious savages." But the more exposed settlements dreaded the consequences of full-scale war, and new towns like Sandusky faced extinction as settlers moved away. Even in Cincinnati, alarmed citizens expected an Indian attack.[66] Worthington's awareness of the state's vulnerable position persuaded him to vote against the declaration of war in June, and his partner in the Senate, Alexander Campbell, would have done so, too, had he not been kept at home by the serious illness of a child.[67]

Public opinion within Ohio as a whole was less cautious. The general assembly passed resolutions in December 1811 that basically ignored the Indians and focused on Britain's maritime measures; these, it asserted, damaged American rights to "life, liberty and property," and "such ignominy and insult" must be resisted. The people of Ohio, the assembly pronounced, were willing to suffer every hardship and privation and would "not shrink from the danger of war." In private, Republican legislators recognized the menace of "the Savages of the Wabash," but this was a risk they were willing to take. In general, public men seemed confident that the militia could defend them and help the regular army to conquer Canada, Britain's one hostage to fortune within striking distance. In April, Governor Meigs had no difficulty in recruiting 1,200 volunteers to march to Detroit to help General Hull in the event of war, and Lewis Cass thought he could easily have raised "ten times the number." Worthington's vote in June against total war was widely criticized, Worthington himself was burned in effigy, and only his subsequent prompt, firm, and active support of the efficient prosecution of the war preserved his political standing. Indeed, John Hamm thought that, had the demand for war been disappointed once again, Madison could not hope to carry Ohio in the forthcoming presidential election.[68] Ohio was awash with a "bellicose nationalism" that demanded a reassertion of the nation's will to preserve its self-respect and its sense of unity and destiny.[69]

The harsh realities of military power quickly revealed the naïveté of the warmongers. In August the U.S. army under General Hull surrendered at Detroit, the military posts at Mackinac and Chicago fell, Fort Wayne was besieged, and Indians began to flock to the British standard. In such circumstances, as Governor Meigs had foreseen, "the Frontiers of Ohio will be harassed by the murderous incursions of numerous Savages." The Western Reserve was flooded with rumors that the British and Indians were "coming down the Lake, both by land and water, pillaging, marauding and destroying everything on the southern shore." From Cleveland an observer reported that "the settlements to [the] west are all broken up . . . the poor defenceless inhabitants are arriving here every hour." General Harrison, arriving at Piqua to pick up the pieces, found "the whole country in dreadful alarm."[70] The consequence was a rush to arms, a "rising in mass" (as the Urbana newspaper put it, in yet another French Revolutionary reference),[71] as subordinate commanders called out their militia units. In practice, the enemy did not cross the Maumee in force, the strategically critical Fort Wayne was relieved, the volunteers disbanded, and Ohioans became caught up in hauling, selling, supplying, and outfitting, as Harrison made his long preparations for the advance against Detroit and the British post at Malden.

The following year saw a real invasion of Ohio. Hopes that Detroit would be

Ohio in the War of 1812

quickly retaken were dispelled by Winchester's disaster at the Raisin River in January 1813, and Harrison had to build the key defensive posts of Fort Meigs at the lower rapids of the Maumee River and Fort Stephenson on the lower Sandusky. In May the British marched to the Maumee in force, besieging Fort Meigs with a larger army than Harrison could concentrate. Perhaps 3,000 men now sprang to arms in Ohio, their march choking every road to the north, though they contributed little to the fort's relief. In July a second invasion threatened both forts and forced yet another call for "an immediate and voluntary recourse to arms." On this occasion 4,000 militia were called out by Governor Meigs, but once more the British withdrew before the Ohioans saw action.[72] The threats, panics, and bloodshed of 1812–13 had a harrowing effect on Ohioans, as country areas found themselves stripped of men by some sudden emergency. As one eyewitness recalled, "The horrors and fearful sufferings of the first year of the war can never be forgotten by the people of that generation."[73]

In the event, the building of a navy at Presque Isle near Erie, Pennsylvania, transformed Ohio's strategic situation. Perry's victory at Put-in-Bay in September 1813 gave the Americans control of Lake Erie and so made the British position at Detroit and Malden untenable. Harrison's invasion of Upper Canada and the defeat and slaughter of Tecumseh at the battle of the Thames in October finally brought the Indian threat to an end, and Harrison had the final honor and glory of bringing to a close an Indian war that had lasted for almost forty years.

Now the Ohio settlers turned their attention to the dangers that threatened the country in other regions, especially as the British navy prepared to mount seaborne invasions against the Atlantic and Gulf Coasts. At stake was not only national security but even some of Ohio's territory, if ever Britain made good its demand for an Indian buffer state in the Old Northwest. To Congressman John McLean the military disasters, financial breakdown, and political paralysis in Washington appeared to threaten "national destruction" and the collapse of democratic self-government. By the last weeks of 1814 the republic was facing its darkest hour, unable to defend even its capital, and the whole Mississippi Valley trembled at the future if ever Britain should secure control of New Orleans.[74]

All in all, the war was a disturbing experience for Ohioans, and became the overwhelming public concern. James B. Finley remembered how "this excitement, all-pervading and demoralizing as it was, operated disastrously to religion": as soon as "the war spirit . . . entered into many professors of religion, . . . they began to lose their religion"—and even took up drinking again. The newspapers were filled with military and diplomatic news and paid little attention to elections. As the Federalist newspaper at Franklinton remarked, the contest for office in 1812 was not "near as animated as it would have been, had not the events of the war given the electioneering gentry something else to do."[75] In the circumstances there was relatively little political controversy throughout much of Ohio, as public opinion agreed on the need for a vigorous prosecution of the war, and in many places after 1812 incumbents tended to win reelection by ever-increasing margins. The general assemblies of the war years were marked by "an unusual degree of harmony and good understanding," and Duncan McArthur could see "nothing like party spirit among the members." However divided the nation as a whole, however divided the Republicans in Congress, Ohio's spokesmen and representatives in Washington lined up behind the war effort, and if sometimes they dissented from the administration's proposals, they did so in the interests of securing a more effective prosecution of the war.[76]

The most striking political result of the international crisis, however, was the response of the Federalists in most parts of Ohio. Before 1812, they had been deeply critical of Madison's policy. They advocated military and naval preparations, which they claimed would have made the European belligerents show more regard for neutral rights. The Federalists were perfectly willing to contemplate war, as long as it was directed against France as much as Britain. They had strong reservations about a land attack on Canada, but were willing to arm American merchantmen as John Adams had against France. Such firmness they contrasted with Madison's pusillanimity and his disingenuousness in accepting Napoleon's spurious gestures of conciliation.[77]

But, however critical, most Ohio Federalists were willing to rally round their country's cause whenever it seemed threatened by external aggression. In 1807 Federalists were appalled by the Chesapeake incident, and in Cincinnati Jacob Burnet—even while fighting local Republicans (literally, "with a large bludgeon"!)—helped to compose the resolutions passed by a public meeting in condemnation of Britain. In January 1812 the Federalists in the assembly joined the Republicans in voting a loyal address to the president in that hour of trial, and the enthusiasm with which everyone in southwestern Ohio undertook war preparations in April 1812 convinced Lewis Cass that "the artificial distinctions of party are lost in the general name of Americans." In Chillicothe the first reports of the Henry correspondence—which apparently revealed that eastern Federalists had been plotting with Britain—shocked local Federalists, who said they would "change politicks" if it proved true, although they soon began to suspect an administration trick. By 1812 their newspaper, the *Supporter*, reflected a growing distaste for Britain, advocated strong measures, and finally applauded Congress for taking "a firm and decided stand—they have *declared war*, and however we may differ in political sentiments it now becomes the duty of every citizen to cling to his country and rise or fall with it."[78]

Most Ohio Federalists supported the war effort, especially when it seemed to threaten their own communities. Dayton lay uncomfortably close to the frontier and soon became a base for military operations; not surprisingly, the Federalist *Ohio Centinel*, edited in Dayton by Jacob Burnet's brother Isaac, insisted that every citizen must obey the call of country, "with no distinction of party." In Cincinnati, leading Federalists such as William C. Schenck volunteered to fight; indeed, the local militia was led by the Federalist John S. Gano. Unpopular at first, Gano became one of Harrison's most reliable assistants. Even the intensely Federalist students at Ohio University in Athens turned out as mounted volunteers during one invasion scare, although their squadron was ordered to disband after two days' journey.[79]

At Franklinton the hitherto intemperate Federalist James B. Gardiner, of Marietta fame, had opened a newspaper in June 1812. Although no supporter of the administration and certainly "not among the vehement and infuriated clamorists for war," Gardiner wished "every well-meaning and patriotic American to rally round the standard of his country—to throw aside, for the present, all private and political prejudices." Thereafter Franklinton became headquarters of the Northwestern Army, and Gardiner found his paper much in demand as a source of news from the front. Like most other Federalist spokesmen in Ohio, he became severely critical of what he saw as the disloyalty of some Federalists and "blue lights" in New England.[80] However convincingly recent historians may have emphasized the united opposition of the Federalist party during the war, notably in Congress, many Federalists in Ohio drew a clear distinction between their own patriotism and the obstructionism of their counterparts in the East.[81]

REPUBLICANISM RELENTS

Similar nationalistic attitudes also ensured that the war crisis would heal—or smooth over—some of the divisions within the state Republican party. As Wyllys Silliman said in January 1812, "Important as these Subjects [of state politics] are to the people of this State, they are lost when contrasted with the great and important objects which engross the attention of the national government." Leading Democrats, in particular, thought it less important to fight for the principle of the Sweeping Resolution and legislative supremacy than to maintain the state's loyal support for the Madison administration and its foreign policy. In Washington and fully aware of the impending national crisis, Worthington had endeavored in the months before the declaration of war to restore good relations with Governor Meigs, while both Worthington and Congressman Morrow rejected the suggestion that one of them should contest Meigs's reelection.[82]

The governor, for his part, had tried to stand above faction, rejecting conservative demands that he refuse to operate under the commissioning law of 1810, even though such moderate pragmatism was criticized as "milk and water politicks." On the other hand, he made now and then "a little bit of a federal appointment," which did not always please "*red hot* democrats." The more cynical regarded the governor's efforts during the spring of 1812 to raise, train, and supply extra troops for Detroit as his "Electioneering campaign." But there can be no reasonable doubt that Meigs's efforts to organize the defense of the state after Hull's surrender were tireless and marked him out as the most efficient and energetic of Ohio's early governors.[83] His reelection in 1812 was contested primarily by rivals in the western and middle parts, who found a Tammany and antijudiciary man, Thomas Scott, to run against him, but Meigs romped home with 60 percent of the vote, including some Federalist support.[84]

More important to most Republicans was the need to keep the national government in sound hands. Many Federalists in Ohio may have supported the war, but signs of recalcitrance elsewhere and the behavior of the opposition in Congress persuaded even such moderate Republicans as James Kilbourne that Federalists could not be trusted. Initially, Isaac Van Horne feared that popular opposition to the Sweeping Resolution would "eventually give the Federalists an ascendancy in the Election of Members of Congress" in 1812, as the price of their cooperation with the so-called Independent Republicans or Quids. However, the Democrats found it easy to outbid the Federalists in the selection of candidates, since they were happy to acquiesce in the election of moderates and conservatives who were considered sound, pro-war Republicans.[85] In the Cincinnati district, Ethan Stone ran for Congress as an advocate for a vigorous war effort, having demonstrated his reliability by active military service in the months before the election. But he was damned as a Federalist and met with overwhelming defeat at the hands of the sole Republican candidate, John McLean, from Warren County, who gained three-fourths of the vote in Stone's own Hamilton County. Even a hint of doubt about a candidate's enthusiasm for the war was enough to secure defeat, as happened to General Simon Perkins, nominally a Republican, in the special congressional election held on the Western Reserve in April 1813. All those elected to Congress in 1812–13 supported the war effort and were driven by Federalist recalcitrance in Congress to oppose party conciliation.[86]

The same was true in the presidential election of 1812. By October many prominent Ohioans were grumbling about the military and administrative incompetence of the powers that be, and a ticket was organized for De Witt Clinton by Republicans eager for a more vigorous prosecution of the war. This movement received energetic support, and some parts of the state were flooded with "electioneering pamphlets." However, Clinton was damned in Ohio by the open Federalist backing he received in other states, and doubts about the political overtones of his candidacy merely served to confirm the commitment of faithful Republicans to the incumbent. Malcontent editors deplored this "infatuation," which made it "treason to lisp a sentence against the divinity and infallibility of James Madison."[87] To some extent this loyalty may have been encouraged, as some claimed, by the high level of government expenditures in the state, as army contractors forced up the prices of local produce.[88]

But pro-administration sentiment still had to be coordinated, and two tickets appeared for Madison: a Quid one named in Chillicothe and a Tammany one from Zanesville. Some Democratic leaders feared deceit and called on the Quid nominees to state publicly whom they personally supported. However satisfactory the answers, the existence of two Madisonian tickets could still let in the Clintonian ticket, and so the Tammany men at Zanesville issued a circular confirming that their ticket had received the most Republican endorsements and had been "publicly sanctioned by delegate meetings." The circular warned against "the intrigues of federalism and quiddism" and called on Republicans to concentrate their votes on the recommended ticket.[89] The voters heeded the call in what was the most exciting presidential election between 1800 and 1824, and the Tammany ticket took over 60 percent of the votes cast, twice as many as the Clintonian ticket. Although Tammany candidates for other offices were rejected, the voters accepted Tammany guidance in the presidential election, since the loyalty of the radicals to the national administration could not be impugned.[90]

Despite the pressure of war, factional tensions had not died away entirely. The radicals continued to suspect the political probity of the Independent Republicans and feared their "quiddish" inclination to conciliate Federalism. In the legislative session of 1812–13, members disagreed over the wording of resolutions approving the course of the general government: passages critical of the New England Federalists were "warmly opposed by all the members of *dark & suspicious politicks.*" In the end, resolutions approving the government's war policy were passed with solid Republican backing, but even Federalists could support resolutions that condemned France as well as Britain and emphasized the need for patriotic unity. In the election of a U.S. senator to succeed Alexander Campbell, Hamm was "anxious to concentrate the Democratic strength on behalf of one candidate," for he expected that "the strength of parties will, probably, be tried." Federalists and Quids tried to organize a strong rival candidacy, but, to the relief of the Democrats, the well-tested Morrow won easily, 63–18.[91] Again, when the next Senate vacancy arose in December 1814, the Zanesville leaders tried to organize a Tammany candidature, and they were willing to sacrifice eastern Ohio's claim to the Senate seat if in return they could have a sound Tammany man, such as Ethan Allen Brown of Cincinnati. In the end, however, only candidates acceptable to more moderate Republicans were voted for. Significantly, after 1811 no legislative caucus met to unite the party, in either senatorial or gubernatorial elections, since few people believed with John Hamm that a caucus decision could carry any force.[92]

At the local level, intraparty conflict had not died, either. In Fairfield County, a "Tammany ticket" was named in 1812 and "carried altogether." In Ross County, persisting tensions between Worthington's regulars and "the Creighton faction" influenced a special congressional election in 1813. When he maneuvered to have Creighton, the anti-Tammany candidate, ordered to the front, Worthington was accused of depriving the voters of a free choice; as a result, "the public pulse" beat even higher than "when we buried St. Tammany," and Creighton duly carried the district.[93] Similarly, in Coshocton County, the local elections of 1814 were fought between Tammany and the opponents of "the Great Council Fire," with each faction offering a "genuine republican ticket" named by a delegate convention.[94] There was even something of a Tammany revival in 1814, notably in Cincinnati where the society was resuscitated and a newspaper dedicated to its principles, *The Spirit of the West*, began publication in July 1814.[95]

The Tammany revival in Hamilton County was undoubtedly prompted by the alarm of some Democrats at the sight of party fellows supporting firm Federalists. Immediately after the declaration of war, a public meeting in Cincinnati decided—"in that spirit of unanimity which the present interesting state of the nation requires"—that a single municipal, all-party Fourth of July celebration should be held. On this almost unprecedented occasion, "the different political parties" agreed, for the sake of patriotic unity, to forego the expression of "their peculiar political sentiments." According to Dr. Daniel Drake, it was now the deliberate policy of the Republicans in Cincinnati "to promote union," which resulted in a further nonpartisan celebration in 1813, with only the most trivial compromises of principle in the toasts drunk.[96]

As a consequence, local elections in Hamilton aroused little excitement and the anti-Tammany victors of 1811 were easily reelected in 1812, 1813, and 1814. By 1813 partisanship had declined sufficiently for a county delegate convention not to meet—for the first time in a decade—and the various tickets were all privately nominated. Then in 1814 a Republican ticket appeared that included the Federalist Jacob Burnet, who had been prominent in declarations of support for the army and the authorities and had even advanced eight hundred dollars of his own money to help recruit and furnish troops in 1812. The Tammany Society tried to rouse old party feeling against this Federalist candidacy, and a delegate convention met to draw up an alternative ticket. But opposition could be raised only against Burnet, the incumbents were reelected virtually unanimously, and even Burnet won election—by twelve votes.[97] In the assembly, the speaker pro tem was criticized for appointing Burnet to several committees, but Burnet won favor by his active support of the war and was even considered for the U.S. Senate. To John McLean in Washington, Burnet's "Americanism" stood in stark contrast to Federalist behavior in Congress. In 1815 Burnet was reelected by his overwhelmingly Republican Hamilton County constituency, essentially without formal opposition.[98]

Equally impressive were the signs elsewhere that firm Federalists were willing to vote for Republicans who had earlier been outspoken enemies. In Chillicothe, the Federalist newspaper backed Duncan McArthur's candidacy for Congress in 1812, even though "he has always been attached to the democratic party." Partly because of McArthur's record as an Indian fighter, the writer believed that "no man . . . more fully enjoys the confidence of both parties"—and McArthur duly received a virtually unanimous vote throughout the district, including even Washington County. The Republican victor of 1812 in the Cincinnati district, the politic John McLean, was reelected in 1814, reportedly winning the support of every voter who went to the polls.[99]

Most striking, however, was the Federalists' conversion to a full appreciation of Thomas Worthington's virtues. The disapproval publicly voiced by some Republicans in 1812 and 1813 of his vote against war simply assisted in destroying his reputation as a party man; Federalists now praised him as an independent statesman. In 1814 he was nominated for governor by a meeting in Chillicothe of "a number of republican citizens from various parts of the state" who had come together for the meeting of the federal court. In the election Worthington received broad support, winning over 72 percent of the popular vote and carrying most counties. Such unity had not been seen in a gubernatorial election since Tiffin's reelection in 1805. Some old Federalist strongholds voted for Worthington, or at least—as in Washington County—refused to vote against him. The main opposition came from the southwestern counties, but even in that quarter Worthington could win support—ironically, from the Tammany men, who wanted a true Democratic Republican for governor. However contrary their points of view, under the pressure of war men of different faiths could agree on the need for "an ABLE STATESMAN, wise in council, and valiant in the field"—and come up with the same name.[100]

This rallying behind established leaders within the state was quite compatible with a growing disenchantment among some Republicans with an incompetent national administration. For example, Benjamin Tappan was so disillusioned by his war service as an officer in the last months of 1812 that he resigned and refused to serve again, even at the head of a regiment. He blamed the army's problems on the inefficiency of the commissariat, and he pestered Washington with proposals for reform and claims for reimbursement of the money he had spent securing arms and provisions on his own account. Such complaints were common and explain the reluctance of loyal Republicans from Ohio to support uncritically the measures proposed by their national leaders.[101]

As the burden of war increased, issues of finance and taxation began to cause misgivings at home and in Congress. So, too, did the iniquities of the militia draft and the harsh and arbitrary punishments of martial law. Disenchantment with a war so clearly identified as Republican weakened party commitment, especially, it seems, among Methodists and Germans. Indeed, the failures of the war effort disillusioned even some renowned Republicans. By August 1814, Tammany protagonist Thomas Scott was predicting national disgrace and a Federalist administration. Worthington himself began to despair by fall 1814 and even suggested privately that only the election of a Federalist majority in Congress could save the republic![102]

Clearly, the War of 1812 had made nonsense of the old party alignments. Existing factional conflicts within the Republican party had been mollified, but the allegiance of Ohio Republicans to the national leadership and satisfaction with their measures had diminished. More strikingly, antagonism between Federalists and Republicans seemed pointless when both entered the army; as Samuel Williams said of Chillicothe, "Party politics were merged into patriotism." Even before the war, the Cincinnati *Liberty Hall* distinguished between "British Federalists and American Federalists," recognizing that "a great portion of the latter will before long assimilate to and unite with the Republican party, with whom, indeed, they are now in unison as to feeling and sentiment on all national questions."[103] Most Ohio Federalists probably fell into this category, and for them "party spirit" was becoming a thing of the past.

Yet the war did not have the same impact everywhere. Like the struggle over St. Tammany, it divided Ohio into two political spheres, each displaying a distinctive partisan response to the crisis. In southwestern, central, and northern Ohio—areas hostile to Tammany and close to the war—partisanship virtually collapsed. By contrast, in the southeastern parts of the state, as we shall see, the Federalists simply refused to assimilate or support the war effort and so provoked a reinvigoration of the old party conflict, even in the darkest days of crisis. This bifurcation in the state's experience of parties would have significant—and long-term—consequences for the development of party politics in Ohio.

ℱEDERALISM AND THE ORIGINS OF
𝑀ODERN 𝒫OLITICS

Judgments on the nature of "party" during James Madison's presidency depend largely on the Federalists. Did they offer any kind of effective opposition? Given their ideological viewpoint, could they behave as a political party? If the opposition party was ineffective, could a system of party conflict of any kind be said to exist? In most of Ohio, where Federalists were few and far between, politics were ceasing to operate on a party basis, although partisanship continued to affect political language, political discourse, and appointments. But in eastern— and especially southeastern—Ohio, Federalists survived in sufficient numbers to provide energetic local opposition during the war years, and their effectiveness forced politicians and voters on both sides to behave in ways predictive of the Second Party System. Antiquated attitudes toward party began to change in this heated political context, and some political publicists in Ohio, like their counterparts in Pennsylvania and New York, developed further the argument that parties were not an evil to be scorned, despised, and avoided.[1]

REFRACTORY MINORITY PEOPLE

By the time of his death in April 1840, Charles Hammond was widely recognized as the sharpest of political observers. His reputation was based largely on his editorship of the *Cincinnati Gazette,* 1824–40, during which he became one of the most cogent and forthright of Whig spokesmen. Thomas Ewing thought his editorials "well judged and direct, with the point and brevity of Swift and more than the correctness of Addison." Daniel Webster thought him "the greatest genius that ever wielded an editorial pen." Intensely partisan yet generous to a fault, Hammond could maintain warm friendships with even the most intemperate of his opponents, although he also incurred bitter personal hostility.[2] As a lawyer with an acute grasp of constitutional issues, Hammond won the praise of learned men as distinguished and as different as Thomas Jefferson and John Marshall. He was respected by John Quincy Adams, who as president offered him a seat on the Supreme Court. Hammond refused because he knew that his nomination would not be confirmed.[3] His career was still dogged by one disadvantage which prevented him from attaining the eminent positions that his talents merited: not only had he been a Federalist but he had defiantly opposed the War of 1812.

Born near Baltimore in 1778 to an Episcopalian and Loyalist farming family, and brought up in hard circumstances in the panhandle of western Virginia, Hammond became a Federalist long before moving to Ohio. According to an early biographer, "He had been trained in the political school of George Washington and the excitement which . . . accompanied the whiskey rebellion falling at the most susceptible period of the life of the young man . . . made an impression upon his opinions which no after events of his life ever changed and very little modified."[4] First moving to the Northwest Territory in 1801, he intervened in the contest over statehood with some well-directed articles defending St. Clair against Republican charges of tyranny. Fellow Federalists long remembered the effectiveness of his spirited writing in the run-up to the elections for the constitutional convention in 1802, when he unsuccessfully offered himself as a candidate in Belmont County.[5]

The sharpness of his contributions to the press of western Pennsylvania and Virginia brought frequent troubles on his head: he was "cowskinned," publicly pelted with rotten eggs, and threatened with a horsewhipping. He returned to Ohio politics in 1809 and made a reputation as a "toothache politician," criticizing Democrats and defending the judiciary, notably in his widely discussed "Letters to J. Sloane." In 1811, writing as "Calpurnius," he attracted widespread attention with a series of articles attacking leading Sweepers and Tammanyites; his shrewd sallies and near-slanderous personal abuse prompted verbal discharges from the likes of Lewis Cass and Edward Tiffin. To Hammond, the private lives and personalities of politicians were fair game for a journalist, since "every false and hollow-hearted demagogue," every "knave in private life," should be exposed to prevent his advancement in public life. His later application of this philosophy in 1828 to Andrew Jackson's marital irregularities was to bring national notoriety to the "grey-haired slanderer."[6]

Hammond's determination to stand up for sound policy and correct principle inspired him to devise means of effectively opposing the Madison administration. He was believed to be behind an ostensibly nonpartisan newspaper, the *Belmont Repository,* which appeared in St. Clairsville in December 1811, and certainly he used the columns of this "new vehicle of disaffection" to argue that the national interest required the preservation of peace with Britain.[7] This attitude made him oppose military preparations in 1812 that he regarded as unconstitutional and a declaration of war that he thought lunatic. By 1813 he had determined to "resist the Administration in a spirit of desperation, as a man bereft of all hope and reckless of what may befall him." Accordingly, he began another newspaper in St. Clairsville in May 1813 that became the leading mouthpiece for irreconcilable Federalism in Ohio. Through the columns of the *Ohio Federalist,* he blasted the war as senseless, the administration as futile, and the "Democrats" as self-seeking, unscrupulous, unprincipled demagogues. The war, he insisted, could not achieve its objectives and would destroy national resources; the burden fell on the "great body of the people" who could not afford the $120 fine for refusing to serve; only those who sought office or gained government contracts benefited from the conflict. Inevitably Hammond became known as "the only Tory editor" in Ohio, and stood accused of expecting the Star or the Garter from the Prince Regent! The advice of the Fathers, he was reminded, was "TO HANG ALL TORIES."[8]

Although Hammond stood out as the "paragon of infamy," many other Federalists underwent a sharpening of their party consciousness during the war. On the Western Reserve, for example, "a goodly number of Federalists" believed that they had been too "languid in their exertions" and now "must make their stand." The rising Yankee lawyer Elisha Whittlesey, who had seen active service at the front in 1812 as a brigade major until he was taken seriously ill, agreed that "the little scurrilous Democratic papers with which this State is cursed should no longer remain uncontradicted," and so he canvassed subscriptions and put his hand into his own pocket for the *Ohio Federalist.* Hammond could not print enough copies to meet demand.[9]

This heightening of Federalist passion is most obvious in private correspondence. Even the young Thomas Ewing and his fellow Federalist students at Ohio University in Athens were "inflamed" by "the infatuated conduct of the present administration," although they were also willing to serve their turn in the militia. Ewing and his friends hunted for material to "give the Dems . . . a side swipe," loving to quote Fingal: "From dunghills deep of sable hue / Our dirt-bred patriots spring to view." These passions continued even after the war, sustained partly by news of Napoleon's return from Elba, and one friend from Athens hoped that Ewing, now Philemon Beecher's law student, would "make the Democratics of Lancaster tremble under the powerful exhortations of your tongue."[10]

This sharpening sense of partisanship could occasion some strictly two-party elections in Ohio, especially in the disastrous last year of the war when many Federalists thought they saw signs of "Returning Sanity" in the elections in other states. Some of the Ohio congressional battles of 1814 were undoubtedly fought along party lines. For example, in the district stretching from the Scioto Valley to Marietta, the 1814 election was essentially a conflict between two Chillicothe candidates, the firm if conservative Republican William Creighton Jr. and the old Federalist Levin Belt.[11] And although at least five candidates ran in the Dayton and Lancaster district, the election was widely perceived as essentially between the incumbent Republican, James Kilbourne of Worthington, and the Federalist (if pro-war) Philemon Beecher; in Miami and Montgomery Counties these two headed party tickets that were voted for with considerable regularity. As in 1812, these congressional elections attracted significantly more voters than any other election, suggesting the enhanced saliency of national contests during wartime.[12]

Yet such conflicts could be sustained by the Federalists only in unusual local circumstances. For the most part, the Federalists were in so small a minority that they had no alternative but to look for allies among the ranks of the local Republican majority—and that meant playing down partisanship, preaching antipartyism, and supporting the war. Any other course spelled disaster, since it would serve merely to reunite the Republicans and deprive Federalists of whatever slight influence they might otherwise enjoy. This simple political truth was well illustrated by the experience of Muskingum County during the war years.

In this influential county, the leaders of Tammany had survived the disasters of the 1811–12 general assembly. The state capital may have moved back to the Scioto, but Isaac Van Horne, John Hamm, and friends had beaten off the attempts of their opponents in the assembly to repay their legislative meddling by undermining Democratic control of the county. Federalism remained a force locally, however, especially among those with money to invest: in 1812 local Federalists defeated Van Horne's friends in the stockholders' election of directors of the new Bank of Muskingum.[13] The declaration of war proved popular, though, and local Democratic leaders cashed in by forming the Silk Stocking Company of volunteers, named for the famous troop of that name in the Revolutionary War, but when called to the front after Hull's surrender, they refused on the grounds that their services were needed at home to win the election for the administration![14] In the fall, two sound Tammany men were elected state representatives, and Van Horne could, with justice, congratulate himself on gaining "an increasing majority annually, against a host of Fedl. Tavern keepers, store keepers &c. &c. whose intrigues and exertions . . . are not exceeded in any other County in the state."[15]

The popularity of the war in Muskingum placed the Federalist minority in a delicate situation. When they established a party press, the *Zanesville Express,* in December 1812, specifically to scrutinize the conduct of this just but unnecessary war, the editors carefully adopted a moderate tone and pursued a nominally nonpartisan course; their stated aim was to attract the support of those "professedly opposed to us in politics" who were willing to rise "above those narrow prejudices of party, which enchain many political zealots." The reward for restraint came when Republican dissidents opposed the regular nomination in 1813, for the *Express* could speak for an amalgamationist movement that threatened the regulars' control of the county. The *Express* insisted that the delegate convention was called only to rubber-stamp a ticket already named privately by "the *Muskingum junto*, alias the *trio aristocrats* of this county." Party machinery, it claimed, was merely a device for preserving "the unnatural influence of family influence and arrangement." Voters should feel free to disobey the convention's nomination, for "all Tammany principles and delegated tickets," all attempts to discipline voters, were "a direct attack" on the privilege of voting. In the face of all the canvassing efforts of the Democrats, the amalgamationist "Opposition Ticket" was elected over the "Delegate Ticket" by a good margin.[16]

But party feelings bristled beneath the surface, as when men came to blows in Zanesville at the celebration over Perry's victory on Lake Erie. The *Muskingum Messenger* launched a partisan crusade designed to expose the Federalism of the *Express*, so hypocritically cloaked by pseudo-Republican language. At the same time, the *Express* came under pressure from hard-line Federalists, who wished it to take a more openly partisan line and reveal more frankly the iniquities and incompetence of the party in power. The disasters of the war by the fall of 1814 had persuaded them to run their own "Federal Republican" ticket, which they named "in caucus." The only consequence, however, was to enable the regular Republicans to keep a hold on dissenting movements within their ranks and line up the voters behind the delegate-convention ticket. In an election that saw a high degree of ticket voting, the Democratic ticket carried by a 4:1 margin. Once more the Federalists had learned that there was no future in competing in their own right.[17]

Muskingum's experience was not unusual: in Guernsey County, an attempt in 1814 to invigorate the local Federalist organization merely served to reunite a divided Republican party.[18] In general, the centers of Federalism in central and eastern Ohio, such as Granville in Licking County or the town of Coshocton,[19] were swamped by the firm, if far from united, Republicanism of the countryside, while on the Western Reserve the Federalists were too few to put up effective resistance in elections. There were, however, some exceptional local situations in eastern Ohio that made a Federalist bid for power seem almost a duty, and what made Charles Hammond so prominent was the fact that he had a local constituency large enough to support his newspaper and elect him to the assembly.

THE CULMINATION OF PARTY

Irreconcilable Federalism flourished in two sorts of constituencies. First, and most prominently, what distinguished Hammond's Belmont County and neighboring Jefferson and Harrison Counties were their sizable settlements of Quakers. These communities had been growing rapidly since 1803, made up most notably of Friends from North Carolina who wished to escape the neighborhood of slavery. Traditionally Federalist when not apathetic, the Quakers had been willing to support Republican attempts to preserve peace.[20] Once war broke out and the general assembly refused to allow Quakers exemption from military duty, they opposed the war and became Federalists "as a matter of course." As a child, William Dean Howells's father lived in the Quaker settlement at Mount Pleasant in Jefferson County; naturally he "fell in with this [antiwar] spirit, and . . . was of course called a Tory and British by older ones who thus amused themselves at my childish earnestness." Local Quakers refused to perform military service and were liable to heavy fines as a consequence. Even at the news of victory at New Orleans, "the Quakers kept dark and dumb, and were abused for it, of course."[21]

In 1813 Quaker votes in Belmont and Jefferson Counties elected Hammond and other Federalists to the assembly, where they protested against the war and opposed its vigorous prosecution. Although narrowly defeated in 1814, Federalists could find consolation in an underlying growth in voting support that Hammond predicted would become overwhelming, given another twelve months of disastrous and burdensome war. This was not to be, but once more in 1815 the embittered Belmont Federalists offered a full county ticket, headed by Hammond; once more it swept the Quaker townships, but was defeated on a strict party vote by thirty votes overall. The Federalists of Jefferson and Belmont were still considered unusually heated and partisan even as late as 1816.[22]

The strength of feeling among the Quakers encouraged Federalist ambitions to win a congressional seat in eastern Ohio. The newly created fourth district included these Quaker areas and gave hope to Federalist minorities in Steubenville, Coshocton, Springfield-Putnam, and Zanesville. Accordingly, they nominated the wealthy and distinguished Bezaleel Wells of Steubenville, long a popular Federalist candidate, frequently proposed for governor, to face the official Republican nominee, James Caldwell of Zanesville. Yet this district was divided by a sectional conflict over the routing of the planned National Road: the northern area wished the road to strike the Ohio River opposite Steubenville, as originally intended; the southern portion, from St. Clairsville to Zanesville, preferred Wheeling. At first, Republican candidates from Steubenville offered to run in opposition to Zanesville's Caldwell, but desisted in the face of the Federalist challenge. Wells received much support from Federalists, even where interested in the southern route; the Republicans, even in the Steubenville region, supported the official candidate and, standing united, carried the day in both 1812 and 1814. This willingness to ignore local interest and accept the official party nomination offered strong proof of the force of the national party division in eastern Ohio at this time. Partly as a result of it, the National Road was built to Wheeling, and Steubenville Republicans soon complained that they had made "a great sacrifice at the altar of party."[23]

The Federalist challenge stimulated turnouts in these counties to unprecedented levels—to 65 and even 70 percent in Belmont County—between 1811 and 1815[24] and compelled local Republicans to reinvigorate their party machine. Early in 1815, Benjamin Tappan brought in a distinguished young editor to the Steubenville *Western Herald,* James Wilson, who had edited the Philadelphia *Aurora* while its proprietor, William Duane, served in the war. Together, Tappan and Wilson intended to destroy Federalism in eastern Ohio by frontal assault.[25] Throughout this area south of the Reserve, delegate conventions were regularly summoned, and their nominations well supported, wherever and whenever the Federalist threat seemed serious. Indeed, in the fourth congressional district a *district* nominating convention was called in 1812 to settle the claims of Steubenville and Zanesville to have the nomination—even though historians have usually said that district nominating conventions for congressional elections were unknown in Ohio before 1828. In 1814 no convention was called, as the incumbent Caldwell was willing to run again, but in 1816 a further district convention was summoned to decide on his successor. To ensure justice and secure the popular will, seats and votes in the convention were allotted according to each county's population. At the same time some Democrats in eastern Ohio were beginning to advocate a *national* nominating convention to choose the party's candidate in the presidential election. Clearly a close partisan contest was provoking the virtual adoption of the most advanced organizational techniques of the Jacksonian period in some parts of Ohio.[26]

The development of a party conflict akin to that of the Second Party System was most marked in the other sort of constituency where Federalism persisted—the older New England settlements of the Ohio Company, notably Washington County itself. Although Ohio's first county remained predominantly Republican, the local Republican party was demoralized. Federalists had carried the county in the 1808 presidential election, and the economic distress they had exploited then persisted. As elsewhere in Ohio, the Republicans lost their coherence in 1809 and had to jostle their "tools . . . into office, in the hurry of an election." A Republican convention met in 1810, but its intentions were perverted when the friends of one of its nominees, Samuel P. Hildreth, did a deal with the leading Federalist, William Rufus Putnam, and both were elected to the general assembly.[27]

In 1811, the lines were more clearly drawn between the "Democratic Ticket" and the "Federal and American Republican Ticket," and the returns reveal a high level of ticket voting. Again Putnam narrowly carried the county, only to be defeated in Athens County, which shared the senatorship for which he was running.[28] In December 1811, the Republican *Ohio Gazette* collapsed after four years of financial difficulties, giving a monopoly of printed communication to the Federalist Caleb Emerson's impressive *Western Spectator*, which had replaced the earlier idiosyncratic *Commentator* in October 1810. No wonder that by June 1812 leading Republicans were putting their heads together to find ways of promoting local party unity, reducing jealousies, drawing their full support to the polls, and so reestablishing their full ascendancy.[29]

Their embarrassment arose, in large part, from the eagerness with which the Federalists were adopting Republican techniques. In 1810 one Federalist called upon his party to make formal nominations, not as "a mere electioneering manoeuvre, calculated to mislead and confound, but as a fair and honest mode of proceeding, that the people on the day of election may not be taken by surprise." Thereafter, for five years, the Federalists always had a clearly identified ticket in the field, the product, though, of a private or public meeting rather than of a convention, and they advocated their nomination with great energy. In the last days before the 1811 election, according to the Marietta *Ohio Gazette,* Federalists were "to be seen before day light . . . —Printing offices besieged in and out of doors—Feds buying democratic News Papers—'a dollar for your paper, sir'—'No, sir'—all flying-tickets, hand-bills, Sunday newspapers, runners and horses, Merchants, Taylors, Priests, Deacons, Blacksmiths and Coblers [*sic*]—all agoing with the federal sign manual."[30]

By this time passions ran deep. Emerson's *Spectator,* from the beginning, had blasted the Republicans as "Napoleonites" who wished to incorporate the republic within Bonaparte's Continental System and establish a party despotism in order to prevent criticism of a ruinous policy. When war was declared, Emerson reprinted as a pamphlet the antiwar address of the Federalists in Congress to their constituents. Predicting disaster, Marietta Federalists privately blamed "our national misfortunes" on "that cursed Gallicmania, which perverted the mind of Mr. Jefferson & . . . his humble successor," as well as on "the imbecillity [*sic*] of our Government" and its incompetent measures. In this spirit, the elections of 1812 became a clear contest between the "Peace Ticket" and the "War Ticket" in Washington County.[31] When the state authorities decided not to call for volunteers but to resort to a draft on the militia in order to fulfill their military obligations, the *Spectator* insisted that their motive was to ensure that as many Federalists as Republicans went off to the frontier to fight; otherwise, it claimed, the departure of Republican volunteers would have jeopardized the party's success in the county elections. As for the conscripted Federalists, they were rumored to be badly treated by their officers and, as suspected "Tories," were never risked in battle—at least according to local tradition.[32]

With everything they valued at stake, the Republicans pressed their organizational efforts even further. In June 1812 their leaders began to establish a system of popularly elected standing committees of correspondence in each township. Their task was to contradict local slanders, persuade the young, serve as township delegates in the county convention, and ensure a high turnout on the day of election. Only by some such plan of union and action could the Republican interest overwhelm the "malice, slanders, & zeal of our political adversaries."[33] The lack of a party press was overcome in April 1813 when a new editor, David Everett, was brought in from Boston to establish the firmly Republican *American Friend* in support of the "just and necessary" war; the position of this press strengthened when Emerson's *Spectator* collapsed in July.[34]

In elections local Republicans accepted the spirit of the *Friend*'s masthead: "United We Stand, Divided We Fall." The nominations of delegate conventions were accepted as authoritative and binding. In cases where representative offices were shared with Athens County, careful arrangements were made to balance the ticket between the two counties. No independent Republican intervened to prevent a straight race against the Federalist nominees in a series of strict party elections that continued through 1815. Turnout increased markedly, with over 72 percent voting in 1812 and over 61 percent in 1814, in spite of the absence of those voters serving in the war. In these regular elections the Republicans were uniformly successful, although in a special election for state senator in December 1814, at the darkest hour of the republic's fortunes, the Federalist candidate won by eight percentage points in a light poll.[35]

The closeness of the contests was a measure of Federalist combativeness. The "friends of the Washingtonian system" took seriously Caleb Emerson's advice to emulate "the decided and invariable System of the Democrats."[36] Most notably, the Federalists introduced the Washington Benevolent Society, a Federalist counterpart to St. Tammany. Devoted ostensibly to promoting humanitarian welfare and social discourse, this organization was openly described by its members as an attempt "to change or overturn the present Administration" by encouraging Federalist cooperation if not by actually electioneering. The Society "for the County of Washington and State of Ohio" was founded in August 1813 in Marietta and immediately began to encourage the foundation of other branches. By May 1814 there were six branch societies in Washington

County, one of them boasting 387 members in 1816, and a further branch in the New England settlement of Springfield-Putnam in Muskingum County. All were strongly Federalist in membership and sentiment, and some must have included a high proportion of local Federalist voters; their effectiveness as a motivating and mobilizing agency should not be underestimated. With justifiable sarcasm, the Zanesville Democratic newspaper commented, "As these *benevolent societies* are unquestionably instituted with the *very benevolent intention* of combining to overthrow our present government and administration, the anti-Tammanyites in and about Zanesville will have an opportunity of showing their consistency by joining this secret society."[37]

In the Washington County elections of 1811–15, candidates were clearly labeled as party men, and the voters tended to vote strict party tickets. In 1814 the Federalists refused to oppose Worthington for governor, but otherwise ticket voting was almost universal. Similarly, most voters must have persisted in voting for the same party throughout. The evidence of individual voter behavior from Adams Township reveals a complex situation, with relatively few voters turning out in all three of the elections for which township records of this period survive; however, two-thirds of those who voted in 1811 and 1814 voted the same way, as did 55.88 percent of those who voted in both 1814 and 1815, when there was a marked swing to the Republicans. The aggregate data from all the townships from 1812 through 1815—displayed in table 7.1—is rather more impressive, showing high levels of interval-level correlation between the elections. Indeed, 90 percent of the distribution of party strength among the townships in 1814 and 1815 can be explained by the distribution in the preceding county election, suggesting an extraordinarily high degree of consistency and persistence in voter loyalties in the mass, at least for a short period.[38] Although the changes in township boundaries make it impossible to correlate statistically the distribution of party strength with that of ten years earlier, it is clear that the two parties found their strength in much the same localities as they had in 1804 and 1808, at earlier moments of undoubted two-party confrontation.

The rival Fourth of July celebrations in 1815 showed how contemporaries perceived this heightened two-party battle. If hostilities did not become so blatant as in Zanesville, in Marietta there was a deep sense of social conflict. One local Federalist reported how, on the great day, the members of the Washington Benevolent Society marched to the large meeting house where they heard an oration by William Rufus Putnam and sang several hymns and psalms. "The society then formed, the banners were all placed and we marched to a bower built by Nature where we partook of an 'extreme' dinner—the cloth being removed 30 or 40 toasts were drank with the best of wine . . . decency and decorum prevailed. 130 members present." Then "the young Gentlemen &

Table 7.1

**Proportion of Township Vote Won by Republican Party,
Washington County, 1812–1815**

	1812	1813	1814	1815
Grandview	55.84	96.97	100.00	100.00
Wesley	77.77	75.00	78.95	75.00
Roxbury	60.90	80.56	73.68	83.33
Deerfield	68.75	75.87	No return	68.75
Newport	66.66	75.00	80.85	75.47
Marietta	64.00	74.51	68.67	70.76
Warren	50.00	75.76	75.86	72.22
Waterford	58.04	44.74	54.63	62.35
Fearing	52.17	56.90	50.00	52.38
Adams	48.91	50.00	50.00	60.71
Union	49.38	50.00	38.98	53.57
Salem	51.16	40.00	56.25	40.74
Wooster	40.32	40.00	40.91	43.64
Belpre	9.87	4.69	5.48	8.75
Washington County	52.05	57.88	58.51	57.70

Sources: Abstract of Votes, 1812, Campus Martius Collection, Ohio Historical Society; Marietta *American Friend*, Oct. 30, 1813, Oct. 22, 1814; Abstract of Votes, 1814, 1815, Washington County Courthouse, Marietta.

Note: Townships ranked according to overall Republican preference.

Ladies of nobility of Town & Country" proceeded to Campus Martius where "we partook of an excellent dish of Tea prepared by the Ladies own hands and served by two Negroes employed for that purpose." During these festivities the young Federalists saw something rather different: "The ruffscruffs of the earth collected together and stalking through the streets one after another in couples and their piper jogging along before. . . . This was a composition of Ignorance, rascality, indolence and poverty, 3 thirds of them were in their shirt sleeves, 2 thirds barefooted, one third bareass-d. Perhaps you will ask who these were—I will answer the Democrats of the County of Washington." For one young Federalist at least, the county's political conflict remained cast along precisely the same Hogarthian social and partisan lines as it had at the time of statehood.[39]

In southeastern Ohio, the effect of international crisis and the war was to intensify, not dilute, party spirit among committed Federalists. The womenfolk sometimes ostracized the wives of Republican politicians, as in Steubenville in 1809; their men frequently excluded even Quid and Independent Republicans from their Fourth of July celebrations, as in Zanesville in 1811.[40] The Federalists were regularly tempted to take a distinctive party line, either in the press or in elections, even though more political mileage could be found in tacit cooperation with Independent Republicans.

Furthermore, even after the triple disasters of the Hartford Convention, the battle of New Orleans, and the Treaty of Ghent undermined their criticism of the Republican war effort, they tried to maintain—and extend—the party battle. In March 1815, established presses such as the *Zanesville Express* "still wielded . . . their weapons of war . . . with an acrimonious spirit." The Federalist John Saxton founded the *Ohio Repository* in Canton, and young Federalists took over the *Western Spy* in Cincinnati and reprinted some of Hammond's articles with enthusiasm. An abortive attempt was even made to transform Gardiner's Franklinton press into a Federalist state newspaper, but under new editorship, with a new title—the *Columbian Gazette*—and across the river in the new state capital.[41] In the bitterly divided counties on the eastern margin of the state, this partisan commitment carried over into the fall elections of 1815, which were once more fought along strict party lines. The initial response of these Federalists to peace abroad was to maintain the war against Republican irresponsibility at home.

BECOMING A PEOPLE'S PARTY

The party battles of 1811–15 saw significant changes taking place in the character of the Federalist party. Traditionally *Federalism* has been viewed as a synonym for *elitism* and the Federalists as being stuck in a mold of eighteenth-century organicism. They undoubtedly disapproved of the Democrats' extravagant claims on behalf of both party and democracy, but their ideological stance did not prevent them from adjusting to the new political climate. There is ample evidence that many Federalists—and not just the "young" ones celebrated by David Hackett Fischer—were capable of recognizing the needs of majority building in a democratic polity. Although their minority position made it necessary to appeal for allies among the majority party—so stressing the undesirability of existing party divisions—the Federalists also found themselves becoming the natural means of expression for local protest movements. In 1802 those opposed to statehood for whatever reason, in 1808 those injured by the embargo, in 1813–14 those suffering from the war—all turned to the opposition party almost as a matter of course. Inevitably, therefore, active Federalists by 1815 were evolving into a political party somewhat different from the demoralized and ineffective fragments of a decade earlier.[42]

In these disputes and contests Democratic critics constantly accused the Federalists of favoring aristocracy or even monarchy over democracy. In part, this was semantic obfuscation, since Federalist descriptions of Democracy as a "hellish mist" or worse always referred either to their opponents ("the Democracy") or to a doctrine of unrestrained popular government. Federalists themselves were committed to the principle of balanced government in which popular rule had a legitimate place, but one limited by the structure and law of the Constitution. What they feared, above all, was an all-powerful government dominated by unprincipled demagogues who had seduced a populace deluded by party names: such a government could swiftly slip into aristocracy or tyranny, as Napoleon had demonstrated in France. "Democracy," in this meaning, could prove to be "but one step from Monarchy," and then the people might find—like the French before them—that their liberty consisted of high taxation and conscription into the tyrant's armies.[43] But in preferring the popular will to be restrained by guarantees of property and liberty, the Federalists were scarcely erecting a distinctive party ideology, as the many Republicans who voted with them on the judicial and sweeping issues demonstrated.

Otherwise by 1812 the Ohio Federalists had few reservations about the right of the people to rule. They did not, even privately, wish to introduce a more limited franchise; as Ephraim Cutler confirmed in 1819, they may in 1802 have doubted the wisdom of a universal male suffrage, but their doubts had soon been "intirely [sic] done away." Hammond may have favored a freeholder-cum-householder qualification for town elections, but only because municipal government primarily involved taxation on local property, and he never questioned popular rights in more important elections. What Federalists refused to accept was that the people could never make a mistake: as Whittlesey said in 1809, vox populi may be vox Dei, but sometimes "God . . . got on the wrong side."[44]

For this reason Federalists opposed pledges—which, "if lived up to, make a mere automaton of the Representative"—and instructions by the people, which could make representatives "merely slaves to their opinion." In 1816 Hammond was to object vigorously to the doctrines advanced in 1816 by William Henry Harrison and "the Tammany squad at Cincinnati," who regarded a congressman as the agent of his constituents and under a "moral obligation to execute their will." For Federalists, the representative was of necessity in the best position to judge what to support and how to vote, and he should have the courage of his convictions; it was, however, essential for him to inform the electorate of his views on public matters, to help them choose their best representative. The Federalists had nothing but scorn for a congressman, like John McLean in 1816, who, when the people disapproved of a particular vote, offered to change it next time; what he ought to do was resign and allow the people to choose a man of different principles. Behind all Federalist views lay a belief in permanent truths, which a constitution must uphold and a politician must adhere to according to his best lights. Those truths did not change according to popular whim, although one might hope that proper education would teach the people to recognize them more readily.[45]

Federalists therefore took great pains to explain their ideas to the people. The newspapers they established between 1810 and 1813 devoted far more space to editorializing and discussing great issues than did the Republican papers; Hammond even produced learned disquisitions on political philosophy in his critiques of "Democracy" in 1815 and 1816. In this way the Federalists claimed to show greater respect for the people than many Democrats who flattered voters merely to use them for their own purposes. Especially despicable were those Democrats who had earlier deserted Federalism, for such apostates—as Ephraim Cutler said of Lewis Cass—appeared to follow the simple maxim, "The majority are always wrong, I go with them. They are immoral and I can shape them for my own advantage." By contrast, faithful Federalists believed that the people were capable of doing right.[46]

Nothing in this outlook prevented the Federalists from exploiting whatever electoral opportunities came their way. In Muskingum County, in 1814, leading local Democrats had the vote of a prominent Irishman rejected because he was unnaturalized; in the township elections of 1815, Federalist spokesmen joined with their amalgamationist allies to exploit the resentment felt by the Zanesville Irish. Similarly, in Jefferson County in the same year, Federalist politicians openly wooed Irish votes, and James Wilson had to conjure up memories of Federalist nativism to hold them in line.[47]

The Federalists had a far more powerful electoral weapon in their standard argument that the Republican party had degenerated into a new "aristocracy." Party managers, they claimed, used their influence to ensure that their friends gained "good snug fat offices," and behaved as though they had a prescriptive right—as "legitimate" as the claims of European monarchs—to control the process of nomination; thus "all that were not within the pale of their peculiar and favorite influence" stood no chance of securing office. The fact that nominations were made by popularly elected conventions made no difference, for the conventions merely ratified a ticket already secretly chosen by the party managers. From this point of view, conventions were no different from caucuses, since in most cases Republican predominance made nomination tantamount to election.[48]

Such attacks on party "aristocracy" gave a natural sympathy with all those distant from power, all who felt their interests overlooked. Thus, in election appeals, the Federalists naturally identified themselves with "the clod-hoppers of the country, who consider more making their bread than of managing their fellow citizens." As in Ross County in 1809, Federalists could mock their opponents as "too lazy to labour in the cornfield or at shoe-making." As in Mont-gomery County, they could publicly sympathize with hard-pressed purchasers of public lands in 1808 and accuse Congress in 1810 of doing nothing but "pick the people's pockets."[49] In Belmont County in 1813 Hammond successfully directed his electoral appeal to farmers and "producers" against "lawyers, doc-tors, merchants" and "idle-young men, educated in habits of extravagance, without means of gaining an honest living." The war, he argued, meant gain for officeholders and the rich, but it subjected "the great body of the people to ruin, misery and death." He pointed up the oppressive burden of the "drafts on the militia," the shortages, the taxes, and he excoriated the Democrats for blessing a plague of taxgatherers on the land. This grievance resulted in a "great hue and cry about taxes" in some places in 1815, as the state tried to collect enough money to pay its wartime liabilities to the federal government.[50]

This social discontent was especially vocal from 1813 onwards in Muskin-gum County, where the Federalist press became the natural vehicle for local protests from aggrieved farmers and artisans. In 1815, for example, "Republican Farmers and Mechanics" refused to follow their party leaders, and they held not only their own Independence Day celebration but even their own rival nomi-nating convention. The reason was, they said, the "general complaint among the laboring part of the community, who are the source of government, that the nomination heretofore has been made by a designing few, in Zanesville and its vicinity"; instead, "the honest farmer and mechanic . . . ought to rule the destinies of this country in future." The regular Republicans denounced this movement as playing the Federalist game, even if that party had no ticket in the field, but in the end this uprising of "the common people," backed by the Federalist press, succeeded in defeating the officeholding "aristocracy" that men believed dominated the county. Although never benefiting as an exclusive party, the Federalists of Muskingum formed part of a malcontent combination that continued to challenge local Democratic predominance in the contests of 1816 and 1817.[51]

The Federalists also took the lead in criticizing the "growing evil of bank incorporations." The rage for making new banks had begun in Ohio a couple of years after the chartering of the first bank in 1808, and it was further stimulated by the demise of the Bank of the United States in 1811 and the financial pressures generated by the war effort. The needs of Harrison's army forced up prices, and the shortage of specie encouraged the use of credit. The direct taxes imposed by Washington prompted further borrowing by individuals, while increased pur-chases of land after 1813 created a demand for loans that could be provided only by paper money. The larger local banks were conservatively run and benefited from the large sums of specie deposited in their vaults, but they inevitably succumbed to the general suspension of specie payments in the last months of the war, along with the rash of small, unchartered, paper-issuing institutions.[52]

Banks inevitably bore the blame for the growing flood of irredeemable paper money and the changes in monetary values. A few Republicans questioned the desirability of "monied aristocracies" and advocated taxing bank profits, but the main criticism during the war came from Federalist publicists, especially as Republican politicians were prominent among the defenders—and directors—of banks. One correspondent in a Federalist newspaper pointed to the spread of banks as a sign of the unhappy state of the country in 1814, and Hammond became the leading spokesman for legal controls on state banking. When a law he drafted taxing banks and prohibiting unauthorized banknotes was passed by the legislature in February 1815, a writer in the Chillicothe *Fredonian* attacked "the Charles Hammond law" as a Federalist measure as repressive as the Alien and Sedition Acts! Correspondents in the highly Democratic Steubenville *Western Herald* condemned this "foolish law against the banks," and when Hammond criticized banks founded by Quakers in Jefferson and Columbiana Counties, his Republican opponents tried to arouse Quaker opposition in Belmont to his reelection: "I don't care a fig about thy politics . . . but the bank must go on." On this issue, Federalist rather than Republican publicists were initially more in sympathy with the trend of popular opinion.[53]

Similarly, after 1815 the Federalists led the way in voicing the widespread suspicion that Republican "aristocrats" in power were intent on lining their own pockets. In 1816 the Ohio general assembly was widely criticized for raising its members' wages from two to three dollars a day. This issue was soon overwhelmed by news that congressmen had voted themselves twelve dollars per day: "There is republicanism and economy for you!" cried the *Ohio Federalist,* charging that "an aristocracy of wealth and extravagance" had sprung up in Washington, where congressmen were rapidly sucked into "the fashionable dissipation and extravagance of the city." Although not all Federalists approved, its active leaders were at the forefront of the popular uproar at this enormity, which in Ohio as elsewhere decisively demonstrated the power of public opinion.[54]

Hammond, in particular, used his newspaper and his position in the general assembly to denounce the abuse of power. In 1817, when still perceived as "the leader of the opposition party in the state," he challenged the election of two congressmen on the grounds that they held federal office at the time of election, and he almost secured the rejection of the regular Republican Samuel Herrick—with strong support in Congress from southern Republicans.[55] Hammond also campaigned against state legislators who appointed themselves to office, in violation of the state constitution. As a state representative in 1818, he gained enough Republican support for the Ohio house to pass a resolution establishing his point. But when the legislature, on a joint secret ballot, then elected two of its members to new circuits of the common pleas courts, he issued an address to the people about this "infamous intrigue." His campaign considerably embarrassed leading Republicans—including Herrick in his bid for reelection—and raised issues about the uses of legislative patronage that troubled elections in several counties in 1818 and 1819. So firmly did Hammond advocate these popular causes that even his old enemy James Wilson came to believe that Hammond, "although still calling himself a federalist, . . . was a better Democrat than many of those who howled Democracy the loudest."[56]

Exclusion from power had put the Federalists into a position that made them the natural champions of the discontented and resentful—not unlike the Jacksonian Democrats in some places in the late 1820s. Of course, the electoral reward for the Federalists' efforts were strictly limited. They suffered from the simple fact that many of the discontented could not bring themselves to vote openly for Federalist candidates; the protests of 1816 would result in a change of one set of Republican representatives for another, not in the election of Federalists. In most parts of the state, political success continued to require firm commitment to the national administration, and ambitious and talented Federalists like Hammond knew that, as long as they maintained their attachment to the opposition, they were "without any chance" of attaining the positions to which they aspired. Moreover, there was no point in maintaining a local opposition, however vigorously, when there was no chance of broader success—especially when the focus and purposes of partisan identity were on national affairs.

The Federalists, therefore, faced a dilemma. They were confident of their own righteousness and competence and were willing to act as a party where they could, but they could succeed only by concealing their identity and supporting Republican dissidents. Federalists could find some satisfaction, at least rhetorically, by blaming the Republicans' failings upon their excessive partisanship and by emphasizing the need for right-minded men to come together to elect better governors. But blasting party opponents for being partisan meant using antiparty arguments in partisan ways—and that was just typical of the way in which politicians on all sides exploited the antiparty tradition.

DELUSIVE SONGS OF ANTIPARTYISM

Contemporary writers and politicians commonly ridiculed the idea that the existence of organized parties could be healthy for the perpetuation of republican liberty. As Richard Hofstadter has shown, a powerful cultural tradition taught that parties endangered the republican experiment because they stood in the way of a proper, responsible concern for the welfare of the whole community, and few contemporaries were willing to argue in favor of a political system in which two organized parties regularly competed for power and occasionally changed places.[57] Yet the antiparty creed was not monolithic: different political elements—Democratic, Independent Republican, and Federalist—placed emphasis on different parts of the creed at different times and, in so doing, were creating the elements of a full-blown partisan theory.

The Democratic elements in the Republican party had long argued in favor of their own right to maintain a permanent party organization. Since the statehood campaign, the Democratic societies of Hamilton County had maintained that a clearly organized system of focusing the party's support on the requisite number of candidates would not only keep Federalists from power but also provide the electorate with the means of ensuring that it was presented with the ticket and the candidates that a majority wanted. Because the Republican party represented the bulk of the people, its nominating mechanisms provided a means of expression for the community; in particular, the delegate system gave an opportunity for isolated farmers and humble men to make their voices heard. However, once a majority of the electorate in many counties began to reject the authority of delegate nominations, Democratic spokesmen had to formulate a more carefully developed justification for tight party organization, although their attitudes and beliefs were to become fully explicit only after 1815 when the postwar spirit of national consensus began to undermine the very spirit of partisanship itself.

Yet even while justifying their own partisanship, the Democrats denied the legitimacy of fixed, organized party opposition. In circumstances of Republican ascendancy, they were arguing, in effect, for a one-party state in which the people's government and a democratic political system were reinforced by party mechanisms. Like other Jeffersonian Republicans, they thought of themselves as representing the country, the overwhelming mass of decent Americans, and so once they had power, opposition should naturally cease. Democrats could not accept the legitimacy of opposition to the people's government partly because they did not distinguish clearly between the system of government as constituted and the current administration of that government; hence their presumption that Federalists must wish to overthrow the constitutional system and reestablish monarchy, to introduce the alien and corrupt forms of the Britain that Federalists adulated.

When war came, such a blinkered attitude proved downright intolerant. All opposition was expected to cease. Democrats demanded a "Union of all Americans against the common enemy—They who are not for us are against us." Edward Tiffin thought it "high time those [Federalist] Gentry should be curbed . . .

our Country should be purged of all enemies to a Government, which has been emphatically styled 'the World's best hope.' " John Hamm and Isaac Van Horne were less gracious: when they called for an end to party conflict in 1812, they meant that the Federalists should supinely accept whatever the government did. In 1814 their colleague, David Chambers of the *Muskingum Messenger,* denounced "the spirit of party, in times of peril like the present," and even quoted Washington's Farewell Address in his denial of legitimacy to the opposition.[58] These Republicans had little sense that a permanent organized opposition could play a legitimate and responsible role in a republican polity, little sense that parties should see themselves as part of a system in which they alternated with their rivals in the enjoyment of office and power.

By contrast, the Independent Republicans were more willing to accept that moderate, patriotic Federalists had a reasonable point of view. These Independents believed that their own obedience to party was limited to the specific purposes for which they had established their partisan allegiance, and they were unwilling to follow the party into areas of state policy that they thought beyond its legitimate concern. Their success in 1812 had depended on the support of Federalists, and they were attracted by an antiparty ideology that reduced both the embarrassment of joining with nominal opponents and their own dependence on men whose excessive partisan commitment they could not approve. Hence the Independent or conservative governors of 1808–14—Huntington and Meigs—claimed to understand partisan differences and respect honest disagreement, and insisted that such differences must be discussed sensibly in a spirit of liberality and without "asperity of animadversion" or a desire to exclude.[59]

Various impulses contributed to the strength of this version of antipartyism. One was a desire for national unity, especially at a time of international peril. As Benjamin Ruggles declared in Marietta in 1809, excessive partisanship allied to state pride could "tear down the whole splendid edifice of [federal] government erected by the wisdom and valor of our fathers, and bury the whole nation under its ruins." In December 1814 Worthington, in his new role as statesman, expressed a view of parties scarcely different from that of Huntington and Meigs: party divisions can be salutary, he told the general assembly, but when party spirit replaces patriotism, the essential interests of the country are sacrificed. Only "the baneful effects of party divisions" could explain the disasters of the war, and he called on the people of Ohio, in the country's hour of need, to throw off "the intemperate indulgence of party spirit."[60]

Another concern was to restore communal harmony, to smother a partisanship that disrupted social relations; hence the significance of the Independents' policy of turning township meetings and county nominating conventions into meetings of the whole community, open to everyone regardless of partisan affiliation. But besides this urge for consensus and harmony, the antiparty out-look of the Independents also expressed an individualistic and liberal demand for freedom of opinion. They disliked the sense that others were dictating how they should think and behave, regardless of whether the dictator was an exclu-sive society—as for so long in Cincinnati—or a party mogul behaving like Wor-thington in the congressional election of 1813. A Cincinnati writer of 1811 feared that if the militant Democrats had their way, "the dogmas of the party then become the *criterion*" which every supporter has to judge by, and so the individ-ual's "god-like faculty of *Reason* . . . is lost." The editors of the *Independent Press,* opening in Lancaster in 1812, wished to be "the keepers of our own reason, . . . Independent, unbiased by party clamor," and so able to "form our own opin-ions on men and measures, with truth and sound policy as our only guides." Samuel Huntington, while governor, had insisted that "diversity in political sentiment is neither pernicious nor useless," as long as there is no intolerance or party dictation; the contest of ideas stimulates vigilance and aids the discovery of truth. This notion of a marketplace of ideas, preferably supplied by news-papers that printed both sides of a question, strongly appealed to many anti-party spokesmen and somewhat contradicted the consensual tradition.[61]

For the Federalists, the antiparty rhetoric that filled the columns of their newspapers served slightly different purposes. Undeniably, it represented a genuine anxiety about the political health of a republic whose people placed incompetent men in power and then supported them through thick and thin. This they blamed on the gullibility of the people, who were too easily misled by names and labels. If only "the people were wise! and would look to the conduct, not the *professions* of men," wished the Chillicothe *Supporter.* "Then the words *Federalists, lawyers, republicans,* &c. would lose their *magic charms,* and truth would prevail over error." Instead, irresponsible politicians curried popular favor, pandered to popular prejudices, and presented everything in partisan terms. As Hammond complained, parties consistently put forward their most popular men rather than their most capable. The republic needed firm leaders who were willing to do their duty, even when unpopular, and to present politi-cal affairs to the people in their true light. As it was, party machinery served merely to keep power within a few restricted hands. Even popularly chosen conventions were often devices merely to ratify a ticket already secretly chosen by the party managers. By these means, power fell into the hands of a few fortunate men, and this new "aristocracy" was then kept in power by the blind support of their followers. Even Revolutionary heroes, when they would not accept party dictation, were damned as traitors and the country was denied their services, while the power of government was misused to suppress dissi-dence and "to oppress the refractory minority people."[62]

This analysis effectively explained to Federalists why the electorate rejected them and what could be done about it. The most basic need was to educate the electorate, and it is no accident that Federalists, as the 1810s wore on, became increasingly drawn into movements for moral reform and publicly financed common schools. In the shorter term they could use their press to publicize the evils and shortcomings of the ruling party and to appeal to allies among the ranks of the local Republican majority; in this respect their antiparty rhetoric, with its attacks on party dictation and contempt for the new "aristocracy" of party managers, usefully appealed to discontented Republicans who were tempted toward an independent course. But, beyond that, there was nothing in the Federalists' antiparty outlook that was inherently opposed to party action, as long as the leaders of their party were concerned primarily with the public welfare, and as long as the party nomination was only a recommendation and not a limitation on the electorate's freedom of choice. Indeed, some of the values that the Federalists asserted—liberty of opinion, access to public office, and political opportunity, the need to elect the best men, the duty of defending the public interest—encouraged coordinated effort on the part of right-minded men. As a Republican in Guernsey County complained in 1814, the moment these apostles of antipartyism thought they could "elect men of their own politics, . . . they eulogise the delegate system, appoint committees, subcommittees, [and] take up their candidates in the most formal manner." As proof, he pointed to "the conduct of the opposition in this state" as well as in some eastern states.[63]

From this point of view, it is not surprising that the Federalists insisted that organized opposition was justified, even during the war. The Chillicothe *Supporter*, at the outbreak of a war it did not oppose, pronounced, "Political parties will not, and ought not to cease. They are often carried to excess, but they are not without their use, and, we believe, are in a degree necessarily essential to the very existence of freedom." Other Federalist editors were aroused when Republicans disagreed. In the final issue of the *Western Spectator*, Caleb Emerson complained of "the doctrines of despotism advanced by the tools of the administration." Charles Hammond started the *Ohio Federalist* because he objected to the Democratic doctrine that criticism must not be allowed in time of war, and so "by the exercise of my rights I practically demonstrated their existence." Hammond was particularly effective in defending political liberty in the face of self-righteous Democratic doubts about the legitimacy of opposition. He shrewdly depicted David Chambers of the *Muskingum Messenger* as belonging to "that class of politicians who identify their party with the country, and who consider every measure directed against the party as a species of high treason. He looks upon the agents employed or appointed to administer the government, as the government itself, and hence he interprets every attempt to expose the imbecility and wretchedness of the administration, as an attack upon the [system of] government." Federalist spokesmen in Ohio insisted on making that distinction and recognized that it logically required them to obey all constitutional measures passed by the government of the day. They rejected the obstructionism of their eastern colleagues, but insisted on their right to work for electoral defeat of the party in power. In this way the Federalists, at least in Ohio, made a decisive contribution to the development and acceptance of the concept of a loyal opposition, and so helped to ensure the ultimate acceptance of the legitimacy of political parties.[64]

Clearly these differing views, attitudes, and practices prevalent among Ohioans in the early 1810s fell well short of acceptance of a mass two-party system such as clearly existed in the United States by the 1840s. Most people felt that permanent, organized opposition was an unnecessary evil, and they looked forward to a situation in which old wounds were healed, disagreements forgotten, and a national consensus looking forward to the welfare of the general good established. Yet they also believed in freedom of speech, freedom of political activity, and freedom of elections, and since the Revolution they had been developing the organizational devices that made it possible to defeat governments at the polls.

At the same time Americans were divided, mistrusting the political and social purposes of some of their fellow citizens so deeply that they were unwilling to allow them to govern, or recapture government, without serious challenge. As a result they had organized political formations that can only be described as parties, even if they were not quite the same as later parties. The fact that people at the time did not understand, appreciate, or value the behavior patterns in which they had become caught up does not prove that the patterns did not exist. Not for the first or last time, ideas and perceptions had yet to catch up with reality.[65]

Beneath antiparty rhetoric commonly lurked a partisan reality. The condemnation of intolerant partyism expressed by most Federalists itself bore witness to the existence of partisan behavior and even partisan values on the side of their most extreme opponents. Even those Republicans who insisted on their independence of party dogma and party dictation hastened to own their allegiance to the national party whenever challenged by intraparty rivals. Thus Thomas D. Webb, editor of the first newspaper on the Western Reserve, the Warren *Trump of Fame,* refused in 1812 to state his political creed in his prospectus, although he assured readers that he was "no monarchist, no aristocrat," and he opened his paper to "decent communications of any political faith." When criticized for his vagueness, he explained that he did not want to be branded "a party man"—but added that he had opposed Jay's Treaty and John Adams's measures, had supported Mr. Jefferson's administration, and now was strongly in favor of Mr. Madison's war![66] For all the pressures toward nonpartisan cooperation in many parts of the state, national party distinction between Federalist and Republican continued to retain real emotional significance for politicians, voters, and customers.

THE SPADE OF OBLIVION

John C. Wright was to gain considerable distinction: in Congress in the 1820s, on the Ohio Supreme Court in the 1830s, and as a Cincinnati Whig editor in the 1840s. Born in New England, by 1816 he was a successful young Republican lawyer in Steubenville, where he lived close by his brother-in-law, Benjamin Tappan. He had always been a less committed partisan than Tappan and, while working on a Federalist newspaper in western New York a decade earlier, had argued for a softening of party asperities. He got on well with Federalists, notably Charles Hammond, and cooperated with them during his several attempts to win a seat in Congress after the war. In the summer of 1817 he undertook a trip to the eastern states, where he discovered that at last "the bitterness of party is dying away." In New York, De Witt Clinton's election "seems to have hushed up the animosities of party." As for Connecticut, "*Party* seems there to be *breaking* down," and in New England as a whole, men seemed to have forgotten that "President Monro was elected by a party," as even Federalists proved "most attentive" to the president on his tour of goodwill. Wright rejoiced that "the day is approaching when the zeal, the heat, the passion, prejudice & blind infatuation of party, mean, pitiful and degrading party, is subsiding and the door opening for considering the substantial interests of the Country."[67]

The decline in party feeling to which Wright bore witness, the rapid spread of Good Feelings in the postwar afterglow, demonstrates the extraordinary importance of policy issues in provoking and maintaining the party division of the previous twenty years. Party differences before 1815 had gained their saliency from the sense that the whole future of the Republic was at stake, in what David Chambers called "this stupendous age of revolutions." The common linking of Republicanism with France and of Federalism with Britain made the party conflict seem but a continuation of the struggle taking place in Europe; each party suspected its rival of wishing to introduce the political and social forms of its European associate—be they jacobinical or monarchical—into the United States. Most Republicans had no great liking for Napoleon, but they saw him as fighting against British usurpations which, as it happened, threatened

American integrity and independence. The Federalists themselves believed that "a war with England is not so much to be deprecated as an Alliance (its necessary consequence) with France," for France had shown an insatiable appetite for gobbling up friendly republics. With the fate of the world in balance and the outcome of an age of revolutions to be decided, both parties had felt they could not leave the fate of the republic in the hands of those whose purposes, they feared, were un-American. Such ideological polarity was exaggerated, and it neglected the common commitment of both parties to the Constitution, to the republic, to federalism, and to representative democracy, but the emotional overloading can be understood in the context of a new republic struggling for survival in a world of warring giants.[68]

The political issues, and the divisions which they drove through the political nation before 1815, were so clearly a product of the French Revolution and the Napoleonic Wars that heightened party feeling could not be expected to survive unscathed the coming of peace and restoration. As a widely reprinted article from the *National Register* said, American party divisions had derived from the "tremendous political volcano" in Europe which had involved "the whole civilized world so deeply." With the final passing of those commotions, politics could be expected to be more "exclusively American than they have hitherto been." Moreover, as partisan suspicion of the other party's loyalty to an independent American federal republic declined, so Ohioans increasingly appreciated that all Americans shared a common set of political values. As a result, nonpartisan Fourth of July celebrations now became common as never before, not only in western and central Ohio but even in party-torn eastern Ohio. By 1816 men of both parties could listen to the same orators without fear of hearing unacceptable versions of history and current affairs, while in Steubenville even Benjamin Tappan could toast a "union of parties on American principles."[69]

Likewise, differences over domestic policy diminished, as the national Republican party came to adopt policies directed at rectifying the internal weaknesses revealed by the war. In December 1815 President Madison's annual message proposed a stronger navy, the encouragement of commerce, the reestablishment of a national currency, and measures to improve the country's capacity to defend itself. Federalists eagerly approved the proposals as a welcome departure from the traditional Republican emphasis on cheap, weak government. The *Zanesville Express* rejoiced "to find our national government falling upon a system of measures which remind us of former times." By January the paper was claiming that the message, with its blend of federal measures and republican principles, was the first that all parties could agree upon. By August, the *Express* and the *Ohio Federalist* concurred that, in view of the

Republicans' "adoption of good old Washington principles," there was no need to oppose them as long as they nominated "honourable and capable men."[70]

The changing focus of public life after 1815 also aided the process of party reconciliation, for politics became less central as other obsessions arose. Local religious activity, for example, caught fire once more after the war. As Thomas S. Hinde said of the Chillicothe region, "The tremulous motions of the late calamitous war had subsided, peace reigned, the Gospel spread most astonishingly." The Methodists organized camp meetings in all parts of Ohio and established ten traveling preachers for the Ohio District; they roused "religious interest" even in nominally Presbyterian and Congregationalist towns such as Steubenville and Marietta, and most denominations benefited from the greater religious awareness.[71]

However, the churches now competed for adherents, and revival stimulated both theological controversy and denominational strife. The Methodist campaign "waked up opposition," James B. Finley remembered, "and the sluggish artillery of Calvinism was brought to bear upon our ranks." Besides fighting Presbyterians and Congregationalists, especially in the Scotch-Irish and New Englander areas, the Methodists competed with New Light immersionists ("great on argument"), with Universalists, and with infidels, irreligious ruffians, and whiskey drinkers. Even within their own ranks there were bitter arguments over Arian and Pelagian doctrines, which were prevalent in some parts of Ohio, and by 1819 "radicalism" was turning some Methodists against some of the denomination's traditional methods. Such disputes and controversies could divide whole neighborhoods, as in parts of eastern Ohio where arguments over free will and predestination became the major public concern. Even in Federalist Dayton, the old ruling groups were overtaken after 1814 by the rise of evangelicalism within the local Presbyterian church.[72]

The rise of evangelical religion may have been a response to the increasing importance, in the first years of peace, of money making. The war had stimulated economic growth in many parts of Ohio, and the sense of buoyancy was sustained by the huge increase of migration to the state. New settlers expanded the market for agricultural produce, pushed up land values, and created a need for an expanded currency and other banking facilities. Community leaders who, like James Kilbourne, had originally been conscious of moral and religious purposes were increasingly attracted into profitable business enterprises that were not necessarily in keeping with those purposes. This "money mania" gripped even normally sensible men, including Dr. Daniel Drake, who was tempted to borrow heavily to invest in overly ambitious commercial activities. Land speculation and "town making" became the general rage.[73]

In many places, new companies and partnerships of many kinds—mercantile, manufacturing, and financial—drew together men of capital and influence regardless of their partisan differences. In Cincinnati, a closely knit economic elite dominated municipal affairs, with Republicans as renowned as William Henry Harrison and James Findlay increasingly entwining their interests—in commerce, banking, manufacturing, and landed pursuits—with those of Federalists such as Jacob Burnet. Local banks commonly drew their directors from both sides of the political divide: there were objections in Washington in 1817 when Burnet was proposed as president of the Cincinnati branch of the new Bank of the United States, and Harrison had to vouch for the Republicanism of the majority of the proposed directors.[74]

In eastern Ohio immediately south of the Western Reserve, economic affairs had always been dominated by a group of men who were largely Federalist in origin and headed by Bezaleel Wells of Steubenville. Increasingly after 1815, this business elite attracted to its ranks a number of prominent local Republicans, including partisans previously as determined as John Sloane and Benjamin Tappan. Their political prestige helped the elite to establish a local political dominance that was beneficial to the furtherance of their interest in land, banks, and, above all, wool. In Stark County, centered on Canton, the elite was not replaced, as Elkins and McKitrick would have it, by petty local boosters; rather, the county's politics came to be dominated after 1815 by a regional elite, located outside the county but commanding the local economy—and much of political life.[75]

Ohio political alignments responded remarkably quickly to the passing of an unusual international and domestic situation and the arrival of a brave new world of internal expansion. Independent Republicans had long wished to cooperate with Federalists on matters of domestic government, and now the obstacles seemed removed. In Muskingum County, some Republicans formed themselves into a secret benevolent and political organization called the Round Ring Society, which aimed "to bury Party Spirit with the Spade of Oblivion." In February 1816, its members voted unanimously to amalgamate with the Washington Benevolent Society, since "really there appears nothing lately so discordant in our respective Creeds. . . . In fact, we approximate so near in religion, morality and even politics, that [we] can see no good reason that we should any longer be kept asunder."[76]

As befitted their antiparty rhetoric, it was the Federalists in Ohio who initiated the process of political reconciliation, insisting that "the days of dissension . . . have passed by." Even in southeastern Ohio, Federalist spokesmen made clear their willingness to drop their opposition to the national administration. In Washington County in 1816, the members of the Washington Benevolent Society invited all admirers of the great man to join its Fourth of

July celebration, without distinction of party: thus "the spirit of party shall give place to the indulgence of social affections." When the county's Republican party insisted on holding its own celebration and made formal nominations for the fall elections, the local Federalists did not object; they refrained from making a counternomination and helped to elect a Republican congressman, Levi Barber of Marietta. Again, in 1817, Republicans were elected in the county "without opposition," and by 1818 both parties could join together to honor Congressman Barber and toast "More patriotism, and less party spirit."[77]

In southwestern Ohio, of course, the healing process continued the process of party fusion that had marked the war years. Dr. William Goforth had left Cincinnati a decade earlier because his radical politics had alienated his wealthy clientele; when he returned from Louisiana in January 1817, "the lapse of a few weeks was sufficient to evince that the political feelings of former times had subsided, and that his practice would soon become lucrative and respectable." The tone of the Cincinnati press changed, as radical Democratic sheets such as the *Spirit of the West* disappeared in 1815 and both major newspapers, the *Liberty Hall* and *Western Spy,* fell under the control of partnerships that included Federalist sympathizers. The latter paper, edited by the young Micajah T. Williams, could on occasions criticize the cant of some Democratic politicians, but its masthead proclaimed its ideal: "Unwarped by Party Rage, to Live like Brothers."[78]

In the congressional election of 1816, the overwhelming concern in Hamilton County—despite some rumbles of discontent—was to demonstrate popular confidence in Harrison's military record after Congress's refusal to vote him a medal of honor. As the county's war hero, Harrison won three-quarters of its votes (and 57 percent in the district), with the support not only of the county delegate convention but also of "a number of the leading Federalists, . . . a detachment from all parties and Religions whatsoever, and . . . many of the army folks."[79]

In Ross County, too, factional as well as party differences became less acute: the Chillicothe Democrats' mouthpiece, the *Scioto Gazette,* developed a more reasoned and moderate tone after its takeover by John Bailhache of the Independent Republican *Fredonian* in 1815; the *Supporter* shifted from Federalism to nonpartisanship and so prepared the way for the amalgamated *Supporter and Scioto Gazette* in 1821. In the new state capital, several newspapers were trying to establish themselves, including the conservative *Western Intelligencer,* which in 1817 became the moderate *Columbus Gazette* and ultimately, in 1825, evolved into the *Ohio State Journal.* Moreover, in this congressional district—located, in the incumbent James Kilbourne's words, "on the late frontier and lines of savage war"—appeals to party discipline could not prevent several Republicans from running in the 1816 election, opening the door for the election of Philemon Beecher as Ohio's first Federalist congressman.[80]

The ultimate sign that Federalists no longer opposed Republicans on grounds of principle came when Ohio's Federalist leaders refused to make the presidential contest of 1816 interesting. In January, the Republicans held a "grand caucus" at Chillicothe, the temporary state capital, and named a slate of electoral college candidates who, it was presumed, would vote for the candidate named by the congressional caucus, preferably James Monroe. Despite scattered grumblings about party dictation, even the *Muskingum Messenger* conceded that "we hear of no opposition in this state" to the ticket, although some votes were cast against Monroe in Quaker areas.[81]

Some Federalists in southeastern Ohio endeavored to resist the contagion of Good Feelings in 1816. In Washington County, Paul Fearing urged the Washington Benevolent Society to stand firm against Jacobins. In Belmont County, the *Ohio Federalist* continued to take the offensive against Democratic editors during 1816 and 1817, producing some probing philosophical and historical analyses of Democratic ideology. Hammond aimed "solely to expose those who insist upon keeping up the strife of party," but he acknowledged that joining in controversy also kept party animosities alive. Contrary to his advice, local Federalists "dragged" him into running for the general assembly in 1816, which made him "the only man in the state nominated for an elective office by the federalists, *as a party.*" The Republican delegate convention named a party ticket but could not prevent Hammond's election. However, the following year a newspaper correspondent claimed it was "generally agreed that there is no good reason for any longer keeping alive the party distinctions which have agitated this county so much," and suggested a nomination "upon which I think parties may fairly unite." Belmont, accordingly, sent two Republicans and two Federalists, including Hammond, to the general assembly in 1817 and 1818. After 1816 no Republican convention met in Belmont to determine nominations for the county elections, and in 1818 Hammond decided it was time to discontinue the *Ohio Federalist.*[82]

As in New England, the new president's goodwill tour of 1817 provided a suitable symbol of reconciliation. When Monroe visited Ohio, Federalists scrambled with Republicans to welcome him "as members of the American family." At Lancaster, Philemon Beecher chaired the welcoming committee. In Chillicothe, the Federalist mayor, Levin Belt, doggedly prevented Thomas Worthington from monopolizing the affair and insisted that the president must be formally honored by local dignitaries. At the civic reception, Belt publicly complimented Monroe on demonstrating by his presence how the person of the president adds to "the strong cement of union" and so forms "a barrier to civil feuds." Hammond, at the *Ohio Federalist,* echoed the general gratification.[83]

Overall, the main credit for the ending of old arguments belonged to the Federalists. In most local situations they had taken the initiative in offering the olive branch. In part, this represented a fulfillment of their antiparty ideals, but it was also motivated by pragmatic calculations. Hammond had always criticized party spirit chiefly on the grounds that it prevented the people from electing the best men from both parties—Federalists because of partisan prejudice, Republicans because party conflict led parties to choose as candidates their most popular rather than their best men. He looked forward to a time "when the only questions concerning a candidate shall be, is he honest? Is he capable? Is he faithful to the constitution?" Above all, such an attitude would end a situation in which Federalists were automatically excluded from office, and so "encrease [sic] the chance of future usefulness" for himself and others. As Shaw Livermore has argued, the great concern for Federalist politicians after 1815 was to somehow shuffle off the disadvantage that forever excluded them from public office.[84]

For what was the point in maintaining the Federalist party if it could never win? Spokesmen in Ohio agreed that it was "high time for the Federalists to give up an opposition which only serves to heighten the asperities of party spirit, and exhibit the thinness of their ranks."[85] Conscious of their minority position within the structure of voter loyalties, the Federalists recognized that popular prejudices against them made it unlikely that they could attract fresh support to their party, especially since their associates elsewhere had become branded with disloyalty to the republic during a war that had ended so happily. As with most minority parties that no longer have an enemy worth fighting, Federalist politicians could see no future in a party formation that promised only defeat.

Yet what of their opponents, who had learned what benefits their party coherence had brought both to the republic and to themselves? Such parties have usually shown an extraordinary ability to survive, even when the situation that originally gave them meaning has passed away. The collapse of the First Party System after the war suggests powerfully that this era of party conflict was fundamentally different from later ones and did not generate the sort of popular commitment which has made party ties so lasting in subsequent decades. But did, in fact, those first parties collapse with the ease and completeness that historians have assumed? Did ordinary Federalists forget their old party so easily, and were the Republicans so keen to accept them? Or had a web of emotion and common experience created, for many people, a lasting sense of allegiance to a particular partisan identity? And had political passion burned those loyalties and antipathies so deep that they were never ever quite to be forgotten?

8

Good Feelings and Partisanship,
1816–1821

No period is so misunderstood, and its significance for American party history so underestimated, as the laughably misnamed "Era of Good Feelings." There can be no doubt that, for a short time after 1815, political passions abated, formal organized opposition to the Republican party disappeared, and a national consensus seemed to exist on the leading issues of the day. Yet the decline in the force of the old party division does not necessarily show the weakness of the old party loyalties or the overriding power of antipartyism, since the decline was due not merely to Good Feelings but also to powerful new sources of internal disagreement at the local level which ripped at the unity of both parties. In spite of these forces, moreover, the old party division never completely disappeared, for it remained a significant, if far from general, organizing principle of political behavior. The old loyalties were, in fact, not overridden until a multifaceted crisis hit state and nation in 1818–19 which, in the next three years, destroyed Good Feelings, provoked severe sectional controversy, and, in the end, created a new political cleavage of mighty significance for the future.

Politics without Parties

Since statehood, over much of Ohio, local elections had frequently been fought on a nonpartisan basis, simply because Federalists had been too weak to provide an effective challenge at the county level. Experience of party concerns had been aroused only in statewide or district elections when partisans recognized the danger of Federalists sneaking into power through Republican divisions. With the decline of party after 1815, however, the experience of "no-party" elections became more widespread, and modes of behavior that had always existed somewhere in the state became the common practice. As a consequence, many young politicians who entered the state after 1815 believed that partisanship had not influenced the conduct of politics in Ohio before the rise of Jacksonianism in the 1820s.[1]

At the state level, it proved ever more difficult after 1815 to organize nominations and campaigns, and gubernatorial elections became little more than one-sided popularity contests. This situation benefited incumbent governors, with Thomas Worthington garnering two-thirds of the vote in 1816 and Ethan Allen Brown almost three-quarters in 1820. In contests to replace retiring governors, the greatest advantage was to have run before (and so become known), as Brown had two years before his triumph of 1818. In 1816 and 1818, the successful candidate benefited from nomination by a Republican meeting in Columbus, but by 1820 no advantage was to be gained from such dictation from a capital widely identified as dominated by its own boosters. A candidate could always gain some momentum from nomination by county conventions, as Brown did in 1818, but conventions and other meetings still needed a hint as to who would win support elsewhere. Such hints tended to come through men with statewide contacts, sometimes the judges but more often a county's state representatives. As Judge Calvin Pease would tell one gubernatorial aspirant in 1822, the opinions of legislators "have considerable weight with people who are not personally acquainted with candidates."[2]

Within the assembly, there were no clear-cut or fixed alignments in these years, and after 1816 the earlier factional divisions within the Republican party had largely ceased to operate. Little legislation of general interest was passed, and most measures concerned private and local interests: elections to office, the creation of judicial circuits, the establishment of new counties and county seats, and the chartering of banks. Special interest groups sent paid lobbyists to Columbus to secure the measures they required, and "a seat in the lobby of this state" became almost as influential as one in the general assembly itself. "Log-rolling" proved more than ever a chief technique for getting measures through, and all sorts of groupings operated in the politics and management of business.[3]

Regional groupings became more significant than earlier, with the traditional balance between east and west influencing the distribution of advantage and the election of statewide officers, especially judges and U.S. senators. The Scioto Valley continued to be identified as a separate interest, while increasingly the Western Reserve made itself felt as the "northern interest."[4] Religious groupings were also perceived as important, especially in appointments, as in December 1818 when "the Methodist interest" was considered "very strong" and likely to affect an election to the supreme court. These alignments cut across each other, as in 1819 when another legislator could identify the support for a measure as including not only "the methodists' and quakers' interest" but also "almost all the northward interest."[5] Otherwise, the shifting groupings were difficult to identify and often based on personal connection.

Nonpartisan elections had always been common in some parts of the state in local elections, especially since 1812. But now, even in those counties where delegate nominating conventions had regularly been used, enough voters ignored their recommendations in 1816 for their authority, as in Franklin County, to prove "abortive," and thereafter they became less frequent. In Hamilton County, a delegate convention met in 1816 and 1817, but its authority was successfully disputed on both occasions.[6] Indeed, accusations of management could make nomination by a delegate convention a positive disadvantage, and candidates were often advised to avoid being "set up by a caucus" or formal meeting lest they be dismissed as the favorite of some officeholding clique or "family connexion." Self-nomination or nomination by friends soon appeared to be "the only respectable and popular mode of obtaining the public approbation" and became conspicuously more common and even, some claimed, customary.[7]

In this situation, local politicians developed many techniques for winning over the popular vote. One device was to place an unpopular candidate on a ticket with more acceptable names; another was to announce a nonserious candidacy by someone who would attract support away from an opponent. Treating was traditional in some counties, although it probably served to bring out voters rather than to buy votes. Electioneering by the candidate himself became increasingly common, although some clearly felt that a candidate risked losing votes if he asked for support too blatantly. Handbills circulated, especially on the eve of an election, allowing no time for lies to be contradicted. Slander was, indeed, "too frequently resorted to," with many commentators objecting to scurrilous attacks on the personal character of opponents—and some candidates seeking redress by their own physical efforts. Not surprisingly, one New Englander found Ohio elections reminiscent of the "intreague [sic] and strategies" used in the southern states, marked not only by nocturnal caucuses, slander, and animosities but also by "the carrying of weapons, mobs, and gougings."[8]

With the breakdown of party, county politics became a struggle of personal interests and local factions, and power lay increasingly in the hands—as one newspaper correspondent claimed in 1816—of "those men who possess local influence sufficient to cause such persons as they *choose*, to be elected." Increasingly, nominations came from small groups of men gathered together for other purposes: county courts, grand juries, militia officers. Some commentators detected a distinct decline of popular interest in public affairs and an increase in elite political influence in the first years of Good Feelings.[9]

U.S. Census 1820

· 250 Rural population

• 2,500 Urban population

0   miles   100

Ohio Counties and Population Distribution in 1820. *Source:* Utter, *Frontier State,* 220.

Yet it continued to be widely recognized that the power of influential men depended on their ability to persuade the electorate. In Geauga County the Paine family dominated public office, but in 1816 they faced a popular challenge that they overcame only by using all the arts of "the loquacious, sycophantic and insinuating, bar-room politician." In 1818 John C. Wright reported that opposition in Columbiana County to Ethan Allen Brown's gubernatorial campaign came from "divers great men," but he doubted whether "these gentry" could carry the county; despite their opposition, Brown won over three-quarters of Columbiana's vote. In 1819, as Hammond remarked, many candidates for the assembly who initially favored revising the state constitution "totally changed sides" when they began to campaign among the people and realized how unpopular the proposal was. In practice it would seem true, as one newspaper writer said in 1819, that men of influence usually had less command over the votes of others than they often claimed, and under the pressure of Ohio's Bank War and the panic of 1819 elites found their political control well and truly challenged.[10]

Looking back, men were to regard the years following the second war against Britain as a golden age of political calm. Supreme Court Justice Humphrey Howe Leavitt, who had settled in 1816 as a young lawyer in Harrison County (formerly the western part of Jefferson County), recalled that in the next few years "there were literally no parties, and consequently no political turmoil [or] strife." This view is correct as regards conventional two-party conflict, but forgets how popular turmoil increased in these years, with voter turnouts after 1818 beginning to show a marked increase that would continue for a decade. Even the decline of party was itself a cause of controversy, as traditional regular Democrats in southeastern Ohio fought to resist the progress of Good Feelings.[11]

LEGITIMATE DEMOCRACY

Even after 1816, some faithful Republicans were determined to resist the insidious progress of Good Feelings. The group of strict Democrats at Zanesville, clustered round Isaac Van Horne, John Hamm, David Chambers, and the *Muskingum Messenger,* endeavored to preserve the authority of the old party and its traditional authority. As a result, opponents sometimes dubbed them the "Legitimates," in sarcastic reference to the monarchist restorations in Europe in 1814 and 1815. They were reinforced by experienced Democratic editor James Wilson at the Steubenville *Western Herald,* and by David Smith, who started the *Ohio Monitor* at Columbus in May 1816 with a view to making it "the democratic state paper" in resistance to the amalgamationist tendencies of other central Ohio newspapers.[12] Between them, these publicists tried to keep party sensitivities alive and began to erect an explicit justification for maintaining Democratic party organization even in the postwar glow of Good Feelings.

Their primary objective was to prevent the Federalists from regaining power. The war, the Legitimates believed, had demonstrated not only the disloyalty of the Federalists but also their preference for a country where "office and emolument is exclusively confined to a pampered nobility, clergy, and pensioners of the crown, who have . . . no reluctance at furnishing the crown liberally with the national resources." The best interests of the people, therefore, dictated that Federalists should be kept out of legislatures, where they had shown such skill in subverting true Republicanism. The danger was demonstrated when the Federalists managed to "smuggle a man into Congress" in

1816, for Philemon Beecher was elected in the fifth district with only 21 percent of the vote, in the face of seven Republican rivals. "No delegates were chosen to fix upon a candidate—no consultation of the people in one part of the district with those in other parts"—the names of ten candidates put before the people by one means or another—and the result, as the *Muskingum Messenger* bemoaned, "A federalist is chosen in a district in which three fourths of the people are republicans!"[13]

Even when the Federalists spoke honeyed words and ceased opposition, many Democrats distrusted them. As one Federalist pointed out in 1817, the Good Feelings obvious among the nationally prominent politicians were "distressing and odious to the subalterns" of the Democratic party: "At the same time that their principal leaders . . . seem inclined to a general armistice, *the third and fourth rate politicians* are as full of fight and fury as ever." In Steubenville, writers in the *Western Herald* could concede that "in these times . . . devotion to party is not the only test for office," but they still insisted that voters should trust only "a republican or a democrat at heart," who was attached to the rights of the people. Furthermore, Democratic editors warned there was no evidence that Federalists had sincerely given up their principles. As a young Zanesville lawyer, Appleton Downer, told his father in Connecticut in 1817, Federalists "are as bitter here as anywhere. . . . They all pretend to be republican and praise Mr. Monroe most outrageously. . . . It is all a trick."[14]

Even when there were no Federalist candidates in the field, the Legitimates and their friends advocated maintaining party organization, simply because delegate conventions ensured that elections accurately reflected the popular will. The *Muskingum Messenger* made much of the deficiency of the Ohio constitution in allowing candidates to be elected by a mere plurality, whereas "most of the States" required "a majority of the *whole number of votes* given." This defect opened the possibility that an unpopular candidate might be elected, and small selfish interests could even improve their own chances by deliberately multiplying the number of candidates. But this perversion of the electoral process could not happen if there was "*previous consultation* among the electors," which allowed all views to be considered so that "*the men best qualified*" may be named. Small meetings "in conclave" or "in private *caucus*" were not suitable for this purpose, since they were "rank aristocracy—rank dictation to the people." Delegate conventions were far superior because they held their appointment from the people and acted in public; according to the *Muskingum Messenger* in 1817, the "*Delegation Plan* . . . is the best and *only* method of ascertaining the wishes of the people," which was why usually "their constituents . . . have discernment enough to support the nomination." By focusing votes on the most generally acceptable character, delegate meetings helped to ensure that the successful candidate would secure the approbation of an absolute majority.[15]

In this way, delegate nominations ensured that elections were truly representative of the people at large. Increasingly, after 1816, Democrats accepted that conventions were now called less as party meetings than as representations of the community as a whole, although they could safely presume that most of the voters were Republicans. Such conventions allowed the people to choose the representatives and officials who were most committed to a disinterested protection of the general welfare, and party mechanisms served to promote the communal good of society. Thus the office-seeking proclivities of "the aspiring and ambitious demagogue" who pushed himself forward could be checked, and a more obscure, unassuming character unrelated to dominant cliques could be selected. After all, those "living at a distance from town" had as much right to be a candidate as any resident of the county seat. Finally, the system of delegate conventions prevented the "evils which ensue from the distraction of public sentiment at elections." If the representatives of the people met together to choose their candidates in advance of the election campaign, the general will would be known and the campaign would, accordingly, be less disruptive of communal peace. This emphasis on unanimity and "concord" shows not merely how far the advocates of permanent party organization had to accommodate to Good Feelings in the postwar years, but also the consensual assumptions that increasingly underlay their populistic rhetoric.[16]

Yet after 1815 the Legitimates found huge difficulties in persuading even those who advocated these partisan principles to accept party discipline in all circumstances. For example, problems arose because the people of the congressional district embracing both Zanesville and Steubenville divided over the proposed route of the National Road. A Zanesville congressman had been elected in 1812 and 1814, and President Madison had subsequently decided that the Road should strike the Ohio at Wheeling, on line for Zanesville, rather than at Steubenville—although some said the decision owed less to the Zanesville congressman's representations than to Henry Clay's susceptibility to the charms of a young lady in Wheeling whom he visited when traveling between Kentucky and Washington![17]

Infuriated by the decision, a delegate convention in Jefferson County in 1816 nominated John C. Wright of Steubenville to be the next congressman. However, as Hammond said, "Among the Legitimates of Zanesville (your masters) Herrick stands in the line of succession." As in 1812, a district delegate convention was called, which duly nominated Samuel Herrick—and party regulars in the northern counties promptly refused to accept the decision. James Wilson, at the Steubenville *Western Herald*, was embarrassed to explain why the formal mechanisms of the party were not to be obeyed on this occasion, and he resorted to the argument that the district convention had been unrepresentative and captured by a selfish interest group. Thus even party loyalists were divided by a sectional issue, and Steubenville Republicans dismissed "the legitimate denunciation against those who excite divisions" as a device to help Zanesville retain its hold on the congressional seat. In the end, the Legitimate Herrick won on a sectional vote: he received nearly 90 percent of the votes on the future route of the National Road, but less than 20 percent in the previously loyal Republican counties in the northern part of the district.[18]

This alienation of the Steubenville Democrats typified a growing division within the more extreme wing of the Republican party: the regulars and the democrats, who up to that point had been identified together, now had different priorities. Some of the more doctrinaire Democrats had come to feel that the national party was losing sight of its original principles and becoming a machine to help the few monopolize office and the advantages of power. This view was openly expressed by James Wilson, who, as editorial assistant to William Duane at the Philadelphia *Aurora*, had written the key editorial which had marked the emergence of the "Old School" faction among the Democrats of Pennsylvania, highly critical of men in power. While blasting away in the Steubenville *Western Herald* at the Federalists in 1815–16, he also began to criticize his own party's intention of nominating its next presidential candidate by means of a congressional caucus. Like Duane, Wilson believed that such a nomination was a usurpation of power by the few, partly because it gave control of the election to those in charge at Washington, but mainly because a proper and binding nomination could be made only by a set of delegates specifically chosen by the people for that task.[19]

Such a view caused deep misgivings among those Ohio Democrats who placed party regularity and party unity before all other considerations. Isaac Van Horne, as leader of the Zanesville Legitimates, complained to Wilson's main patron in Steubenville, Benjamin Tappan, that Wilson was taking a course "calculated, . . . not to consolidate & unite the Republicans, but to engender discord and disunion." Since the United States was ever divided into only two parties, "an attempt to divide the Republican party, if successful, must inevitably result in raising the Federal party into power." Hence the highest obligation was to support the congressional caucus nomination, if one were made. "The mode of nominating a candidate by the Republicans in Congress," Van Horne thought, "(if not the least exceptionable) [is] the least inconvenient to them as a party; and I may add, the most likely to meet the public sentiment—for if we should adopt the mode of sending delegates from each state for the express purpose, the inattention of some and the intrigues of others would be more likely to excite irritation & scism [*sic*], and consequently less liable to meet the public opinion."[20]

The event justified Van Horne's faith, for fears that the intriguers at Washington would nominate William H. Crawford of Georgia, or someone equally unpalatable, proved wrong. Those, like Wilson, who were prepared to rebel against the nomination if James Monroe were not named could not object to the result, and Wilson had to approve the nomination while regretting the means. The *Muskingum Messenger* acknowledged that many Republicans had "ever been opposed to congressional caucusses, from an idea that the interference of the legislative branch of government in the choice of President is improper and an infringement of the rights of the people. But . . . long before the congressional nomination, popular sentiment had emphatically designated Mr. Monroe as the next President; and it certainly cannot detract from the merit of this selection by the people that it has been confirmed by their representatives."[21]

In this controversy, Democratic critics were taking ground akin to that of the Federalists, who complained loudly about the congressional caucuses of 1812 and 1816. Admittedly, the Federalists objected to all nominations by extra-constitutional, partisan groups, and insisted that caucuses and conventions were essentially the same and equally objectionable. The "old school" Democrats accepted the rightfulness of party nominations, as long as they were decided in the open by properly elected delegates. But both challenged the established way of nominating presidents and insisted that control of elections must be given back to the people. Both sides could agree with Hammond's prediction in 1816 that "the caucus business is now in its last stage. I do not believe our next President will be nominated by a caucus."[22]

Party mechanisms may not have carried the authority they once enjoyed, but these regular Republicans were reluctant to give them up in their own county politics, especially as, on occasion, the voters responded favorably. In Muskingum County, for example, the resistance that the Legitimates experienced from "independent Republicans" in 1816 and 1817 persuaded them to drop the "Delegate plan" in 1818, although they still hoped to persuade local Republicans of "the necessity of early seeking a rallying point, to which all their movements shall be steadily directed." Their adjustment to popular opinion helped to reestablish their control, and in 1819 they summoned a full county meeting representing all the townships, but not through elected delegates. The meeting named a ticket to be supported "by all consistent democrats—by all those who have heretofore taken the delegate nominations for their guide," and secured the election of a leading Legitimate, Samuel Sullivan, by an overwhelming majority.[23] Similarly, in the congressional election of 1818, they had claimed—with justification—that the perennial Steubenville candidate, John C. Wright, was receiving support from Federalists all over the district, and so the Legitimates persuaded enough Republicans in the northern counties, especially in Coshocton County, to desert Wright and support the "Delegate" nominee, the incumbent Samuel Herrick. Coshocton's transfer from the Wright column gave Herrick his margin of victory in what the *Messenger* called "a triumph of *democratic republicanism* over a combination of Federalism, quidism [*sic*], apostasy and personal spite."[24]

Throughout the counties served by the Zanesville *Muskingum Messenger*, in fact, regular Democrats persistently resorted to properly elected delegate nominating conventions. From 1817 through 1819, the "Delegate plan" was adopted in a number of eastern counties, including Coshocton, Tuscarawas, and Guernsey. In 1818, according to the *Messenger*, "The Delegate Plan is this year practised in Belmont, Franklin, Washington, and several other counties in this state; and, we believe, very generally, in the state of Pennsylvania." In Licking County, too, "a delegate meeting" named a ticket that succeeded in electing five of its six nominees.

Indeed, in the counties of central Ohio, there was a strong incentive to call some sort of nominating meeting in 1818 in order to effect agreement on a Republican candidate to oppose the reelection of Beecher in the fifth congressional district. Republican meetings in Licking, Franklin, Delaware, and Champaign all named Joseph Vance, who had been identified in 1816 as "long . . . an inflexible Republican" and acceptable to party men. They expected his election "by a great majority"—if "the delusive song of '[no]-partyism' has not lulled the democrats asleep." Party slang grew so bitter that it resulted in challenges to a duel between William Doherty and Thomas Ewing, Beecher's law partner and protégé. Vance won clear majorities in most counties, but could not withstand the overwhelming popularity of Beecher in his home county of Fairfield, the most populous in the district.[25]

Where such efforts to preserve party regularity persisted, there was a tendency to force opponents of all political shades into some sort of "amalgamation." In 1818 conservative Republicans in Urbana and Dayton organized for the Federalist Beecher, in order to offset the efforts of party regulars in other parts of the district. In the fourth congressional district, John C. Wright had failed to attract Federalist support in the southern counties in 1816 because he had branded himself by initially entering the delegate convention nominating process. In 1818, however, the efforts of the Legitimates to secure Samuel Herrick's reelection forced Federalists and Republican dissidents into a "new combination" supporting Wright, thus transforming him into something more than a sectional candidate representing Steubenville. In 1820, when the Legitimates nominated the former editor of the *Messenger,* David Chambers, to succeed Herrick, their opponents, Federalist and Republican, held a joint caucus with representatives from each county to decide on a single candidate to oppose him. These short-term coalitions could, as in Guernsey County, mark the beginnings of a cooperation that would lead to a new party division in the 1820s, but more immediately they reflected the widespread antagonism to those who would keep old party differences alive.[26]

The location and strength of old-party resistance to Good Feelings may be measured by James Wilson's analysis of the state's political press in June 1818. Out of twenty-seven newspapers, only six, he thought, "avow and support democratic principles": David Smith's *Ohio Monitor* at the state capital, and five presses in eastern Ohio south of the Western Reserve. Yet the *Monitor* doubted whether three of those five were genuinely Democratic, and in any case all except the *Western Herald* and *Muskingum Messenger* faced financial difficulties. So, too, did the *Ohio Monitor* when Smith lost the state printing in 1819. Of the other twenty-one newspapers, according to Wilson, many were "anything or nothing, some singing Lullaby, and others up for sale! What a falling off."[27]

As a consequence of "Lullaby," editors who were opening new presses or taking over old newspapers no longer bothered to make a profession of their political faith. As the editors of the new *Cleaveland Herald* wrote in 1819, they were no less attached than others to the present national government, no less committed to the principles of "the equal rights of man, the supremacy of the people, an attachment to our common country, and a cordial friendship for our republican institutions." But "an acknowledgement of their correctness is only echoing the general voice of the American people. All parties make the same profession, all subscribe to the same fundamental principles of civil liberty; and a minute detail of the maxims by which we shall be governed . . . would be wasting the time of the reader." Such statements implied, as the Steubenville *Western Herald* warned in 1818, that the "union of two parties" could result in "principles of all kinds [being] amalgamated in what Dr. Johnson calls 'a porridge of politics.' "[28] This collapse in political morality suggested that the good old Republican party was quietly passing away—or was it bleeding to death from internal hemorrhages?

SCHISM, ARISTOCRACY, AND BANKS

The decline of traditional party feeling, apparently inexorable even in the face of "legitimist" resistance, resulted not merely from the disappearance of the old partisan issues. For the decade after 1810 also saw both the exacerbation of long-disruptive influences and the emergence of new issues that divided the Republican majority along new lines, and the Federalists, too. Together these forces operated not merely to disrupt local and state parties; they also caused great disillusionment with national politicians and prompted even some strict party men to think about politics in novel ways and unconventional categories.

Essentially the old political yardsticks were being overwhelmed by the rapid development of Ohio, especially after the military victories of 1813. The 1810 Census had astonished Ohioans when it revealed that they had gained an "unparalleled population of 227,843 inhabitants in so short a period." If the war interrupted that process, by the end of 1813 Niles could report that already "a mighty population is pouring into Ohio, since the capture and dispersion of the allied savages." In the years that followed "the tide of emigration set . . . strongly westward," and the population was to double in the course of the decade. Interior and outlying areas began to fill and so reduced the significance of the older centers: by the 1810s, more than half the people lived in interior counties, distant from the influence of Cincinnati, Chillicothe, and other major centers, even though urban areas were growing slightly more rapidly than the remainder of this overwhelmingly rural state.[29] If anything, isolated and self-sufficient frontier settlements increased, even as population growth reduced isolation in older areas; and many homogeneous communities—notably of New Englanders, Quakers, and Germans—experienced some settlement by people of different backgrounds, if not within their midst, then close at hand and rubbing shoulders. As society became more complex, so political relationships became more complicated and the old Democratic Republican party found itself ripped apart.

Various dissensions within the dominant party had their roots in ethno-cultural tensions that party feeling had for the most part managed to contain before 1812. In July 1817 one observer in Cincinnati saw society becoming divided and "the people too clanish [sic]"; he perceived a "general spirit of distinction . . . building up wide walls and partitions between the Philadelphian, the New-Englander, the Kentuckian and the Southernman." New Englanders were considered especially standoffish, and in Columbus "A Yankee Tavern" opened in 1818 specifically to cater to their needs and those of their representatives. New Englanders and Pennsylvania Dutch especially despised each other; one young emigrant from Connecticut commented in 1816 on how the Dutch in Pennsylvania "cordially hate what they call the Yankees, and the moment they see one, they bristle up like a cat when she sees a dog approaching her." Unprejudiced himself, of course, he noticed "how little these people are raised above the brutes." Such strains made ticket building a difficult matter for party organizers, and one proponent of delegate conventions thought them the only way of forming the "closest political union between the New-Englander, the Dutchman, the Kentuckian and others."[30]

The most conspicuous signs of ethnic political fallout occurred in eastern

Ohio. In 1816, New Englanders of the Western Reserve contested the sixth congressional district with the more culturally variegated but equally Republican groups from Pennsylvania who were settling across the backbone of the state immediately south of the Reserve. The Dutch in that area commonly proved apathetic about politics and voting, but when a Stark County representative, John Harris, voted against making the state laws available in German, they flooded to the polls in 1816 to defeat this fellow Republican.[31] Recent immigrants represented a further difficulty: although not allowed to vote under the 1809 Act, in some areas of eastern Ohio township officers had customarily allowed them to do so. However, factional disputes could lead to judges of election suddenly refusing their votes, as in Jefferson County in 1816, and consternation intensified when the state supreme court, manned by Republicans, upheld the verdict in Steubenville in 1817. Such disputes confirmed the tendency of Irish immigrants to support local dissident movements, as in Zanesville, although by 1820 they were becoming divided between Catholic and Protestant as the *Express* sought to exploit their religious antagonisms.[32]

Postwar elections more obviously involved the strain of social discontent that Federalists had endeavored to exploit during the war. Many ordinary people simply felt that the same men had held power too long and were growing fat on the public purse. This prejudice underlay the explosion over Congress's Compensation Act of 1816, when the agitation initiated by Federalist pressmen was soon taken over by a host of primarily Democratic editors and politicians. This measure aroused more popular concern in 1816 than either the major legislative enactments of this Congress or the presidential election. On the Western Reserve "there was much excitement," and appropriate songs passed around:

> O, would you hear what roaring cheer
> They had at Uncle Sam's Congress, O;
> How they gabbled so gay as they doubled their pay,
> And doubled the people's taxes, O.

Regular politicians agreed the law must be repealed, but did not see this as a reason for voting against any incumbent Republican. Many incumbents, however, including John McLean, recognized that a vote for the Compensation Act was an obstacle to election success or political influence in the immediate future, as candidates throughout Ohio were called upon for—and gave—pledges to repeal the law. Ohio was one of the states in which not one incumbent congressman was reelected.[33]

These social and political tensions which so threatened to overwhelm traditional party lines were seriously exacerbated by the floods of depreciating paper money issued by the growing number of banks. In the immediate postwar years, banking expanded hugely and an "almost universal spirit of speculation . . . prevailed." According to the Methodist preacher James B. Finley,

> A money mania seemed to have seized, like an epidemic, the entire people. Every body went to banking. Within the bounds of our circuit [made up of three eastern counties] there were no less than nine banking establishments, seven of them within the county of Jefferson, and one of them said to have been kept in a lady's chest. All were engaged in issuing paper, while every incorporated town, village or company went to work issuing notes. But it did not stop here. Tavern-keepers, merchants, butchers, bakers—every body seemed to have become bankers.[34]

Leading Republicans were prominent among the directors of these banks, and the Republican press showed little evidence of antibank sentiment before late 1815. Some proposed taxes on bank stock, but prominent men were reluctant to do anything that might deter inward investment.[35] However, even during the war some legislators opposed the creation of "a dangerous monopolizing aristocracy" through the chartering of banks, and such sentiments became more widespread as shinplasters flooded the state and unchartered banks issued their own paper trash. Newspapers around the state began to condemn banking as a device whereby a man could make loans at a profitable rate of interest, pay off his debts without laying out a cent of real money, and preserve his own capital while refusing to redeem the notes he had put into circulation. Such a situation inevitably created a considerable difference of opinion within the Democratic Republican party, and the establishment of a new bank in Steubenville played some role in causing a breach among the Republicans of Jefferson County that resulted in rival Democratic tickets competing at the polls in 1815.[36]

Attitudes toward banking were, in truth, confused and far from polarized as yet. Some opponents of expansion, like Alfred Kelley, wished to refuse further charters—in order, it was suspected, to spare existing banks from competition in a lucrative business. Charles Hammond was more critical of existing banks but favored chartering some new banks, since his main concern was the creation of a sufficient, sound, and properly regulated banking system in place of the rash of unchartered and inadequately based institutions that plagued Ohio. Both elements could agree on the "bonus law" that Hammond drafted and a Republican legislature passed in February 1816: this measure incorporated twelve new banks, extended all bank charters to 1843, prohibited all others from banking functions, and guaranteed the state an income from bank profits. This constructive approach aimed to weaken the ranks of the unchartered and pro-vide chartered banks where they could satisfy genuine needs, although the measure scarcely ensured effective suppression of the unchartered banks.[37]

The opponents of regulation were equally divided. Some were "enemies of banking establishments of all kinds" and did not wish to see the state counte-nance and so to some extent underwrite them. Others wanted to see unlimited banking and used the Democratic rhetoric of "equal rights" to justify their antimonopoly attitude: "Why should one class of the community be debarred from privileges granted to others?" Bray Hammond has associated hostility toward established banks in the Jackson period with the selfish ambitions of rival entrepreneurs; in Ohio there is more evidence for that view in the debates of the 1810s than can be found twenty years later.[38]

The forces favoring banking expansion rapidly overwhelmed the attempt at regulation. Still more banks were chartered, although within the terms of Ham-mond's bonus law, and by 1817 the number had reached twenty-one. This rapid expansion was not solidly based, especially as banks often made loans to their own directors to help them pay in their stock! Paper money began to submerge some parts of the state, and the discount in Philadelphia on Ohio banknotes rose to 15 percent for authorized banks and 25 percent for unchartered banks. However, the resumption of specie payments in spring 1817 improved the credit of the banks and forced them to be more conservative in their note issues. John C. Wright, returning from his eastern trip in 1817, observed that although there was none of the destitution seen in the seaboard states, times were hard in Ohio, "for *money* is so scarce, & the little circulating medium we have is such vile & worthless trash, that it seems almost impossible to transact any business in the Country." As a result, the general assembly was crowded with yet more applica-tions for banking charters, and "the majority in the house is very large in favor of chartering banking companies." Contemplating the great paper money rage and speculative fever in the Northwest in 1818, the British traveler James Flint decided that state legislatures were imposing an excessive number of banks on the people because so many of the legislators were themselves directly interested in banking concerns.[39]

Even before the crash of November 1818, a popular reaction had set in, especially in counties flooded with shinplasters. The press increasingly crit-icized banks as swindling institutions that impoverished farmers and threat-ened a financial and commercial collapse. Even in Muskingum County, the formerly pro-bank *Messenger* had opened its columns to bank critics by the summer of 1817, but could not prevent the "independent republicans" from linking the abuses of banking monopolies with the political control of party regulars. Candidates were questioned about their views on banking and "exclusive privileges," and the issue may have helped the independent ticket to succeed in that election. In any case, by 1818 the *Messenger* had changed its tune and now insisted that the root of Ohio's problems lay in the swindling institutions that obscured "the difference between *rags* and *money!*" Such issues influenced elections in other parts of the state, too: in Cincinnati, for example, one Republican candidate in the congressional elections of 1818 was bitterly attacked for operating an unchartered bank and so contributing to the considerable overissue of banknotes in the area.[40]

Evidently, even before the crash, as Hammond himself said in 1818, the leading issues of the day divided men in both parties. Republicans recognized this and saw the difficulty of ensuring that men in power would indeed pursue policies that their constituents considered "republican." In the congressional elections of 1818, one politician argued in favor of electing "a genuine republican, who will not be induced to support any party or measure unless it is grounded on principle." He thought it "too much the fashion of the present day to determine on a man's principles by his attachment to certain political parties—in this way every thing may pass for republicanism and principles be lost sight of entirely." He thought it "obvious to every one that what is now called [the] republican party has got so great a majority that if every thing done by it is called republican measures, let it partake of republican principles or not, there is great danger of abuses by men in power." This argument, hostile to partisan discipline, was all the more significant for coming from a Democrat, John Sloane, who had previously been firmly aligned with the more radical and partisan section of his party.[41] Clearly, the leading issues of the day divided opinion along lines that did not match the division between Federalist and Republican, even before the great crisis of 1819–21.

A MATTER OF STATE PRIDE

By 1819 the sense that something was amiss, that the Republican party was in some way going astray, was not only pervasive; it was changing—and sharpening—its focus. Evils at the local level were overshadowed by menaces from outside, and it became a commonplace that the majority in Congress could no longer be trusted to pursue genuine Republican policies or honor the original purposes of the republic. This sentiment came to a head in 1819–21 with Ohio's Bank War and the Missouri controversy, which saw Ohioans close their ranks in an unprecedented display of unity and so made old party divisions quite irrelevant.

Initially, the national bank was not a major issue in Ohio. The rechartering of the first Bank of the United States in 1811 had been opposed largely because of traditional Republican party ideology, and both senators had voted decisively against renewal. During the war, however, most of Ohio's public men recognized the need for a national bank to sustain public credit and improve the means of exchange, and the state's congressional delegation, with some misgivings, uniformly supported the various bank measures proposed. Several of them had strong reservations about the "Mammoth Bank Bill" of 1816, however, and the delegation divided on its final passage.[42] There was little hostile reaction at home, since initially (as Jacob Burnet later recalled) prejudice against the institution in Ohio was "neither general nor strong." Many hoped that a strong national bank would speed up the postwar resumption of specie payments and constructively supplement (and even control) the state's banking facilities. Several towns competed to have branches established in their midst, although, after a struggle reminiscent of statehood, only Chillicothe and Cincinnati succeeded.[43]

Actual experience of the Bank's blessings made even strong supporters change their minds. The Second Bank of the United States was more loosely managed and more irresponsible in its note issues than most local banks, but it was underwritten by the U.S. Treasury's willingness to accept its notes in payment of land sales and government dues. According to Burnet, the branch president, the Cincinnati directors tried to pursue sensible policies but were required to accept dubious local paper money paid into the local land office. The policy of the parent bank forced them to loan out that paper locally, thus underwriting excessive issues of paper money by the smaller banks in and around Cincinnati and so fueling a speculative overexpansion in the region. Then, in the summer of 1818, the parent bank ordered the Cincinnati branch to curtail drastically and placed restrictions on the kinds of notes (including some of its own) that it would accept in settlement of debts. The result was the banking collapse of November 1818 in Cincinnati, followed by the land office's decision to accept only specie and national bank notes in payment for land— which, in effect, stopped public land sales. Local banks in other parts of the state, finding their specie drained, in self-protection suspended specie payments and called in loans. Not unnaturally, their necessities were blamed on the Bank of the United States, and local bankers and those hostile to all banks joined in attacking the main villain of the piece.[44]

Some critics maintained that the state bankers were trying to divert popular hostility from themselves. If so, they scarcely succeeded. Paper money collapsed in value, business ground to a halt, forced sales of property became a common sight—and cries arose for positive action against local banks and bankers. Public meetings threatened to invade banks and unlock the specie they refused to pay out in return for their depreciated notes; local people signed forms of agreements refusing to accept notes issued by defaulting banks; and when State Treasurer Samuel Sullivan announced in July 1820 that taxes must be paid in specie, at least one public meeting declared that taxes would not be paid at all unless the local banks resumed specie payments. By the elections of 1819 and 1820, nominating meetings were resolving—like one township meeting of "farmers" in Muskingum County—that "we will not vote for any person to fill any office of honor, profit or trust, who has, or has had any connexion as president, cashier or director, of any bank, or who countenances the banking system." The protesters wanted laws to prevent bankers from buying up their own notes at depreciated values, to compel specie payments, and to repeal the charters of defaulting banks.[45]

The problem was that the legislature could do little about the local banks at that moment without reducing the currency, embarrassing businessmen, and deflating the economy even more. State bankers may have been blaming the Bank for a disaster of their own making, and yet it was a reasonable target. Its operations had become unduly oppressive, as it deprived the local banks of the specie reserves upon which their note issues depended; as John McLean said, no individual bank could "withstand a hostile policy" from the Bank. The sight of wagonloads of specie being hauled eastward to Philadelphia in 1819 was bound to infuriate Ohio public opinion, even if the root cause was the imbalance of federal receipts and expenditures within the state. Inevitably, the Bank appeared to be a gigantic swindle designed to take money from Ohioans for the benefit of an eastern aristocracy of "brokers, shavers and speculators." According to the *Ohio Monitor,* "Under the pretence of a bank, they have organized a banditti, to strip and insult us." After the banking collapse of November 1818, popular hatred of exploitation by a privileged aristocracy turned naturally against eastern monied men who added to their sins the constitutional crime of destroying Ohio's ability to manage its own internal affairs.[46]

There was one obvious way of preventing the Bank from gaining control of all financial operations in Ohio, destroying the local banks, and subjecting the state to monetarist policies decided in Philadelphia: bring the Bank's branches in Ohio under the system of control that had been worked out for the state's private banks. By imposing a tax on the branches, the state would not only secure a revenue but also destroy the branches' unfair advantages over the state banks, thus perhaps inducing the closure of the branches by the parent bank. Hence the law passed in February 1819 to tax the Bank was in no way a defiance of the federal government or its legislation. The general assembly simply operated on the assumption that Congress could not deprive a state of its power to tax and that no bank should be exempted from the taxation that its competitors had to bear. Nor did the Supreme Court's decision in *McCulloch v. Maryland* the following month affect the issue: if the Supreme Court had declared that states could not tax the Bank of the United States, clearly it had not reviewed a case as compelling as that of Ohio; and the sovereign state had a perfect right to pass a law, enforce collection of the tax, and then wait to be heard in its own right. This was not "nullification," since the Bank was not an agency of the federal government, nor was it under the government's control or responsible to it; it was a private commercial institution, a "Band of Brokers" to be treated as a "natural individual citizen," and the controversy was one "between a non tax payer and a publick officer who distrains property on the refusal to pay."[47]

This standpoint had already brought together state bankers fearful of oppression by the Bank, antibankers hostile to paper money and privileged institutions, and those devoted to states' rights and strict construction of the Constitution. From the beginning of serious discussion in December 1817, the Bank's friends were a minority in the Ohio house, though not in the state senate, and thanks to the Bank's deflationary measures during the summer, most of those were weeded out in the elections of 1818, which were virtually a plebiscite on the issue. As the Steubenville *Western Herald* reported, "Those members of the last assembly who were suspected of being friendly to the U.S. bank have been dismissed from the confidence of the people." The whole delegation from Ross County, including directors of the Chillicothe branch bank such as Duncan McArthur, had been defeated, while "the gentlemen elected to the legislature are known to be pointedly inimical to that institution."[48]

The outpouring of popular vitriol against banks in 1818 resulted in an assertion of popular control over state representatives. Public meetings and delegate conventions insisted on tying the hands of those they elected: many representatives arrived in Columbus under strict instructions from their constituents to vote against the Bank, and some complained that they had no instructions on how to vote on other matters of dispute in the assembly![49] One consequence, therefore, of Ohio's Bank War was that candidates became more concerned than ever with adjusting their views to those of the voters. This was a lesson that pro-Bank politicians learned to their cost.

Thomas Worthington concluded his governorship in December 1818 by both advocating an expansion of banking facilities to meet the financial crisis and opposing taxation of the Bank branches. Two months later he was defeated for the Senate by a political nonentity, William Trimble ("a Nice young man but two [*sic*] much of a Boy"), and consigned to the political wilderness for the next three years. As Secretary of the Treasury William H. Crawford observed, Worthington had "fallen victim to the paroxysm which has convulsed the western country in relation to the U.S.B."[50] His successor as governor was Ethan Allen Brown, another Tammany man but from Cincinnati and since 1810 a state supreme court judge. Although previously considered by Hammond "the negative kind of character that gives no offence," Brown came out strongly on banking questions. As governor, he consistently opposed any extension of bank and paper credit and steadfastly supported the state's action in the forthcoming trial of strength with the Bank of the United States.[51]

The "crowbar law," imposing an annual tax of $50,000 on each branch of the Bank in Ohio, passed in February 1819 with only three dissident votes in the house. When state officials entered and seized money in the Chillicothe branch, "no paper in the state . . . said anything in condemnation but the *Cincinnati Inquisitor* and the *Muskingum Messenger,*" the one of "little influence" and the other "actuated by personal pique."[52] The state's action was once more the issue in the elections of 1819 and resulted in the election to the house of "a large majority of anti-Bankites." In many counties, delegate conventions met to ensure a clear agreement on explicit anti-Bank candidates, and those named had to announce their convictions and accept instructions to vote for firm action against the Bank. In Ross County the successful candidates issued a "Declaration of Independence against the United States Bank," while in Muskingum the anti-Bank candidate for the state senate defeated the pro-Bank candidate by a 7:3 margin.[53]

But it was Cincinnati and its vicinity that felt the consequences of the Bank's behavior most critically. As Harrison's son-in-law reported in November 1818, "This place & all the country round are almost in a state of mutiny and insurrection in consequence of the Banks shutting up their vaults." The fall elections of 1818 had seen the defeat of candidates too closely connected with banking, and only those hostile to the Bank could hope to be elected. When the eminent Harrison was himself nominated for state senator by the county convention in 1819, the Cincinnati delegates objected because he was a director of the Cincinnati branch and an earlier opponent of taxing the Bank. A public meeting in the city attended by over a thousand voters made a rival nomination of a known opponent of banking, James Gazlay, justifying its action as the expression of the rights of "the laboring and industrious classes" against "aristocratic power." Harrison had to take a firm anti-Bank stance in order to win an election that demonstrated how insecure was the business elite's control in the city.[54]

In the legislature, Harrison preached compromise and argued against insisting on a right that the Supreme Court, however questionably, had found unconstitutional. But then the "mammoth Bank . . . required the poor Devils at Cincinnati to renew their notes and pay the reductions and discounts at Chillicothe [*sic*]" and, when they demurred, put "the whole debts in suit." This news reached Columbus "opportunely to brace [Harrison's] resolution" just as he was about to question further the state's course of action. In any case, with an election to the Senate coming up, keen observers felt "Gen. H. will hardly *venture* upon open hos[t]ility" to the state's policy "so long as he is reaching for the senatorial tid bit." His association with an unpopular interest was enough to ensure his defeat, and the triumph of "radical" elements in Cincinnati and Hamilton County in the early 1820s destroyed—for the time being—the home base of what had seemed a distinguished political career of great potentiality.[55]

Harrison's failure—like the eclipse of Worthington—was a symptom of a growing popular discontent with politicians as a whole and with the professional classes that provided most representatives and officeholders. To many, it appeared that the professional classes too often benefited from special privileges supported by the law; lawyers in particular seemed increasingly to dominate legislatures and pass laws that created business for them—especially as they enjoyed the fees collected from the increased litigation consequent upon the crash. In 1819 James Wilson had blamed the failure of the proposal for a new constitutional convention partly on the general supposition that it was "a manoeuvre on the part of the lawyers to make a *splendid judiciary*." In 1820, one newspaper correspondent in Cuyahoga County opposed two prominent candidates on the grounds that they were lawyers, and lawyers, by definition, did not understand the needs of the community. Instead, he proposed a substantial farmer—"that class who are the very vitals of the commonwealth"—who, of course, won handsomely. Politicians were assumed to be growing rich off the people's taxes and the bribes of bankers whose charters they enacted. Such suspicions inevitably attached primarily to men in office, who, by definition, were Republicans.[56]

Throughout these disputes, prominent Federalists were openly aligned behind the state's radical stance in hostility to the Bank—even though support for a national bank was originally one of the touchstones of Federalism. From the start, Hammond objected to the excessive power that the Second Bank had over the state banks, fearing that "all our best interests" were now placed "at the mercy of Stockjobbers and Brokers, mostly foreign agents, without morals or social feelings of any kind whatever which can induce them to assimilate with us." An early advocate of taxing the branches, Hammond disapproved of the Supreme Court's decision in *McCulloch v. Maryland*. Confessing himself "too much a state sovereignty man at present" to accept the Court's current claims to review decisions of state supreme courts, he became Ohio's most effective spokesman on the constitutional issue, even writing articles for his old enemy at the Steubenville *Western Herald* as well as for major Republican newspapers in Baltimore and Washington.[57]

Hammond was frequently consulted by Governor Brown, and he wrote the "masterly and convincing" committee report on the Bank case that the general assembly adopted by overwhelming majorities in January 1821. There was little discussion on the report and its proposals, since there was no need "to effect a change in the public sentiment," and even Hammond's proposal to withdraw the protection of Ohio's laws from the Bank of the United States passed by substantial majorities. Throughout this session Hammond was, in effect, leader of the house, critically examining every proposition. As one member later recalled, "His influence with the members was very considerable and was dependent on his integrity and intelligence solely, as there existed no party organization at that time in the Legislature."[58] Most significantly, leaders of the Virginia states' rights school wrote Hammond expressing their approval of his constitutional arguments—not only Thomas Ritchie and John Taylor of Caroline, but also his venerable former bête noire, Thomas Jefferson.[59]

Other Federalists took a similar stand. Congressman Beecher thought the tax imposed on the branches excessive, but he wished to see it enforced in order to contest to the full the constitutional pretensions of the Bank men. The states, he thought, must provide a constitutional remedy "before the monster shall have bound the nation to the car of a monied aristocracy." Jacob Burnet presided over the Cincinnati branch but disapproved of the mother bank's policy, which he found publicly and personally disastrous. A conspicuous sufferer from the crash, Burnet appreciated the plight of the small farmers who were buying federal land on credit. He devised a scheme to save their lands, canvassed support for it throughout the West, and saw it pass into law as the federal Relief Act of 1821. In July 1821 Burnet was appointed pro tem to the state supreme court by Governor Brown, who acknowledged that "the appointment may not be pleasing to some *exclusive* republicans, who may surmise that I am therefore becoming federalist," but pointed out that the legally accomplished Burnet "professes to entertain similar views with my own in regard to 'the vital consequences to the nation . . . of the subject of federal judicial supremacy.' "[60]

In the assembly the next winter, supporters of rival claimants tried "to engender the spirit of party" and "made a Tammany jab" against Burnet, but this "effort to excite old party feelings" offended "the good sense of the House," which "rejected the effort to create, or revive, the[se] distinctions." Burnet's appointment was overwhelmingly confirmed by a Republican legislature impressed by the virtues of some Federalists.[61] Ohio's Bank War had created a sense of internal unity that helped to override old party feelings—and so reinforced Ohio's growing sense of sectional distinctiveness.

THE MOST FEARFUL CRISIS

The years between 1819 and 1821 generated new political pressures because of the combination of two major crises affecting the whole country. The Missouri crisis split the nation asunder for a moment and created a conscious division between North and South. Simultaneously, the panic of 1819 and the subsequent depression had a double impact. In the short term, social tensions came to a head and caused political turmoil in many localities, but did not impinge directly on national political attitudes. In the longer term, however, economic distress bred a demand in the West for national policies capable of improving economic conditions. When this solution was resisted by older states, a strong sense of resentment developed in the Northwest, which now looked forward to the time when its growing strength would allow it, and its allies in the Middle Atlantic states, to impose these policies on the national government. These twin crises, coming on top of the Bank War, generated in Ohio a sense of being distinctly western and distinctly northern, which divided the state from the Republicans in other states with whom a majority of Ohioans had previously acted in national politics.

By 1819 a decade of commercial restriction, war, and then floods of British imports had persuaded most vocal Ohioans of the need to create a strong internal market by adopting a policy of high protective tariffs. At the same time they also appreciated their need for federal assistance to improve communications within the state and with the eastern seaboard. All over Ohio, by 1818–19, public meetings, newspaper correspondents, agricultural societies, congressional candidates, and the general assembly were resolving that national independence, moral and social health, and economic recovery depended on adopting a policy of high protective tariffs and federally financed internal improvements.[62]

Then, in 1820, Congress rejected the tariff increases proposed by Henry Baldwin of Pittsburgh, thanks to the hostility of a suspicious South and the commercial interests of New England. At the same time, Ohio requested the federal government to sell it, on easy credit terms, some of the millions of acres recently purchased from the Indians of northwestern Ohio, in order to help the state build canals to link the Ohio River with Lake Erie. The Senate rejected the proposal on the grounds that a state should never become the debtor of the federal government. Similarly, Congress showed no signs of granting money to build the long-promised National Road west of Wheeling, Virginia, although it did authorize the location of the route across Ohio.[63]

Ohio's representatives blamed Congress's obstructions upon, in John W. Campbell's words, the "astonishing . . . jealousy" with which "the Western interests are viewed by many" in Washington. Governor Brown was infuriated by "this disposition in the East and South to impede our improvement: it tends to weaken the affection of the people N.W. of the River Ohio, whose strength is growing too mighty to be treated with contempt." The census of 1820 revealed that Ohio's population had increased by one-quarter of a million since 1810, reaching 581,434. This would give the state, in the reapportionment of 1822, fourteen congressmen and sixteen electoral college votes—fewer only than New York, Pennsylvania, and Virginia. If experience suggested that national politics had become, at bottom, a struggle for sectional advantage, then Ohio politicians would use their new political strength to override the selfishness of the eastern seaboard and gain some satisfaction from Washington.[64]

This growing sense of sectional distinctiveness was further crystallized by the controversy that arose when Missouri applied for admission to the Union as a slave state. Antislavery sentiment—in the limited sense of believing that slavery was an evil institution—had been powerful in Ohio since before statehood. Ephraim Brown, a New Hampshire–born farmer in Trumbull County, remarked in 1807 that he had been "taught from my cradle to despise Slavery and will never forget to teach my children . . . the same lesson." In Marietta, the *Western Spectator* ran, during 1811–12, a long series of bitterly antislavery articles written specially for it. The abolitionist sentiments of the Quakers produced the Union Humane Society, organized in eastern Ohio in 1816 by Charles Osborn and Benjamin Lundy. Aiming to build nonsectarian support, the society openly denounced slavery, advocated gradual emancipation, agitated for the repeal of the state's black laws, and opposed schemes for colonizing free blacks abroad.[65] Similarly, some of the more evangelical congregations in the state voiced vigorous antislavery sentiments, most notably the evangelical Presbyterians in some southwestern river counties. So widespread was this antislavery feeling that the call for a state constitutional convention in 1819 was defeated in the referendum primarily because of popular fears of a plot to introduce slavery into Ohio. These suspicions were thought "groundless," because "the aversion to slavery [in Ohio] is deeprooted and universal. If there should be some individuals who would wish to introduce a slave population among us, . . . the bare suggestion of the idea would forever ruin their influence."[66]

Yet Ohioans also recognized that they could do little about the existence of slavery in the southern states. They accommodated to its existence by allowing slave owners to bring their slaves with them while visiting the state, and their newspapers, even on the Western Reserve, printed fugitive slave advertisements.[67] At the same time Ohioans quietly appreciated that slavery prevented the mass migration of Negroes into their own state, and the Black Law of 1807 had been designed to discourage free black immigration. When, in 1819, about three hundred slaves in Virginia belonging to an Englishman, Samuel Gist, were freed and settled in Brown County, in southwestern Ohio, there were voluble protests locally against the introduction of a "depraved and ignorant . . . set of people," and although they received some charitable assistance from the Quakers, these black settlers were ostracized and even persecuted by their neighbors.[68]

In view of such common attitudes, Ohio's representatives had not shown
the highest concern or unity of view when Missouri's application for statehood
first came before Congress in the 1818–19 session. The whole Ohio delegation,
with one exception, voted in favor of the first proposal of the Tallmadge amendment—that no more slaves should be introduced into Missouri. But the delegation split down the middle in both houses on the second part of the Tallmadge
amendment. Three out of six congressmen, together with Harrison in the
Senate, voted to confine in chains the slaves already in Missouri and to allow the
movement of slaves into the new Arkansas Territory.[69]

But then the prospect of slavery expanding into the territories of the Louisiana Purchase roused public opinion back home in 1819 and 1820 as no one had
anticipated—and more than some historians have allowed. The *Cleaveland
Herald* believed that no question agitated in Congress had "excited more interest and anxiety, in the minds of the people of the United States, we believe, . . .
since the formation of the Federal Constitution—in the ultimate result of
which, depends our national character as acknowledging and guaranteeing
universal, civil and religious freedom to all mankind." Public meetings were
held, notably in Cincinnati and in the eastern counties, that petitioned Congress and instructed congressmen to prevent slavery from spreading across the
Mississippi. Thomas Ewing urged Philemon Beecher—his law partner, patron,
and congressman—to take a firmer antislavery line than he had in the previous
session: if he could conscientiously oppose the admission of Missouri, "an
appropriate and spirited speech from you on that subject would do much for
you with the people—the question with regard to our own constitution aroused
them, and no detail of the question will now pass them unheeded."[70]

Active and responsible politicians saw great complexities and greater menaces in the situation. Fearing disunion, some members of the general assembly
and some representatives in Washington advocated allowing the retention of
slavery as long as no more slaves were introduced. According to later reports,
the Ohio delegation privately favored Henry Clay's compromise, although instructions from their constituents prevented them from voting for Missouri's
admission as a slave state. They all supported the Thomas amendment prohibiting slavery north of 36°30', and Senator Trimble even tried to get the prohibition extended to all lands yet to be organized in the West. In marked contrast
with the previous session, the Ohio delegation voted as a bloc to remove slavery
from Missouri and restrict it elsewhere in the West as far as possible.[71]

At home, the delegation won praise for its faithfulness to its constituents'
views—as Benjamin Tappan said, "not one *dough faced traitor* amongst them"—
but many people were horrified by the South's triumph in extending slavery.
Some newspapers in eastern Ohio now refused to print fugitive slave advertise-

ments, and on the Western Reserve a Virginian who recaptured two runaway slaves was himself arrested and found guilty of kidnapping. Congressional candidates were questioned to ensure that they were of sound sentiments, and one especially outspoken correspondent in the Marietta Republican newspaper demanded "a pledge from every candidate who would receive the public suffrage; that however *modified*, however *disguised*, however *coupled*—that slavery shall be prohibited from extending its desolating and debasing current beyond the limits of the old states."[72]

Yet, among some Republicans, there persisted a heightened sense of the need to end the controversy and restore sectional harmony. Harrison greatly feared that northern interference with the rights of the slave states would "produce a state of discord and jealousy that will, in the end, prove fatal to the UNION." In this spirit, newspapers in Cincinnati, Chillicothe, and Zanesville refused to stop publishing fugitive advertisements: they wished to restore good relations with the South and to discourage settlement by blacks—"nuisances to society, destroying our peace and quiet, as is frequently the case in this part of the state."[73] The same newspapers also felt that the Missouri question had become "a political poney to ride into Congress on." John Bailhache, editor of the Chillicothe *Scioto Gazette*, condemned "the attempts now making to excite the feelings of the people, in the northern and middle States." He not only suspected them to be maneuvers by a Federalist party that was trying to restore its fortunes, but thought them "misguided" at a time when the nation needed moderation. To this end the *Muskingum Messenger* preached the need to adhere to the old Democratic Republican party, since parties of some kind were inevitable in a republic and, as the Cleveland paper said, "No parties are so dangerous to the Union . . . as geographical ones."[74]

The newspapers that advanced such conciliatory arguments soon found themselves branded by local rivals as advocates for slavery. At Steubenville, James Wilson—whose columns during the crisis had shown him fearful for the Union and the Republican party, and hence not averse to compromise—was swept along by the embittered antislavery tide among his readers: his sentiments became more antislavery, and he accused slave owners of defying the Declaration of Independence. Wilson attacked moderate editors, applauded the defeat in other northern states of the congressional "dough faces," and called for efforts to prevent Missouri's formal admission to the Union.[75] During the session of 1820–21, the Ohio delegation in Washington voted consistently against accepting Missouri's constitution and against the "*conscience* plaster" compromise that Clay fudged up for the final "hypocritical" settlement of the issue in 1821.[76]

But even this was far from the end of the matter, as the more ambivalent congressmen of 1819 discovered. The careers of Beecher, Harrison, and Morrow were haunted in the next few years by memories of their pro-slavery votes of 1819.[77] Beyond that, Ohioans had learned that the national government was no longer manned by those with whom they could identify, as they had under Jefferson and during the war, and they found themselves in direct confrontation with a section that had traditionally provided trusted national party leadership. Many Republicans agreed with the *Western Herald*'s desire for a free-state candidate to challenge Monroe's reelection in 1820. Hammond, for his part, wanted "a Northern President, whether J. Q. Adams or D. Clinton, or any body rather than that things should remain as they are." The sectional crisis had raised such transcendent issues that he believed "a new state of parties must grow out of it."[78]

The maneuverings before the presidential election of 1824 demonstrated that Ohioans wanted a president who could represent views that were both northern and western. Since men antithetical to those views dominated the Republican party in Congress, Ohioans would not accept any nomination made by a caucus dominated by its enemies. Even distinguished politicians long devoted to the party—like Worthington and Harrison—recognized the strength of public opinion. According to John Sloane, any politician who supported a Virginia candidate in 1824 risked his political career—as the Zanesville Legitimates would discover to their cost. As Beecher rejoiced, "*Party, party, party* names have not their usual charm," and out of the new alignments made to elect a president in 1824–25 would emerge a new system of party conflict.[79]

PERSISTENCE OF PARTY

To all appearances, by the early 1820s the Republican party, inside and outside Ohio, had fallen apart. The state was developing, in the midst of sectional crisis, a strong sense of internal unity. Federalists were being elected to high office by predominantly Republican state legislatures. Most elections involved negligible partisan activity. Yet, in spite of the antiparty atmosphere, the memory of earlier partisanship persisted, and men continued to use the "Federalist" and "Republican" labels. More to the point, in those parts of the state where the early party conflict had bitten deep, some politicians and voters endeavored, with some success, to structure electoral contests along old party lines.

The strength of inertia behind the old party structures assured the outcome of the 1820 presidential election, despite the sectional crisis. The Steubenville *Western Herald* may have made "soft insinuations" that a free-state president would be more satisfactory to northern sensibilities, but there is no contemporary evidence of an opposition ticket in Ohio explicitly in favor of a rival candidate. Instead, popular contempt made voting "a mere farce," with the people voting—if at all—"in sport for tag, rag, and bobtail" as presidential electors. Everyone agreed that there was no alternative to the reelection of the incumbent, despite the dissatisfaction with the current regime. As Representative John Sloane said, the administration might be weak, inefficient, and lacking influence in Congress, but it understood "the management of electioneering" so well that "all popular men are broken down in the northern states." Moreover, it had secured an effective control over the operations of the Republicans of New England, too many of whom had "grown up under the care of Madison's and Monroe's administration" and so were "too much the creatures of courtly power." In this way Monroe was "able to ride in at another election without opposition," simply because the party's traditions provided for a predictable outcome at a time when any alternative might prove less acceptable.[80]

Even in local elections in places where Good Feelings had apparently long triumphed, Ohio politicians occasionally attempted to structure electoral contests along old party lines. The old slang was still used in Butler County in 1821, when one aspirant was accused of being the Tammany candidate; and, indeed, Tammany societies still survived in parts of southwestern Ohio. Delegate conventions continued to meet, and some newspaper correspondents expressed faith in their propriety. In the heated Hamilton County elections of 1820, two slates were put forward—one the "Delegate nomination," the other the "Nomination by the Cincinnati Delegates." Another delegate convention met the next year, headed by two Tammany men, but its recommendation was not accepted, partly because not every township was represented.[81] Such devices lacked the authority they had once enjoyed, but in some places—notably in southeastern Ohio—a party nomination and an appeal to old party passions could still carry an election, despite the breakdown of the old national parties.

At first sight, elections in Washington County displayed all the features of the "no-party" model. Under the impress of Good Feelings and regional self-awareness, amalgamation had proceeded here more rapidly than in many other eastern counties. The architect Joseph Barker, a well-known Federalist and builder of Aaron Burr's boats in 1806, had been elected to the state house of representatives in 1818 without much fuss. In 1819 Barker was replaced by fellow Federalist Ephraim Cutler, who later recalled that, by that time, "the party heat had become much cooler than what had prevailed since 1803, and no party measures were agitated." In the assembly Cutler created a stir in the house over the state land tax, arguing forcefully that the existing system of assessment bore unfairly on the less well endowed hilly regions of southeastern Ohio, in comparison with rapidly developing agricultural areas such as the lower Miami Valley. At the same time as Cutler defended local interests, the Missouri controversy created an even greater sense of local Yankee solidarity.[82]

Yet in 1820 a county delegate convention was organized in the good old party mode, and it nominated a full ticket of sound Republicans. Cutler and Barker, both up for election, were carefully excluded. The "Independent Electors of Marietta" then called a public meeting to investigate this proceeding— and duly confirmed the delegate nominations. There followed, in the columns of the only county newspaper, a controversy as bitter as any the county had seen. Fierce attacks were made on the men accused of controlling the local Republican party and dominating office; they were indicted as a corrupt, monopolizing aristocracy—in rhetorical terms of which any later Jacksonian would have been proud. Cutler and Barker were duly brought forward as opposition candidates and gained some support from independent Republicans. They were not, however, publicly damned as Federalists by their "regular" opponents—presumably because Federalist support was required to reelect Levi Barber, the Washington County candidate, to Congress. The Federalists themselves divided, because some local leaders, notably William Rufus Putnam, remained proud of their long resistance to the Democratic "office-seeking confederacy" and believed that Cutler had begun to work too closely with their historic opponents.

These divisions within both old parties, and the intervention of other privately nominated candidates, prevented a simple repeat of the more obviously two-party elections of the war years. The delegate convention's ticket failed to win outright majorities, although it elected five of its seven nominees. But then the result for the house of representatives was challenged and a special election called for December; Cutler now withdrew in order to allow Barker a straight race against the previously successful Republican. The subsequent two-horse race produced a distribution of votes among the townships remarkably similar to that seen in the elections of 1814 and 1815—and the Republican was returned with 61.59 percent, the party's traditional proportion of the local vote.[83]

The next year, 1821, leading Marietta Republicans issued a broadside warning that Federalists had not yet in any way renounced their political creed. "The Amalgamation of parties," it insisted, "has recently been the favorite theme of FEDERALISTS, who, availing themselves of the prevailing sentiments favorable to political toleration, are insidiously gaining an ascendancy in our councils, which may terminate in the total subversion of republican institutions." The previous year's elections had shown that "the spirit of Federalism had only slumbered," for "the leaders of the Federal party" had successfully "rallied their adherents" in the Washington County. The Republican leaders therefore called for township meetings "composed of the democratic republicans exclusively" to name delegates to meet in convention and name a slate of candidates—which duly happened. Once more, the convention's nominees were attacked for abusing power, although on this occasion a rival "Independent Ticket" was named to concentrate the votes of the opposition. Once more, the delegate nomination won, and Cutler lost, by a vote which in two-thirds of the townships was similar to that of the previous December.[84]

In 1822 the Marietta Republicans again called a delegate convention, but for some reason it did not meet. Instead, a Republican meeting in Marietta named a ticket that excluded Federalists. Then, on the eve of the election, a broadside announced that Cutler was not a candidate—a "base falsehood" which twenty-three Federalists of Belpre claimed "outstrips all the electioneering tricks that can be met with in the annals of Jacobin perfidy." Cutler still won overwhelmingly, with Belpre providing—as it almost always had done—an almost unanimous vote for the two Federalist candidates. By now, however, the likely adoption of a state canal scheme made tax reform crucial to Washington County and its neighbors, as Cutler had convincingly argued in the press before the election. In 1823, in spite of a rival, privately made "republican nomination," he gained promotion to the state senate, where he finally succeeded in securing the measures for which he had struggled so long in the face of partisan prejudice. By 1825 "even the democrats of *high* and *low* order" in the county spoke well of him—"but not all."[85]

Other counties in eastern Ohio also maintained, or revived, old party machinery in the early 1820s. Morgan County had been created in 1817 mainly from Washington and still shared two house seats with its mother county. Each year between 1820 and 1823 the Morgan Republicans held a delegate convention that named one candidate for the house, whom the Washington Republicans accepted in return for Morgan's support for the nominee of the Washington delegates. Ironically, in 1821 each county gave overwhelming majorities to the regular nominee of the other county, while marginally preferring its own "Independent" candidate; thus, the regulars triumphed in house elections because delegate nominations impressed voters at a distance much more than those who were more likely to know the nominees![86]

Similarly, Coshocton, Tuscarawas, and Guernsey Counties were linked in some elections for the general assembly, and they coordinated their nominations through party meetings. When conflicting names were put forward in 1823, the Coshocton candidate withdrew so as to avoid "a division of the republican interest in this district." Coshocton itself had a long tradition of delegate conventions, which were designed to keep power out of the hands of amalgamationist opponents who, according to the regulars, were "in reality federal." In 1820 the convention named township vigilance committees to distribute tickets, "persuade the people to turn out," and "watch the polls on the day of election." These efforts to preserve the old machinery proved successful at the polls, certainly in Coshocton in 1820 and 1822.[87]

In neighboring counties the same impulse met with more mixed response. In Tuscarawas, for example, James Patrick had operated the *Tuscarawas Chronicle* since 1819 "decidedly in favor of the class of Republicans termed *democratic.*" In 1820 and 1821, however, the delegate system became a bone of contention and seems to have been "dispensed with, by agreement." But then, in 1822, a public meeting "agreed to make one more effort to revive the spirit of republican nomination by the people," but could not generate general acceptance of the ticket it named.[88] In Guernsey County, after 1817, no delegate convention was summoned, but regular county meetings were held and candidates were commonly identified as legitimate or amalgamationist. Supporters of the latter sometimes insisted on attending all county meetings, causing much confusion; in 1822 the Democratic Republicans of Guernsey were driven to ask—in vain— that their meeting "not be disturbed by those who are not entitled to the appellation of Democrats, as heretofore."[89]

Even in Belmont County, Good Feelings and amalgamation had failed to obliterate the loyalties and commitments of the old party system. In the late 1810s, on every occasion when he had chosen to run, Belmont voters had happily returned Charles Hammond to the general assembly along with old Republicans, and they had elected another prominent Federalist, the lawyer David Jennings, to the state senate in 1819 and 1821. Yet the old parties remained conscious of their traditional identities: the 1820 congressional election was something of a party contest, with most of the county supporting the Legitimate candidate, whereas Wright "got very few but federal votes." Still, in 1821, Republican leaders in Belmont could debate whether the congressional candidate of the Zanesville Legitimates was of sound enough principles to justify party support in the county. In that same year Republicans and militia officers opposed the reelection of Jennings to the state senate "upon account of his vote in favor of excusing the Quakers from mustering," but the sole effect was to "bring such a host of them to the polls, as to secure Jennings his election."[90]

Then in 1822 Hammond ran for Congress in the newly created district of Belmont, Guernsey, Morgan, and Monroe Counties. A Republican district convention unanimously nominated the same John Patterson who had beaten Hammond for the state senate in the strictly partisan Belmont election of 1815. Although the two had cooperated since that time, Patterson now attacked Hammond for his Federalism, and the day after the election Hammond conceded that "Democracy, Republicanism, whatever you may chuse to call it, has made a violent and I suppose successful effort." After this defeat Hammond decided to leave eastern Ohio, where a Federalist past was such a liability, and make a fresh start the next year in amalgamationist Cincinnati.[91]

After his defeat, professional colleagues, including Republicans, pressed

Hammond to become a candidate for the vacancy on the Ohio Supreme Court occasioned by John McLean's appointment, in October 1822, as commissioner of the General Land Office in Washington. Hammond was willing to accept election by the legislature, but he refused to be hawked about or considered an active candidate. As he said privately, "I cannot be elected. The same feeling and sentiment that sent Patterson to Congress from the district prevails in the Legislature in at least the same extent, and will prevail to make Herrick judge rather than me." Although the attempt to rouse old party feeling against Burnet's appointment had backfired in the previous session, Hammond was right: a second Federalist on the supreme court was more than the legislature could safely stomach. Instead, the assembly chose a sound Republican, Charles R. Sherman, whose sons would become more widely known than any of them. Other major appointments that came up at this time, like the federal posts of marshal and district attorney, also attracted some strong Federalist candidates, but most state politicians, most of the Ohio delegation in Congress, and the president of the United States were careful not to support "any one suspected of the crying sin of federalism."[92]

In fact, old party considerations permeated everywhere, even if politics no longer operated along party lines. The *Cleaveland Herald* may have stated that "the old divisions of parties are but little known in this quarter," but it then immediately urged local voters to support only sound Republicans![93] The congressional election of 1820 in which the Federalist Beecher was at last narrowly defeated by Joseph Vance was not strictly speaking a party election, with four serious candidates attracting mainly localized support. But several newspapers wrote about it as though it were a contest between "a firm Democratic Republican" and a "blue-light" Federalist, and voters were called on to remember their feelings of the war years.[94] Even in cases where there was less of a semblance of political and electoral groupings cast along strict party lines, the fact that public men continued to identify each other by national party labels shows that the old landmarks still served to organize thought and feeling about political events, issues, and personalities. Federalists may have given up formal opposition to the governments of the day, but privately, like William Rufus Putnam in 1820, they retained pride in their Federalism and scorned the self-seeking Jacobins who misled the people. Conversely, it was awareness that the Federalist spirit had not died which persuaded regular Democrats to maintain party organization. Even election conflicts that at first glance appear to be purely personal— and irresponsible in their scurrility—often turn out to have some past history of partisan hostility lying behind them.[95] The old loyalties had not died and would prove a force that could yet influence the outcome of elections at all levels.

JACKSONIAN PERSPECTIVES

By 1830, few of the party labels, few of the loyalties, few of the political friendships and enmities that had existed before 1820 had any relevance to the current political behavior of Ohioans. Benjamin Tappan no longer belonged to the same party as his former protégé, James Wilson, who now found himself on the same side of the party fence as his earlier antagonist, Charles Hammond. During the 1813–14 assembly, Hammond had come to blows with Duncan McArthur; they were now political allies.[1] Former Tammany men had divided—even Isaac Van Horne and John Hamm now voted different ways—and Federalists could be found on both sides. Collections of political correspondence commonly attest this change, as old political friendships died and new ones took their place. In many counties the disappearance of old party newspapers and the emergence of new ones in the course of the decade likewise demonstrated the transformation that had come over the basic political and electoral cleavage in the state.

Essentially a new pattern of party conflict had arisen out of the great crisis that gripped state and nation in the early 1820s. In 1824, for the first time, Ohioans refused to follow the lead of the national Republican party, which they now believed to be controlled by a hostile sectional interest. Rejecting the nomination of the congressional caucus, they looked for a presidential candidate who expressed their particular outlook on national affairs—someone who was both northern and western. Unfortunately, they could find no viable candidate who combined both qualities, but they supported the alliance of John Quincy Adams and Henry Clay in 1825, which gave them a nonslaveholding president at the head of an administration committed to economic policies acceptable to the West.[2]

Threatening, at first, a supremacy as great as that of the Jeffersonian Republicans, this new dispensation roused considerable opposition. In southwestern

Ohio many people refused to support anything involving Henry Clay, whom locals associated with the thieving Bank of the United States; Andrew Jackson provided a suitable western alternative. Throughout the state, many Irish and Germans preferred Jackson to a New Englander. By 1828 Ohio had divided into two camps, supporting President Adams and General Jackson, respectively, and the excitement of close two-party competition drew into presidential politics the alienated backcountry farmers who had learned in the panic and depression to suspect politicians of all kinds—except those dressed as national heroes, like Jackson. The narrow Jacksonian success of 1828 guaranteed that the state would now experience a prolonged period of two-party conflict more evenly balanced and penetrating more fully into local politics than anything experienced before 1820. By the late 1830s this electoral division had evolved into the classic party confrontation between Whigs and Democrats, which permeated politics at all levels and drew voters to elections in incredible numbers.[3]

This new two-party division, which had appeared in almost every state by 1838, seems to bear little relation to the contests of the Jeffersonian period. Yet appearances are deceptive. Compared with the Second Party System, the politics of the earlier period certainly did not constitute a "party system" in any meaningful sense of the term, and yet they were more like later party conflicts than earlier experiences of factional conflict.[4] In the late 1820s and 1830s, Ohio election campaigns were more vigorous and perhaps more uniform in their organization, and they provoked more popular interest, especially in presidential elections. Yet older politicians recognized that their partisanship, vitriol, and passion were no greater than in the early years of the state. Almost everything had been foreshadowed in some way.

Certainly "democracy" was scarcely new in the 1820s. Undoubtedly, social strife and popular grievances were voiced more openly in the early part of the decade than before, and common folk subsequently turned out to vote in national elections in unprecedented numbers. But the distribution of power had not changed fundamentally since statehood, and the door to popular participation was no wider in 1828 than it had been twenty-five years earlier. When Jacksonians in Ohio warned of the threat of aristocracy, of an elite seizing power, they were not appealing to a new democratic spirit but to a feeling that democracy as known for twenty-five years was in danger.[5] If this reflected anything, it was not a more democratic society but a more socially and economically variegated one, in which popular concern with sectional interests had tended to put power into the hands of incumbents.

Similarly, the campaign against the caucus in 1824 did not express some new populist demand that the people be allowed to determine nominations. In many parts of the state, voters had been able to play a role in the nominating process since the statehood contest, and there was nothing novel in the idea of holding delegate nominating conventions. The 1824 campaign against the congressional caucus drew on political traditions that were well established in Ohio. Democratic Republicans had long believed that the only valid nominations were those sanctioned by primary meetings of the people, a belief that had produced the proposal for a national nominating convention in 1816. On the other hand, Federalists and Independent Republicans had long objected to party dictation, insisting that party nominations ought not to forestall the voter's freedom of choice. In 1824, in their eyes, a party device was being used to persuade old party men to vote for the representative of a hostile sectional interest. This second line of criticism operated against conventions as much as caucuses, for, as Martin Van Buren acknowledged in 1827, either served the purpose of directing a party's supporters toward a single agreed candidate.[6]

The traditional nature of partisan electoral techniques meant that the Jacksonian Democrats did not have a monopoly on good organizational practice in the 1820s. Their opponents had as much practical experience at state and local levels, and they often showed greater eagerness to use delegate conventions; in Ohio, the supporters of Adams and Clay were more concerned with maintaining a proper delegate system in the true Jeffersonian tradition, with decisions coming up from the localities. If anything, the Jacksonian Democrats in Ohio proved more centralist and directive in their organizational pattern and often less interested in allowing grassroots initiative in nominations and election structure than the Jeffersonian Republicans had been.[7]

The common background of Jeffersonian politics ensured that politicians on both sides of the new divide of the 1820s would struggle to claim exclusive possession of the old Republican mantle. In Ohio, Jacksonian claims in 1828 to be the exclusive heirs of Mr. Jefferson's party were met with hoots of derision: how could a set of men who numbered in their midst Federalists as prominent as the vituperative editor James B. Gardiner—or Elijah Hayward, who had applied to be secretary of the infamous Hartford Convention of 1814—be considered good Republicans? Undeniably, many men of sound Democratic credentials, such as John Sloane or James Wilson, had moved naturally into the Adams-Clay camp, without any sense of betraying past principles.

Overall, though, the Jacksonians more successfully claimed the inheritance. After all, they were the country party, criticizing men in power. Their opponent was called Adams, and their own candidate had some claims to be considered the second Jefferson. Jackson stood apart from the ordinary crowd of politicians, having given up power and status to return to his farm. He embodied the natural virtue of farming men, such as Mr. Jefferson had extolled. He was not a beneficiary of Washington patronage politics, and his popular image promised a return to the days of original democracy before party devices and the private intrigue of party managers perverted the people's choice. Above all, he did not have to prove his Republican credentials, in spite of some dubious points in his past; he had fought the British in times which had tried the souls of loyal Jeffersonians. If by 1828 memories of 1812 had become a touchstone of political soundness, Jackson passed the test with flying colors.

In other words, Jackson's appeal was deeply conservative, arousing nostalgic recollections of days when things were simpler. He represented patriotism at a time of sectional and partisan discord, and wholesome purity at a time of perceived moral decay. So, too, the old Republican party was recalled as a means of ensuring political virtue, and its devices were seen as the system for re-establishing sound politics. Many people were unhappy with what they saw as a decline in political morality and public standards. But far from this change being blamed on the revival of national political contests, some men saw the revival of partisanship as a possible cure. This sense lay behind some unusual efforts to revive the old Republican nominating machinery in Ohio in the mid-1820s.

In 1825 and 1826, the old delegate system reappeared in at least two Ohio counties. Historians have interpreted these movements as the beginnings of local Jackson party organization, on the assumption that conventions were new to the Ohio of the 1820s. Yet Jackson's name was not mentioned by the organizers of the conventions, which were supported by some men who would never declare for Jackson. In Hamilton County, some participants saw the 1825 convention as a means of healing wounds in the body politic inflicted by the previous year's presidential election. Columbia Township deliberately sent to the convention three delegates who had each supported a different presidential candidate in 1824, with the object of "reconciling those political differences which originated in the late Presidential election, or rather as it should seem to forget all parties."[8]

In Belmont County, protagonists of delegate conventions in 1825 and 1826 claimed the device would mitigate sectional and partisan differences within the county. It would reduce rancor and bickering, and end the disgusting sight of candidates electioneering for themselves and trying to bribe voters with promises. Furthermore, effective power would return to the farmers, who, under the informal system of private nominations, never bothered to see that good candidates were brought forward. In other words, although private and self-nominations had become the usual practice in the county, many old Republicans still looked back to the brave days of the Good Old Party. Moreover, in all parts of Ohio, men regretted the evils that had entered elections during the last decade, and they believed that old-party mechanisms would reduce the sectional ill will and social antagonism, the self-promotion, slander, and personal abuse, the disorder and inebriation increasingly apparent at election time.[9] Some men still hoped that the consensual predominance of the old Democratic Republican party could be revived by resorting to its nominating procedures; however futile or disingenuous their hopes, the arguments they used demonstrate the widespread respect in which the old party was still widely held.

These curious movements demonstrated how Republican nominating machinery had come to be seen as a means of promoting communal harmony by the 1810s. Whatever their original partisan purposes, advocates of delegate conventions began to insist that their value lay in the opportunity they provided for men to talk through their preferences and come to a generally acceptable consensus in advance of an election. The argument was specious, of course, since the persisting use of conventions at a time of easy Republican predominance was itself a cause of strife in many localities. But some Republicans saw that such devices provided an opportunity to preserve decent and responsible political behavior and so avoid the rampant self-seeking that threatened to become the mark of elections at all levels.

Thus when Jacksonians called themselves the Democratic Republicans in 1827–28, they were not conjuring up some new political principle of democracy but associating themselves with the good old ways. Of course, some older men saw the Jacksonians as responsible for the decline they detected in standards of political life rather than the solution to it. James Heaton, for example, long a committed Tammany man in Butler County, condemned the self-exhibitionism and the appeal to passions that he witnessed. The solution, he thought, lay in supporting a well-qualified, high-minded statesman such as Adams, who recognized the needs of the West and the nation for an active federal government, and he damned the Jacksonians as opportunistic self-seekers who supported popular personalities rather than sound policy. For such men, Jacksonian claims to be the old Republican party reborn were just a further example of their deceit.[10]

Certainly there was good reason for Heaton's skepticism. Republicans and Federalists could be found on both sides, and the distribution of the Ohio vote in 1828 showed little obvious reflection of voting behavior before 1816. Nor had the earlier state conflict over the judiciary and St. Tammany foreshadowed the new alignments. The distribution of votes in the crucial state election of 1812 did not correlate with that of the presidential election of 1828, and prominent individuals were equally divided. Some notable Democrats of 1812 did become Jacksonians, as did Benjamin Tappan and John Hamm, but they joined with former supporters of the judiciary such as John W. Campbell and Robert Lucas. Similarly, some leaders of the judicial party strengthened the Adams-Clay

ranks—men such as Duncan McArthur, William Creighton Jr., Benjamin Ruggles, and Calvin Pease—as did keen Democratic Republicans such as James
Wilson, Francis Dunlavy, and John Sloane. But then the limits of judicial power
and major issues of democracy were scarcely an issue in Ohio after 1815 and
certainly not after 1822.

Such skepticism did not prevent the Jacksonians from describing themselves as good Republicans, refighting the struggle of 1800. When Benjamin
Tappan called himself a "Democrat" in the later period, he was specifically
associating himself with Mr. Jefferson's party; for him, even "hickory" was a
symbol of resistance to Federalist tyranny dating back to the 1790s. Moreover,
after the 1828 election, leading Jacksonians claimed they owed their victory to
their old Republicanism as much as anything. The *St. Clairsville Gazette* declared that "the old landmarks had been blazed afresh," and it was the duty of
Jacksonians to "keep the line drawn." In 1829 the state party justified the extension of party conflict into local elections on the grounds that this was the way of
the good old party, while county conventions were the "established system of
Republican nominations." Even their partisanship they credited to Jefferson's
Democratic party.[11]

Surprisingly, in some localities, the Jacksonians could justifiably pose as the
legitimate heirs of the Jeffersonians. This was the case especially in southeastern
Ohio, where the old party conflict had burned deep among voters, as even
Adams men sometimes acknowledged. Alexander Armstrong, for example, had
edited the St. Clairsville opposition paper from 1811 to 1824, for much of that
time in conjunction with Charles Hammond, and in due course he had become
a prominent Adams man; in 1828 he took it for granted that, in Belmont
County, "the Jackson and old Democratic party" (to which he was "personally
obnoxious") was one and the same thing.[12] Certainly Jacksonians agreed. In
1830 John Hamm proudly told a local Jacksonian celebration that the history of
Muskingum County "for twenty years back" demonstrated that "the Democratic Republican party . . . have continued to maintain the same political principles . . . without having been jostled out of their rightful political course."[13]

In reality, of course, the story was much more complicated. The regular
Republicans had been divided by the crisis of the early 1820s and the issues of
the 1824 presidential election, and those among the Legitimates who turned to
Jackson did so only slowly and reluctantly. Initially their campaign on his behalf
struggled limply—until they discovered that the old party cries had the power
to arouse local voters in their favor. In key counties such as Muskingum, Belmont, and Washington, the Jacksonians could fairly point out that local Federalists had almost uniformly become Adams men and were openly rejoicing in
their prospects of power under the amalgamating regime of President Adams.[14]

Local Democratic voters responded, establishing in Belmont and Washington Counties, for example, a significant rank-order correlation between the partisan township pattern of voting of 1815 and that established in 1828—of the order of +0.79 and +0.88, respectively. In Washington County, the Jacksonians did not adopt the Old Republican appeal until after their abysmal failure in the local elections of 1827. Then, over the next twelve months their vote increased markedly, and about half of the distribution by townships of that increase can be explained by the distribution of Republican party strength nearly fifteen years before.[15]

These clear signs suggest that, for many people, the party loyalties created by 1815 had the ability to persist and influence voting behavior in the very different conditions of the Jacksonian period. Just as, after 1856, loyalty to the Whig party and antagonism to former Democrats would affect the new Republican party through the Civil War and beyond, so the course of Jacksonian electoral politics would be repeatedly affected by constant reference back to Jeffersonian conflicts. In the end, many Jacksonians would come to see the battles of the late 1830s as a reenactment of the original party struggle. Of course, this was a mighty oversimplification, and the appeal to old party loyalties was only one of several perceptible forces operating on men's choices in the 1820s and 1830s. In Ohio, the old party pattern cannot be discerned in the overall voting returns because it was overlaid by more recent cleavages, but that does not mean it was not a determining force of some importance. The interaction between the new political forces of the 1820s and the reassertion of old allegiances in the late twenties was complex, and the full, revealing tale cannot be told on this occasion.

But, significantly, old Republican revivalism was a major force only in certain constituencies where the Federalist threat was still a fairly recent memory. In southwestern, central, and northeastern Ohio, the sense of partisan unity had begun to weaken even before 1812, and the experience of invasion had weakened it further. In such places the Federalists had demonstrated their patriotism and their trustworthiness. As William Henry Harrison told the state senate in 1820, the unpatriotic extremism of some Federalists, notably in the eastern states, should not be allowed to prejudice Ohioans against "that mild, consistent federalism between which and Republicanism there is only a shade in difference, which in the late war actuated the conduct of . . . the greater part of our own federalists."[16]

In fact, the War of 1812 became the great touchstone of political reliability, the true test of patriotic republicanism. The real enemies, for some Jacksonians, were "those opposed to bearing arms, and such as endeavoured to paralyze the energies of the government in our late contest with Great Britain." In much of

Ohio after 1815, whenever a politician was accused of having been a Federalist, it was more than a sufficient reply that he had volunteered and fought bravely during the war. In December 1828, the Adams-Clay majority in the general assembly sought a candidate for the U.S. Senate. The talented Charles Hammond seemed the obvious choice, especially in light of his services to popular causes since 1815 and to the Adams party more recently, but some Adams members of the assembly dared not vote for such a pronounced opponent of the war. As one Jacksonian member reported, "Some few of the Republican members that have *strayed* into the Administration ranks do say that they will not vote for . . . a known Federalist." Yet they could vote for, and elect, Jacob Burnet. The difference between the two candidates was simply their stance on the war: one was the most outspoken opponent, the other a staunch supporter. In Ohio as in Maryland and New York, it was the "Republican and Patriotic Federalists" who built successful political careers after 1816.[17]

Thus, in practice, loyalties forged before 1812 could influence behavior after 1825. Politicians eager to attract voters into their own phalanx found that appeals often had to be made in terms of the old parties, that language and symbols and ideas learned during the conflicts of Jefferson and Madison's day still had the power to move voters. On the whole, appeals to past national identifications were far more important than any reference to struggles internal to Ohio, because so many new voters of 1828 had no memory or knowledge of past Ohio politics, since they were either young or newcomers to the state, or both. The persistence of popular partisan loyalties formed in earlier decades in a very different situation proved just how deeply those old party loyalties had burned. As a result, the conflicts of the 1830s would be increasingly perceived— however inaccurately—in terms of the earlier party battle.

The one thing that has always kept party division alive has been memory. Mutual antagonism continues because it already exists. Parties fight because they are separated by recollections of earlier fights. Thus the critical question is why they began to fight each other in the first place: what was the original cause? Surely it took something deeply divisive, something that raised questions about the future of the whole nation, something of profundity and emotional force. In its beginnings the party division had to be issue-directed, even if the subsequent party system has not necessarily been so concerned with policy differences. That original cleavage, as it happens, came in the 1790s when the radicalism of the French Revolution polarized the American political nation, at a time of international peril in a world at war, in a critical period when the very future of the republic seemed at stake.

NOTES

The following abbreviations are used in the notes:

Locations

AAS	American Antiquarian Society, Worcester, Massachusetts
CHS	Cincinnati Historical Society
LC	Library of Congress
LCHS	Lake County Historical Society, Mentor
NYPL	New York Public Library
MC	Dawes Memorial Library, Marietta College
OHS	Ohio Historical Society Library and Archives, Columbus
RCHS	Ross County Historical Society, Chillicothe
WRHS	Western Reserve Historical Society, Cleveland
WCC	Washington County Courthouse, Marietta
WSU	Wright State University Archives, Dayton

Manuscript Collections

BTP	Benjamin Tappan Papers, LC or OHS
CERP	Charles E. Rice Papers, OHS
CHP	Charles Hammond Papers, OHS
EABP	Ethan Allen Brown Papers, OHS
ECP	Ephraim Cutler Papers, MC
SPHP	Samuel Prescott Hildreth Papers, MC
SWP	Samuel Williams Papers, RCHS
TWP	Thomas Worthington Papers, LC, OHS, or RCHS
VFM	Vertical File Material, OHS

PREFACE

1. Some of the most impressive recent studies of the early republic focus on newly opening areas and concentrate on political culture, power relationships, and social

character. Most of them do not primarily concern themselves with the issues of partisan behavior raised here, among which may be numbered Cayton, *Frontier Republic* (1986); Slaughter, *Whiskey Rebellion* (1986); Randolph A. Roth, *The Democratic Dilemma: Religion, Reform, and the Social Order in the Connecticut River Valley of Vermont, 1791–1850* (New York: Cambridge University Press, 1987); Alan Taylor, *Liberty Men and Great Proprietors* (1990); and Aron, *How the West Was Lost* (1996). For a notable exception that, in a different local context, incidentally comes to conclusions about the changing nature of politics and parties that comport with those reported in this work, see Alan Taylor's brilliant *William Cooper's Town: Power and Persuasion on the Frontier of the Early American Republic* (1995), esp. 232–33, 286–87, 357–62.

2. Quoted in Silbey, *American Political Nation,* 16.

INTRODUCTION: PARTY AND DEMOCRACY IN A FRONTIER REPUBLIC

1. Cotton, "From Rhode Island to Ohio," 253–54; Martin, *Franklin County,* 335–36. The objectionable lines came from Joel Barlow, *The Columbiad, a Poem,* 2 vols. (Philadelphia, 1809), 1:399.

2. Martin, *Franklin County,* 340–41; Cummings, *Ohio's Capitols at Columbus,* 7–8, 13–14. Ludlow himself composed the lines inscribed on the tablet over the east (or back) door, a photograph of which appears in Utter, *Frontier State,* 300.

3. Cotton, "From Rhode Island to Ohio," 250–51; Church, *Early History of Zanesville,* 48–49, 147, and passim; Schneider, *Y-Bridge City,* 59–66, 70, 115, 178. Cotton claimed that the population of Zanesville was only 200–300, which is surely too low since, according to *Niles' Weekly Register* 2 (Mar. 14, 1812): 31, it had passed 1,000 by 1812; the confusion no doubt arises from different definitions of the boundaries of the town. For the political struggle to control the bank, see Arius Nye to Horace Nye, Sept. 8, 1812, VFM 634, OHS.

4. *Zanesville Express,* July 13, 27, Aug. 10, 1815.

5. Chambers, *Political Parties in a New Nation;* Fischer, *Revolution of American Conservatism.* The concept of a "First Party System" was introduced by McCormick, *Second American Party System,* 19–31, and Goodman, "First Party System." Subsequent works reinforcing the concept include Banner, *To the Hartford Convention;* Broussard, *Southern Federalists;* Hoadley, *Origins of American Political Parties;* and notably Bohmer, "The Maryland Electorate and the Concept of a Party System in the Early National Period." For later party systems, see McCormick, *Second American Party System,* and Kleppner, *Third Electoral System.*

6. Ketcham, *Presidents above Party,* 209; Sharp, *American Politics in the Early Republic,* 7.

7. Formisano, "Deferential-Participant Politics," "Federalists and Republicans," and *Transformation of Political Culture.* See also James Sterling Young, *Washington Community,* 110–42; Nichols, *Invention of the American Political Parties,* 199–247.

8. See Formisano, "Deferential-Participant Politics" and "Federalists and Republicans." The term "preparty party system" is proposed by Kleppner, *Third Electoral System,* 19. The persistence of the older-style "patrician order" is emphasized by, among others,

Marshall, "Strange Stillbirth of the Whig Party"; Heale, *Making of American Politics;* Formisano, *Transformation of Political Culture;* and Silbey, *American Political Nation.*

9. Hofstadter, *Idea of a Party System,* esp. chap. 5; Formisano, "Federalists and Republicans," 68; Silbey, *American Political Nation,* 14–16; Cayton and Onuf, *Midwest and the Nation,* 68–69.

10. Chambers and Burnham, eds., *American Party Systems;* Kleppner et al., *Evolution of Electoral Systems;* Richard L. McCormick, *The Party Period and Public Policy: American Politics from the Age of Jackson to the Progressive Era* (New York: Oxford University Press, 1986); Joel Silbey, "Beyond Realignment and Realignment Theory: American Political Eras, 1789–1989," in *The End of Realignment?* edited by Byron Schafer (Madison: University of Wisconsin Press, 1991), esp. 5–8.

11. Formisano, "Federalists and Republicans," 34, 57, 58. For the comparably limited nature of later party systems, see Kleppner, *Third Electoral System;* Kleppner et al., *Evolution of Electoral Systems;* and Silbey, *American Political Nation.*

12. Sharp, *American Politics in the Early Republic,* 8–10, 297 n. 56; Wallace, "Changing Concepts of Party." Formisano, "Deferential-Participant Politics," 476, 481, 486, prefers the contemporary word "interests" to describe the formations of the Jeffersonian era; I have not found much evidence of the term being used in Ohio, certainly not after 1800.

13. Formisano, "Federalists and Republicans," 67–68; Pocock, "A Candidate I'll Surely Be," 56–62; Marshall, "Strange Stillbirth," 452–53. Formisano, "Deferential-Participant Politics," 480, has pointed out that the rise of conventions "is interwoven with the decline of deference."

14. Amy Bridges, *A City in the Republic: Antebellum New York and the Origins of Machine Politics* (New York: Cambridge University Press, 1984), 61. For the "republican synthesis," see Robert E. Shalhope, "Republicanism and Early American Historiography," *William and Mary Quarterly* 39 (1982): 334–56; Isaac Kramnick, "Republican Revisionism Revisited," *American Historical Review* 87 (1982): 629–64; Daniel T. Rodgers, "Republicanism: The Career of a Concept," *Journal of American History* 79 (1992): 11–38; and the symposia that appear in *American Quarterly* 37 (1985) and *Proceedings of the American Antiquarian Society* 102 (1992).

15. Wallace, "Changing Concepts of Party," 453. For a nice example of George Washington's antiparty attitudes being expressed in terms that acknowledged the prevalence of party in 1799, see Wood, *Radicalism of the American Revolution,* 366.

16. Jefferson's Inaugural Address, reprinted in Commager, ed., *Documents of American History,* 187. For assumptions that party ideological differences were not clearly defined and that terminology was consensual, see Formisano, "Deferential-Participant Politics," 477, and Pocock, "A Candidate I'll Surely Be."

17. Formisano, *Transformation of Political Culture;* Young, *Washington Community;* Marshall, "Strange Stillbirth." The assumption is too common to require further reference, but for a recent passing example, see Richard J. Carwardine, *Evangelicals and Politics in Antebellum America* (New Haven: Yale University Press, 1993), 5–8.

18. Gary B. Nash, "The Transformation of Urban Politics, 1700–1765," *Journal of American History* 60 (1973): 605–32, and *The Urban Crucible: Social Change, Political*

Consciousness, and the Origins of the American Revolution (Cambridge: Harvard University Press, 1979); Richard Alan Ryerson, *The Revolution Is Now Begun: The Radical Committees of Philadelphia, 1765–1776* (Philadelphia: University of Pennsylvania Press, 1978); Edward Countryman, *A People in Motion: The American Revolution and Political Society in New York, 1760–1790* (Baltimore: Johns Hopkins University Press, 1981); J. R. Pole, *The Gift of Government: Political Responsibility from the English Restoration to American Independence* (Athens: University of Georgia Press, 1983), 117–31; John M. Murrin, "Political Development," in *Colonial British America: Essays in the New History of the Early Modern Era,* ed. Jack P. Greene and J. R. Pole (Baltimore: Johns Hopkins University Press, 1984), 442–45; Richard R. Beeman, "Deference, Republicanism, and the Emergence of Popular Politics in Eighteenth-Century America," *William and Mary Quarterly* 49 (1992): 401–30; Benjamin H. Newcomb, *Political Partisanship in the American Middle Colonies, 1700–1776* (Baton Rouge: Louisiana State University Press, 1995).

19. Wood, *Creation of the American Republic,* 391–564; Robert A. Rutland, *The Ordeal of the Constitution* (Norman: University of Oklahoma Press, 1966); Jack N. Rackove, "The Structure of Politics at the Accession of George Washington," in *Beyond Confederation: Origins of the Constitution and American National Identity,* ed. Richard Beeman, Stephen Botein, and Edward C. Carter II (Chapel Hill: University of North Carolina Press, 1987), 261–94. See also Jackson Turner Main, "Government by the People: The American Revolution and the Democratization of the Legislatures," *William and Mary Quarterly* 23 (1966): 391–407, and *Political Parties before the Constitution* (Chapel Hill: University of North Carolina Press, 1973).

20. Formisano, "Deferential-Participant Politics," 483–84; Wood, *Creation of the American Republic,* 70–90, 162–96, 476–83. For Virginia, see Isaac, *Transformation of Virginia;* Beeman, *Old Dominion in the New Nation,* 33–41; and Beeman, *Evolution of the Southern Backcountry.*

21. Wood, *Radicalism of the American Revolution,* esp. 298–305; Appleby, *Capitalism and a New Social Order.*

22. The whole Northwest Territory contained 9,106 adult white males in 1801, according to my calculations, but 948 of them were in Wayne County, which is now in Michigan. U.S. Census, Second Census. For the calculation of adult white males throughout this work, see Ratcliffe, "Voter Turnout in Early Ohio," 228–31.

23. Espy, "Memorandums of a Tour," 22; U.S. Census, *Census for 1820.* North Carolina had the fourth largest total population in 1820, but in calculating federal representation, its slave population was, of course, reduced to three-fifths, thus dropping that state to fifth place.

24. McCormick, *Second American Party System,* 257; Formisano, "Federalists and Republicans," 60; Pocock, "A Candidate I'll Surely Be," 67. See also Feller, "Benjamin Tappan," 69, and even Fischer, *Revolution of American Conservatism,* 202–3.

25. Formisano, "Deferential-Participant Politics," 480; Pocock, "A Candidate I'll Surely Be," 60, 67, 205 n. 71.

26. Cayton, *Frontier Republic,* esp. chaps. 6 and 7; Brown and Cayton, eds., *Pursuit of Public Power,* xi.

27. Of Cayton's many stimulating contributions, see his *Frontier Republic* and, in particular, "Land, Power, and Reputation."

28. Brown, "Samuel Huntington," "Ohio Federalists, 1803–1815," and "Political Culture."

29. Brown, "Political Culture," 1; Ratcliffe, "Voter Turnout," 225–28, and "Ohio's Missing Presidential Election Returns."

30. Young, *Washington Community;* Pocock, "A Candidate I'll Surely Be."

31. Winkle, *Politics of Community;* Pocock, "A Candidate I'll Surely Be," 65.

CHAPTER 1. PARTISANSHIP UNDER THE *Ancien Régime*, 1793–1802

1. Thomas P. Abernethy, *From Frontier to Plantation in Tennessee: A Study in Frontier Democracy* (Chapel Hill: University of North Carolina Press, 1932); White, *Politics on the Southwestern Frontier;* Owens, "Pattern and Structure in Western Territorial Politics," 161–79. For recent applications of this interpretation to Ohio, see Brown, "Frontier Politics"; Bloom, "Congressional Delegates from the Northwest Territory"; Cayton, *Frontier Republic,* 33–91.

2. Thomas Rogers Sr. in Martzolff, "Reminiscences of a Pioneer," 196, 199–202. See also McDonald, *Biographical Sketches;* Finley, *Autobiography,* 100–103, 127–33; Massie, *Nathaniel Massie;* Cramer, "Duncan McArthur."

3. Berkhofer, "Northwest Ordinance and the Principle of Territorial Evolution," 45–55.

4. Albrecht, "Peaceable Kingdom."

5. Clarence E. Carter, *Territorial Papers,* 2:470; Burnet, "Letters," 11–12; Goodwin, "Development of the Miami Country," 491–92. St. Clair put the population of the whole Territory at 15,000 in 1795–96. Burnet, *Notes,* 31.

6. Finley, *Autobiography,* 109; Burnet, "Letters," 19–21, and *Notes,* 57–58, 290–91.

7. Elkins and McKitrick, "A Meaning for Turner's Frontier."

8. Smith, *St. Clair Papers,* 1:190–91; Burnet, *Notes,* 57–58, 290–91; Carter, *Territorial Papers,* 2:293–94, 343–47, 433–34, 442–50, 647–48. See also Downes, *Frontier Ohio,* 131–46, 170–71; Brown, "Frontier Politics," 61–63, 94–99, and "Timothy Pickering and the Northwest Territory," 120.

9. St. Clair to the president, 1790, in Smith, *St. Clair Papers,* 2:179; *Centinel of the North-Western Territory,* Nov. 30, 1793, and Aug. 16, Sept. 20, 27, Oct. 4, 11, 18, Nov. 29, 1794.

10. St. Clair to Henry Knox, May 1, 1790, in Smith, *St. Clair Papers,* 2:140. See also Putnam to Timothy Pickering, Aug. 30, 1794, in Buell, *Memoirs of Rufus Putnam,* 393–94; Carter, *Territorial Papers,* 2:481–86, 500–505, 586, 604, 652. For the importance of the postal service in informing frontier communities and binding them into the national polity, see John, *Spreading the News,* 31–42.

11. Cincinnati *Centinel,* Nov. 9, 1793.

12. *Centinel,* Mar. 8, May 10, July 12, Aug. 2, 1794. Stewart, *Opposition Press of the Federalist Period,* 884, errs in describing the *Centinel* as "Little politics; perhaps impartial."

13. *Centinel,* July 11, 18, 1795.

14. Ibid. "Ça Ira" was a French revolutionary song predicting the certain destruction of all aristocrats.

15. *Centinel,* Nov. 30, 1793; Nov. 29, 1794; Jan. 31, 1795; Downes, *Frontier Ohio,* 178–80. The polarizing impact on American opinion of the radical phase of the French Revolution in 1793–95 has been underlined in recent years by Hoadley, *Origins of American Political Parties;* Klein, *Unification of a Slave State,* 203–37; Elkins and McKitrick, *Age of Federalism;* and Sharp, *American Politics in the Early Republic.*

16. Formisano, "Deferential-Participant Politics," 476, points up the need to discover how quickly distant localities responded to the issues raised by national elites in the 1790s.

17. Burnet, "Letters" and *Notes,* esp. 299, 314, 342 n. See also De Chambrun, *Cincinnati,* 98; Martzolff, "Autobiography of Thomas Ewing," 162.

18. Smith, *St. Clair Papers,* esp. 1:196–97, 201–2, 2:320–21; Carter, *Territorial Papers,* 2:458–59, 460–61, 523; Smith, "Monarchists and Jacobins," 193.

19. St. Clair to Ross, June 21, 1798, and Ross to St. Clair, July 5, 1798, in Smith, *St. Clair Papers,* 1:186–87, 2:423. See also Tinkcom, *Republicans and Federalists in Pennsylvania,* 24–41, 148–49.

20. Cayton, "'A Quiet Independence,'" 5–32, esp. 16. See also Cayton, *Frontier Republic,* 12–32, and "Land, Power and Reputation," 273–74.

21. Cutler and Cutler, *Manasseh Cutler,* 522; Cayton, "Contours of Power," 106, 116–17.

22. John Mathews to Increase Mathews, Apr. 15, 1797, and Paul Fearing to W. W. Parson, Apr. 10, 1799, SPHP; Ephraim Cutler, "Copy of manuscript prepared for Dr. S. P. Hildreth," ECP.

23. Rufus Putnam to Fisher Ames, 1790, in Buell, *Memoirs of Rufus Putnam,* 243; Carter, *Territorial Papers,* 2:338–39, 578, 622; Hildreth, *Biographical and Historical Memoirs,* 410–13; Downes, *Frontier Ohio,* 141. For the squatters of the early 1780s, see "Papers Relating to the First White Settlers in Ohio," Western Reserve Historical Society *Tract* 6 (1871): 1–8, and Downes, "Ohio's Squatter Governor."

24. John Smith to Jefferson, April 6, 1807, John Smith Papers, CHS; Burnet, *Notes,* 342 n.

25. Sargent to Secretary of State Pickering, Sept. 30, 1796, and Aug. 14, 1797, in Carter, *Territorial Papers,* 2:578, 622–23; also 338–39, 611. See also Tinkom, *Republicans and Federalists in Pennsylvania,* 149–50.

26. Buell, *Memoirs of Rufus Putnam,* 386–91, 411–12; Cayton, "Contours of Power," 115–19, and *Frontier Republic,* 26–27, 33–35, 47–50; Rohrbough, *Trans-Appalachian Frontier,* 116–17.

27. Cincinnati *Centinel,* Oct. 18, Dec. 6, 1794; July 25, Dec. 5, 1795. For a similar situation in western Virginia, see Risjord, "Virginia Federalists," 499–502; and for western Pennsylvania, see Slaughter, *Whiskey Rebellion.* The word "country" was commonly used at the time to mean immediate locality or neighborhood or region, as Thomas Paine explained in *Common Sense.*

28. Burnet, *Notes*, 342 n; Cincinnati *Freeman's Journal*, Mar. 5, 1799; Smith, *St. Clair Papers*, 2:431–32; St. Clair to his son Daniel, 1798, in William Henry Smith, "Familiar Talk," 194.

29. Smith, *St. Clair Papers*, 1:213, 2:484–85; Chillicothe *Scioto Gazette*, Nov. 20, 1800; Burnet, *Notes*, 299, 314, 342 n.

30. Cincinnati *Centinel*, Feb. 20, 1796; "Address to the Citizens of the Different Counties of the Eastern District of the North Western Territory," [December 1797], SPHP, reprinted in Julia Perkins Cutler, *Ephraim Cutler*, 319–20. See also Downes, *Frontier Ohio*, 180–86.

31. Burnet, *Notes*, 342 n, which I read to refer to 1796 rather than 1800. See also ibid., 57–58, 290–91, 294–96; McBride, *Pioneer Biography*, 1:28–29, 97–98, 110, 112–13, 147.

32. Burnet to Timothy Walker, Sept. 27, 1843, Burnet Papers, CHS, [5–6]; St. Clair to John Adams, Jan. 27, 1800, in Smith, *St. Clair Papers*, 2:488. See also Burnet, *Notes*, 57–58, 290–91; Corry, *William M'Millan;* and Brown, "William McMillan and the Conservative Cincinnati Jeffersonians."

33. Morris, *Thomas Morris*, 19–21; Dunlevy, *Miami Baptist Association*, 96–119, and Dunlevy, newspaper sketch (presumably from Lebanon *Western Star*, 1867), copy appended to Josiah Morrow, "Life of Judge Francis Dunlavy," ms., Josiah Morrow Papers, CHS.

34. Katzenberger, "Major David Ziegler," esp. 133.

35. Cincinnati *Centinel*, Feb. 20, 1796; Massie, *Nathaniel Massie*, 68–69. For the father, see Estelle Wade Spining, "Notes Concerning Judge William Goforth" (ms., CHS), and Cincinnati *Western Spy*, Mar. 16, 1803; and for the son, see Mansfield, *Daniel Drake*, 50–53, 71, and Cincinnati *Western Spy*, June 13, 1817. Contrary to many statements, it was the judge-father, not the doctor-son, who was a member of the 1802 constitutional convention, congressional candidate in 1803, and presidential elector in 1804.

36. Cincinnati *Western Spy*, July 8, 1801; J. C. Symmes to Griffin Greene, Jan. 21, 1802, SPHP.

37. Cincinnati *Centinel*, Feb. 27, 1796; Smith, *St. Clair Papers*, 2:442–43; *Western Spy*, July 9, Aug. 13, 1800. Few copies of the Cincinnati *Freeman's Journal* (1796–1800) survive after its first seven months, but see the copy of Mar. 5, 1799, for its moderate Republicanism.

38. Benjamin Tappan, "Notes on Howe's *Historical Collections*" (1847), ms., BTP, OHS. See also Ratcliffe, "Autobiography of Benjamin Tappan," 122–32.

39. [Birchard], "Benjamin Tappan," 540; Tappan, "Comments on Burnet's *Notes on the Northwestern Territory*" (1847), ms., BTP, OHS, [p. 2]; Ratcliffe, "Benjamin Tappan," 109–13. Feller, "Benjamin Tappan," concentrates on the 1820s and underestimates the enduring power of Tappan's earlier commitment.

40. Ratcliffe, "Benjamin Tappan," 115, 117, 120–23; Tappan, "Comments on Burnet's *Notes*," [4].

41. [Benjamin Tappan], "Oration, 4 July 1801, Deld. at Hudson," BTP, LC. For the importance of traditional "Country" ideology, see Banning, *Jeffersonian Persuasion*, and Slaughter, *Whiskey Rebellion*, 125–42.

42. Elisha Tracy to Samuel Huntington, May 15, 1802, Mar. 20, 1803, in Benton, "Huntington Correspondence," 79, 82.

43. Burnet, *Notes*, 289, 298–99; Brown, "Frontier Politics," 166–69. For individual voting, see pollsheet for the territorial election in Hamilton County, Dec. 17, 1798, CHS. This source does not sustain the claim in Grupenhoff, "Politics and the Rise of Political Parties," 59–60, that this was a partisan election with marked ticket voting; the five winners got 417, 357, 303, 228, and 190, respectively. No relevant copies survive of the local newspaper, *Freeman's Journal.*

44. Smith, *St. Clair Papers,* 2:441, 446–52.

45. Sol Silbey to Paul Fearing, Oct. 3, 1799, SPHP. The territorial legislatures are well analyzed in Brown, "Frontier Politics," 171–77, 189–96, 237–47. Historians emphasizing partisan considerations in Harrison's election include Goebel, *Harrison,* 41–42; Bond, *Foundations of Ohio,* 447; Grupenhoff, "Politics and the Rise of Political Parties," 65–68; and Bloom, "Congressional Delegates," 7–10.

46. Barnhart, "Letters of Harrison to Worthington," 54; [Peter], *Private Memoir of Thomas Worthington,* 39.

47. St. Clair to Ross, December 1799, in Smith, *St. Clair Papers,* 2:483; Downes, *Frontier Ohio,* 147–76. For an imaginative re-creation of the Republican leaders' worldview, see Cayton, *Frontier Republic,* 51–61, though he goes considerably farther than the evidence really justifies, certainly in relation to the period before 1800.

48. St. Clair to James Ross, December 1799, in Smith, *St. Clair Papers,* 2:483; Burnet, "Letters," 99. See also Smith, *St. Clair Papers,* 2:484–85, 495; Massie, *Nathaniel Massie,* 67–69. Sears, *Thomas Worthington,* 46–53, exaggerates the partisan nature of territorial politics without producing evidence of clear Republican commitment on Worthington's part at this time. The Worthington Papers, as far as I can see, do not clarify the issue.

49. St. Clair to James Ross, December 1799, in Smith, *St. Clair Papers,* 2:480; Burnet, *Notes,* 321–22, 374–78; Worthington to Massie, [Dec.] 23, 1799, TWP, and to R. J. Meigs Sr., Feb. 23, 1801, SPHP. See also Gilmore, *Edward Tiffin,* 43, and Massie, *Nathaniel Massie,* 66–68, 72–73, 154.

50. Ratcliffe, "Benjamin Tappan," 134, 136–37 (though the events remembered there probably took place in 1800, not 1801 as the foolish editor claimed, 137 n. 54).

51. Brown, "Frontier Politics," 197. See also ibid., 189–96; Burnet, *Notes,* 306, 316–18; Smith, *St. Clair Papers,* 2:501–16, 524–25; and Hildreth, *Pioneer History,* 347–48.

52. [Dr.] William Goforth to Jefferson, Jan. 5, 1802, in Carter, *Territorial Papers,* 3:198–201. See also Cayton, "Contours of Power," 115–19, and *Frontier Republic,* 26–27, 33–35, 47–50; Rohrbough, *Trans-Appalachian Frontier,* 116–17.

53. Whittlesey, *Early History of Cleveland,* 358–60; Ratcliffe, "Voter Turnout," 232; Williamson, *American Suffrage,* 117–18.

54. Chase, *Statutes of Ohio,* 1:241–43; Smith, *St. Clair Papers,* 2:505–6. See also Chillicothe *Scioto Gazette,* Oct. 10, 1800; *Western Spy,* July 31, 1802; Burnet, *Notes,* 323.

55. Chase, *Statutes of Ohio,* 1:241–43.

56. Pollsheets for territorial election held in Hamilton County, Sept. 12, 1799; *Western Spy,* Sept. 3, 1799; Chase, *Statutes of Ohio,* 1:241.

57. Ratcliffe, "Benjamin Tappan," 135–36.

58. [Dr.] William Goforth to Worthington, Aug. 29, 1803, CERP; *Western Spy*, June 13, 1817. For eastern Ohio, see Ratcliffe, "Benjamin Tappan," 134–36, and Heald, *Bezaleel Wells.*

59. This situation has led many historians to describe known Republicans as Federalists at this time; for references, see Ratcliffe, "Experience of Revolution," 194 n. 25. For this characteristic of the *ancien régime,* see Wood, *Radicalism of the American Revolution,* 77–92.

60. *Western Spy,* Aug. 30, 1816; Burnet, "Letters," 132 n, and *Notes,* 342 n; Cleaves, *Old Tippecanoe,* 27.

61. Goebel, *Harrison,* 36–52; Cleaves, *Old Tippecanoe,* 26–32; Brown, "Frontier Politics," 148–50, 179–81; Barnhart, "Letters of Harrison to Worthington," 54, 56, 58. It is often said that Symmes objected to Anna's marriage to Harrison, yet surviving letters suggest that there was not a serious breach, e.g., J. C. Symmes to Dayton, Aug. 10, 1796, Symmes Papers.

62. Cox, "Torrence Papers," 2:23, 35; Blair, "James Findlay," 1–3.

63. Michael Baldwin, *To the Electors of the State of Ohio,* June 7, 1803, broadside, RCHS; Cincinnati *Liberty Hall,* Apr. 3, 1811. See also Worthington's correspondence, 1793–1800, TWP, OHS; Sears, *Thomas Worthington,* esp. 36–43; and Cayton, "Contours of Power," 117–18.

64. Timothy Phelps to George Tod, May 21, 1802, George Tod Papers. See also Tod to Huntington, Jan. 14, 1802, Nov. 2, 1802, Huntington Papers, WRHS; Smith, *St. Clair Papers,* 2:547–48, 584–85.

65. McMillan to Fearing, Oct. 16, 1800, SPHP. For the division plans and the sectional logroll, see Downes, *Frontier Ohio,* 186–200.

66. Beecher to Worthington, Jan. 14, 1802, TWP. Cayton, *Frontier Republic,* 82, errs in describing Beecher as a Republican.

67. For a comparative approach, see Owens, "Pattern and Structure in Western Territorial Politics."

68. Conlin, *Simon Perkins,* 30–35; Burnet, "Letters," 129, and *Notes,* 336–38, 494–96; Este, *Jacob Burnet.*

69. St. Clair to [James Ross?], Jan. 21, 1799 [misdated 1789], St. Clair Papers, OHS, and St. Clair to Ross, December 1799, in Smith, *St. Clair Papers,* 2:481–83.

70. John Fowler to Massie, Jan. 29, 1802, in Massie, *Nathaniel Massie,* 188; ms. in Worthington's hand (apparently a submission to Congress in 1802), TWP, RCHS. See also Onuf, "From Constitution to Higher Law," 5–14, and *Statehood and Union,* 67–87.

71. James Ross to St. Clair, Jan. 18, 1798, St. Clair Papers, OHS; S. T. Mason to Worthington, Feb. 5, 1801, in Smith, *St. Clair Papers,* 2:531.

72. Barnhart, "Letters of Harrison to Worthington," 56–59; Massie, *Nathaniel Massie,* 184–87; Brown, "Frontier Politics," 179–81, 185. In these instances the decisive influence was often Timothy Pickering, who took a special interest in Northwestern affairs. Carter, *Territorial Papers,* 3:74, 81; Brown, "Timothy Pickering and the Northwest Territory."

73. Secretary of the Treasury [Albert Gallatin] to Worthington, Aug. 7, 1801, in Carter, *Territorial Papers*, 3:160. See also Byrd to Worthington, Dec. 4, 1802, TWP.

74. John Smith to Jefferson, Apr. 6, 1807, Smith Papers; *Western Spy*, Feb. 9, 1807. See also Burnet to Timothy Walker, Sept. 27, 1843, Burnet Papers, [9–10]; Burnet, *Notes*, 342 n.

75. Interpretations that stress patronage as the key consideration include Burnet, *Notes*; Smith, *St. Clair Papers*; Downes, *Frontier Ohio*, 216–25; and Cayton, "Contours of Power," and *Frontier Republic*.

76. Smith, *St. Clair Papers*, 2:563–75, 581–85. See also Dudley Woodbridge Jr. to James Backus, Feb. 17, 1802, and Paul Fearing to Dudley Woodbridge Sr., Feb. 28, 1802, Backus-Woodbridge Papers; Worthington to R. J. Meigs, Dec. 20, 1801, J. C. Symmes to Griffin Greene, Jan. 21, 1802, and B. I. Gilman to Fearing, Feb. 20, 1802, SPHP; and Downes, "Thomas Jefferson and the Removal of Governor St. Clair," esp. 67–72.

77. Worthington to Abraham Baldwin, Nov. 30, 1801, TWP, LC. See also Massie, *Nathaniel Massie*, 185, and Smith, *St. Clair Papers*, 1:238.

78. St. Clair to Dudley Woodbridge, Dec. 24, 1801, and Fearing, Dec. 25, 1801, Jan. 15, 1802; Smith, *St. Clair Papers*, 2:548–51, 557–58. See also Fearing to Cutler, Dec. 9, 1801, ECP, and Burnet to Fearing, Sept. 27, 1843, Burnet Papers.

79. Fearing to St. Clair, Jan. 18, 1802, in Smith, *St. Clair Papers*, 2:559, and Fearing to Ephraim Cutler, Jan. 18, 1802, in Julia Perkins Cutler, *Ephraim Cutler*, 61–62. See also Smith, *St. Clair Papers*, 2:548–50, 557–58; Brown, "William McMillan," 128–30. McMillan agreed to go, but then postponed his departure because the trip seemed pointless. Return Jonathan Meigs Jr. did go to Washington, but he was seeking office from Jefferson and was soon persuaded to back statehood. The Republican agents, Worthington and Baldwin, also set out without firm guarantees that their expenses would be covered and, indeed, "not a cent was ever made up or paid to them." But then they too had hopes of personal advantage from presidential favor. *Scioto Gazette*, Sept. 18, 1802.

80. Manasseh Cutler to Cutler, Feb. 1, 1802, and Fearing to Cutler, Jan. 18, 1802, in Cutler, *Ephraim Cutler*, 62, 65; Burnet, *Notes*, 494–96. See also Sears, *Thomas Worthington*, 81–85, 90; Brown, "Frontier Politics," 257–62; Bloom, "Congressional Delegates," 16–17.

81. Pritchard to Worthington, Mar. 23, 1802, and Symmes to Worthington, June 24, 1802, TWP, OHS; Worthington to Nathaniel Macon, [June] 1802, quoted in Downes, "Jefferson and the Removal of St. Clair," 72; Worthington to Massie, Jan. 17, 1802, TWP, OHS, and to Albert Gallatin, May 17, 1802, in Carter, *Territorial Papers*, 3:224–25.

82. Smith, *St. Clair Papers*, 1:240–46, 2:601 n; Brown, "Frontier Politics," 268–69; Massie, *Nathaniel Massie*, 215; and Byrd to Jefferson, Oct. 15, 1802, Jefferson Papers. See also Carter, *Territorial Papers*, 3:240–42, 533–35.

83. Tiffin to Worthington, Mar. 20, 1802, in Smith, *St. Clair Papers*, 2:575; Dudley Woodbridge Jr. to James Backus, Feb. 17, 1802, Backus-Woodbridge Papers; B. I. Gilman to Fearing, Feb. 20, 1802, SPHP.

84. Worthington to Massie, Mar. 5, 1802, and C. W. Byrd to Massie, May 20, June 20, 1802, in Massie, *Nathaniel Massie*, 200–203, 205, 210; C. W. Byrd to Jefferson, Oct. 15, 1802, Jefferson Papers, transcripts, RCHS; Jeremiah Morrow's statement, Jan. 20, 1848, in

Benjamin Tappan's ms. comments on Burnet's *Notes on the North-Western Territory,* BTP, OHS. See also Worthington to [W. B. Giles?], Mar. 30, 1802, TWP, RCHS; Downes, "Jefferson and the Removal of St. Clair," 72–73. The second assembly had adjourned until the fourth Monday of November, but St. Clair agreed that it should not meet until after the convention, by which time St. Clair's removal had changed the situation. Burnet, "Letters," 75, 79; Grupenhoff, "Politics and the Rise of Political Parties," 131.

85. Worthington to W. B. Giles, Nov. 17, 1802, John Smith to Thomas Jefferson, Nov. 9, 1802, in Carter, *Territorial Papers,* 3:254–58; Smith, *St. Clair Papers,* 2:599–601.

86. John Smith to Worthington, Jan. 17, 1803, TWP, OHS. See also Carter, *Territorial Papers,* 3:254–59; Downes, "Jefferson and Removal of St. Clair," 73–77.

Chapter 2. The Democratic Revolution of 1802

1. William Goforth to Jefferson, Jan. 5, 1802, in Carter, *Territorial Papers,* 3:198–201. The idea is developed in Ratcliffe, "Experience of Revolution," esp. 187–92. For hope for an English revolution in the early 1770s, see Pauline Maier, *From Resistance to Revolution: Colonial Radicals and the Development of American Opposition, 1765–1776* (London, 1973).

2. Deference to influential men survived most commonly where it was associated with group membership and group solidarity. Formisano, "Deferential-Participant Politics," 484. Thus a traditional elitist establishment appeared in Dayton, which retained its character as a Presbyterian stronghold until the late 1810s. See Pocock, "Evangelical Frontier," and "Popular Roots of Jacksonian Democracy," 492–96.

3. Cayton, "Contours of Power," and *Frontier Republic,* 25–43.

4. This analysis follows the distinction between three forms of frontier settlement— ethnocultural communities, commercial localities, and universal frontier society—suggested by Rohrbough, *Trans-Appalachian Frontier,* 134. For traditional cultural acceptance of deference to superiors as right and proper, see J. G. A. Pocock, "The Classical Theory of Deference," *American Historical Review* 81 (1976): 516–23.

5. Benton, "Ohio Company of Associates," 70–72; Shannon, "Ohio Company and the Meaning of Opportunity," 393–94, 406–13.

6. Burnet, "Letters," 72, and *Notes,* 394–96. See also Chillicothe *Scioto Gazette,* Sept. 18, 1802; Downes, *Frontier Ohio,* 60–68, 73–76, 83–87; and Shannon, "This Unpleasant Business," 15–30.

7. Soltow, "Inequality amidst Abundance," 133–51. I have put a gloss on this article's statistics slightly different from that of the original.

8. I owe this point to Carl Engel of the Lake County Historical Society. For other hesitations over Soltow's use of the 1810 tax figures, see chap. 4, p. 271.

9. Elkins and McKitrick, "A Meaning for Turner's Frontier," 336–37. For Symmes, see Burnet, "Letters," 135–47, 152–58; Bond, *Correspondence of John Cleves Symmes;* Downes, *Frontier Ohio,* 86, 181–82, 190–92.

10. Carter, *Territorial Papers,* 3:16–18, 46–47.

11. Chillicothe *Freeman's Chronicle,* Sept. 5, 12, 19, 26, 1800; Smith, *St. Clair Papers,* 1:214, 2:451, 543–47; Burnet, *Notes,* 330.

12. Cincinnati *Western Spy,* Feb. 4, 1801; Burnet, *Notes,* 306, 332–33.

13. Wilgus, "Evolution of Township Government in Ohio," 406–7; Smith, *St. Clair Papers,* 2:436–38, 545–47; Burnet, *Notes,* 306; Carter, *Territorial Papers,* 1:327; Bond, *Foundations of Ohio,* 418, 458–59, 460, 465–66; Downes, *Frontier Ohio,* 68, 163 n.

14. For the conduct of elections, see pollsheets for the territorial election in Hamilton County, Dec. 17, 1798, Sept. 12, 1799, CHS; Chillicothe *Freeman's Journal,* September 1800; Cincinnati *Western Spy,* September–October 1800.

15. *Western Spy,* Aug. 21, Oct. 20, 1802; Smith, *St. Clair Papers,* 2:531, 560; Downes, *Frontier Ohio,* 207, 210–12, 244.

16. E. Wadsworth to E. Paine, Sept. 27, 1801, reprinted in *Summit Beacon,* Aug. 12, 1857, clipping in Whittlesey Papers; Downes, *Frontier Ohio,* 182–85, 205–16; Smith, *St. Clair Papers,* 2:524–25, 549–50; William Ludlow to Tiffin, Dec. 22, 1801, TWP; Ratcliffe, "Benjamin Tappan," 137.

17. St. Clair to Timothy Pickering, Mar. 30, 1802, in Smith, *St. Clair Papers,* 2:495; Joseph Darlinton to Paul Fearing, March 1802, SPHP. See also William Creighton Jr. to Worthington, Jan. 30, 1802, and Worthington to Massie, Mar. 5, 1802, TWP, OHS.

18. David Vance to Worthington, Feb. 19, 1802, and Massie to Worthington, Feb. 19, 1802, TWP, OHS; Burnet to Fearing, Jan. 19, 1802, SPHP.

19. Ms. in Worthington's hand (apparently a submission to Congress in 1802), TWP, RCHS. See also Worthington's letters in Massie, *Nathaniel Massie,* 191–92, 194–98, 200–203.

20. Michael Baldwin to Worthington, Mar. 25, 1802, and Duncan McArthur to Worthington, Dec. 24, 1802, TWP, OHS. See also Smith, *St. Clair Papers,* 2:536; Burnet, "Letters," 76–77, and *Notes,* 338–40, 342–49, 364–69. Worthington's efforts to modify the terms in 1802 and 1803 are documented in TWP, RCHS; see also Feller, *Public Lands in Jacksonian Politics,* 8–9.

21. Massie to Worthington, Feb. 19, 1802, David Vance to Worthington, Mar. 20, 1802, Worthington to Massie, Mar. 5, 1802, TWP, OHS. See also Smith, *St. Clair Papers,* 1:227, 2:549–51, 581; Burnet, *Notes,* 348; and Carter, *Territorial Papers,* 3:187.

22. Worthington to [W. B. Giles?], Mar. 20, 1802, TWP, OHS. For typical confusion, see *Western Spy,* July 24, 31, Aug. 7, 21, 1802.

23. Smith, *St. Clair Papers,* 1:147, 209, 218, 2:482 (quotation), 501, 519, 582; Downes, *Frontier Ohio,* 151; Williamson, *American Suffrage,* 181, 218–19; Berkhofer, "Northwest Ordinance and the Principle of Territorial Evolution," 45–55. St. Clair's political views are caricatured in Sears, "Political Philosophy of Arthur St. Clair," and in Brown, "Ohio Federalists," 261.

24. Duncan McArthur to Worthington, Mar. 16, 1799, TWP, OHS; Chillicothe *Freeman's Chronicle,* Sept. 5, 1800; Chillicothe *Scioto Gazette,* Sept. 18, 1802; Tiffin to Worthington, Feb. 1, 1802, TWP, OHS.

25. Michael Baldwin to Worthington, Apr. 2, 1802, and Duncan McArthur, reported in Massie to Worthington, Oct. 1, 1802, CERP. The name of the candidate referred to by Baldwin is elided in the original; Tiffin is my guess.

26. *Scioto Gazette,* Aug. 21, 28, Sept. 4, 11, 18, Oct. 16, 1802; Jonathan Mills Thornton, *Politics and Power in A Slave Society: Alabama, 1800–1860* (Baton Rouge: Louisiana State University Press, 1978), 72.

27. Pritchard to Worthington, Mar. 23, 1802, TWP, OHS. See also Heald, *Bezaleel Wells,* 36–37, 43–45; and Stuckey, "Formation of Leadership Groups in a Frontier Town," 24–66, which is the best corrective to the misleading account of Welles in Elkins and McKitrick, "A Meaning for Turner's Frontier," 350–51. Fischer, *Revolution of American Conservatism,* 409, is just wrong.

28. Pritchard to Worthington, Oct. 23, 1802, TWP, OHS.

29. Marietta *Ohio Gazette,* Jan. 1, Sept. 7, 1802, Apr. 24, 1806; proceedings of county convention for forming a state, Marietta, June 17, 1801, SPHP. Claims by Hooper, *Ohio Journalism,* 21–22, and Brown, "Frontier Politics," 233, 328, 398, that Silliman and the Marietta *Ohio Gazette* were Democratic Republican are mistaken. Silliman to E. Cutler and W. R. Putnam, Marietta, Dec. 22, 1801, ECP; Burnet to Timothy Walker, Oct. 5, 1843, Burnet Papers; Downes, *Frontier Ohio,* 218. For Silliman's background, see Evans, *Scioto County,* 56, and Aronson, *Status and Kinship,* 72.

30. Worthington to Massie, Jan. 17, 1802, in Massie, *Nathaniel Massie,* 181. See also Meigs Jr. to Cutler, Dec. 8, 1801, in Julia Perkins Cutler, *Ephraim Cutler,* 58–61; Worthington to Meigs, Dec. 20, 1801, SPHP.

31. B. I. Gilman to Fearing, Jan. 14, Feb. 4, 20, 1802, SPHP; Ephraim Cutler to Manasseh Cutler, Aug. 31, 1802, ECP. See also J. C. Symmes to Griffin Greene, Jan. 21, 1802, SPHP; Dudley Woodbridge Jr. to James Backus, Feb. 17, 1802, Backus-Woodbridge Collection; and, for Greene, see Joseph Barker, *Recollections of the First Settlement of Ohio,* 49. The main beneficiary locally of the new federal dispensation was the elder Return Jonathan Meigs, whom Jefferson appointed Cherokee Indian agent and agent of the War Department in Tennessee in May 1801—thus simplifying our tale after this chapter.

32. *Western Spy,* Sept. 3, 10, 1799, Oct. 20, 1802; pollsheet for territorial election in Hamilton County, Sept. 12, 1799, CHS; Henry Howe, *Historical Collections* (centennial edition), 1:754.

33. St. Clair to Fearing, Feb. 17, 1801, Worthington to Fearing, Jan. 28, 1801, SPHP; William Creighton Jr. to Worthington, Jan. 30, 1802, TWP, OHS.

34. Daniel Symmes, reported in J. C. Symmes to Worthington, June 24, 1802, TWP, RCHS, and Massie to Worthington, Oct. 1, 1802, TWP, OHS, and in Smith, *St. Clair Papers,* 1:242, 2:591; Jacob White to Massie, Aug. 15, 1802, Massie Family Papers (Collection 965), OHS.

35. *Western Spy,* July 31, Sept. 18, 1802. See also Link, *Democratic-Republican Societies;* Sharp, *American Politics in the Early Republic,* 100–101; and, for England, see John Brewer, *Party Ideology and Popular Politics at the Accession of George III* (Cambridge: Cambridge University Press, 1976).

36. *Western Spy,* May 1, July 3, 10, Aug. 21, 1802; Robert McClure to Worthington, Mar. 4, 1802, TWP, OHS; Pocock, "Popular Roots of Jacksonian Democracy," 503. The num-

ber of Republican societies is variously given as nineteen or seventeen; the discrepancy may arise because two of them were probably in Clermont County, which had been newly carved out of Hamilton.

37. *Western Spy,* Aug. 28, Sept. 11, 18, 25, Oct. 2, 1802.

38. Ratcliffe, "Voter Turnout in Early Ohio," 231–32.

39. Ibid., 233–37.

40. Burnet, *Notes,* 341 n; *Scioto Gazette,* July 24, 1802.

41. John Armstrong to Tiffin, Feb. 13, 1802, Edward Tiffin Papers, OHS; James Caldwell to Worthington, Mar. 8, 1802; Francis Dunlavy to Worthington, Aug. 12, 1802, CERP; Cutler, *Ephraim Cutler,* 68.

42. Burnet, *Notes,* 378, 341 n.

43. *Scioto Gazette,* June 5, 12, Sept. 4, 11, 1802; Samuel Huntington Jr. to Turhand Kirtland, Dec. 3, 1802, reprinted in Conlin, *Simon Perkins,* 53–54. For Finley, see Smith, *St. Clair Papers,* 2:495, 565; little is known about Grubb.

44. J. C. Symmes to Worthington, June 24, 1802, TWP, RCHS; *Scioto Gazette,* Sept. 11, 1802.

45. Smith, *St. Clair Papers,* 2:565 n; Thomas Scott, "Memoir of Hon. Thomas Scott, Chillicothe, Ohio, By Himself," ms., RCHS.

46. Smith, *St. Clair Papers,* 1:241, 2:565, 571–72, 586; Downes, *Frontier Ohio,* 242–46; Pocock, "A Candidate I'll Surely Be," 64, 53. For a comparative view, see Cunningham, *Jeffersonian Republicans,* 144–261, and *Jeffersonian Republicans in Power,* 125–202; and Prince, *New Jersey's Jeffersonian Republicans,* 62.

47. Bond, "Memoirs of Benjamin Van Cleve," 65; Worthington to Fearing, Jan. 28, 1801, and to [Meigs Jr.?], May 25, 1802, SPHP.

48. Worthington to the president, Jan. 30, 1802, in Smith, *St. Clair Papers,* 2:569–570. The editor, William Henry Smith, could imagine "the broad smile that must have spread over the face of Thomas Jefferson when he read that solemn accusation from the pen of his ambitious political manager in the new Republican State." Ibid., 569, n.2.

49. Smith, *St. Clair Papers,* 2:587–90; *Western Spy,* Aug. 28, 1802. See also *Western Spy,* Oct. 2, 9, 1802; Burnet, *Notes,* 501.

50. *Scioto Gazette,* Sept. 25, 1802; *Western Spy,* Aug. 28, Sept. 11, 18, 25, Oct. 2, 1802.

51. *Western Spy,* Oct. 20, 1802.

52. Morris, *Thomas Morris,* 20; St. Clair to Woodbridge, Dec. 24, 1801, in Smith, *St. Clair Papers,* 2:548. Smith has sometimes been described as unpopular in Cincinnati because, it is presumed, of a business connection with Symmes, e.g., by Downes, *Frontier Ohio,* 87, and Brown, "Frontier Politics," 153–54. The main evidence cited for his unpopularity is this quotation from St. Clair, in which the phrase "go down" is taken to mean "fail" or "be rejected." It is more likely to mean "be swallowed" or "find acceptance," which was a long established usage by 1800 and certainly fits the context of the letter much better. Other meanings were already known. *The Oxford English Dictionary* (2d ed.), 20 vols. (Oxford: Clarendon Press, 1989), 6:627.

53. C. W. Byrd to Massie, June 20, 1802, in Massie, *Nathaniel Massie,* 210–11; Smith, *St. Clair Papers,* 2:572; *Western Spy,* Oct. 20, 1802.

54. *Scioto Gazette,* Aug. 28, Sept. 4, 11, Oct. 16, 1802. I can find no evidence that the convention actually met, *contra* Pocock, "A Candidate I'll Surely Be," 53.

55. For the Western Reserve, Ratcliffe, "Benjamin Tappan," 137–38, and Conlin, *Simon Perkins,* 53. For Fairfield, see Jacob Beck to Charles E. Rice, Nov. 7, 1894, CERP.

56. Marietta *Ohio Gazette,* Sept. 28, 1802. See also Downes, "Thomas Jefferson and the Removal of Governor St. Clair," 73, 76–77; Carter, *Territorial Papers,* 3:254.

57. Cayton, *Frontier State,* 12–32.

58. Proceedings of a county convention for forming a state, Marietta, June 17, 1801, SPHP; Cutler, *Ephraim Cutler,* 68.

59. R. J. Meigs [Sr.] to Massie and to Worthington, Jan. 15, 1801, in Massie, *Nathaniel Massie,* 166–68, and Smith, *St. Clair Papers,* 2:527–28; Meigs [probably Jr.] to Worthington, Nov. 20, 1801, TWP, RCHS; Gilman to Fearing, Jan. 14, Feb. 4, 20, 1802, SPHP.

60. R. J. Meigs [Sr.] to Massie, Jan. 15, 1801, in Massie, *Nathaniel Massie,* 166–68; R. J. Meigs [Sr.] to Worthington, Jan. 15, 1801, in Smith, *St. Clair Papers,* 2:527–28; R. J. Meigs Jr. to Worthington, Marietta, 18 May 1802, TWP, OHS; Cutler, reported in Worthington to [Meigs Jr.], May 25, 1802, SPHP.

61. B. I. Gilman to Fearing, Jan. 14, 4, Feb. 20, 1802, SPHP; Fearing to Cutler, Feb. 3, 19, 1802, ECP, and in Cutler, *Ephraim Cutler,* 63–65.

62. Daniel Symmes, quoted in J. C. Symmes to Worthington, June 24, 1802, TWP, RCHS and in Smith, *St. Clair Papers,* 1:242. The *Western Spy and Hamilton Gazette* had appeared in May 1799 as a rival to the more Republican *Freeman's Journal.* Early in 1800, Freeman moved his paper to the more promising location of Chillicothe, where the paper changed hands and became the *Scioto Gazette* before the year was out. Hooper, *Ohio Journalism,* 14–15. Most of the extant political pamphlets and broadsides published in Cincinnati and Marietta in 1802 expressed Federalist arguments.

63. Paul Fearing to St. Clair, May 1, 1802, in Smith, *St. Clair Papers,* 2:583 and Carter, *Territorial Papers,* 3:220–21. For the conventions, see proceedings of county convention for forming a state, Marietta, June 17, 1801, SPHP; Cutler, *Ephraim Cutler,* 65–66.

64. Worthington to Massie, May 26, 1802, in Massie, *Nathaniel Massie,* 207; John S. Gano to St. Clair, Nov. 15, 1800, in Smith, *St. Clair Papers,* 2:524; Putnam to Worthington, Oct. 20, 1800, and William Ludlow to Tiffin, Dec. 22, 1801, TWP, OHS.

65. Smith, *St. Clair Papers,* 2:548–49, 557–58; Dudley Woodbridge to Fearing, Jan. 14, 1802, SPHP.

66. *Scioto Gazette,* Aug. 21, Sept. 4, 18, 1802.

67. Ephraim Cutler to Manasseh Cutler, Aug. 31, 1802, ECP; Cutler, *Ephraim Cutler,* 65–67.

68. B. I. Gilman to Fearing, Feb. 20, 1802, SPHP; Dudley Woodbridge Jr. to James Backus, Feb. 17, 1802, and Paul Fearing to Dudley Woodbridge Sr., Feb. 28, 1802, Backus-Woodbridge Papers; James Pritchard to Worthington, Oct. 23, 1802, TWP, OHS; Cutler, *Ephraim Cutler,* 68.

69. Burnet to Cutler, Sept. 26, 1847, ECP; Cutler, *Ephraim Cutler,* 68–69. For the question of submitting the constitution to the voters, see chap. 1, pp. 42–43.

70. Massie, *Nathaniel Massie,* 88–90.

71. Cutler, *Ephraim Cutler*, 69–71, 73–74. This volume, pp. 68–82, reprints recollections of the convention "written in a very desultory manner in the old age of Ephraim Cutler," who died in 1853; this published version derives from several ms. accounts (some of which give extra details) in ECP. Roll calls are recorded in the *Journal of the Convention of the Territory of the United States North-west of the Ohio River* (Chillicothe, 1802), which is reprinted in Ryan, "From Charter to Constitution," 80–132; page references here are to the latter version. Most of the Federalists voted together in thirty-six of the forty-five recorded roll calls—five or six of them on twenty-three occasions, and all seven together on thirteen occasions. Although one or two other delegates are sometimes associated with the Federalists, notably Samuel Huntington, and Cutler refers to ten men voting on that side, only seven can be clearly identified as Federalists. Worthington had analyzed the convention as twenty-six decided Republicans, seven Federalists, and two doubtful. Downes, "Jefferson and the Removal of St. Clair," 76–77. For the Tennessee constitution, see Barnhart, *Valley of Democracy.*

72. Cutler, *Ephraim Cutler*, 70, 71, 73; Samuel Huntington Jr. to Turhand Kirtland, Dec. 3, 1802, in Conlin, *Simon Perkins*, 53–54; *Western Spy*, Dec. 2, 1802. Another delegate, Philip Gatch, remembered that "in general, unanimity prevailed among the members of the Convention." Connor, *Methodist Trail Blazer*, 206, 209.

73. Ephraim Cutler to George Ewing, [early November 1802], quoted in Martzolff, "Autobiography of Thomas Ewing," 152. As Ewing was quoting from memory sixty-seven years after the event, this evidence must be treated cautiously; Ewing said he could not remember the final figure, which I have deduced.

74. *Scioto Gazette*, June 12, Sept. 4, 1802; Ephraim Cutler, July Fourth Oration, [Waterford], 1802, ms., ECP; Marietta *Ohio Gazette*, Oct. 4, 1802; Burnet, *Notes*, 359–60. Burnet added that "experience has shown that the danger was not as serious as was anticipated."

75. *Western Spy*, Sept. 18, 1802.

76. *Scioto Gazette*, Aug. 28, June 5, 1802; "Some of the People" to Worthington, Pickaway and Green Townships, Oct. 11, 1802, TWP, RCHS.

77. *Scioto Gazette*, July 17, 1802; *Western Spy*, Aug. 21, 1802. For Highland County, see Finley, *Autobiography*, 150; Trimble, *Autobiography and Correspondence*, 70–73; Kilbourn, *Ohio Gazetteer* (11th ed., 1833), 342.

78. Dunlevy, *Miami Baptist Association*, 57; Connor, *Methodist Trail Blazer*, 206–7; Cutler, *Ephraim Cutler*, 69. Of those on the Society ticket, Byrd tended to vote with the Virginian group, while Judge William Goforth voted fairly conservatively on most issues.

79. Cutler, *Ephraim Cutler*, 70–73. Cutler's account of the maneuverings over the judiciary article is supported by contemporary evidence in *Western Spy*, Dec. 1, 1802, and Samuel Huntington Jr. to Worthington, Oct. 3 [30?], 1803, TWP, OHS.

80. Burnet, *Notes*, 354; Ryan, "From Charter to Constitution," 111; Cutler, *Ephraim Cutler*, 74–77; *Western Spy*, Oct. 2, 1802; *Scioto Gazette*, Aug. 28, Sept. 11, 18, 1802. Cutler's account has been much criticized, for example in Gilmore, *Edward Tiffin*, 70–77, and Thurston, "1802 Constitutional Convention and the Status of the Negro," 24 n. 20.

However, the critics sometimes confuse proceedings in committee (which Cutler is talking about) with proceedings in the full convention, for which there is a formal record. Nor was there an improbable inconsistency in a Republican voting both for this supposed proposal of Jefferson's and for antislavery measures later in the convention. For the Jeffersonian belief that diffusion would lead to slavery's destruction, see William W. Freehling, *The Road to Disunion: Secessionists at Bay, 1776–1854* (New York: Oxford University Press, 1990).

81. Ryan, "From Charter to Constitution," 113, 114, 122, 124–25. Thurston, "1802 Constitutional Convention and the Status of the Negro," is a valuable survey of the evidence, but errs in some identifications and in its conclusion that there was no significant difference between party members in voting on racial issues. All seven undoubted Federalists voted in favor of prohibiting indentures that might covertly allow the holding of slaves, whereas the Republicans divided 14–12. Thurston's pro-Negro groups included the members from Hamilton County and those from Clermont County. See Thurston, 21, 27–28, 33.

82. Ryan, "From Charter to Constitution," 103, 104, 113–14, 122; Worthington to [W. B. Giles?], Mar. 20, 1802, TWP, RCHS; Samuel Huntington to Turhand Kirtland, Dec. 3, 1802, in Conlin, *Simon Perkins*, 54. Edward Tiffin left no voting record because he was president of the convention, but he may be bracketed with Worthington on the strength of his statement to the voters in the *Scioto Gazette*, Aug. 28, 1802. For the assumption that these men opposed the wide distribution of political power, see Cayton, *Frontier Republic*.

83. *Scioto Gazette*, Aug. 28, 1802; *Western Spy*, July 24, 1802; "Some of the People" to Worthington, Pickaway and Green Townships, Oct. 11, 1802, TWP, RCHS.

84. Ryan, "From Charter to Constitution," 113–14, 122; constitution, article IV:1, 5; Cutler, draft article for the Marietta *American Friend* [1819], ECP. The constitution is widely reprinted, notably in Ryan, "From Charter to Constitution"; for the obligation to labor on the roads, see Chase, *Statutes of Ohio*, 1:262–63, 338–39.

85. Constitution, article I:2, 4, 7, 10, 15, 19, article IV:1, 2, article VII:2, article VIII:16, 19; Heale, *Making of American Politics*, 123.

86. James H. Hitchman, ed., "John Jay Janney and his 'Recollections of Thomas Corwin,'" *Ohio History* 73 (1964): 109; *Scioto Gazette*, Aug. 28, 1802; Joseph Darlington, May 1830, in Kilbourn, *Geography of Ohio*, 72; Cutler, *Ephraim Cutler*, 78.

87. Smith, *St. Clair Papers*, 2:488–89, 519; Martzolff, "Autobiography of Thomas Ewing," 152; constitution, article I:5. A senator had to be five years older and to have resided in the district one year longer. For the long debate on this point in the Kentucky convention of 1799, see Coward, *Kentucky in the New Republic*, 146–50.

88. Ryan, "From Charter to Constitution," 105–9, 111–12, 126; constitution, article I:19, article VII:4; Burnet, *Notes*, 358.

89. *Scioto Gazette*, Aug. 28, 1802. See also Levin Belt to Fearing, Dec. 3, 1802, SPHP; Burnet, *Notes*, 357–58.

90. Foote, quoted in Morris, *Thomas Morris*, 45.

91. Faragher, *Sugar Creek*, 141, 145–46, 154.

CHAPTER 3. THE MERIDIAN HEIGHT OF PARTY, 1803–1804

1. Massie to Worthington, Dec. 8, 1802, and Worthington to Massie, Dec. 25, 1802, Jan. 6, 1803, in Massie, *Nathaniel Massie*, 219–22; Abraham Baldwin to Huntington, Mar. 5, 1803, Samuel Huntington Papers; Fearing to Cutler, Jan. 20, 1803, ECP; Meigs Jr. to Worthington, Jan. 31, 1803, TWP, OHS.

2. Chillicothe *Scioto Gazette,* Jan. 15, 26, Feb. 26, 1803. For the 1803 caucus, see Steubenville *Western Herald,* Aug. 23, 1806; Chillicothe *Supporter,* Jan. 26, 1809; Thomas Scott, "Memoir of Hon. Thomas Scott, Chillicothe, Ohio, by Himself," ms., SWP, [19–20].

3. Tiffin to Worthington, Dec. 24, 1802, and William Goforth to Worthington, Dec. 24, 1802, CERP; Tiffin to Worthington, Jan. 7, 1803, TWP, OHS; Cincinnati *Western Spy,* Dec. 8, 1802, Jan. 5, 12, 19, 1803; *Scioto Gazette,* Jan. 8, 15, 1803.

4. Tiffin to Worthington, Jan. 7, 24, 1803, TWP, OHS.

5. In addition, one vote was given to Elias Langham for Congress. Cincinnati *Western Spy,* May 11, 18, 25, June 22, 29, Aug. 3, 1803; Worthington to Goforth, May 25, 1803, reprinted in John S. Williams, *American Pioneer* 2 (1843): 89. See also Huntington to Worthington, May 2, 1803, TWP, OHS.

6. *Scioto Gazette,* Jan. 22, 1803; Pritchard to Worthington, June 24, Oct. 31, 1803, TWP, OHS. For statewide results by county, see *Scioto Gazette,* June 25, July 2, 9, Aug. 3, 1803.

7. Silliman's tergiversation is difficult to date, but he was named as Republican candidate for the assembly in the elections of January 1803, though Worthington still had to be reassured of his soundness in February, a month before he was elected president judge by the general assembly. B. I. Gilman to Fearing, Feb. 14, 1803, SPHP; Meigs [Jr.] to Worthington, Mar. 5, 1803, TWP, OHS; Gilkey, *Ohio Hundred Year Book,* 494.

8. Meigs Jr. to Worthington, Jan. 31, 1803, TWP, OHS; *Scioto Gazette,* Jan. 22, Feb. 26, 1803; abstracts and pollbooks, Washington County, WCC.

9. Scott, "Memoir of Thomas Scott," [19–20].

10. Ohio constitution, article II:16, article III:2, 3, article V; article VI:2.

11. Chase, *Statutes of Ohio,* 1:352–78.

12. Constitution, article VI:1, 3, 4; Chase, *Statutes of Ohio,* 1:272–73, 352–78. Cayton, "Land, Power, and Reputation," 285, surely errs in saying, "The beauty of the Ohio constitution was the way in which it decentralized government into the hands of local leaders."

13. Belt to Fearing, Feb. 14, 1803, SPHP; Chillicothe *Supporter,* Jan. 26, 1809. This is a much earlier use of "logroll" than that normally given as the earliest known use, which is *Niles' Weekly Register* 24 (June 7, 1823): 210–11. *The Oxford English Dictionary,* 2d ed., 20 vols. (Oxford: Clarendon Press, 1989), 8:1114.

14. *Western Spy,* June 15, Sept. 28, 1803.

15. *Western Spy,* Sept. 7, 28, Oct. 12, 19, 1803, Sept. 7, 1804; Huntington to Worthington, Oct. 3 [30?], 1803, William Creighton Jr. to Worthington, Oct. 17, 1803, McArthur to Worthington, Oct. 21, 1803, Tiffin to Worthington, Oct. 24, Nov. 2, 1803, and Samuel

Carpenter to Worthington, Nov. 7, 1803, TWP, OHS. Cf. Utter, "Ohio Politics and Politicians," 31, 39, 41–42.

16. David Abbot to Worthington, Jan. 17, 1804, Tiffin to Worthington, Dec. 8, 1803, Jan. 9, 1803 [1804], Massie to Worthington, Feb. 1, 1804, McArthur to Worthington, TWP, OHS. See also W. Jackson to Griffin Greene, Jan. 13, 1804, SPHP.

17. Chase, *Statutes of Ohio*, 1:399, 410–12.

18. Silliman to Worthington, Dec. 29, 1803, and Massie to Worthington, Feb. 1, 1804, TWP, OHS.

19. Tiffin to Worthington, Dec. 26, 1803, Jan. 13, 1804, Silliman to Worthington, Nov. 2, 1803; see also Samuel Carpenter to Worthington, Nov. 7, 1803, TWP, OHS.

20. McCormick, "Political Development and the Second Party System," 109–11.

21. Tiffin to Worthington, Feb. 20, 1804; *Scioto Gazette,* Sept. 24, Oct. 8, 1804; Carpenter to Worthington, Nov. 7, 1803, TWP, OHS.

22. *Western Spy,* Sept. 26, Oct. 17, 1804.

23. Tiffin to Worthington, Nov. 11, Dec. 24, 1804; see also McArthur to Worthington, Dec. 21, 1804, Jan. 10, 1806, TWP, OHS, and Gilkey, *Ohio Hundred Year Book,* 496. For the results, see *Scioto Gazette,* Nov. 12, 19, 1804.

24. Daniel Symmes and others to Worthington, May 31, 1804, CERP; *Western Spy,* Oct. 17, Nov. 7, 1804. See also J. W. Browne to Worthington, [July 31, 1804], TWP, RCHS; *Scioto Gazette,* Sept. 24, Oct. 29, Nov. 5, 19, 1804; Massie, *Nathaniel Massie,* 230.

25. Steubenville *Western Herald,* Aug. 23, 1806.

26. The Pearson coefficient of correlation between the two distributions is 0.74 ($r^2 = 0.54$). Abstracts of votes, Washington County, 1803, and pollbooks and tallysheets for Adams Township, 1804–5, WCC. The Adams Township returns (and those for Newport Township) are unusual in that the clerks of election for many years after 1803 misinterpreted the law on elections and kept their pollbooks and tallysheets in a way that revealed which candidates each voter selected.

27. *Western Spy,* Oct. 19, 1803, Oct. 17, Nov. 7, 1804; Washington *National Intelligencer,* Nov. 19, 1804. See also James Pritchard to Worthington, Jefferson County, Oct. 31, 1803, TWP, OHS; and abstract of votes, Montgomery County, October 1803, WSU.

28. Tiffin to Worthington, Jan. 14, 1803, TWP, OHS; *Scioto Gazette,* Oct. 8, 1804; Cincinnati *Liberty Hall,* Sept. 30, 1806.

29. *Western Spy,* June 15, 1803. See also Ratcliffe, "Voter Turnout in Early Ohio," 241–42.

30. Calvin Pease to Huntington, May 21, 1803, Huntington Papers, LCHS. See also Martin Baum to Fearing, May 2, 1803, SPHP; Paul Fearing, David Putnam and W. R. Putnam to Huntington, May 9, 1803, Huntington Papers, WRHS; Jacob Burnet and others to Massie, May 9, 1803, in Massie, *Nathaniel Massie,* 227–28.

31. Tiffin to Worthington, Jan. 14, 18, 1803, TWP, OHS; *Scioto Gazette,* Jan. 15, 22, Feb. 26, 1803.

32. *Scioto Gazette,* Oct. 1 (quotation), 24, Nov. 12, 1804; Byrd to Worthington, Nov. 23, 1804, TWP, OHS. See also *Western Spy,* Oct. 17, 31, 1804.

33. The emphasis on cultural differences between different groups of settlers dates back to Chaddock, *Ohio before 1850;* Power, *Planting Corn Belt Culture;* and Barnhart's "Southern Element in the Leadership of the Old Northwest," "Southern Influence in the Formation of Ohio," and *Valley of Democracy.*

34. Cayton, *Frontier Republic,* and especially "Land, Power and Reputation." Some other recent writing tends to express the conflict in cruder terms akin to the older tradition, as, for example, in Brown, "Ohio Federalists," esp. 266 n. Etcheson, *Emerging Midwest,* is erected on the assumption that upland southerners in the Old Northwest were culturally distinctive, but rather proves the opposite.

35. Michaux, *Travels to the West;* Jessup N. Couch, diary, Sept. 11, 1804 through May 26, 1805, VFM 1672, OHS, entry for Oct. 12, 1804; [Cutler], *Topographical Description,* 22–23; Joseph Barker, *Recollections,* 39–51.

36. Harris, *Journal of a Tour,* 58–59. The cleavage within the county is made obvious in [Mathews], *Washington County:* compare 499, 556–60, 684–87, 608–13, 711–15, 580–86, 634–40, 622–29, with 565–72, 593–99, 685–89, 655–60, 700–702.

37. Barnhart's account of the constitutional convention in his "Southern Influence in the Formation of Ohio" assumes that ethnocultural divisions were what mattered in producing voting alignments, which he cannot then adequately explain.

38. Hudson, "North American Origins of Middlewestern Populations," esp. 407–11; James M. Berquist, "Tracing the Origins of a Midwestern Culture: The Case of Central Indiana," *Indiana Magazine of History* 77 (1981), 10–11.

39. Elisha Tracy to Samuel Huntington Jr., Hartford, Conn., May 15, 1802, in Benton, "Huntington Correspondence," 79; Huntington to Worthington, Cleveland, Jan. 18, 1803, TWP, OHS; Brown, "Samuel Huntington," 422.

40. J. Cook to Jefferson, Oct. 21, 1801, quoted in Fischer, *Revolution of American Conservatism,* 218 n; Meigs Jr. to Worthington, May 18, 1802, TWP, OHS.

41. S. Wilkeson, "Early Recollections of the West," 206–17; Steubenville *Western Herald,* Oct. 11, 1806. See also Hunter, "Pathfinders of Jefferson County," 208–9; Dunaway, "Pennsylvania as an Early Distributing Center," 113–14; Slaughter, *Whiskey Rebellion.*

42. *Western Spy,* July 24, Oct. 2, 1802; Brown, "Frontier Politics," 312, 356 n. 16. For the Virginia Military District, see Hutchinson, "Bounty Lands," and E. D. Mansfield's draft of vol. 2 of his memoirs (ms., E. D. Mansfield Papers), 1–2.

43. Martzolff, "Rev. Paul Henkel's Journal," 175–94; abstracts of votes, Montgomery County, 1803–26, WSU.

44. Cuming, *Sketches of a Tour,* 74; Yeager, "Religion in Ohio," 25–26; Ashe, *Travels in America,* 1:257.

45. Steubenville *Western Herald,* July 4, 1807; B. I. Gilman to Paul Fearing, Feb. 20, 1802, SPHP.

46. Tappan to Nancy Tappan, Jan. 22, 1804, BTP, LC, ellipsis in original; Smith to Worthington, June 30, 1806, TWP, OHS. See also *Scioto Gazette,* June 25, 1801; Cartwright, *Backwoods Preacher,* 42; Brown, "Ohio Federalists," 273. Etcheson identifies the statehood movement in Ohio with upland southerners, but agrees that no easy identi-

fication can be made between party support and the regional origins of settlers. Etcheson, *Emerging Midwest*, 10–12, 40.

47. Lipson, *Freemasonry in Federalist Connecticut*.

48. Calvin Pease to Tappan, Apr. 28, July 25, 1799, BTP, LC; Badger, *Memoir*, 26–27. See also Ratcliffe, "Benjamin Tappan," 112–13, 118–19, 128–30.

49. Riddle, "Rise of the Antislavery Sentiment," 151–52; Cartwright, *Backwoods Preacher*, 42–44; Finley, *Sketches of Western Methodism*, 454–57.

50. Bushnell, *Granville*, and Utter, *Granville*; Berquist and Bowers, "Kilbourn's Episcopal Haven," and *New Eden*, viii, 41–45, 67–69.

51. James Pritchard to Worthington, Oct. 23, 1802, John Sloane to Worthington, Aug. 6, 1808, TWP, OHS. See also Smith, "The Quakers," and Burke and Bensch, "Mount Pleasant and the Early Quakers."

52. Yeager, "Religion in Ohio," 9–10, 12–15, 21–23; Finley, *Western Methodism*, 102. See also Kennedy, *Plan of Union;* Josiah Morrow's chapter on "Presbyterians, New Lights and Shakers," in his ms. biography of Francis Dunlavy, Morrow Papers; and for Dayton, see Pocock, "Evangelical Frontier."

53. Finley, *Western Methodism*, 73–79, 85–89, 102, 183, 195–97, 347, and *Autobiography*, 165–77, 362–68; John Marshall Barker, *Ohio Methodism*, 82–96, 116–18, 123, 136–37, 144–53, 306–447; Dunlevy, *Miami Baptist Association*, 41ff., 154; Downes, *Frontier Ohio*, 88–100; Yeager, "Religion in Ohio," esp. 3–8, 16–17, 28, 30. For Virginia, see Isaac, *Transformation of Virginia*.

54. Finley, *Western Methodism*, 60, 260–87, and *Autobiography*, 127, 130–33; Scott, "Memoir of Thomas Scott," SWP. Worthington is sometimes described as a Quaker: his father came of Quaker stock but was ejected for marrying a non-Quaker, and his sister Mary (Mrs. Tiffin) was a committed Methodist. Worthington himself attended Methodist and Presbyterian churches regularly, Quaker meetings occasionally. Sears, *Thomas Worthington*, 43–45.

55. Dunlevy, *Miami Baptist Association*, 96–119, 147–65; Estelle Wade Spining, "Notes Concerning Judge William Goforth," (ms., CHS).

56. Ephraim Cutler's Notes and Autobiographical Sketches, ECP, contain this story, which was omitted from the published version in Cutler, *Ephraim Cutler*, 67–68. For Gatch, see Connor, *Methodist Trail Blazer*.

57. J. C. Symmes to Jonathan Dayton, Nov. 25, 1788, in Bond, *Correspondence of John Cleves Symmes*, 50–51; Williams, *American Pioneer* 1 (1842): 40; Dunlevy, *Miami Baptist Association*, esp. 30–37; Yeager, "Religion in Ohio," 7–8.

58. Finley, *Western Methodism*, 88–89, 102 (quotation), 455–58; Cayton, "Language Gives Way to Feelings," 43. See also Cartwright, *Backwoods Preacher*, 24–52, 61; Yeager, "Religion in Ohio," 5–7; John Marshall Barker, *Ohio Methodism*, 123.

59. Charles C. Cole, *The Social Ideas of the Northern Evangelists, 1826–1860* (New York, 1954), 13–14, claims that only one person in fifteen was connected with a Protestant church in 1800.

60. Cartwright, *Backwoods Preacher*, 30–32, 35–36, 40, 62–63; Finley, *Autobiography,*

245–52. See also Utter, *Frontier State,* 362–63, 382–83; Boase, "Moral Policemen"; Rohrer, "Battling the Master Vice," 1–5; and for the territorial period, see Cincinnati *Centinel,* Dec. 6, 1794, Jan. 10, 17, Sept. 19, 1795.

61. Marietta *Ohio Gazette,* Sept. 29, 1808.

62. W. R. Southward, *Chillicothe in 1811: Reminiscences of an Old Merchant* (1866; reprint, Chillicothe: David K. Webb, 1950), [8]; Katzenberger, "Major David Ziegler," 133. See also Alfred Young, *Democratic Republicans of New York,* 363.

63. Drake, *Notices concerning Cincinnati,* 30–31; *Western Spy,* June 22, Oct. 12, 1803, Sept. 26, 1804. See also Alfred Young, "The Mechanics and the Jeffersonians: New York, 1789–1801," *Labor History* 5 (1964): 247–76.

64. *Western Spy,* July 9, Aug. 13, 1800; *History of Ross and Highland Counties,* 73.

65. Michaux, *Travels to the West,* 89–90; Cuming, *Sketches of a Tour,* 106.

66. Cutler to Manasseh Cutler, Aug. 31, 1802, ECP; B. I. Gilman to Fearing, Feb. 20, 1802, SPHP. See also Tiffin to Worthington, Jan. 24, 1803, TWP, OHS; *Scioto Gazette,* Oct. 24, 1804.

67. Dudley Woodbridge to Fearing, Jan. 14, 1802, SPHP, and Cutler, *Ephraim Cutler,* 55 n; Marietta *Ohio Gazette,* Aug. 17, 1802. See also Smith, *St. Clair Papers,* 2: 549–50.

68. Pollbooks for Newport and Adams Townships, Oct. 12, 1802, Marietta College; *Western Spy,* Oct. 20, 1802.

69. Burnet to Fearing, Jan. 19, 1802, and B. I. Gilman to Fearing, Feb. 20, 1802, SPHP. See also Downes, *Frontier Ohio,* 155–63.

70. *Western Spy,* Aug. 27, Sept. 3, 10, Oct. 2, 1800, Aug. 21, 1802; *Scioto Gazette,* Aug. 28, 1802.

71. *Western Spy,* July 3, 1802, and *Scioto Gazette,* July 3, 1802; Jared Mansfield to William Lyon Jr., Feb. 20, 1804, Jared Mansfield Papers. For the broader scene, see Fischer, *Revolution of American Conservatism,* 201–26; Dauer, *Adams Federalists,* 7, 18–25, 275–87. See also Kelley, *Cultural Pattern in American Politics,* 109–40; Young, *Democratic Republicans of New York,* 468–95; Broussard, *Southern Federalists,* 375–80.

72. Michaux, *Travels to the West,* 111; Worthington to [Meigs Jr.], May 25, 1802, SPHP. See also Banning, *Jeffersonian Persuasion,* and compare Appleby, "Commercial Farming and the 'Agrarian Myth'" and *Capitalism and a New Social Order,* esp. 39–50.

73. *Western Spy,* May 25, 1803.

74. Ratcliffe, "Voter Turnout in Early Ohio," 244.

75. See, e.g., Republican Address, Cincinnati *Liberty Hall,* Aug. 13, 1808.

76. Formisano, *Transformation of Political Culture,* applies the term to the whole period from the 1790s to the 1820s.

77. Wilkeson, "Early Recollections of the West," 217; Cutler, July 4 oration, 1802, ECP; *Scioto Gazette,* Oct. 23, 1800, Jan. 8, 1801. For the significance of the passion and emotional frenzy of politics at this period, see Smelser, "The Federalist Period as an Age of Passion," and "Jacobin Phrenzy"; John R. Howe Jr., "Republican Thought and the Political Violence of the 1790s."

78. Hendrik V. Booraem, *The Formation of the Republican Party in New York: Politics and Conscience in the Antebellum North* (New York, 1983), 221.

CHAPTER 4. THE STRUCTURE OF POLITICS AFTER THE ACCESSION TO STATEHOOD

1. Burnet, *Notes on the North-Western Territory;* William Henry Smith, *St. Clair Papers.*

2. Cayton, *Frontier Republic;* Cayton and Onuf, *Midwest and the Nation.*

3. Buel, *Securing the Revolution,* 75.

4. Smith, *St. Clair Papers,* 2:482.

5. Soltow, "Inequality amidst Abundance," 142–43, and "Tocqueville's View of the Northwest in 1835," 139. Soltow's figures for wealth distribution in 1825 and 1835 do not show great change from 1810. See also Soltow, "Progress and Mobility among Ohio Propertyholders, 1810–1825," 414–15.

6. Finley, *Autobiography,* 122–23; St. Clair to Paul Fearing, Dec. 25, 1801, in Carter, *Territorial Papers,* 3:187. See also Cayton, "Land, Power and Reputation," 275–82; Cramer, "Duncan McArthur," 1–10; Shannon, "This Unpleasant Business," 15–30.

7. Brown, "Samuel Huntington." In 1804 Huntington owned 98 acres, compared with the 4,968 reported in 1810.

8. William Creighton Jr. to Worthington, Mar. 5, 1804, TWP, OHS; J. C. Symmes to Charles Wilkins Short, Feb. 23, Apr. 9, 1810, in Bond, ed., *Intimate Letters of Symmes,* 37–38; Hildreth, *Genealogical and Biographical Sketches,* 191, 196. See also Judge Carter, *Old Court House,* for "amusing" stories of the legal profession.

9. Soltow, "Inequality amidst Abundance," 140–41. Soltow's figures are not beyond dispute, because the tax lists show who paid the tax rather than who owned the land. Some landowners were also agents for nonresidents, and the records do not clearly indicate who owned the land upon which they were paying taxes. Philip Gatch is recorded in 1810 as paying taxes on 5,127 acres in Clermont County, which is rather more than his biography shows him to have owned in that county. In 1810–11 Simon Perkins acted as agent for a number of Connecticut proprietors, not one of whom is listed in the tax records for 1810, and he paid some taxes in his own name on 3,000 acres he probably did not own. Connor, *Methodist Trail Blazer,* 186, 217–19, 234; Benton, "Connecticut Land Company," 197–99; Conlin, *Simon Perkins,* 57.

10. Soltow, "Inequality amidst Abundance," 141, 150–51. Soltow exaggerates the median holding for the constitutional convention by excluding from his calculations Edward Tiffin (who owned 720 acres), John Wilson (115 acres), and John Reily (9 acres), though there can be little doubt about the identification. Like Soltow, I have assessed the landed property of individual delegates from Petty, *Ohio 1810 Tax Duplicate.*

11. Ashe, *Travels in America,* 1:203; Wade, *Urban Frontier,* 77–79; Kantzer, "Municipal Legislation in Ohio," 17–21, 53–54, 74, 78–79; Pocock, "Evangelical Frontier," 238–40. Most relevant studies of community power structure relate to Cincinnati after 1815; see

Aaron, *Cincinnati*, 58–59; Farrell, "Cincinnati in the Early Jackson Era," 177–78, and Flack, "Who Governed Cincinnati?"

12. Brown, "Samuel Huntington," 431; *History of Geauga and Lake Counties*, 196 (quotation); Wilgus, "Evolution of Township Government in Ohio," 407–9. The power to levy local taxation was given back to township trustees in 1810.

13. For the significance of the county court system, see Cayton, "Land, Power, and Reputation," 281–82; Coward, *Kentucky in the New Republic*. For Reily, see McBride, *Pioneer Biography*, 1:51, 56. The appointive nature of Ohio local government before the 1820s has been exaggerated by some authors; for a corrective, see Andrews, *Washington County*, 78–82; Rose, *Ohio Government*, 54, 73, 74.

14. Winkle, *Politics of Community*, and "Ohio's Informal Polling Place"; Chase, *Statutes of Ohio*, 1:365, 622.

15. Ratcliffe, "Voter Turnout in Early Ohio," 234–36; Pocock, "A Candidate I'll Surely Be," 65–66. There is much room for further research on election practices before the period Winkle has studied most thoroughly.

16. Ratcliffe, "Benjamin Tappan," 140. See also Grupenhoff, "Politics and the Rise of Political Parties,"155 n, 187–88; Stuckey, "Formation of Leadership Groups in a Frontier Town," 71–76, 88.

17. Jared Mansfield to William Lyon Jr., Feb. 20, 1804, Jared Mansfield Papers, OHS; Ashe, *Travels in America*, 1:298. See also Chillicothe *Scioto Gazette*, Feb. 26, 1803; Mansfield, *Personal Memories*, 5–6; Cutler, *Ephraim Cutler*, 65–66, 84–85; Buell, *Memoirs of Rufus Putnam*, 125–26, 439.

18. Pritchard to Worthington, June 24, Oct. 31, 1803, Samuel Carpenter to Worthington, Nov. 7, 1803, TWP, OHS; Rohrbough, *Land Office Business*, 183–84.

19. *Scioto Gazette*, Jan. 15, 1803; McArthur to Worthington, Jan. 17, 1803, TWP. For the "Chillicothe Junto" in recent writing, see especially Cayton, "Land, Power, and Reputation," and Brown, "Chillicothe's Elite," 101–23.

20. Henry Howe, *Historical Collections* (1847), 434, 436–37. See also James Flint, *Letters from America*, 122, speaking of 1804 or 1806; Martzolff, "Rev. Paul Henkel's Journal," 185, 187–88, 193; [Cutler], *Topographical Description*, 10, 41.

21. McArthur to Worthington, Mar. 16, 1799, TWP, OHS; M. Baldwin, *To the Electors of the State of Ohio*, June 7, 1803, broadside, TWP, RCHS.

22. Abraham Shepherd to Worthington, Feb. 13, 1799, TWP, OHS; *Scioto Gazette*, Sept. 4, 11, 18, Oct. 16, 1802; Baldwin to Worthington, Mar. 25, 1802, TWP, OHS, and Apr. 2, 1802, CERP; *Plain Truth and Very Plain Dealing, To the Citizens of Ross County, "By their deeds ye shall know them,"* [fall 1802], broadside, RCHS. In September 1802 Worthington called Langham "a man lost to every sense of honesty or honor." Clarence E. Carter, *Territorial Papers*, 3:244–47.

23. Burnet to Timothy Walker, Oct. 3, 1843, Burnet Papers, CHS, [3]; *Ross and Highland Counties*, 73–74; Thomas Scott, "Memoir of Hon. Thomas Scott, Chillicothe, Ohio, By Himself," ms., SWP; Howe, *Historical Collections* (1896), 2:517; Tiffin to Worthington, Dec. 24, 1802, John S. Wills to Worthington, Dec. 29, 1802, and William Creighton Jr. to Worthington, Mar. 5, 1804, TWP, OHS. For Worthington's relations

with Baldwin on their trip to Washington in 1801–2, see Massie, *Nathaniel Massie,* 176–77, 181–82, 204. For an interesting discussion that somewhat romanticizes and exaggerates the significance of Baldwin, see Cayton, "The Failure of Michael Baldwin." Baldwin was basically an upper-class rowdy—Prince Hal without the reformation—who drank himself to ruin and an early death in 1810. Chillicothe *Independent Republican,* Mar. 15, 1810.

24. M. Baldwin, *To the Electors of the State of Ohio,* June 7, 1803, and A Friend to Langham and Baldwin [probably Duncan McArthur], *To the Electors of the State of Ohio,* [1803], broadsides, RCHS; *Scioto Gazette,* May 21, June 25, 1803.

25. Silliman to Worthington, Nov. 2, 1803; McArthur to Worthington, Oct. 21, 1803; Tiffin to Worthington, Nov. 2, 1803, Jan. 9, 1803 [1804], Jan. 13, 19, Feb. 17, 20, 1804, TWP, OHS.

26. Tiffin to Worthington, Feb. 17, 20, 1804, Jan. 8, 1806, Jan. 3, 1807, TWP, OHS; *Scioto Gazette,* Oct. 15, 1804.

27. *History of Ross and Highland Counties,* 73; Fitch, *Breaking with Burr,* 158; Scott, "Memoir of Thomas Scott"; and election return, Nov. 4, 1808, SWP.

28. *Scioto Gazette,* May 21, 1803; M. Baldwin, *To the Electors of the State of Ohio,* June 7, 1803, broadside, RCHS; Tiffin to Worthington, Jan. 3, 1807, TWP, OHS.

29. *Scioto Gazette,* May 22, 1806; Cincinnati *Western Spy,* Aug. 23, Oct. 7, 1806; Steubenville *Western Herald,* Aug. 23, Sept. 13, 1806.

30. Tiffin to Worthington, Feb. 17, Nov. 11, Dec. 5, 1804, Jan. 8, 1806, Jan. 3, 9, 1807; McArthur to Worthington, Jan. 10, 1806; Silliman to Worthington, Jan. 2, 6, 1807, TWP, OHS. See also *Scioto Gazette,* Oct. 15, Nov. 5, 1804, Oct. 24, 1805, Oct. 23, 1806. I am not clear when Baldwin ceased to be U.S. district attorney and became marshal.

31. W. R. Putnam to John May, Aug. 10, 1805, in Benton, "Ohio Company of Associates," 187, 179–221. For tax policy, see Bogart, *Financial History of Ohio,* 181–86, and Utter, "Ohio Politics and Politicians," 67–68.

32. Ratcliffe, "Benjamin Tappan," 140; Tappan to Sloane, Nov. 25, 1805, BTP, OHS; Benton, "Huntington Correspondence," 86.

33. Ratcliffe, "Benjamin Tappan," 140. See also Elijah Backus to Elijah Wadsworth, July 20, 1804, Wadsworth Papers; Backus to Tappan, Aug. 24, 1804, BTP, LC; Cincinnati *Western Spy,* Nov. 7, 1804; Benton, "Connecticut Land Company," 190–91. For the company's influence before 1803, see Benton, "Huntington Correspondence," 65–67, 77.

34. Tappan to John Sloane, Nov. 28, 1805, BTP, OHS; Turhand Kirtland to Henry Champion Sr., Oct. 2, Nov. 23, 1808, in Benton, "Connecticut Land Company," 190–91, 193–94. For the change in the tax law, see Tiffin to Worthington, Jan. 2, 29, 1806, TWP, OHS. The Connecticut Land Company dissolved in January 1809.

35. *Scioto Gazette,* Oct. 23, 1800; Perkins to Benjamin Gorham, Sept. 3, 1805, in Conlin, *Simon Perkins,* 57.

36. Bond, *Intimate Letters of Symmes,* 37–38; Carter, *Territorial Papers,* 3:97; Rohrbough, *Land Office Business,* 23, 183.

37. Silliman to Tiffin, May 18, 1803, Tiffin Papers; Silliman to Worthington, Nov. 2, 1803, TWP, OHS.

38. Samuel Carpenter to Worthington, Nov. 7, 1803, TWP, OHS; John Harris, "A Brief Sketch of Stark County," VFM 498, OHS, 2, 12; Marietta *Commentator,* Aug. 25, 1808. See also Rohrbough, *Land Office Business,* 23, 183–84; Stuckey, "Formation of Leadership Groups in a Frontier Town," 71–72.

39. Carter, *Territorial Papers,* 3:241; Gallagher and Patera, *Post Offices of Ohio,* 8, 17.

40. Josiah Morrow, "Francis Dunlavy," Morrow Papers; Benjamin Ruggles to Peter Hitchcock, July 27, 1810, CERP; McBride, *Pioneer Biography,* 1:51–52 (quotation).

41. Benjamin Tupper to Worthington, Feb. 20, 1804, TWP, OHS.

42. Jared Mansfield to Albert Gallatin, Sept. 8, 1806, Nov. 27, 1807, Jan. 24, 1812, quoted in Rohrbough, *Land Office Business,* 46, 181.

43. William Creighton Jr. to Worthington, Mar. 5, 1804, TWP, OHS; J. C. Symmes to Charles Wilkins Short, Feb. 23, Apr. 9, 1810, in Bond, *Intimate Letters of Symmes,* 37–38; Hildreth, *Genealogical and Biographical Sketches,* 191, 196.

44. Tiffin to Worthington, Dec. 5, 1804, Dec. 18, 1806, TWP, OHS. See also the letters of December 1804 through February 1805, in Benton, "Huntington Correspondence," 94–95, 98–99, 100–101.

45. Steubenville *Western Herald,* Aug. 23, Sept. 13, 1806; Chillicothe *Ohio Herald,* June 28, 1806; Marietta *Ohio Gazette,* July 21, 1808, speaking of 1807.

46. Tiffin to Worthington, Dec. 18, 1806, Jan. 3, 9, 25, 1807; Cass to Worthington, Jan. 4, 1807; Silliman to Worthington, Jan. 6, 1807, TWP, OHS; *Western Spy,* Jan. 6, 19, 1807.

47. For the linkage of personal and regional loyalties with partisanship, see Cayton and Onuf, *Midwest and the Nation,* 69, and Brown and Cayton, *Pursuit of Public Power,* ix, 3–9.

48. Creighton to Worthington, Mar. 5, 1804, Massie to Worthington, Feb. 1, 1804, TWP, OHS.

49. Tiffin to Worthington, Jan. 29, 1806; Steubenville *Western Herald,* Aug. 23, 1806; Cincinnati *Liberty Hall,* Nov. 4, 1806; *Scioto Gazette,* Nov. 13, 1806.

50. Steubenville *Western Herald,* Aug. 30, Sept. 20, 27, 1806.

51. Huntington to Worthington, Jan. 18, 1803, TWP, OHS; Ratcliffe, "Benjamin Tappan," 138; Benjamin Tappan Sr. to Tappan, Apr. 22, 1803, BTP, LC.

52. Elisha Tracy to Huntington, Norwich, Conn., Feb. 4, Nov. 15, 1805, in Benton, "Huntington Correspondence," 95–97, 102–3; Case, "Early Settlement of Warren," 11–13. See also Tappan to Jonathan Sloane, Nov. 28, 1805, BTP, OHS; Tappan to Nancy Tappan, Oct. 6, Nov. 9, 1806, and Sloane to Tappan, Jan. 25, 1808, BTP, LC.

53. [Charles Williams], "Auto-Sketch," 378; Cutler, *Ephraim Cutler,* 96, 101–2; Dwight, *Journey to Ohio,* 16. See also Harris, "A Brief Sketch of Stark County," VFM 498, OHS, 3.

54. John Heckenwelder to John Matthews, Gnadenhutten, Nov. 28, Dec. 12, 25, 1807, Jan. 8, 1808, SPHP.

55. Chase, *Statutes of Ohio,* 1:623; Conlin, *Simon Perkins,* 55–59, esp. 56; and Brown, "Frontier Politics," 290, 387. In Cincinnati, for example, dissident politicians exploited hostility to foreigners, and Republicans of British birth found their national origins held against them. Cincinnati *Liberty Hall Handbill Extra,* Oct. 7, 1806; *Western Spy,* Feb. 9, 1807; *Liberty Hall,* Oct. 8, 1808; *Western Spy Extra,* Oct. 8, 1808.

56. Cincinnati *Liberty Hall,* May 21, 1808; Finley, *Sketches of Western Methodism,* 353, 457–58, 460–61. See also Finley, *Autobiography,* 154, 240–41, 252; Cartwright, *Backwoods Preacher,* 38–39.

57. William Woodbridge to John Sloane, Mar. 30, 1826, Sloane Papers, OHS.

CHAPTER 5. THE REPUBLICAN ASCENDANCY, 1805–1809

1. Jean H. Baker, *The Politics of Continuity: Maryland Political Parties from 1858 to 1870* (Baltimore: Johns Hopkins University Press, 1973), 77; Kleppner, *Third Electoral System,* 257–97.

2. Ashe, *Travels in America,* 2:175–76, 210–11, 242–43, 251–54. See also Taylor, "Agrarian Discontent," 471–74, 484.

3. Chillicothe *Supporter,* Dec. 16, 1809, Oct. 6, 27, 1808. For the withdrawal of the Federalists, see Cutler, *Ephraim Cutler,* 84, 114; Buell, *Memoirs of Rufus Putnam,* 125; Heald, *Bezaleel Wells,* 45; Noyes, *Family History,* 1:272. The "old"/"young" dichotomy is drawn from Fischer, *Revolution of American Conservatism.*

4. John Sloane to Benjamin Tappan, Jan. 1, 30, 1806, BTP, LC; William Creighton Jr. to Worthington, Dec. 18, 1806, TWP, OHS.

5. Cincinnati *Western Spy,* Oct. 16, 1805; Chillicothe *Scioto Gazette,* Oct. 24, 1805, Oct. 17, 23, Nov. 13, 1806; Cincinnati *Liberty Hall,* Feb. 3, 1806.

6. Caldwell, *Belmont and Jefferson Counties,* 178. See also James Hedges to J. H. Larwill, Dec. 6, 1808, Larwill Family Papers, OHS; Ratcliffe, "Benjamin Tappan," 143–44; Stuckey, "Formation of Leadership Groups in a Frontier Town," 33–45; Heald, *Bezaleel Wells,* 73, 78, 92–97.

7. Tiffin to Worthington, Jan. 29, 1806, Worthington to Massie, Feb. 16, 1806, Timothy Buell to Worthington, Feb. 22, 1806, TWP, OHS; Massie, *Nathaniel Massie,* 233; Steubenville *Western Herald,* Sept. 20, 1806.

8. Worthington to Huntington, Mar. 14, 1806, in Benton, "Huntington Correspondence," 106; Cincinnati *Liberty Hall,* June 16, Oct. 28, 1806; *Scioto Gazette,* Oct. 17, 23, Nov. 13, 1806.

9. Huntington to Worthington, Feb. 15, 1806, TWP, OHS; Steubenville *Western Herald,* Sept. 13, Oct. 11, 1806.

10. Tiffin to Worthington, Dec. 18, 1806, Jan. 3, 9, 1807; Cass to Worthington, Jan. 4, 1807; Silliman to Worthington, Jan. 6, 1807, TWP, OHS.

11. Tiffin to Smith, Mar. 8, 1806, Tiffin Papers, OHS; Tiffin to Worthington, Jan. 25, Feb. 5, 1807, TWP, OHS. See also Utter, *Frontier State,* 42–43; Ratcliffe, "Voter Turnout in Early Ohio," 235.

12. Sears, *Thomas Worthington,* 145–46; Beecher to William Lytle, June 11, 1808, William Lytle correspondence, Lytle Family Papers. For fuller discussion of the 1807 and 1808 elections, see the last section of this chapter.

13. Ratcliffe, "Voter Turnout," 239–40; *Scioto Gazette,* Oct. 15, 1804.

14. *Western Spy,* Sept. 11, 18, 1805; Cunningham, *Jeffersonian Republicans in Power,* 196–200. It is commonly argued that nominations at this period came from the top down; see, for example, Formisano, "Federalists and Republicans," 67–68.

15. Cass to Worthington, Aug. 14, 1807, TWP, OHS; *Western Spy*, Aug. 30, Sept. 20, 1806; John Harris, "A Brief Sketch of Stark County," VFM 498, OHS, 10–11. Pocock, "A Candidate I'll Surely Be," 59, claims that the conventions were not partisan but designed to "gauge the consensus of the entire county." This became increasingly true after 1810, but was not the case before, except in Federalist Washington County in 1801–2.

16. *Scioto Gazette*, Sept. 24, Nov. 19, 1804, May 22, 1806, Aug. 21, Sept. 3, 1807, July 10, 1809. Brown, "Early Political Culture," 7–12, exaggerates the number of counties that had organized corresponding societies and regularly held delegate conventions. Pocock, "A Candidate I'll Surely Be," 61, claims that a delegate convention was held in Ross County in 1806; the evidence cited shows that a public Republican nominating meeting had been called, but not one specifically organized on the delegate system used in some other counties. *Scioto Gazette*, May 22, 1806.

17. *Scioto Gazette*, Apr. 17, 1806; Cunningham, *Jeffersonian Republicans in Power*, 199. See also Steubenville *Western Herald*, Sept. 20, 1806.

18. Marietta *Ohio Gazette*, Sept. 18, 1806; Cincinnati *Liberty Hall*, Sept. 15, 1806; Silliman to Worthington, Zanesville, July 29, 1808, TWP, OHS.

19. Heale, *Presidential Quest*, 83. Cf. Prince, *New Jersey's Jeffersonian Republicans*, 71ff.

20. Ashe, *Travels in 1806*, 2:172–78, 209–11, 223, 242–43, 251–57. See also *Western Spy*, June 13, 1817, and Mansfield, *Daniel Drake*, 51–52, 71; Hildreth, "Voyage from Marietta to New Orleans in 1805," 25. Ashe sold the fossil bones to Liverpool Museum in England and never sent Goforth a penny.

21. J. C. Symmes to Peyton Short, Cincinnati, Feb. 28, 1805, in Bond, *Intimate Letters of Symmes*, 69; *Western Spy*, Aug. 7, 1805; Grupenhoff, "Politics and the Rise of Political Parties," 136–37.

22. *Western Spy*, Oct. 17, 1804, Sept. 18, Oct. 9, 1805, Oct. 21, 1806; *Liberty Hall*, Mar. 24, Apr. 14, 1806. See also *Scioto Gazette*, Oct. 23, 1806, and Grupenhoff, "Politics and the Rise of Political Parties," 157–62. Grupenhoff's pioneering study of local politics often overgeneralizes and makes claims which go beyond the evidence it cites, as, for example, in its claim that Federalists as early as 1805–6 were infiltrating the societies: ibid., 143, 148–49.

23. *Liberty Hall*, Mar. 24, Apr. 26, June 30, July 21, Sept. 30, and *Liberty Hall* "Handbill Extra," Oct. 7, 1806.

24. *Liberty Hall*, Apr. 14, June 30, July 7, 1806; Tiffin to Worthington, Feb. 5, 1807, TWP, OHS. See also Grupenhoff, "Politics and the Rise of Political Parties," 161–62.

25. Tiffin to Worthington, Dec. 14, 1804, TWP, OHS; John Nimmo, Deposition, Feb. 25, 1808, Smith Papers; Grupenhoff, "Politics and the Rise of Political Parties," 138–39, 166–67.

26. *Western Spy*, Feb. 9, 1807, and *Liberty Hall*, Jan. 20, Feb. 3, Mar. 2, 1807; *Scioto Gazette*, Feb. 5, 1807. See also Grupenhoff, "Politics and the Rise of Political Parties," 166–71, and Pitcher, "John Smith."

27. *Liberty Hall*, Sept. 8, 21, 28, Oct. 6, 16, 26, 1807.

28. *Liberty Hall*, Jan. 11, 17, Sept. 24, Oct. 1, 8, 22, 29, 1808; *Spy Extra*, Oct. 8, 1808. Some proceedings of the town society are revealed in testimony collected by Smith,

though most members refused to make depositions if it meant violating the society's rules of secrecy. See Questions by John Smith to Jacob Fowlbe and His Answers, John Nimmo's deposition, Feb. 25, and Smith to Harper and Key, Feb. 27, 1808, Smith Papers.

29. *Liberty Hall*, Sept. 28, Oct. 6, 1807.

30. Cincinnati *Whig*, May 11, 1809, and *Liberty Hall*, March–April, Oct. 18, 1809. See also Grupenhoff, "Politics and the Rise of Political Parties," 177–79.

31. Steubenville *Western Herald*, May 2, 9, July 4, 19, 1807; Daniel Symmes and others to Worthington, May 31, 1804, CERP; *Liberty Hall*, Sept. 28, 1807.

32. *Liberty Hall* Handbill Extra, Oct. 7, 1806; *Scioto Gazette*, May 22, 1806.

33. *Liberty Hall* Handbill Extra, Oct. 7, 1806; Steubenville *Western Herald*, Aug. 23, 1806; Worthington to Massie, Feb. 16, 1806, TWP, OHS; *Liberty Hall*, July 7, Sept. 28, 1807.

34. *Liberty Hall*, Dec. 4, 1804, Aug. 13, 1808; Chillicothe *Ohio Herald*, Aug. 23, 1806; Steubenville *Western Herald*, Oct. 10, 1807.

35. Marietta *Ohio Gazette*, Sept. 22, 1808; *Western Spy*, Feb. 9, 1807, *Spy Extra*, Oct. 8, 1808, and *Liberty Hall*, Sept. 17, 1808. See also Steubenville *Western Herald*, Oct. 11, 1806.

36. Ketcham, *Presidents above Party*, 119.

37. Utter, "Judicial Review in Early Ohio," and "Ohio and the English Common Law"; Cayton, *Frontier Republic*, 96–106; and, for a national perspective, Ellis, *Jeffersonian Crisis*.

38. Ephraim Quinby to Worthington, Dec. 24, 1808, TWP, OHS.

39. Tiffin to Worthington, Jan. 3, 9, 1807, TWP, OHS; Sloane to Tappan, Jan. 25, 1808, BTP, LC. See also Utter, "Judicial Review," 8–9, 12–15, 18, 22–24.

40. Tappan to Worthington, Sept. 15, 1808, Quinby to Worthington, Dec. 24, 1808, TWP, OHS; John Thompson to J. H. Larwill, Sept. 27, 1808, William C. Larwill Papers.

41. Ellis, *Jeffersonian Crisis*; John Ashworth, *"Agrarians" and "Aristocrats": Party Political Ideology in the United States, 1837–1846* (London: Royal Historical Society, 1983).

42. Steubenville *Western Herald*, July 19, 1807, Jan. 29, 1808; Sloane to Worthington, Aug. 6, 1808, TWP, OHS; J. W. Browne to Tiffin, June 4, 1808, Tiffin Papers, WRHS. Burnet, an old acquaintance of Burr's, was retained to defend him in his trial at Chillicothe; see *Quarterly Publications of the Historical and Philosophical Society of Ohio* 9 (1914): 68. Cayton, *Frontier Republic*, 90–94, exaggerates the extent of popular support for Burr.

43. Fischer, *Revolution of American Conservatism*. The Federalist revival in Ohio has been pointed out previously in Ratcliffe, "Experience of Revolution," 211–19, and Brown, "Ohio Federalists," 261–82.

44. Marietta *Commentator*, Sept. 16, 1807; J. C. Symmes to Meigs, Cincinnati, Oct. 20, 1806, SPHP.

45. Steubenville *Western Herald*, Sept. 13 through Oct. 11, 1806; Pitcher, "John Smith," 82; Utter, "Ohio Politics and Politicians," 51.

46. Cass to Worthington, Jan. 4, 1807, Silliman to Worthington, Jan. 6, 1807, TWP, OHS; *Liberty Hall*, Oct. 6, 1807; Marietta *Ohio Gazette*, Nov. 10, 1808.

47. Steubenville *Western Herald*, Aug. 23, 30, 1807; Cincinnati *Liberty Hall*, July 27, Aug. 3, 12, 1807; Brown, "Ohio Federalists," 265.

48. Ratcliffe, "Experience of Revolution," 203.

49. Tiffin to Worthington, Chillicothe, Jan. 25, Feb. 5, 1807, TWP, OHS.

50. Worthington to Meigs, Dec. 12, 1806; Tiffin to Worthington, Nov. 18, 1807; R. J. Meigs Jr., Statement, Dec. 14, 1807, TWP, RCHS. This is a more serious case against Meigs than that usually stated. For a warning of Meigs's ambition and unreliability, see Smith to Worthington, June 30, 1806, TWP, OHS.

51. Tiffin to Worthington, Jan. 25, Feb. 5, 1807, TWP, OHS; *Liberty Hall*, Sept. 14, 1807. For Tiffin's interventions against Massie in Clermont and Ross Counties, see William Lytle to Massie, May 29, Sept. 23, 1807, and William Lyon to Massie, Oct. 2, 1807, Massie Papers.

52. Sears, *Thomas Worthington*, 141–42; Massie, *Nathaniel Massie*, 93–100, 245–49. I know of no evidence that Massie's challenge was decided on by a party caucus, as claimed by Grupenhoff, "Politics and the Rise of Political Parties," 165, and Sears, *Thomas Worthington*, 141–42; see Massie, *Nathaniel Massie*, 248, where Worthington says only that he had consulted with friends.

53. *Liberty Hall*, July 21, Aug. 18, Sept. 8, 14, 28, 1807. See also Steubenville *Western Herald*, Sept. 12, 26, 1807; Elias Glover to E. A. Brown, May 29, Aug. 17, 1807, EABP; and Cass to Worthington, Aug. 14, 1807, TWP, OHS.

54. Sloane to Tappan, Sept. 4, 1807, BTP, LC; Chillicothe *Supporter*, Aug. 18, 1809. For Massie, see Utter, "Judicial Review," 6 n. 8.

55. Utter, *Frontier State*, 42–43; Brown, "Frontier Politics," 344–49, and "Samuel Huntington," 432. John W. Campbell later commented that, in 1810, Meigs was "denounced as the Federal candidate by men who, three years before, had sustained him with energy for his republicanism." Campbell, *Biographical Sketches*, 70.

56. John Mathews and others to Massie, Sept. 15, 1807, in Massie, *Nathaniel Massie*, 248, 249; abstract of votes, Washington County, WCC; and, for Fairfield, Cincinnati *Liberty Hall*, Oct. 24, 1807. Granville was still part of Fairfield, as Licking County was not created until 1808.

57. Steubenville *Western Herald*, Sept. 12, 26, Oct. 3, 10, 17, 1807. The Jefferson County result was confused, early reports giving the advantage to Massie, 430 to 389, whereas the result reported to the assembly gave it to Meigs, 430 to 457. This was apparently the first time since 1803 that the county failed to elect the entire regular ticket.

58. *Journal of the Senate of the State of Ohio, 1807–8*, 7, 8, 16–17; Campbell, *Biographical Sketches*, 70; Brown, "Frontier Politics," 373–74.

59. Chillicothe *Fredonian*, June 6, 1807; Marietta *Commentator*, Sept. 16, 1807. See also *American Friend and Marietta Gazette*, Sept. 27, 1828, and *Marietta and Washington County Pilot*, Oct. 11, 1828.

60. Sloane to Tappan, Jan. 25, 1808, BTP, LC; J. C. Symmes to E. A. Brown, Jan. 11, 1808, in Bond, *Intimate Letters of Symmes*, 129, 131. See also Creighton to Worthington, Jan. 5, 1807, TWP, RCHS; Chillicothe *Supporter*, Aug. 11, 1810. Sprigg had resigned his Ohio judgeship in order to take up a federal appointment in a western territory, but had disliked it, resigned, and returned to Ohio. *Liberty Hall*, Aug. 29, 1810.

61. Chillicothe *Supporter*, Oct. 6, 27, 1808. The Dayton paper was *The Dayton Repertory*, edited by Isaac G. Burnet, Jacob's brother.

62. J. W. Browne to his son, June 26, 1808, Browne Papers. See also Steubenville *Western Herald,* Jan. 8, 1808; Lebanon *Western Star,* June 30, 1808; *Scioto Gazette,* July 19, 1808.

63. Silliman to Worthington, July 29, 1808; see also Morrow to Worthington, Dec. 7, 1808, TWP, OHS.

64. Taylor, "Agrarian Discontent," 485, 487–93, 494 n. Cf. Appleby, *Capitalism and a New Social Order,* 39–50.

65. Ashe, *Travels in 1806,* 1:292–98, 308, 2:45; Henry Howe, *Historical Collections* (1900), 2:785. See also Baldwin, "Shipbuilding on the Western Waters," 36–43.

66. Hildreth, *Genealogical and Biographical Sketches,* 191–97; Andrews, *Washington County,* 64.

67. Putnam to John May, May 7, Sept. 22, Oct. 21, 1808, in Benton, "Ohio Company of Associates," 202, 203, 205.

68. Marietta *Ohio Gazette,* Aug. 25, Sept. 15, 22, Nov. 10, 1808; Chillicothe *Supporter,* Oct. 20, Nov. 17, 1808; the doggerel is quoted in Hulbert, "Western Ship-Building," 732. The *Gazette* ascribed the Federalist victory in Washington County to the failure of Republicans to vote.

69. Sloane to Worthington, July 7, 1808, TWP, OHS; Steubenville *Western Herald,* Jan. 15, 1808; Howe, *Historical Collections* (1900), 1:599; Martzolff, "Autobiography of Thomas Ewing," 162. Lyman Beecher's father had five wives and twelve children; when his mother died, he was brought up by a maternal uncle and aunt. See Lyman Beecher Stowe, *Saints, Sinners, and Beechers* (Indianapolis: Bobbs-Merrill, 1934), 24–25. I remain somewhat skeptical of the relationship, since Philemon and Lyman were born in the same year, presumably of different mothers.

70. Sloane to Worthington, July 7, Aug. 6, 1808, TWP, OHS, and to Tappan, July 11, 1808, BTP, LC.

71. Sloane to Worthington, July 7, 1808, TWP, OHS; Tiffin to Huntington, July 29, 1808, in Benton, "Huntington Correspondence," 120, 122–23. For Huntington's frustrated ambition, see Brown, "Huntington," 426–31.

72. Ephraim Quinby to Worthington, Dec. 24, 1808, TWP, OHS; Chillicothe *Supporter,* Aug. 11, 1810; Marietta *Ohio Gazette,* Sept. 22, 1808. See also Tappan to Worthington, Sept. 15, 1818, TWP, OHS, and Huntington to Burnet, Oct. 30, 1808, CERP.

73. Sloane to Tappan, July 11, 1808, BTP, LC; *Liberty Hall,* July 9, Aug. 13, Sept. 17, Oct. 22, 1808.

74. Tappan to Worthington, Sept. 15, 1808, Sloane to Worthington, Aug. 20, Oct. 3, 1808, TWP, OHS; James Hedges to Joseph H. Larwill, Oct. 26, 1808, Larwill Family Papers; *Liberty Hall,* Sept. 15, Oct. 1, 8, 22, 1808. See also John Harmon, "Portage County 47 Years Ago" (written 1856), transcript, OHS, and for the statewide result, *Journal of the House of Representatives of the State of Ohio, 1808–9,* 30–31.

75. Tiffin to Worthington, Dec. 9, 1808, TWP, OHS; Chillicothe *Supporter,* Nov. 17, 1808; Sloane to Worthington, Nov. 13, 1808, TWP, OHS. For the distant press reports, see Raleigh, N.C., *The Minerva,* Sept. 29, 1808, and, from Virginia, *Berkeley and Jefferson Intelligencer,* Sept. 23, 1808. I owe these last references to the kindness of Philip Lampi.

76. Huntington to Wadsworth, Aug. 25, 1808, Tiffin to Huntington, Jan. 12, 1809, and Griswold to Huntington, June 19, 1809, in Benton, "Huntington Correspondence," 123–24, 130–35; Marietta *Commentator,* June 24, 1809; *Scioto Gazette,* Apr. 24, 1809. See also Brown, "Frontier Politics," 373–74, 378–79, and "Political Culture," 10, where Griswold is identified as hostile to the Jeffersonian Republicans.

77. Worthington to Huntington, July 29, 1808, in Benton, "Huntington Correspondence," 121–22; Sloane to Tappan, Oct. 1, 1808, BTP, LC.

78. Huntington to Worthington, June 10, 1808, TWP, RCHS; Sloane to Tappan, July 11, Oct. 1, 1808, BTP, LC; Sloane to Worthington, Oct. 3, Nov. 13, 1808, TWP, OHS; Chillicothe *Supporter,* Oct. 20, 27, Nov. 17, 1808.

79. Huntington to Elijah Wadsworth, Aug. 25, 1808, in Benton, "Huntington Correspondence," 123–24; Huntington to Worthington, June 10, 1808, TWP, RCHS; Sloane to Worthington, Oct. 3, 1808, TWP, OHS.

80. Cunningham, *Jeffersonian Republicans in Power,* 199. For returns, see Chillicothe *Supporter,* Nov. 17, 1808; *Liberty Hall,* Nov. 5, 12, 25, 1808; Marietta *Ohio Gazette,* Nov. 10, 1808.

81. *Liberty Hall,* Oct. 22, Nov. 5, 12, 1808; *Western Spy,* June 22, 1803; Marietta *Ohio Gazette,* Nov. 10, 1808; abstracts of votes, Montgomery County, WSU.

82. Jefferson to Harrison, Apr. 28, 1805, in Esarey, *Messages and Papers of Harrison,* 1:127; Chillicothe *Supporter,* October 1808 through November 1812.

CHAPTER 6. THE LIMITS OF PARTISANSHIP, 1809–1814

1. McCormick, *Second American Party System,* 11.

2. Campbell, *Biographical Sketches,* 1–13, 70–71, 124–27, 151–52.

3. Atwater, *History of the State of Ohio,* 3–4, 182–86; Ratcliffe, "Benjamin Tappan," 144–47.

4. William Woodbridge to Paul Fearing, Jan. 20, Feb. 12, 1809, SPHP. For examples of antilawyer rhetoric, see Cincinnati *Western Spy Extra,* Oct. 8, 1808; Chillicothe *Independent Republican,* July 19, 1810; Zanesville *Muskingum Messenger,* in Cincinnati *Liberty Hall,* Aug. 15, 1810. The two new judges were Thomas Scott and Thomas Morris; Huntington had become governor and Meigs had been elected to the Senate in December 1808. Gilkey, *Ohio Hundred Year Book,* 468, 574; Ratcliffe, "Benjamin Tappan," 145–47. For the origins of the dispute, see chap. 5, pp. 135–36.

5. Marietta *Ohio Gazette,* in Chillicothe *Supporter,* Sept. 8, 1809; Hamm to John Fuller, Oct. 1, 1809, Fuller Papers, OHS.

6. Atwater, *History of the State of Ohio,* 182–85. See also Ratcliffe, "Benjamin Tappan," 143–46; Chillicothe *Supporter,* Sept. 29, Dec. 30, 1809.

7. Hamm to E. A. Brown, Feb. 11, 1810, EABP. For the role of state judges in elections, see Benjamin Ruggles to Peter Hitchcock, July 27, 1810, CERP. One or two Federalists gained election as associate judges, notably Paul Fearing in Washington County. Gilkey, *Ohio Hundred Year Book,* 501.

8. Atwater, *History of the State of Ohio,* 185–86. See also Cincinnati *Liberty Hall,*

Aug. 29, 1810; Campbell, *Biographical Sketches*, 70–71; and Ratcliffe, "Benjamin Tappan," 146–47.

9. Robert Lucas to John Clark and John Lucas, Sept. 15, 1810, TWP, RCHS. See also Parish, *Robert Lucas*, 21–24, 91, which stresses the personal conflicts involved.

10. David Griffin to Samuel Williams, June 22, 1811, Tammany Society Records, OHS; Dayton *Ohio Centinel*, in Cincinnati *Liberty Hall*, May 29, 1811.

11. John Thompson to J. H. Larwill, June 5, 1810, W. C. Larwill Papers, OHS.

12. Benjamin Ruggles, *An Oration Delivered at the New Meeting House . . . in Marietta . . . on the Fourth of July, 1809;* Campbell, *Biographical Sketches*, 239–51; Chillicothe *Independent Republican*, Sept. 8, Nov. 20, 27, 1809; St. Clairsville *Impartial Expositor*, Mar. 25, 1809. The other nonpartisan newspapers included the Zanesville *Union* (advertised in Marietta *Commentator*, Apr. 17, 1810), and the first Cincinnati *Advertiser* (first issue, June 13, 1810).

13. *Principles of Union agreed on by the Society of True Americans in Green County, Pennsylvania; Adopted by the New-Boston Branch of True Americans, in Champaign County, Ohio* (Cincinnati, 1810), copy at RCHS. See also Cincinnati *Liberty Hall*, Apr. 17, May 15, July 31, 1811, and John Kerr to Worthington, Dec. 6, 1811, TWP, RCHS.

14. Benjamin Tappan, Oration, Steubenville, July 4, 1810, BTP, LC; communication to Chillicothe Wigwam, Zanesville, Mar. 23, 1811, Tammany Society Records. See also Abraham Shepherd to Worthington, Dec. 30, 1810, TWP, OHS.

15. Constitution of the Tammany Society or Columbian Order, Chillicothe, Month of Worms, the year of discovery 318; J. A. Gibson to Thomas Lloyd, Mar. 9, 1810, and Michael Leib to Worthington, March 1811, Tammany Society Records; Campbell, *Biographical Sketches*, 71. The membership list is written inside the flyleaf of Samuel Williams's personal copy of the *Constitution of the Tammany Society or Columbian Order* (Chillicothe, 1810), at RCHS. See also Utter, "Saint Tammany in Ohio."

16. Chillicothe *Independent Republican*, Mar. 1, Sept. 22, Oct. 4, 13, 1810; *Supporter*, Aug. 11, 25, Sept. 8, 15, 22, 1810; *Fredonian*, Oct. 7, 12, 1812.

17. *Liberty Hall*, Aug. 15, 22, 29, Sept. 12, 26, 1810, Apr. 24, 1811; *Western Spy*, Sept. 15, 22, 29, 1810. See also Grupenhoff, "Politics and the Rise of Political Parties," 177–83.

18. Chillicothe *Independent Republican*, Sept. 27, 1810; Zanesville *Muskingum Messenger*, Aug. 25, 1810; Lebanon *Western Star*, Sept. 29, 1810.

19. Steubenville *Western Herald*, Oct. 17, Dec. 5, 12, 1807; Marietta *Ohio Gazette*, reprinted in Chillicothe *Supporter*, Aug. 11, Sept. 8, 1809; Marietta *Commentator*, in Chillicothe *Supporter*, Oct. 6, 1809.

20. J. P. R. Bureau to Huntington, Mar. 31, 1810, Huntington Papers, OHS; Simon Perkins, Feb. 20, 1809, quoted in Conlin, *Simon Perkins*, 58. For Montgomery County, see abstracts of votes, Montgomery County, 1807–12, WSU; Martzolff, "Rev. Paul Henkel's Journal," 190–92; [Cutler], *Topographical Description;* Henry Howe, *Historical Collections* (1907), 299, 301; Howson, "German Element"; Pocock, "Evangelical Frontier."

21. Chillicothe *Supporter*, June 9, 1811, Aug. 11, Sept. 22, 1810; John McLean to Worthington, Jan. 1, 1811, TWP, RCHS.

22. Tappan to Worthington, Nov. 22, 1811, TWP, OHS. By contrast, Meigs's appeal to

conservative Republicans enabled him to run well in parts of western Ohio—for an eastern man; Jeremiah Morrow to Worthington, Oct. 8, 1810, TWP, OHS.

23. McArthur's statement, in Chillicothe *Fredonian,* Oct. 9, 1811.

24. *Niles' Weekly Register* 2 (Mar. 14, 1812): 31; Marietta *Commentator,* Aug. 25, 1808. See also Church, *Early History of Zanesville.*

25. Marietta *Commentator,* Aug. 25, 1808; Chillicothe *Supporter,* Oct. 27, 1808; Zanesville *Muskingum Messenger,* Aug. 25, 1810, Jan. 2, Feb. 20, 1811; petition to Grand Sachem, July 2, 1810, Tammany Society Records. See also Church, *Early History of Zanesville,* 72–74, 78–82, 93–101, 152–53, 238–40, 242–49, 260–61; Everhart, *Muskingum County,* 141; Schneider, *Y-Bridge City,* 176, 187, 69, 70, 176, 187; and *Samuel Herrick,* 5–8, 20, 23. For Van Horne, see Tinkcom, *Republicans and Federalists in Pennsylvania,* 257–60, 319; and *Biographical Directory of the American Congress,* 1851.

26. Benjamin Hough to Worthington, Dec. 11, 1810, James Caldwell to Worthington, Dec. 15, 1810, Carlos A. Norton to Worthington, Dec. 15, 1810, TWP, OHS. See also Elisha Tracy to Huntington, Feb. 25, 1810, in Benton, "Huntington Correspondence," 141–42.

27. C. A. Norton to Worthington, Dec. 14, 1810, Feb. 1, 1811, TWP, OHS; W. W. Irvin to Brown, Feb. 4, 1811, EABP.

28. Chillicothe *Independent Republican,* Feb. 21, 1811; Samuel W. Williams, "Tammany Society in Ohio," 355, 363; political broadside signed by Isaac Van Horne, Benj. Hough and Samuel Herrick, Zanesville, July 8, 1811, OHS. See also Hamm to Samuel Williams, July 13, 1811, Tammany Society Records. Brown, "Political Culture of Early Ohio," 10–11, claims that the object in creating new wigwams was to "supplant existing Republican Correspondence societies"; the latter, however, were different in purpose from the Tammany societies and, in any case, had only brief and scattered existence outside Hamilton County.

29. Jacob Smith, quoted in Williams, "Tammany Society in Ohio," 365–66; David Griffin to Samuel Williams, June 22, 1811, Tammany Society Records. See also *Liberty Hall,* Feb. 6, May 1, June 26, 1811.

30. William Creighton Jr. to George Tod, June 2, 1811, in Benton, "Huntington Correspondence," 157–58.

31. *Liberty Hall,* May 8, 1811; *Muskingum Messenger,* May 15, 1811; *Western Spy,* May 25, 1811; *Scioto Gazette,* July 10, 1811.

32. *Muskingum Messenger,* Sept. 4, 1811; *Liberty Hall,* May 29, 1811.

33. *Scioto Gazette,* July 10, 1811; Hamm to Worthington, Dec. 14, 1811, TWP, OHS.

34. *Liberty Hall,* May 29, July 31, Aug. 28, Sept. 11, 18, 25, Oct. 16, 1811; *Western Spy,* Aug. 3, Sept. 11, Oct. 12, 1811. See also petition, Sept. 25, 1810, Tammany Society Records.

35. Tiffin to Worthington, Oct. 31, 1811; Hamm to Worthington, Dec. 2, 1811, TWP, OHS.

36. Norton to Worthington, Dec. 2, 1811, Jan. 8, 1812, Hamm to Worthington, Dec. 14, 1811, Van Horne to Worthington, Dec. 12, 1811, Jan. 4, Mar. 11, 1812, Jacob Smith to Worthington, Jan. 9, 1812, Silliman to Worthington, Jan. 12, 1812, Sloane to Worthington, Jan. 24, 1812, TWP, OHS. Many of these letters are reprinted in Knopf, *Document Transcriptions,* vol. 3.

37. Van Horne to Worthington, Mar. 11, 1812, TWP, OHS.

38. McArthur to Massie, Dec. 17, 1811, in Massie, *Nathaniel Massie*, 265–66.

39. This view is expressed most explicitly in Cayton, *Frontier Republic*, and Cayton and Onuf, *Midwest and the Nation*, esp. 68–69.

40. Cayton and Onuf, *Midwest and the Nation*, 69.

41. Hamm to E. A. Brown, Feb. 11, 1810, EABP; Chillicothe *Independent Republican*, Sept. 18, 25, Oct. 25, 1809, Mar. 8, 1810; Cramer, "Duncan McArthur," 23–27. For Buckingham, who was Rufus Putnam's son-in-law, see Van Horne to Meigs, Aug. 4, 1812, Meigs Papers, OHS, and Knopf, *Document Transcriptions*, 2:140; Arius Nye to Horace Nye, Sept. 8, 1812, VFM 634, OHS. For Woodbridge's promotion, see William Carl Klunder, "The Seeds of Popular Sovereignty: Governor Lewis Cass and Michigan Territory," *Michigan Historical Review* 17 (1991): 68–69, 76. See also *Zanesville Express*, Feb. 16, Aug. 3, 1814.

42. Tiffin to Worthington, Oct. 31, 1811, TWP, OHS. For Abbot, see J. P. R. Bureau to Huntington, Mar. 31, 1810, Huntington Papers, OHS, and Hamm to Brown, Feb. 11, 1810, EABP.

43. Tiffin became commissioner of the General Land Office in Washington in April 1812, and then in 1814, at his own request, surveyor general, based in Chillicothe. Cass was made governor of Michigan in October 1813, and his place as U.S. marshal for Ohio was taken by Hamm. Meigs became postmaster general in March 1814. For the expectation that federal office would be given on partisan grounds, see Abraham Shepherd to Worthington, Dec. 30, 1810, TWP, OHS; and for the reward of party activism at the local level, see Hildreth, *Genealogical and Biographical Sketches*, 191, 196, 197, 199.

44. Marietta *Commentator*, Aug. 25, 1808. For Sloane, see Utter, "Ohio Politics and Politicians," 75–77; Brown, "Political Culture," 13.

45. Tiffin to Worthington, Dec. 18, 1806 (includes copy of circular), Jan. 3, 9, 1807, Dec. 9, 1808, Morrow to Worthington, Jan. 16, 1810, Kerr to Worthington, Mar. 3, 1815, TWP, OHS; *Ohio Federalist*, in *Western Spy*, Aug. 2, 1816. For Kerr, see Dickoré, *General Joseph Kerr*.

46. Stagg, *Mr. Madison's War*, 194.

47. *Muskingum Messenger*, Aug. 25, Sept. 1, 15, 29, Oct. 20, Nov. 17, 1813, Sept. 13, 1815.

48. Ratcliffe, "Benjamin Tappan," 140, 142–43; B. Tappan Sr. to Tappan, Feb. 18, 1809, William Tappan to Tappan, Aug. 18, 1810, BTP, LC; Brown, "Samuel Huntington," 432ff.

49. Chase, *Statutes of Ohio*, 1:622. Winkle, *Politics of Community*, and "Ohio's Informal Polling Place."

50. Cayton and Onuf, *Midwest and the Nation*, 68–69.

51. Benjamin D. Pardee, *An Oration Delivered at the Baptist Church, Cincinnati, before the Tammany Society or Columbian Order; Wigwam no. 3, of the State of Ohio on the 13th of the Month of Flowers, Y.D. 324* (Cincinnati: Looker, Palmer and Reynolds, 1816). The thirteen men who signed the petition for a wigwam at Zanesville included one large landowner, one lawyer, one officer of the land office, two silversmiths, one potter, and one stonemason; five of the thirteen do not appear on either the 1810 land tax list or the 1815 federal direct tax list. Petition to Grand Sachem, Zanesville, July 2, 1810, Tam-

many Society Records; Church, *Early History of Zanesville*, esp. 144–45, 241–42; Petty, *Ohio 1810 Tax Duplicate.*

52. Toasts of the Tammany Society, Chillicothe, May 13, 1811, Tammany Society Records; John Miller to Worthington, Dec. 29, 1812, TWP, OHS and Knopf, *Document Transcriptions*, 3:138–39.

53. *Muskingum Messenger*, Sept. 21, 1814, Sept. 15, 1819; *Western Spy*, Aug. 30, 1816. See also Chillicothe *Supporter*, Sept. 3, 17, 1816; Steubenville *Western Herald*, Sept. 20, 1816.

54. *Muskingum Messenger*, Jan. 15, 1812; Ratcliffe, "Benjamin Tappan," 145–47; Sloane to Worthington, Jan. 28, 1812, and John Thompson to Worthington, May 12, 1812, Sloane to Worthington, Jan. 24, 1812, Jacob Smith to Worthington, Jan. 2, 9, 1812, TWP, OHS.

55. Benson, *Concept of Jacksonian Democracy*, 11–46; Formisano, *Transformation of Political Culture*, 18, 196–223, 249–50; Kathleen Smith Kutulowski, "Antimasonry Reexamined: Social Bases of the Grass-Roots Party," *Journal of American History* 71 (1984): 269–93.

56. *Liberty Hall*, Apr. 24, May 22, July 3, 1811; Chillicothe *Independent Republican*, May 9, 1811.

57. *Independent Republican*, Oct. 9, 1809; Boase, "Moral Policemen," 41.

58. *Muskingum Messenger*, Sept. 4, 1811; *Independent Republican*, in *Liberty Hall*, July 24, 1811. See also Samuel Williams, "A Brief Detail, etc.," Chillicothe, Aug. 5–6, 1811, SWP, and proceedings of Quarterly Meeting conference of Deercreek Circuit, Aug. 9–11, 1811, RCHS; Tiffin to Worthington, Oct. 31, 1811, TWP, OHS; and Samuel W. Williams, *Pictures of Early Methodism in Ohio*, 187–214. Cayton, *Frontier Republic*, 59, 107, confuses the Methodist clergyman who resigned from Tammany, Joseph S. Collins of the Chillicothe *Scioto Gazette*, with the famous preacher John Collins, praised in Finley, *Sketches of Western Methodism*, 87, 106–7, 215, 317–29.

59. *Liberty Hall*, Feb. 6, 13, Mar. 27, May 1, 8, Aug. 14, Oct. 2, 1811.

60. James J. Tyler, *Chillicothe and the Beginning of the Grand Lodge of Ohio* (n.p., 1938), 9–16, 23–27; Bullock, *Revolutionary Brotherhood*, esp. 227. Significantly—and ironically—Van Horne was the second officer of the Zanesville lodge.

61. Huntington to Worthington, Feb. 15, 1806, TWP, OHS; Hamm to Brown, June 7, 1811, EABP.

62. *Western Spy*, July 12, 1811. Much of Ohio's surplus produce was still sold to settlers who continued to pour into the state, if not in quite the same numbers as in 1806–8. There is no evidence of Ohioans urging war because they expected it to improve their economic condition; even Taylor, "Agrarian Discontent," 494–95, 500, in arguing the contrary view, concedes that his case has least weight for Ohio. Horsman, "Western War Aims," and Risjord, "1812: Conservatives, War Hawks, and the Nation's Honor," contain nothing to contradict the interpretation advanced here.

63. Barber to Worthington, May 17, 1812, TWP, OHS. See also Sloane to Tappan, Jan. 22, 1810, BTP, LC; and for the urge to self-sufficiency, see *Independent Republican*, Mar. 22, 1810, and *Muskingum Messenger*, Dec. 8, 1810.

64. Finley, *Western Methodism*, 223–30, and *Autobiography*, 219–22; *Muskingum Messenger*, quoted in *Niles' Weekly Register* 2 (Mar. 7, 1812): 32; Esarey, *Messages and Papers*

of Harrison, 1:300, 312, 348, 459, and 2:27; C. A. Norton to Worthington, Dec. 2, 1811, TWP, OHS.

65. Worthington to Meigs, Nov. 30, 1811, Meigs Papers, OHS and TWP, RCHS. See also Stagg, *Mr. Madison's War,* 177–90; and, for varying responses to Tippecanoe, see Tiffin to Worthington, Dec. 11, 1811, TWP, RCHS, and Knopf, *Document Transcriptions,* 3:11, 14, 20, 49. Apparently some Shawnee and Delaware held their winter hunt in central Ohio in 1811–12; Hildreth, *Genealogical and Biographical Sketches,* 196–97.

66. Circleville *Fredonian,* Feb. 26, Mar. 18, 1812; Worthington *Western Intelligencer,* Nov. 20, 1811, May 22, 29, 1812; Daniel Drake to Isaac Drake, May 24, 1812, Jared Mansfield Papers, OHS. See also Esarey, *Messages and Papers of Harrison,* 2:27, 32, 35, 39, 45–49, and Knopf, *Document Transcriptions,* 2:6–9, 185, 3:63–64, 84–85, 87–88, 97.

67. Worthington to ———, November 1812, TWP, RCHS, giving his reasons for voting against the declaration of war; Sears, *Thomas Worthington,* 163–70; Alexander Campbell to Worthington, Apr. 12, 1812, CERP, and June 17, 1812, TWP, OHS. By contrast, Morrow consistently supported the drive for war in the House; Ronald L. Hatzenbuehler, "Party Unity and the Decision for War in the House of Representatives in 1812," *William and Mary Quarterly* 29 (1972): 376.

68. Resolutions, Dec. 26, 1811, in *Niles' Weekly Register* 1 (Jan. 18, 1812): 361–62; James Caldwell to Worthington, Dec. 14, 1811, Silliman to Worthington, Jan. 12, 1812, Cass to Worthington, Apr. 13, 1812, Hamm to Worthington, June 18, 31, 1812, TWP, OHS. See also Knopf, *Document Transcriptions,* 3:18, 89, 98, 103, 122, 128; Stagg, *Mr. Madison's War,* 193–96; and Sears, *Thomas Worthington,* 175–78, 190–92. Ohio congressmen saw maritime issues and national honor as the causes of war; Barlow, "Ohio's Congressmen," 179, 190.

69. Henry Clay to [James Monroe], Lexington, July 29, 1812, in Hopkins and Hargreaves, *Papers of Henry Clay,* 1:697; *Zanesville Express,* Nov. 16, 1814; Millett, "Bellicose Nationalism in Ohio." See also Risjord, "Conservatives, War Hawks, and the Nation's Honor," and Brown, *Republic in Peril.* For the unconvincing argument that the majority of Ohioans were opposed to the declaration of war, see Cady, "Western Opinion and the War of 1812," and Sears, *Thomas Worthington,* 175–78, 190–92.

70. Meigs to General John S. Gano, Apr. 6, 1812, in Hamlin, "Gano Papers," pt. 1, 53–54; Crary, *Pioneer and Personal Reminiscences,* 7; Esarey, *Messages and Papers of Harrison,* 2:108. See also ibid., 2:58–59, 81, 85, 95, and Knopf, *Document Transcriptions,* 2:150, 3:112.

71. Urbana *Farmer's Watch-Tower,* Oct. 28, 1812. The French government had ordered a *levée en masse* to oppose foreign invasion in August 1793.

72. *Western Spy,* July 6, 1813. See also Hamlin, "Gano Papers," pt. 4, 63–65; Knopf, *Document Transcriptions,* 3:166–67, 174, 179, 183; and Stagg, *Mr. Madison's War,* 320–31. The strains of the first year of the war, as well as concern for their families and the profits of supplying the army, made Ohio a poor recruiting ground for the regular army by 1813, and Harrison had to depend for his forward advance almost entirely on the Kentucky volunteers raised by Governor Shelby.

73. Quoted in John Marshall Barker, *Ohio Methodism,* 36. See also Badger, *Memoir,* 126–27, and Knopf, *Document Transcriptions,* 2:70, 80, 203, 3:214–15.

74. See the remarkable letters of McLean to Worthington, December 1814 through February 1815, TWP, RCHS; Barlow, "Ohio's Congressmen," 187–88, 192–93.

75. Finley, *Autobiography*, 258, 266; Franklinton *Freeman's Chronicle*, Sept. 5, 1812. See also Cartwright, *Backwoods Preacher*, 60, 64; Knopf, *Document Transcriptions*, 3:115.

76. Jessup N. Couch to Worthington, Dec. 10, 1813, and McArthur to Worthington, Dec. 8, 1812, TWP, OHS. See also Knopf, *Document Transcriptions*, 3:127, 130, 138–39, 146, 147, 225; Stagg, *Mr. Madison's War*, esp. 294, 316; and Barlow, "Ohio's Congressmen."

77. Marietta *Commentator*, Nov. 25, 1809; Marietta *Western Spectator*, Feb. 26, May 11, 1811; Samuel Finley to Worthington, July 2, 1812, TWP, OHS.

78. *Liberty Hall*, Aug. 12, Nov. 3, 30, 1807; Hamm to Worthington, Dec. 2, 1811, Van Horne to Worthington, Mar. 11, 1812, Lewis Cass to Worthington, Apr. 13, 1812, McArthur to Worthington, Mar. 23, Apr. 7, 1812, Silliman to Worthington, May 12, 1812, TWP, OHS; Chillicothe *Supporter*, July 4, 1812. Brown, "Ohio Federalists," 275–76, errs in saying that the Chillicothe *Fredonian* initially opposed the war; see *Fredonian*, June 30, Sept. 1, Nov. 4, 1812.

79. Dayton *Ohio Centinel*, July 15, 1812; Martzolff, "Autobiography of Thomas Ewing," 157–58. See also Pocock, "Evangelical Frontier," 49–52; Joyner, "William Cortenus Schenck." For Gano, see Smith, *St. Clair Papers*, 2:495, 524; Knopf, *Document Transcriptions*, 3:89; and Hamlin, "Gano Papers."

80. Franklinton *Freeman's Chronicle*, June 24, July 2, 1812, Feb. 11, 1814. Brown, "Ohio Federalists," 274, is misleading on Gardiner and the *Freeman's Chronicle*.

81. Cf. Hickey, "Federalist Party Unity and the War of 1812," and "Federalists and the Coming of War."

82. Silliman to Worthington, Jan. 12, 1812, and C. A. Norton to Worthington, Mar. 4, 1812, TWP, OHS; Worthington to Meigs, Nov. 30, 1811, Meigs Papers, OHS; Worthington to Tod, Mar. 15, 1812, WRHS *Tract*, 39:19; George Jackson to Meigs, Aug. 28, 1812, TWP, RCHS.

83. McArthur to Worthington, Mar. 23, Apr. 7, 1812, TWP, OHS; *Muskingum Messenger*, May 22, Aug. 7, 1811, Sept. 23, 1812. For Meigs as war governor, see Esarey, *Messages and Papers of Harrison*, 2:304, 334–35; Tappan to Brown, Jan. 21, 1819, EABP; Campbell, *Biographical Sketches*, 75–84.

84. Thomas Scott to Tappan, Sept. 23, 1812, and W. W. Irvin to Tappan, Sept. 28, 1812, BTP, LC. See also Knopf, *Document Transcriptions*, 3:68, 81, 82; *Liberty Hall*, Sept. 12, 26, 1812; Beecher to Meigs, Oct. 16, 1812, TWP, RCHS. Sears, *Thomas Worthington*, 156–57, errs in calling Scott the "High Court" candidate.

85. James Kilbourne, "Letter to R. F. Slaughter: An Essay upon the Administration and the Opposition," Washington, June 5, 1813, in *Old Northwest Genealogical Quarterly* 6 (1903): 125; Van Horne to Worthington, Jan. 4, Mar. 11, 1812, and Hamm to Worthington, Dec. 2, 1811, TWP, OHS.

86. *Western Spy*, Sept. 19, Oct. 10, 17, 1812; *Liberty Hall*, Sept. 22, 29, Oct. 6, 14, 1812; Conlin, *Simon Perkins*, 90–94. For the congressional election in the Lancaster-Columbus-Dayton district, see Berquist and Bowers, *New Eden*, 126–30, 145 n. This district was then "entirely upon the frontier"; Kilbourne, "Address to the Electors," 1814,

in *Old Northwest Genealogical Quarterly* 6 (1903): 133. See also Barlow, "Ohio's Congressmen," 177–90, which, among other things, demonstrates that these congressmen did not support administration proposals uncritically.

87. Lebanon *Western Star*, Nov. 6, 1812; *Western Spy*, Oct. 17, 24, 1812. See also W. W. Irvin to Tappan, Sept. 28, 1812, BTP, LC; William Sterret to Cutler, Sept. 17, 1812, ECP; Franklinton *Freeman's Chronicle*, Nov. 14, 1812.

88. Stagg, *Mr. Madison's War*, 219; John McLean to Worthington, Nov. 29, 1812, TWP, RCHS, which also comments on the "great exertions" of Ohio Federalists.

89. "Circular," in Urbana *Farmer's Watch-Tower*, Oct. 28, 1812, and *Liberty Hall*, Oct. 27, 1812. See also the circulars sent to the Quid candidates by McArthur, Worthington, David Kinkead, and Kirker, Oct. 7, 1812, TWP, and in Massie, *Nathaniel Massie*, 266; *Muskingum Messenger*, Nov. 18, 1812; Knopf, *Document Transcriptions*, 2:146, 3:114–15, 217.

90. Chillicothe *Supporter*, Nov. 14, 1812; *Muskingum Messenger*, Nov. 18, 1812; Warren *Trump of Fame*, Dec. 2, 1812. The anti-Tammany Madisonian ticket received 8.6 percent of the votes. A fourth ticket named "Federal" was also announced, but no votes for it are recorded; Franklinton *Freeman's Chronicle*, Oct. 24, 1812. The turnout, at only about 20 percent of adult white males, was the highest between 1804 and 1824; Ratcliffe, "Voter Turnout in Early Ohio," 237, 240–41.

91. Hamm to Worthington, Dec. 13, 1812, Feb. 7, 1813, TWP, OHS; Hamm to Brown, Jan. 6, 1813, EABP; *Zanesville Express*, Jan. 6, 1813; *Journal of the Senate of the State of Ohio, 1812–13*, 114–17.

92. Van Horne, Samuel Herrick, and Hamm to Brown, Dec. 7, 1814, EABP; Peyton Symmes to Van Horne, Herrick, and Hamm, Dec. 11, 1814, VFM 323, OHS; *Zanesville Express*, Dec. 28, 1814. See also Hammond to Tappan, Dec. 14, 1814, BTP, LC; Dickoré, *General Joseph Kerr.*

93. Beecher to Meigs, Oct. 16, 1812, TWP, RCHS; William Sterret to Cutler, Apr. 20, 1813, ECP; Robert Lucas to Worthington, May 10, 1813, C. A. Norton to Worthington, June 1, 1813, and McArthur to Worthington, June 30, 1813, TWP, OHS.

94. C. Johnston to Jeremiah McLene, Oct. 13, 1814, Othniel Looker Papers, OHS; *Muskingum Messenger*, Sept. 7, 28, 1814; *Zanesville Express*, Sept. 14, 28, Oct. 19, 1814.

95. *Western Spy*, June 14, 1814, and Cincinnati *Spirit of the West*, July 26, 1814, Feb. 25, 1815. Historians, including Brown, "Ohio Federalists," 274, have underestimated the survival of the Tammany Societies. For example, the branch in the town of Hamilton continued to meet regularly until at least 1816; see *History and Biographical Cyclopaedia of Butler County*, 104–5.

96. *Western Spy*, July 11, 1812; Daniel Drake to Elizabeth Mansfield, July 7, 1813, and to Jared Mansfield, July 10, 1813, Jared Mansfield Papers, OHS. In this spirit, the *Western Spy* became markedly more tolerant of Federalism; Brown, "Ohio Federalists," 275.

97. *Western Spy*, Oct. 2, 9, 16, 1813; *Spirit of the West*, Sept. 27, Oct. 4, 1814; *Liberty Hall*, Sept. 27, Oct. 4, 18, 1814. For the convention of 1812, see *Liberty Hall*, Sept. 15, 29, 1812. See also Meigs to William Eustis, May 2, 1812, Burnet Papers, CHS, and Burnet, "Letters," 133–34.

98. Charles Hammond to Tappan, Dec. 14, 1814, BTP, LC; Thomas Scott to Brown, Jan. 24, 1815, CERP; Scott to Samuel Williams, Oct. 19, 1814, and James Barnes to Williams, Oct. 26, 1814, SWP; McLean to Worthington, Dec. 30, 1814, TWP, RCHS; *Liberty Hall*, Oct. 16, 1815.

99. Chillicothe *Supporter*, Sept. 10, 1812; *Fredonian*, Oct. 21, 28, 1812; *Liberty Hall*, Oct. 18, 1814; Lebanon *Western Star*, Oct. 20, 1814; Hamilton *Miami Intelligencer*, Oct. 24, 1814. See also Morrow, *Thomas Corwin*, 24; Weisenburger, *John McLean*, 9–16.

100. *Western Spy*, Sept. 17, 1814; Marietta *American Friend*, Oct. 22, 1814; D. Symmes, T. Henderson, M. S. Petit, *Circular*, Cincinnati, Aug. 11, 1814, political broadside, OHS. See also Chillicothe *Supporter*, Aug. 1, 1812; *Zanesville Express*, Jan. 20, 1813, Dec. 7, 1814; *Liberty Hall*, Oct. 4, 1814; Sears, *Thomas Worthington*, 193–95.

101. Tappan to Morrow, Jan. 13, 1813, James Monroe Papers, NYPL (microfilm, OHS), and Ratcliffe, "Benjamin Tappan," 147–53; Campbell, *Biographical Sketches*, 81–84; Barlow, "Ohio Congressmen," 177, 180, 181, 183.

102. Scott to Samuel Williams, Aug. 2, 1814, SWP; Worthington to his wife, September, Oct. 14, 1814, in [Peter], *Private Memoir of Thomas Worthington*, 63–65. See also *Western Spy*, Oct. 9, 1813; *Zanesville Express*, Aug. 24, 1814; Stagg, *Mr. Madison's War*, 456; Banner, *To the Hartford Convention*, 213–15.

103. Williams, *Pictures of Early Methodism in Ohio*, 213; *Liberty Hall*, July 17, 1811.

Chapter 7. Federalism and the Origins of Modern Politics

1. For Pennsylvania and New York, see Phillips, "William Duane, Philadelphia's Democratic Republicans, and the Origins of Modern Politics"; Wallace, "Changing Concepts of Party."

2. Martzolff, "Autobiography of Thomas Ewing," 171–72; Webster, quoted in Harlow, *Serene Cincinnatians*, 121.

3. Jefferson to E. A. Brown, February 1821, copied in Whittlesey to George Tod, Dec. 16, 1821, in Benton, "Huntington Correspondence," 159–60; John Marshall to Hammond, Dec. 28, 1823, CHP; Charles Warren, *The Supreme Court in United States History*, 2 vols. (Boston, 1922), 1:700–701. See also William Henry Smith, *Hammond in His Relations to Clay and Adams*.

4. Marsh, *Charles Hammond*, 12. The fullest treatment is Weisenburger, "Charles Hammond," but see also the memorial letters to W. D. Gallagher, 1840, CHP, and Burnet to Timothy Walker, Oct. 5, 1843, Burnet Papers, CHS.

5. Marietta *Ohio Gazette*, Oct. 19, 1802; Chillicothe *Scioto Gazette*, Sept. 11, 1802. See also Burnet, *Notes*, 321.

6. Chillicothe *Independent Republican*, Jan. 18, 1810, and *Supporter*, Feb. 24, 1810, June–August 1811; Zanesville *Muskingum Messenger*, June 19, July 17, Aug. 7, Oct. 9, 1811; "Part of Prospectus to Ohio Federalist" [1813], CHP; Weisenburger, "Charles Hammond," 345–47; *Cincinnati Advertiser*, Aug. 16, 1828.

7. Roswell Mills to Worthington, Feb. 3, 1812, in Knopf, *Document Transcriptions*, 3:49, 149; St. Clairsville *Belmont Repository*, Dec. 21, 1811, Feb. 29, Mar. 7, 1812.

8. Weisenburger, "Charles Hammond," 347; St. Clairsville *Ohio Federalist,* Sept. 22, 29, 1813, Jan. 5, 1814; Cincinnati *Spirit of the West,* Sept. 6, 1814.

9. *Spirit of the West,* Sept. 6, 1814; Whittlesey to Hammond, Aug. 30, 1813, and Hammond to Whittlesey, July 13, 1813, Whittlesey Papers. See also Badger, *Memoir,* 127–29.

10. William Rufus Browning to Ewing, Jan. 14, 1813, John Hunter to Ewing, Aug. 17, 1813, David B. Spencer to Ewing, Sept. 26, 1813, W. W. Petit to Ewing, Dec. 12, 1813, Jacob Parker to Ewing, Nov. 4, 1815, Ewing Family Papers, LC.

11. Chillicothe *Supporter,* Sept. 24, 1814; "Old Marietta Newspapers," *Marietta Register,* Nov. 13, 1863. See also James Barnes to Samuel Williams, Oct. 26, 1814, SWP.

12. Dayton *Ohio Republican,* Oct. 24, 1814; Ratcliffe, "Voter Turnout in Early Ohio," 244–45. I have discovered a few more election returns for these years since the publication of the latter article; in every case turnout for congressional elections exceeds that for governor and local offices.

13. Arius Nye to Horace Nye, Sept. 8, 1812, VFM 634, OHS.

14. *Zanesville Express,* Feb. 17, 1813, Oct. 5, 12, 1814, Aug. 15, 1816, Sept. 3, 1822. See also Van Horne to Meigs, Aug. 1, 1812, Meigs Papers, OHS, and in Knopf, *Document Transcriptions,* 2:138; Church, *Early History of Zanesville,* 146; and Schneider, *Y-Bridge City,* 69.

15. Van Horne to Worthington, Dec. 9, 1812, TWP, OHS.

16. *Zanesville Express,* Aug. 25, Sept. 1, 15, 29, Oct. 20, 1813. For the editor's moderate partisan views, see Edwin Putnam to J. S. Collins, Mar. 10, 1812, TWP, RCHS.

17. *Zanesville Express,* Mar. 16, Sept. 28, Oct. 5, 1814; *Muskingum Messenger,* Sept. 21, 28, Oct. 5, 19, 1814.

18. *Muskingum Messenger,* Aug. 10, 31, Oct. 19, 1814.

19. Bushnell, *Granville,* 37, 97; for Coshocton, see William Craig to James Pritchard, Sept. 8, 1812, BTP, LC.

20. John Sloane to Worthington, Aug. 6, 1808, TWP, OHS. For these communities, see H. E. Smith, "The Quakers."

21. Howells, *Recollections,* 17, 33–34. See also Conlin, *Simon Perkins,* 77; *Zanesville Express,* Jan. 6, 1813; *Journal of the Senate of the State of Ohio,* 1812–13, 187–90; Knopf, *Document Transcriptions,* 3:151. For a Quaker call for spiritual firmness in the face of wartime fines, see the pamphlet entitled "From Meeting for Sufferings Held at Short Creek, 23–25 Sept. 1813," copy at RCHS.

22. St. Clairsville *Ohio Federalist,* Sept. 29, 1813, Jan. 5, Oct. 19, 1814, July 25, Sept. 19, 1816; Steubenville *Western Herald,* Sept. 29, Oct. 6, 20, 1815, Sept. 20, Oct. 11, 1816. See also Hammond to John C. Wright, Sept. 19, 1816, CHP. For Hammond's formal protest against the war, see *Journal of the Senate of the State of Ohio,* 1813–14, 340–44.

23. *Western Herald,* Sept. 20, 1816. See also correspondence of August–September 1812, BTP, LC; *Muskingum Messenger,* Oct. 5, 26, 1814; *Zanesville Express,* Sept. 28, 1814, Apr. 11, 1816.

24. Ratcliffe, "Voter Turnout," 238–39.

25. James Wilson to Tappan, Jan. 23, 1815, BTP, LC; *Ohio Federalist,* Oct. 26, 1815. See also *Western Herald,* June 14, July 19, 1816. Wilson did not take over the editorship until

April 1815, but he was writing in the *Herald* before then. *Zanesville Express,* Jan. 25, 1815; Weisenburger, "Middle Western Antecedents of Woodrow Wilson," 375–76.

26. Hammond to J. C. Wright, Sept. 19, 1816, CHP; *Western Herald,* Sept. 15, 1815, May 10, Sept. 20, 1816. Cf. Webster, "Democratic Party Organization," 6.

27. "To the Independent Electors" of Washington County, in Chillicothe *Supporter,* Aug. 4, 1810; Marietta *Ohio Gazette,* Oct. 5, 1810; Hildreth, *Genealogical and Biographical Sketches,* 192.

28. Marietta *Western Spectator,* Sept. 21, Oct. 5, 1811, and *Ohio Gazette,* Oct. 14, 1811.

29. S.P. Hildreth and others, circular letter, June 22, 1812, Backus-Woodbridge Papers, OHS. See also Marietta *Ohio Gazette,* May 21, 1810; "Old Marietta Newspapers," *Marietta Register,* June 12, 1863; Brigham, *American Newspapers,* 809–11. Brown, "Ohio Federalists," is not totally reliable on this and other aspects of the years after 1809.

30. "To the Independent Electors" of Washington County, in Chillicothe *Supporter,* Aug. 4, 1810; Marietta *Ohio Gazette,* Oct. 14, 1811.

31. Marietta *Western Spectator,* Oct. 5, 19, 1811, Aug. 29, 1812; B. I. Gilman to Winthrop Sargeant, Dec. 25, 1815, CERP. See also *An Address of Members of the House of Representatives of the Congress of the United States, to Their Constituents, on the Subject of the War with Great Britain* (Marietta, 1812), copy at MC.

32. [Mathews], *Washington County,* 133–34. See also Marietta *Western Spectator,* May 12, 1813; Nahum Ward to Caleb Emerson, Apr. 11, 1814, Emerson Family Papers, WRHS.

33. S. P. Hildreth and others, circular letter, June 22, 1812, Backus-Woodbridge Papers.

34. Marietta *American Friend,* Apr. 24, 1813; Fischer, *Revolution of American Conservatism,* 409, wrongly describes David Everett as a Federalist.

35. Chillicothe *Fredonian,* Oct. 28, 1812; Marietta *American Friend,* Oct. 30, 1813, Sept. 24, 1814, Sept. 15, 1815; *Zanesville Express,* Jan. 5, 1815; "Old Marietta Newspapers," *Marietta Register,* Oct. 30, Nov. 13, 1863.

36. Pelopidas, "To Citizens of Washington County, Friends to Good Order and a Washingtonian System of Government," Emerson Family Papers.

37. *Zanesville Express,* June 8, 1814; *Muskingum Messenger,* Mar. 11, 1814. The accounts in Utter, *Frontier State,* 113–14, Fischer, *Revolution of American Conservatism,* 119, Fox, *Group Bases,* 220–21, and Brown, "Ohio Federalists," 271–72, 274–75, 279, overcount the number of Washington Benevolent Societies in Ohio, because they fail to recognize that the societies at Springfield, Putnam, and Zanesville were all one and the same, and that both that society and the Marietta society were branches of the Washington County society. These same authorities also underestimate the political activism of the societies. See the records of the "Washington Benevolent Society of Washington County and the State of Ohio," Emerson Family Papers; *Zanesville Express,* Mar. 9, July 6, 1814; *Muskingum Messenger,* May 4, 11, 1814; *Ohio Federalist,* Mar. 23, 1815. Brown, in "Ohio Federalists," 271–72, and "Political Culture of Early Ohio," 10, claims that some of these societies were founded between 1809 and 1812; I have found no primary evidence for their existence before 1813.

38. Marietta *American Friend,* Oct. 30, 1813, Oct. 22, 1814; pollbooks for Adams Township, 1811, 1814, 1815, and abstract of votes, 1804, 1814, 1815, WCC; abstract of votes, 1812,

Campus Martius Collection. The Pearson coefficients of correlation for 1813–14 and 1814–15 are 0.95 and 0.94 (r^2 = 0.91 and 0.89), respectively.

39. Luther D. Barker to Ewing, July 26, 1815, EFP. Cf. Ephraim Cutler's description of the Marietta Republicans in 1802 in chap. 3, p. 95.

40. Ratcliffe, "Benjamin Tappan," 143; Hamm to Worthington, July 5, 1811, TWP, OHS.

41. *Muskingum Messenger,* Mar. 29, 1815; Canton *Ohio Repository,* Mar. 30, 1815, in Hooper, *Ohio Journalism,* 44–46, and Heald, *Bezaleel Wells,* 110–11; Cincinnati *Western Spy,* Sept. 13, 1816; *Zanesville Express,* Apr. 20, 1815; Martin, *Franklin County,* 61.

42. For works extending such a view far beyond Ohio, see Fischer, *Revolution of American Conservatism;* Banner, *To the Hartford Convention;* and Broussard, *Southern Federalists.*

43. H. H. Leavitt's letter and J. B. Gardiner's editorial, both written "a few years ago," quoted in Canton *Ohio Repository,* Oct. 10, 1828. See also *Zanesville Express,* 1812–16; *Ohio Federalist,* 1813–16; Ratcliffe, "Experience of Revolution," 221–24.

44. Cutler, draft article for Marietta *American Friend,* 1819, ECP; *Ohio Federalist,* Sept. 4, 1817; Whittlesey to Tappan, Oct. 21, 1809, BTP, LC.

45. Ethan Stone, in *Liberty Hall,* Sept. 29, 1812; Chillicothe *Supporter,* Oct. 26, 1811; *Ohio Federalist,* Sept. 5, 12, Nov. 7, 1816, and as reprinted in *Western Spy,* Aug. 2, Sept. 19, 1816. For a Federalist's acknowledgment that a candidate should answer questions and make his views public before an election, see *Ohio Federalist,* Sept. 29, 1813.

46. Cutler, quoted in George Torrey to Cutler, June 3, 1848, ECP.

47. *Zanesville Express,* Aug. 3, Nov. 9, 1815; Mar. 21, Apr. 18, 1816, Sept. 30, 1818; Church, *Early History of Zanesville,* 103; Steubenville *Western Herald,* Apr. 27, June 15, Aug. 25, Sept. 1, 1815, Sept. 20, 1816.

48. *Zanesville Express,* Sept. 29, 1813, Sept. 7, 1815, Aug. 15, 29, Nov. 7, 1816.

49. *Ohio Federalist,* Mar. 2, 1814; Chillicothe *Supporter,* Sept. 1, 1809; Dayton *Repertory,* Oct. 7, 1808; Dayton *Ohio Centinel,* May 17, 1810.

50. *Ohio Federalist,* Sept. 29, 1813, Jan. 5, 1814, Jan. 5, May 4, June 8, 1815; *Muskingum Messenger,* Aug. 30, 1815.

51. *Zanesville Express,* Sept. 7, July 6, 1815, and 1813–17.

52. Timothy Flint, *Condensed Geography and History,* 2:387–88; Stagg, *Mr. Madison's War,* 218–19; Huntington, *Banking and Currency in Ohio,* 29–40.

53. *Zanesville Express,* Jan. 6, 1813; *Muskingum Messenger,* Feb. 28, 1814; Chillicothe *Fredonian,* Apr. 20, 1815, quoted in *Zanesville Express,* Apr. 27, 1815; Steubenville *Western Herald,* Sept. 22, 1815. See also Wyllys Silliman to Worthington, Jan. 12, 1812, TWP, OHS.

54. *Ohio Federalist,* Mar. 28, 1816, and as reprinted in *Western Spy,* Aug. 2, 1816; *Zanesville Express,* May 30, July 11, Aug. 8, Sept. 5, 1816. See also Skeen, "*Vox Populi, Vox Dei.*"

55. *Samuel Herrick,* 12–19; Levi Barber to Ewing, Aug. 9, 1817 [wrongly cataloged as 1807], Ewing Family Papers; *Niles' Weekly Register* 13 (Dec. 20, 1817): 264–65, 14 (Apr. 4, 1818): 98; *Ohio Federalist,* Apr. 9, 1818; *Zanesville Express,* Oct. 7, 1818; Chester H. Rowell, *A Historical and Legal Digest of All the Contested Election Cases in the House of Representatives, 1789–1901* (Washington, D.C.: Government Printing Service, 1901), 70–73.

56. *Ohio Federalist*, Feb. 5, 1818; Wilson to W. D. Gallagher, Oct. 1, 1840, CHP. See also *Scioto Gazette*, Feb. 12, 1819; Hammond to Wright, Feb. 27, 1819, CHP; *To the Electors of Wayne County*, 1819, broadside, OHS.

57. Hofstadter, *Idea of a Party System*.

58. *Muskingum Messenger*, July 6, 1814; Tiffin to Worthington, Apr. 12, 1812, TWP, RCHS. See also Van Horne to Worthington, Dec. 12, 1811, Dec. 9, 1812 TWP, OHS; Lebanon *Western Star*, Oct. 8, 1812.

59. Governors' messages, *Journal of the Senate of the State of Ohio, 1809–10*, 16, 40.

60. Benjamin Ruggles, *An Oration Delivered at the New Meeting House in Marietta . . . on the Fourth of July, 1809*, 11; Worthington's message, December 1814, *Journal of the Senate of the State of Ohio, 1814–15*, 48–49.

61. Cincinnati *Liberty Hall*, May 29, 1811; "Proposals for extending the circulation of the *Independent Press*, now publishing in the town of Lancaster, Fairfield County (Ohio), June 24, 1812," handbill, AAS; Huntington's message, *Journal of the Senate of the State of Ohio, 1808–9*, 55–60. See also *Zanesville Express*, Feb. 24, 1813, Oct. 5, 1814, Mar. 16, 1815.

62. Chillicothe *Supporter*, Aug. 11, Sept. 22, 1810; *Zanesville Express*, Nov. 16, 1814.

63. *Muskingum Messenger*, Aug. 10, 1814.

64. Chillicothe *Supporter*, July 4, 1812; Marietta *Western Spectator*, July 31, 1813; *Ohio Federalist*, July 2, 1818, June 29, 1814; *Zanesville Express*, Aug. 11, 1813. This aspect of the subject is overlooked by Hofstadter, *Idea of a Party System*.

65. For the argument that "antipartisan theory and partisan reality" can coexist, see Stephen E. Patterson, *Political Parties in Revolutionary Massachusetts* (Madison: University of Wisconsin Press, 1973), chap. 1. For the assumption that they did not coexist in Ohio, see Cayton, *Frontier Republic*, and Cayton and Onuf, *Midwest and the Nation*, esp. 68–69.

66. Hammond to Worthington, Feb. 7, 1812, CHP; Warren *Trump of Fame*, June 9, 1812.

67. Wright to Hammond, July 24, 1817, CHP. See also Wright to Tappan, Jan. 26, 1806, BTP, LC; *Muskingum Messenger*, Sept. 2, 1820; Ratcliffe, "Benjamin Tappan," 147.

68. *Muskingum Messenger*, July 6, 1814; B. I. Gilman to Winthrop Sergeant, Dec. 25, 1812, CERP.

69. Chillicothe *Supporter*, Sept. 17, 1816; *Western Herald*, July 12, 1816.

70. *Zanesville Express*, Dec. 28, 1815, Jan. 11, Aug. 15, 1816. See also *Ohio Federalist*, Sept. 12, 1816, and *Western Spy*, Jan. 3, 1817.

71. Hinde, quoted in Finley, *Sketches of Western Methodism*, 253. See also Finley, *Autobiography*, 268–75, 285–87, 295–301, 344–46, 351–52; Noyes, *Family History*, 2:363–64; Samuel Williams to Rev. John Collins, Feb. 17, 1819, SWP.

72. Finley, *Autobiography*, 228–30, 233–34, 257–58, 268–75, 287–88, 299–300, 346, and *Western Methodism*, 251, 361–63; Pocock, "Evangelical Frontier," 211–25, 240–41, 249.

73. Berquist and Bowers, *New Eden*, 85–171; Finley, *Autobiography*, 273–74; Mansfield, *Daniel Drake*, 102–5, 115–19; Timothy Flint, *Condensed Geography and History*, 2:387–88.

74. Harrison to James Findlay, Jan. 24, 1817, in Cox, "Torrence Papers," 3:105. See also Stevens, "Bank Enterprisers" and "Samuel Watts Davies."

75. Stuckey, "Formation of Leadership Groups in a Frontier Town," 81–89, 96–98; Heald, *Bezaleel Wells*. Elkins and McKitrick, "A Meaning for Turner's Frontier," ignore the persistence of Wells's influence from his Steubenville base.

76. *Muskingum Messenger*, Feb. 28, June 20, 1816; Everhart, *Muskingum County*, 217–18.

77. James B. Gardiner, proposal to publish a weekly in Columbus, VFM 341 (wrongly cataloged as ca. 1838), OHS; Marietta *American Friend*, June 21, Sept. 13, 1816, May 22, 1818; *Zanesville Express*, Aug. 29, 1816; "Old Marietta Newspapers," *Marietta Register*, Nov. 20, 27, 1863.

78. *Western Spy*, June 13, 1817, Aug. 30, 1816. Goforth died in May 1817. See also Brigham, *American Newspapers*, 2:790–94; for Williams, see Scheiber, "Entrepreneurship and Western Development."

79. James Heaton to Brown, Sept. 4, 1816, EABP; *Liberty Hall*, Sept. 9, Oct. 31, 1816. See also *Western Spy*, Aug. 2, 9, 30, Sept. 6, 13, 20, Oct. 18, 1816, Aug. 29, Oct. 10, 17, 1817; political broadsides of 1816, OHS; *Liberty Hall*, Oct. 6, 1817; Cleaves, *Old Tippecanoe*, 232–38.

80. Columbus *Ohio Monitor*, Aug. 22, 29, Sept. 12, 19, Oct. 3, 24, Nov. 7, 1816; Kilbourne, reported in *Old Northwest Genealogical Quarterly* 6 (1903): 139–40. See also *Muskingum Messenger*, Oct. 24, 31, 1816; John Bailhache, "Autobiography" (1855), typescript at AAS, 17–18, 20; Hooper, *Ohio Journalism*, 35–36; Brigham, *American Newspapers*, 785–88, 798–99.

81. *Zanesville Express*, Jan. 25, Aug. 22, Oct. 31, 1816; *Muskingum Messenger*, Oct. 17, 31, 1816; Mount Vernon *Ohio Register*, June 5, Sept. 18, Nov. 6, 1816; *Ohio Federalist*, Nov. 7, 1816.

82. Fearing to the president of the Washington Benevolent Society, July 3, 1816, Campus Martius collection; Hammond to Wright, July 28, 1817, Aug. 2, 1816, CHP; *Western Herald*, Sept. 20, 1816, Oct. 17, 31, 1818; *Ohio Federalist*, Sept. 4, 1817, July 2, 1818.

83. Mount Vernon *Ohio Register*, Sept. 24, 1817; Belt to Worthington, Aug. 28, 1817, TWP, RCHS; *Ohio Federalist*, Sept. 4, 1817 (copy at RCHS). See also *Old Northwest Genealogical Quarterly* 6 (1903): 139–40.

84. *Ohio Federalist*, Sept. 5, 12, Nov. 7, 1816, July 2, 1818; Hammond to Wright, July 28, 1817, Hammond to Worthington, May 18, 1818, CHP; Livermore, *Twilight of Federalism*.

85. *Zanesville Express*, Aug. 15, 1816.

CHAPTER 8. GOOD FEELINGS AND PARTISANSHIP, 1816–1821

1. For example, Leavitt, *Autobiography*; Reemelin, "Reminiscences of Moses Dawson."

2. Pease to Trimble, July 10, 1822, in Trimble, *Autobiography and Correspondence*, 129–30; Still, "Ethan Allen Brown," 52–55, 137–38. Utter, *Frontier State*, 326, and Buley, *Old Northwest*, 2:8–9, err in stating that Trimble defeated Morrow in 1822. Cayton, *Frontier Republic*, 133, exaggerates the role of caucuses in this period. For Columbus, see Pease to Hitchcock, July 3, 1820, Hitchcock Papers.

3. C. P. Beatty to Tappan, Jan. 30, 1820, BTP, LC. See also *History of Fire Lands,* 132–35.

4. Hammond to Wright, Feb. 27, 1819, CHP; Lewis Dille to Hitchcock, Dec. 15, 1818, Jan. 31, 1819, J. H. Larwill to Hitchcock, Feb. 14, 1819, John Thompson to Hitchcock, Feb. 19, 1819, Hitchcock Papers.

5. John Thompson to Hitchcock, Dec. 31, 1818, Hitchcock Papers; Zanesville *Muskingum Messenger,* Sept. 15, 1819. For evidence of a Presbyterian bloc in the assembly in 1822–23, see Ratcliffe, "Benjamin Tappan," 154.

6. Columbus *Ohio Monitor,* Nov. 7, 1816; Cincinnati *Western Spy,* Aug. 2, 9, 30, Sept. 6, 13, 20, Oct. 18, 1816, Aug. 29, Oct. 10, 17, 1817; *Liberty Hall,* Sept. 9, Oct. 31, 1816, Oct. 6, 1817.

7. A. W. Putnam to Ephraim Cutler, Aug. 29, 1820, ECP; Marietta *American Friend,* Sept. 15, 1820; Pocock, "A Candidate I'll Surely Be," 58, 63.

8. Calvin Fletcher to Jesse Fletcher, Nov. 21, 1818, quoted in Power, *Planting Corn Belt Culture,* 2. These generalizations are based on election-time correspondence in county newspapers and on the OHS collection of handbills circulated in local elections between 1818 and 1822, especially those relating to the Wayne County election of 1822. See also Stevens, *Early Jackson Party in Ohio,* 72–73; and Pocock, "A Candidate I'll Surely Be," 56–58, 63–65, 200 n. 3.

9. *Muskingum Messenger,* May 6, 23, 1816; *Zanesville Express,* Feb. 22, 29, 1816; Morrow, *Thomas Corwin,* 24; Pocock, "A Candidate I'll Surely Be," 59. The presidential election of 1816 saw Ohio's lowest ever turnout, at about 5 percent: Ratcliffe, "Voter Turnout in Early Ohio," 241.

10. *Painesville Telegraph,* Oct. 9, 1824; Wright to Brown, Aug. 31, 1818, CHP; Hammond to Tappan, Oct. 10, 1819, BTP, LC; Steubenville *Western Herald,* Oct. 2, 1819.

11. Leavitt, *Autobiography,* 32; Ratcliffe, "Voter Turnout," 241.

12. Columbus *Ohio Monitor,* Dec. 17, 1818.

13. *Muskingum Messenger,* Dec. 22, 1813, May 25, 1814, Aug. 22, Oct. 24, 1816; see also Sept. 4, 1811, Aug. 10, 1814.

14. St. Clairsville *Ohio Federalist,* Sept. 4, 1817; *Muskingum Messenger,* June 20, 1816, June 10, 1818; Steubenville *Western Herald,* June 20, 27, July 11, 1818; Appleton Downer to Dr. Avery Downer, Oct. 15, 1817, VFM 1245, OHS.

15. *Muskingum Messenger,* Sept. 12, Oct. 24, 31, 1816, Sept. 17, 24, 1817.

16. *Muskingum Messenger,* Oct. 24, 31, 1816, Sept. 17, Oct. 1, 1817. See also ibid., Sept. 21, 1814, Aug. 22, 12, Sept. 26, 1816, Sept. 2, 23, 1818, and Columbus *Ohio Monitor,* July 25, Nov. 7, 1816. Thus the idea that party could protect the general good was already a commonplace and not the creation of the Jacksonian period, nor was it peculiar to upland southerners, as claimed in Etcheson, "Private Interest and Public Good."

17. Jordan, *National Road,* 75.

18. Hammond to Wright, Aug. 2, 1816, CHP; *Ohio Federalist,* Sept. 19, 1816; Steubenville *Western Herald,* July 5, Sept. 13, 20, 1816; *Zanesville Express,* Apr. 11, May 9, Aug. 29, 1816; *Muskingum Messenger,* Oct. 3, 24, 1816.

19. *Western Herald,* Sept. 15, 1815; *Ohio Federalist,* Oct. 26, 1815.

20. Van Horne to Tappan, Feb. 16, 1816, BTP, LC.

21. *Muskingum Messenger,* June 13, 1816. See also ibid., Mar. 13, Apr. 17, 1816; *Western Herald,* May 10, 1816.

22. *Ohio Federalist,* Dec. 12, 1816. The opposition to the caucus nomination in Pennsylvania led by Duane is reported in ibid., June 13, Oct. 31, Nov. 21, 1816. The debate over the proper grounds for objecting to caucus nominations may be followed in *Zanesville Express,* Apr. 11, May 16, June 27, 1816, and *Western Herald,* May 31, June 20, July 5, 1816. For other Federalist objections, see Chillicothe *Supporter,* June 6, 1812, Sept. 17, 1816.

23. Columbus *Ohio Monitor,* Sept. 23, 1819; Hammond to Wright, Aug. 2, Sept. 19, 1816; *Muskingum Messenger,* Sept. 2, 1818, Sept. 29, Oct. 6, 1819.

24. *Muskingum Messenger,* Oct. 28, 1818. See also ibid., Sept. 16, 30, Oct. 7, 24, 1818; *Western Herald,* July 11, Oct. 10, 31, 1818; and Hammond to Wright, Aug. 31, Oct. 11, 1818, CHP.

25. *Muskingum Messenger,* Sept. 9, 23, Oct. 21, 1818; Columbus *Ohio Monitor,* Sept. 19, Oct. 3, 1816; *Columbus Gazette,* Dec. 24, 1818. See also ibid., Sept. 24, 1817, Aug. 19, Sept. 2, 23, 30, 1818; *Western Herald,* Sept. 19, 1817, Sept. 4, 1819. For the Doherty-Ewing fracas, see *Ohio Monitor,* Nov. 12, 19, 26, Dec. 3, 1818, and letters and statements, November–December 1818, Ewing Family Papers, LC.

26. Columbus *Ohio Monitor,* Sept. 23, 1819, Sept. 3, 1818; *Muskingum Messenger,* Sept. 2, 30, 1818. For the fourth district, see also ibid., Oct. 24, 1816, Oct. 1, 22, 1817, Sept. 2, 16, Oct. 7, 28, 1818; *Zanesville Express,* Oct. 13, 1816, Sept. 25, Oct. 2, 1817; Hammond to Wright, Oct. 11, 1818, Aug. 6, Oct. 15, Dec. 12, 14, 1820, May 6, Sept. 30, 1821, CHP. See also *Western Herald,* Sept. 9, Nov. 11, 1820.

27. *Western Herald,* June 27, July 11, 1818. See also *Ohio Monitor,* July 23, 1818, and *Muskingum Messenger,* Sept. 8, 1819.

28. *Cleaveland Herald,* Oct. 19, Nov. 2, 1819, in WPA, *Annals of Cleveland,* 2:12, 13; *Western Herald,* June 20, 27, July 11, 1818.

29. Benjamin Hough to Worthington, Jan. 26, 1811, TWP, OHS, and in Knopf, *Document Transcriptions,* 3:1; *Niles' Weekly Register* 5 (Dec. 18, 1813): 263; Chillicothe *Supporter,* June 24, 1817. See also Goodwin, "Development of the Miami Country," 493–94; Grupenhoff, "Politics and the Rise of Political Parties," 150–54.

30. Cincinnati *Western Spy,* July 4, 1817; *Ohio Monitor,* Nov. 17, 1817, Sept. 3, 1818; Dwight L. Smith, "Nine Letters of Nathaniel Dike," 193–99.

31. Stuckey, "Formation of Leadership Groups in a Frontier Town," 35–37, 68, 76, 89–92, 96–97, 136, 202, 240–41, 288–89. For the congressional election, see *Muskingum Messenger,* Oct. 31, 1816, Feb. 13, 1817; Warren *Western Reserve Chronicle,* Nov. 1, 1816.

32. *Western Spy,* Mar. 28, 1818. For competing appeals for the Irish vote in Muskingum, see *Zanesville Express,* Feb. 23, Mar. 1, 15, 22, 1820, and *Muskingum Messenger,* May 20, June 10, July 1, Oct. 10, Dec. 26, 1820. In 1820 the assembly decided that noncitizens may vote in townships where such practices had been condoned for some time. Pocock, "A Candidate I'll Surely Be," 65–66.

33. Crary, *Pioneer and Personal Reminiscences,* 42. See also *Muskingum Messenger,* early August 1816; McLean to Brown, June 20, Aug. 20, 1816, EABP; *Western Herald,* Aug. 23, Sept. 13, 20, 1816; and Skeen, *"Vox Populi, Vox Dei."*

34. Finley, *Autobiography,* 273–74.

35. Silliman to Worthington, Jan. 12, 1812, TWP, OHS. For the directors, see [Mathews], *Washington County,* 373; Everhart, *Muskingum County,* 218.

36. *Zanesville Express,* Jan. 6, 1813; *Western Herald,* June 1 through Oct. 20 (esp. Sept. 22), 1815, and *Ohio Federalist,* Oct. 5, 26, 1815. For examples of criticism, see *Western Spy,* Aug. 2, Sept. 13, 1816, Feb. 28, Mar. 7, Apr. 18, 1817.

37. Hammond to Wright, Jan. 19, Dec. 27, 1816, Feb. 7, 1817, CHP; Huntington, *Banking and Currency,* 44–49.

38. *Ohio Federalist,* Jan. 2, 1817; Timothy Flint, *Condensed Geography and History,* 2:388–89; *Western Herald,* Jan. 10, 1817; Bray Hammond, *Banks and Politics in America from the Revolution to the Civil War* (Princeton: Princeton University Press, 1957).

39. Wright to Hammond, July 24, 1817, CHP; *Columbus Gazette,* Dec. 18, 1817; James Flint, *Letters from America,* 133–36. See also Huntington, *Banking and Currency,* 51, 53, 56.

40. *Muskingum Messenger,* Oct. 22, 1817, Oct. 21, 1818; Everhart, *Muskingum County,* 217; Independence, *To the Electors of the Counties of Warren, Hamilton, Buttler* [sic] *& Preble,* Oct. 12, 1818, political broadside, OHS.

41. *Ohio Federalist,* July 2, 1818; Sloane's statement of 1818, quoted in Wooster *Ohio Oracle,* Sept. 29, 1826.

42. *Liberty Hall,* Jan. 1, Feb. 27, Mar. 6, 1811; Ruggles to [Paul Fearing], Mar. 18, 1816, SPHP. See also Barlow, "Ohio's Congressmen," 186–90; Weisenburger, *John McLean,* 17–18; *Muskingum Messenger,* Apr. 17, 24, May 30, 1816.

43. Burnet, "Letters," 165, and Burnet, *Notes,* 406–8. See also *Western Spy,* Nov. 15, 1816; *Scioto Gazette,* Nov. 28, 1816; Edward Paine Jr. to Hitchcock, Mar. 25, 1818, S. W. Phelps to Hitchcock, Mar. 30, 1818, Hitchcock Papers.

44. Burnet, "Letters," 165–67, and *Notes,* 408–11. See also *Western Herald,* Sept. 12, 1818; David Abbot to Hitchcock, Dec. 23, 1818, CERP; Huntington, *Banking and Currency,* 55–69.

45. *Ohio Monitor,* Nov. 19, 1818; *Muskingum Messenger,* Nov. 18, 1819, Sept. 19, Oct. 3, 1820. See also ibid., Sept. 15, 22, 29, 1819, July 15, Aug. 19, 26, Sept. 2, 12, 19, 1820.

46. McLean to Brown, Jan. 9, 1819, EABP; *Ohio Monitor,* Nov. 26, 1818. See also Chillicothe *Supporter,* Mar. 3, 1819; Hammond to Wright, Apr. 19, 1819, CHP; *Niles' Weekly Register* 16 (1819): 256, 298; *Muskingum Messenger,* Oct. 20, Nov. 18, 1819; *Scioto Gazette,* Jan. 29, Dec. 10, 1819; Leon M. Schur, "The Second Bank of the United States and the Inflation after the War of 1812," *Journal of Political Economy* 68 (1960): esp. 122.

47. Wright to Brown, Nov. 6, 1819, CHP; Worthington to Langdon Cheves, Dec. 2, 1816, TWP, RCHS. This summary of Ohio's case is based on Governor Brown's messages, Hammond's letters, and Ohio newspaper editorials. See also Ryan, "Nullification in Ohio," and Bogart, "Taxation of Second Bank."

48. *Western Herald,* Oct. 31, 1818; Chillicothe *Supporter,* Oct. 21, 1818. See also Fox, "Bank Wars," 263.

49. Leonard Case to Hitchcock, Dec. 3, 1818, Hitchcock Papers; and *Wooster Spectator,* Jan. 13, 1821.

50. William Foulks to Hitchcock, Jan. 31, 1819, Hitchcock Papers; W. H. Crawford to

Worthington, Mar. 13, 1819, TWP, RCHS. See also Sears, *Thomas Worthington*, 208–9, 211; Tuttle, "William Allen Trimble."

51. Hammond to [Wright?], Dec. 27, 1816, CHP; Still, "Ethan Allen Brown," esp. 71–91.

52. *Niles' Weekly Register* 17 (Jan. 1, 1820): 295. See also Still, "Ethan Allen Brown," 71, 74. The "pique" was directed against Hammond, the author of the bill.

53. Wright to Tappan, Jan. 3, 1820, BTP, LC; Chillicothe *Supporter,* Sept. 22, 1819; *Niles' Weekly Register* 17 (Oct. 9, 30, Nov. 6, 1819): 87, 139, 147. Stephen C. Fox is mistaken in seeing these delegate conventions as innovatory: see Fox, "Group Bases of Ohio Political Behavior," 127–29, 428, "Bank Wars," 263–64, and *Group Bases,* 58–61.

54. John Cleves Short to William Short, Nov. 11, 1818, Short Family Papers; *Western Spy,* Sept. 4, 25, Oct. 9, 16, 1819; *Liberty Hall,* Oct. 15, 1819.

55. Hammond to Wright, Dec. 12, 1820, and Wright to Hammond, Dec. 20, 1820, CHP. See also *Liberty Hall and Cincinnati Gazette,* Oct. 19, Dec. 9, 1819; Goebel, *Harrison,* 226–32; Stevens, *Early Jackson Party in Ohio,* 3–47.

56. James Wilson to Brown, Mar. 4, 1819, EABP; *Cleaveland Herald,* in WPA, *Annals of Cleveland,* 3:63–64.

57. Hammond to Worthington, Mar. 24, 1817, and to Wright, Feb. 27, 1819, CHP. See also Hammond to Burnet, July 30, 1817, Burnet Papers; Hammond to Brown, Nov. 4, 1819, CHP; *Ohio Federalist,* Jan. 15, 1818.

58. William Greene to Brown, Jan. 27, 1821, EABP; Whittlesey to W. D. Gallagher, July 23, 1840, CHP.

59. Thomas Ritchie to Ruggles, Jan. 23, 1821, Hammond to Brown, Apr. 23, 1821, Hammond to Wright, Sept. 17, 1821, CHP. See also Whittlesey to George Tod, Dec. 16, 1821, for a copy of Jefferson's letter of February 1821, reprinted in Benton, "Huntington Correspondence," 159–60.

60. Beecher to Brown, Jan. 1, 1819, EABP; Brown to Hammond, Aug. 1, 1821, EABP.

61. Allen Trimble to W. A. Trimble, Dec. 5, 1821, in Trimble, *Autobiography and Correspondence,* 122; Hammond to Wright, Dec. 29, 1821, CHP.

62. *Western Spy,* Sept. 13, 1816, Sept. 5, 1817; *Muskingum Messenger,* June 2, Oct. 6, 1819; *Western Herald,* Oct. 10, 1818, Sept. 4, 1819; Rothbard, *Panic of 1819,* 10, 166, 168.

63. W. A. Trimble to Brown, Dec. 28, 1819, Jan. 29, Mar. 11, Apr. 4, 29, May 3, 10, 1820, EABP; W. A. Trimble to Allen Trimble, Feb. 12, 1820, in Trimble, *Autobiography and Correspondence,* 118–19. See also Bates, *Alfred Kelley,* 24–58; Feller, *Public Lands in Jacksonian Politics,* 40–48.

64. J. W. Campbell to Allen Trimble, Feb. 11, 1819, in Trimble, *Autobiography and Correspondence,* 118; Brown to W. A. Trimble, May 12, 1820, EABP; Feller, *Public Lands,* 31–58.

65. Wing, *Early Years on the Western Reserve,* 24–25; Marietta *Western Spectator,* Mar. 5, 1811 through Feb. 8, 1812; *Circular, to the Advocates of African Emancipation, Who Are Sensible of the Wrongs of Those Unhappy Beings,* St. Clairsville, Jan. 4, 1816, broadside, RCHS. See also Miller, "Union Humane Society"; Ketring, *Charles Osborn,* 34–40; and Dillon, *Benjamin Lundy,* 7–36.

66. *Liberty Hall and Cincinnati Gazette,* Nov. 10, 1817; *Scioto Gazette,* June 11, 1819, and *Supporter,* June 16, 1819; *Muskingum Messenger,* Sept. 15, 1819. See also O'Dell, "Early Antislavery Movement," 179–225, 228–29, 294–300. Moore, *Missouri Controversy,* fails to recognize the strength of antislavery feeling in the North in 1819.

67. Still, "Ethan Allen Brown," 39–41; *Cleaveland Herald,* May 9, 16, July 4, 1820, in WPA, *Annals of Cleveland,* 3:77.

68. *Western Herald,* July 3, 1819, Mar. 25, 1820; *Muskingum Messenger,* July 21, 1819; *History of Brown County,* 591–92. See also O'Dell, "Early Antislavery Sentiment," 146–55, 223–24, 230–32.

69. Moore, *Missouri Controversy,* 52–62; White, *Politics on the Southwestern Frontier,* 11–15. This cleavage did not reflect, as has been suggested, the differences between Ohioans of northern and southern background, since only two of the eight came from a slave state, one of the four New Englanders was sympathetic to slavery, and two of the more antislavery congressmen represented southern-born constituents.

70. *Cleaveland Herald,* Feb. 8, 1820, in WPA, *Annals of Cleveland,* 3:66–67; Ewing to Beecher, Jan. 1, 1820, Ewing Family Papers. See also *Liberty Hall and Cincinnati Gazette,* Dec. 19, 1819; *Muskingum Messenger,* Jan. 26, 1820; Horton Howard to M. T. Williams et al., Dec. 31, 1819, M. T. Williams Papers; Ratcliffe, "Captain James Riley and Antislavery Sentiment," 82.

71. *Scioto Gazette,* Jan. 14, 1820, Apr. 26, 1823; W. A. Trimble to Brown, Jan. 29, 1820, EABP. See also Ratcliffe, "Captain James Riley and Antislavery Sentiment," 84–85; Goebel, *Harrison,* 228–33; and O'Dell, "Early Antislavery Movement," 262–69.

72. Tappan's toast, in *Western Herald,* July 6, 1820; Marietta *American Friend,* Sept. 15, 1820. For the campaign against fugitive advertisements, see *Western Herald,* May 27, July 1, Aug. 12, 19, Sept. 9, 1820; *Cleaveland Herald,* Nov. 14, Dec. 12, 1820, Jan. 2, Mar. 20, 1821, in WPA, *Annals of Cleveland,* 3:77–78, 4:95, 148; Marietta *Register,* Dec. 18, 1863; Eber D. Howe, *Autobiography,* 25; Miller, "Union Humane Society," 99–100.

73. Harrison to James Monroe, June 16, 1823, Monroe Papers; *Muskingum Messenger,* June 10, 1820. See also *Western Spy,* June 22, 1820; *Scioto Gazette,* Nov. 9, 22, 1820.

74. *Muskingum Messenger,* July 15, Dec. 5, 1820; *Scioto Gazette,* Dec. 14, 1820; *Cleaveland Herald,* Mar. 21, 1820, in WPA, *Annals of Cleveland,* 3:67–68.

75. *Zanesville Express,* Apr. 5, 12, 1820; *Western Herald,* December 1819 through March 1820, August through October 1820. See also O'Dell, "Early Antislavery Movement," 269–74, 355–94, and, in general, Adams, *Neglected Period of Anti-Slavery.*

76. Hammond to Wright, Dec. 14, 1820, Feb. 26, 1821, CHP; Sloane to Tappan, Dec. 13, 1820, BTP, LC. See also Moore, *Missouri Controversy,* 144, 145, 156, 158.

77. Lancaster *Ohio Eagle,* Oct. 3, 1822; Harrison to Monroe, June 16, 1823, Monroe Papers; Cincinnati *Independent Press,* Sept. 12, 19, 26, Oct. 3, 8, 1822; Wilson to Worthington, Nov. 17, 1822, TWP, LC; *Delaware Patron,* Sept. 2, 1824. See also O'Dell, "Early Antislavery Sentiment," 258; Morris, *Thomas Morris,* 30–31; Adams, *Neglected Period of Anti-Slavery,* 85.

78. *Cleaveland Herald,* May 2, 1820; Hammond to Wright, Feb. 20, 1820, CHP.

79. Sloane to Hammond, Jan. 1, 1824, BTP; Beecher to Ewing, Feb. 25, 1824, Ewing Family Papers. See also Ratcliffe, "Role of Voters and Issues."

80. *Cleaveland Herald,* May 2, 1820; John C. Wright to Whittlesey, July 19, 1820, Whittlesey Papers; Sloane to Tappan, Mar. 29, Apr. 11, May 4, 1820, BTP, LC. There is a tradition that one-quarter of the votes cast in Ohio were for John Quincy Adams, but extant contemporary evidence suggests that every electoral college candidate favored Monroe. *Liberty Hall,* Sept. 30, Oct. 28, Nov. 29, 1820; *Western Spy,* Sept. 28, 1820. See also Ratcliffe, "Voter Turnout," 241 n. 40.

81. Friends to Liberty, *Fellow Citizens of Butler County,* Sept. 24, 1821, political broadside, OHS; *Liberty Hall and Cincinnati Gazette,* Oct. 5, 1819, Oct. 7, 1820; *Western Spy,* Aug. 10, 1820. For the survival of Tammany in Hamilton County, see *Western Spy,* June 27, 1817, and *Address of the Society of Tammany, or Columbian Order, to Its Absent Members and the Members of Its Various Branches throughout the United States,* reprinted by order of Wigwam no. 3, of the State of Ohio (Cincinnati, 1819), copy at OHS.

82. Marietta *American Friend,* May 22, 1818, Oct. 15, 1819; "Old Marietta Newspapers," *Marietta Register,* Nov. 27, 1863; Cutler, *Ephraim Cutler,* 112–28, 114 (quotation); Andrews, *Washington County,* 59–60; [Mathews], *Washington County,* 108; Nahum Ward to Cutler, Feb. 11, 1820, ECP.

83. Marietta *American Friend,* Aug. 4, Sept. 8, 15, 22, 29, Oct. 6, 13, 20, Dec. 15, 29, 1820. See also W. R. Putnam to Cutler, Oct. 7, 1820, and Cutler to W. R. Putnam, Oct. 14, 1820, ECP. The correlation is identical between each pair of elections, 1814/1820 and 1815/1820, namely r = 0.78 and r^2 = 0.60.

84. S. P. Hildreth et al., circular, Marietta, August 1821, Campus Martius Collection; Marietta *American Friend,* Sept. 7, 14, 28, Oct. 5, 19, 1821.

85. Marietta *American Friend,* Oct. 18, 1822; Nahum Ward to Cutler, Jan. 12, 1825, ECP. See also *American Friend,* Aug. 9, 30, Sept. 13, Oct. 4, 1822, Oct. 9, 30, 1823; Cutler, *Ephraim Cutler,* 133–35, 139–67, 170.

86. *American Friend,* Sept. 8, 15, Oct. 6, 20, 1820, Sept. 7, 28, Oct. 19, 1821, Aug. 16, Sept. 6, Oct. 19, 1822, Aug. 21, Oct. 30, 1823.

87. *Muskingum Messenger,* Aug. 11, 18, Sept. 8, 15, 22, Oct. 6, 1819, Aug. 26, Oct. 17, 1820, Sept. 10, Oct. 22, 1822, Sept. 9, 30, 1823.

88. *Muskingum Messenger,* Sept. 8, 1819, Nov. 14, 1820; New Philadelphia *Tuscarawas Chronicle,* Sept. 29, Dec. 8, 1821, Aug. 17, Sept. 7, Oct. 5, 1822.

89. *Muskingum Messenger,* July 23, Sept. 3, 10, 1822; see also Sept. 9, Oct. 14, 1818, Sept. 22, 29, 1819, Sept. 3, 10, 1822, and Wolfe, *Stories of Guernsey County, Ohio,* 70–71.

90. Hammond to Wright, Oct. 15, 1820, Sept. 30, 1821, CHP; *Scioto Gazette,* Oct. 24, 1821.

91. Hammond to Wright, Oct. 10, Nov. 10, 1822, CHP; *Muskingum Messenger,* July 23, 30, Aug. 20, Sept. 17, 1822; John Patterson to Worthington, Oct. 7, 1815, TWP, OHS.

92. Hammond to Wright, Dec. 15, 20, 1822, CHP; J. C. Wright to Whittlesey, Feb. 11, 1822, Whittlesey Papers. For these appointments, see CHP, BTP, EWP, and esp. EABP, January 1822 through January 1823.

93. *Cleaveland Herald,* July 25, 1820, in WPA, *Annals of Cleveland,* 3:63.

94. *Ohio Monitor,* Sept. 16, Nov. 18, 1820; *Muskingum Messenger,* Sept. 26, Oct. 31, 1820; Dayton *Ohio Watchman,* Oct. 24, 1820.

95. W. R. Putnam to Cutler, Oct. 7, 1820, ECP; *Muskingum Messenger,* July 1, 8, 1820.

EPILOGUE: JACKSONIAN PERSPECTIVES

1. Weisenburger, "Charles Hammond," 350.

2. Ratcliffe, "Role of Voters and Issues."

3. Ratcliffe, "Politics in Jacksonian Ohio," and "Voter Turnout in Early Ohio."

3. Leavitt, *Autobiography;* Reemelin, "Reminiscences of Moses Dawson."

4. Chambers, *Political Parties in a New Nation,* esp. chap. 1.

5. Proceedings of meeting in Wayne County, Ohio, Mar. 14, 1827, Washington, D.C., *United States Telegraph,* Apr. 14, 1827; *The Address, Resolutions and Other Proceedings, of a Public Meeting, Held at the U.S. Court-House, Columbus, Ohio, by Citizens of Franklin County, Favourable to the Election of Andrew Jackson, on the 17th of November, 1827* (Columbus: David Smith, 1827).

6. Martin Van Buren to Thomas Ritchie, Jan. 13, 1827, in Robert V. Remini, ed., *Age of Jackson* (New York: Harper and Row, 1972), 3–7.

7. This and the following paragraphs draw heavily on Ratcliffe, *The Politics of Long Division: Origins of the Second Party System in Ohio, 1819–1828* (forthcoming).

8. Cincinnati *National Republican,* Aug. 16, Sept. 13, Oct. 4, 1825; Remeelin, "Moses Dawson," pt. 5, in *Cincinnati Commercial,* Dec. 18, 1869. The conventions of 1825–26 are misinterpreted as Jacksonian devices in Webster, "Democratic Party Organization," 13–15, and Fox, *Group Bases,* 227.

9. *St. Clairsville Gazette,* Mar. 11, 25, July 29, Aug. 26, Sept. 10, 1826. For dissatisfaction with contemporary campaigns and elections, see also *Newark Advocate,* Sept. 19, 1822; Marietta *American Friend,* Oct. 9, 1823; Cincinnati *Western Tiller,* Oct. 13, 1826.

10. James Heaton, "Old Time Letters," Heaton Papers, LC.

11. Ratcliffe, "Benjamin Tappan," 115, 121; *St. Clairsville Gazette,* Apr. 12, Nov. 8, 1828; Columbus *Ohio State Bulletin,* Aug. 12, Sept. 9, 1829.

12. Alexander Armstrong to Whittlesey, Jan. 10, 1828, Whittlesey Papers. In December 1811 Armstrong founded the *Belmont Repository,* which he amalgamated with Hammond's *Ohio Federalist* in November 1814, and their journalistic cooperation continued even after the demise of the *Ohio Federalist* and Armstrong's commencement of the *Belmont Journal* in August 1818.

13. Columbus *Ohio State Bulletin,* July 21, 1830.

14. *Marietta and Washington County Pilot,* Sept. 6, 1828; *St. Clairsville Gazette,* May 5, Sept. 29, Nov. 10, 1827, May 17, 31, Aug. 31, Sept. 6, 13, Oct. 11, 1828.

15. Pearson coefficient in the latter case is +0.71 (r^2 = 0.51). For the returns, see Steubenville *Western Herald,* Oct. 20, 1815; Zanesville *Muskingum Messenger,* Oct. 25, 1815; abstracts of votes, Washington County, 1815, WCC; Marietta *American Friend,* Oct. 30, 1813, Oct. 22, 1814, Oct. 17, 1827, Oct. 25, Nov. 1, 8, 1828; *Marietta and Washington*

County Pilot, Nov. 15, 1828; St. Clairsville *National Historian,* Nov. 1, 1828; *St. Clairsville Gazette,* Nov. 8, 1828. No election returns survive for Muskingum County in 1828.

16. *Muskingum Messenger,* Jan. 19, 1820.

17. *St. Clairsville Gazette,* June 28, 1828; Joseph H. Larwill to John Larwill, Dec. 10, 1828, Larwill Family Papers; Duff Green to Jackson, June 9, 1827, in John Spencer Bassett, ed., *Correspondence of Andrew Jackson,* 7 vols. (Washington, D.C.: Carnegie Institution, 1926–35), 3:361.

Select Bibliography

Manuscript Collections Consulted

Given the haphazard and scanty nature of published voting returns during this period, the original manuscript records—that is, the township pollbooks and tallysheets and especially the county abstracts of votes—have proved invaluable. I found the most useful voting records for these years in the archives at the University of Cincinnati, Ohio Historical Society, Western Reserve Historical Society, and Wright State University, Dayton, and I stumbled across some pollbooks at Marietta College, at the Cincinnati Historical Society, and in the John Harmon Family Papers at Western Reserve Historical Society. Those seeking the Washington County voting records no longer have to unwrap dusty parcels in the grimy, sweaty attic of the Marietta Courthouse, as microfilm copies are now available at Ohio University in Athens.

Otherwise, some of the most interesting manuscript material in research libraries is to be found in small, scattered collections commonly described as vertical file material. These items are too numerous to list here but are cited in the notes whenever appropriate. The following constitute the major collections that I consulted and in many cases systematically read:

Backus-Woodbridge Papers, OHS
Beecher-Trimble Collection, CHS
Ethan Allen Brown Papers, OHS
John W. Browne Papers, CHS
Jacob Burnet Papers, CHS
Campus Martius Collection, OHS
Maria D. Coffinberry Papers, WRHS
Ephraim Cutler Papers, MC
Caleb Emerson Family Papers, WRHS
Thomas Ewing Family Papers, LC
Thomas Ewing Papers, OHS
John Fuller Papers, OHS

Gano Family Papers, CHS
Charles Hammond Papers, OHS
William Henry Harrison Papers, LC
William Henry Harrison Papers, CHS
William Henry Harrison Papers, NYPL (microfilm, OHS)
James Heaton Papers, LC
Samuel Prescott Hildreth Papers, MC
Peter Hitchcock Family Papers, WRHS
Huntington Papers, LCHS
Samuel Huntington Papers, OHS
Samuel Huntington Papers, WRHS
Thomas Jefferson Papers, transcripts, RCHS
Thomas Kirker Papers, OHS
Larwill Family Papers, OHS
Joseph Larwill Papers, OHS
William C. Larwill Papers, OHS
Othniel Looker Papers, OHS
Lytle Family Papers, CHS
Duncan McArthur Papers, LC (microfilm, OHS)
John McLean Papers, OHS
Edward Deering Mansfield Papers, OHS
Jared Mansfield Papers, OHS
Nathaniel Massie Papers, OHS
Return Jonathan Meigs Jr., Papers, OHS
James Monroe Papers, NYPL (microfilm, OHS)
Josiah Morrow Papers, CHS
Calvin Pease Papers, WRHS
Charles E. Rice Papers, OHS
Arthur St. Clair Papers, OHS
Thomas Scott Papers, RCHS
Short Family Papers, photostats, CHS
John Sloane Papers, OHS
John Smith Papers, CHS
William Henry Smith Papers, OHS
Symmes Papers, Draper Manuscripts, University of Wisconsin
Records of the Tammany Society, OHS
Benjamin Tappan Papers, LC
Benjamin Tappan Papers, OHS
Benjamin Tappan Correspondence, NYPL (microfilm, OHS)
Edward Tiffin Papers, OHS
Edward Tiffin Papers, WRHS
Edward Tiffin Papers, RCHS
George Tod Papers, WRHS

Papers of John Allen Trimble and the Trimble Family, OHS
Allen Trimble Papers, OHS
Allen Trimble Family Papers, WRHS
Elijah Wadsworth Family Papers, WRHS
Elisha Whittlesey Papers, WRHS
Wildman Papers, OHS
Micajah T. Williams Papers, OHS
Samuel Williams Papers, RCHS
Thomas Worthington Papers, LC
Thomas Worthington Papers, OHS
Thomas Worthington Papers, RCHS

NEWSPAPERS CONSULTED

Newspapers provide the fullest information and often the most unusual insights, even in the scanty, amateurish, plagiarist form they took in pioneer Ohio. The essential handbook, without which this project would have been impossible, is Steve Gutgesell's *Guide to Ohio Newspapers, 1793–1973,* although new runs of newspapers have become available and much microfilm has been produced since its publication in 1976. Many copies of Ohio newspapers may be found outside the state that have not survived within it: I have found the Library of Congress and the American Antiquarian Society invaluable. Clarence Brigham's *History and Bibliography of American Newspapers, 1690–1820,* remains indispensable. I have consulted, and in many cases thoroughly read, the following newspapers relevant to this project:

Baltimore
    Niles' Weekly Register, 1811–32
Canton
    Ohio Repository, 1815–28
Chillicothe
    Freeman's Journal and Chillicothe Advertiser, 1800
    Scioto Gazette, 1800–1815, 1827–28
    The Ohio Herald, 1805–6
    The Fredonian, 1807–9, 1811, 1812–15
    The Independent Republican, 1809–11
    The Supporter, 1808–18
    The Scioto Gazette and Fredonian Chronicle, 1815–21
    The Supporter and Scioto Gazette, 1821–27
Cincinnati
    Centinel of the North-Western Territory, 1793–96
    Freeman's Journal, 1796–1800
    Western Spy and Hamilton Gazette, 1799–1805
    Western Spy and Miami Gazette, 1805–9

Cincinnati Whig, 1809–10

The Advertiser, 1810–11

Western Spy, 1810–22

Liberty Hall and Cincinnati Mercury, 1804–11

Liberty Hall, 1811–15

Liberty Hall and Cincinnati Gazette, 1815–28

Spirit of the West, 1814–15

The Inquisitor and Cincinnati Advertiser, 1818–28

Independent Press, 1822–26

The National Republican and Ohio Political Register, 1823–28

Western Tiller, 1826–28

Circleville

The Fredonian, 1811–12

Cleveland

Cleaveland Herald, 1819–32 (also abstracted in Works Progress Administration, *Annals of Cleveland*)

Columbus

Columbus Gazette, 1817–25

Ohio Monitor, 1816–21, 1826–32

Ohio Monitor and Patron of Industry, 1821–26

Ohio State Journal, 1825–32

Dayton

The Dayton Repertory, 1808–9

The Ohio Centinel, 1810–13

Ohio Republican, 1813–16

Ohio Watchman, 1816–20

Delaware

Delaware Patron [and Franklin Chronicle], 1821–24

Franklinton

Freeman's Chronicle, 1812–14

Hamilton

Miami Intelligencer, 1814–16

Lancaster

Western Oracle, 1806–7

Political Observatory and Fairfield Register, 1810–11

Independent Press, 1811–12

Ohio Eagle, 1814–28

Lebanon

The Western Star, 1807–22

Marietta

The Ohio Gazette and Virginia Herald, 1802–11

The Commentator and Marietta Recorder, 1807–10

Western Spectator, 1810–13

American Friend, 1813–23
American Friend and Marietta Gazette, 1823–28
Marietta and Washington County Pilot, 1827–30
Mount Vernon
The Ohio Register, 1814–17
New Lisbon
Ohio Patriot, 1809–28
New Philadelphia
Tuscarawas Chronicle, 1821–27
Newark
The Advocate, 1821–27
St. Clairsville
Impartial Expositor, 1809
Belmont Repository, 1811–12
The Ohio Federalist [and Belmont Repository], 1813–18
St. Clairsville Gazette, 1825–28
National Historian and St. Clairsville Advertiser, 1827–28
Steubenville
Western Herald [and Steubenville Gazette], 1806–20, 1823–24, 1827–28
Urbana
Farmer's Watch-Tower, 1812
Warren
Trump of Fame, 1812–16
Western Reserve Chronicle, 1824–30
Williamsburgh
Western American, 1814–16
Wooster
The Wooster Spectator, 1821
The Ohio Oracle, 1826–27
Worthington
The Western Intelligencer, 1811–12
Franklin Chronicle, 1821
Zanesville
Muskingum Messenger, 1810–30
Zanesville Express, 1812–22
Ohio Republican, 1823–28

PRINTED WORKS

Broadsides, pamphlets, and handbills constitute some of the most interesting electoral material, found notably at the Ohio Historical Society, the American Antiquarian Society, the Ross County Historical Society, and Marietta College. Individual items of this kind are not listed here, but full details appear in the notes wherever specific reference is necessary. The following list includes printed primary works as well as the most relevant secondary literature, although I have not included many works, including county histories and travel accounts, that proved of only incidental value. Works cited only once in the notes are included here—as are some uncited works—if they were important in influencing my understanding of the subject.

Aaron, Daniel. *Cincinnati, Queen City of the West, 1818–1838.* Columbus: Ohio State University Press, 1992.

Adams, Alice Dana. *The Neglected Period of Anti-Slavery in America, 1808–1831.* Boston, 1908.

Albrecht, Carl W. Jr. "The Peaceable Kingdom: Ohio on the Eve of Settlement." *Timeline* 2 (June–July 1985): 18–25.

Aldrich, Lewis C. *History of Erie County, Ohio.* Syracuse, N.Y.: D. Mason, 1889.

Andrews, Israel Ward. *Washington County, and the Early Settlement of Ohio.* Cincinnati: P. G. Thompson, 1877.

Appleby, Joyce. "Commercial Farming and the 'Agrarian Myth' in the Old Republic." *Journal of American History* 68 (1982): 833–49.

———. *Capitalism and a New Social Order: The Republican Vision of the 1790s.* New York: New York University Press, 1984.

Aron, Stephen. *How the West Was Lost: The Transformation of Kentucky from Daniel Boone to Henry Clay.* Baltimore: Johns Hopkins University Press, 1996.

Aronson, Sidney H. *Status and Kinship in the Higher Civil Service: Standards of Selection in the Administrations of John Adams, Thomas Jefferson, and Andrew Jackson.* Cambridge: Harvard University Press, 1964.

Ashe, Thomas. *Travels in America, Performed in 1806. For the Purpose of Exploring the Rivers Alleghany, Monongehela, Ohio and Mississippi, and Ascertaining the Produce and Condition of Their Banks and Vicinity.* 3 vols. London: R. Phillips, 1808.

Atwater, Caleb. *A History of the State of Ohio, Natural and Civil.* Cincinnati: Glezen and Shepard, 1838.

Badger, Joseph. *A Memoir of Rev. Joseph Badger, Containing an Autobiography, and Selections from His Private Journal and Correspondence.* Hudson, Ohio: Sawyer, Ingersoll, 1851.

Baldwin, Leland D. "Shipbuilding on the Western Waters, 1793–1817." *Mississippi Valley Historical Review* 20 (1933–34): 29–44.

Banner, James M. Jr. *To the Hartford Convention: The Federalists and the Origins of Party Politics in Massachusetts, 1789–1815.* New York: Alfred A. Knopf, 1970.

Banning, Lance. *The Jeffersonian Persuasion: Evolution of a Party Ideology.* Ithaca, N.Y.: Cornell University Press, 1978.

Barker, John Marshall. *History of Ohio Methodism: A Study in Social Science.* Cincinnati: Curts and Jennings, 1898.

Barker, Joseph. *Recollections of the First Settlement of Ohio.* Edited by George E. Blazier. Marietta, Ohio: Marietta College, 1958.

Barlow, William R. "Ohio's Congressmen and the War of 1812." *Ohio History* 72 (1963): 175–94.

Barnhart, John D. "The Southern Element in the Leadership of the Old Northwest." *Journal of Southern History* 1 (1935): 186–97.

———. "The Southern Influence in the Formation of Ohio." *Journal of Southern History* 3 (1937): 28–42.

———, ed. "Letters of William H. Harrison to Thomas Worthington, 1799–1813." *Indiana Magazine of History* 47 (1951): 53–84.

———. *Valley of Democracy: The Frontier versus the Plantation in the Ohio Valley, 1775–1818*. Bloomington: Indiana University Press, 1953.

Bartlett, R. J. "The Struggle for Statehood in Ohio." *Ohio Archaeological and Historical Society Publications* 32 (1923): 472–503.

Bates, James L. *Alfred Kelley, His Life and Work*. Columbus: privately printed, 1888.

Beeman, Richard R. *The Old Dominion in the New Nation, 1788–1801*. Lexington: University Press of Kentucky, 1972.

———. *The Evolution of the Southern Backcountry: A Case Study of Lunenburg County, Virginia, 1746–1832*. Philadelphia: University of Pennsylvania Press, 1984.

Benson, Lee. *The Concept of Jacksonian Democracy: New York as a Test Case*. Princeton: Princeton University Press, 1961.

Benton, Elbert J., ed. "Letters from the Samuel Huntington Correspondence, 1800–1812." *Western Reserve Historical Society Tract* 95 (1915): 55–172.

———, ed. "The Connecticut Land Company and Accompanying Papers." *Western Reserve Historical Society Tract* 96 (1916): 59–64, 97–234.

———, ed. "Sidelights on the Ohio Company of Associates, from the John May Papers." *Western Reserve Historical Society Tract* 97 (1917): 63–231.

Berkhofer, Robert H. "The Northwest Ordinance and the Principle of Territorial Evolution." In John Porter Bloom, *American Territorial System*, 45–55.

Berquist, Goodwin, and Paul C. Bowers. "Worthington, Ohio: James Kilbourn's Episcopal Haven on the Western Reserve." *Ohio History* 85 (1976): 247–62.

———, and Paul C. Bowers. *The New Eden: James Kilbourne and the Development of Ohio*. Lanham, Md.: University Press of America, 1983.

Biographical Directory of the American Congress, 1774–1961. Washington, D.C.: Government Printing Office, 1961.

[Birchard, Matthew]. "Political Portraits, with Pen and Pencil, no. 19: Benjamin Tappan, Senator from Ohio." *United States Magazine and Democratic Review* 7 (June 1840): 540–62; 8 (July 1840): 42–51.

Blair, Clifford G. "James Findlay, Politician." M.A. thesis, Ohio State University, 1941.

Bloom, Jo Tice. "The Congressional Delegates from the Northwest Territory, 1799–1803." *Old Northwest* 3 (1977): 3–21.

Bloom, John Porter, ed. *The American Territorial System*. Athens: Ohio University Press, 1973.

Boase, Paul. "Moral Policemen on the Ohio Frontier." *Ohio Historical Quarterly* 68 (1959): 38–53.

Bogart, Ernest L. *Financial History of Ohio*. Urbana: University of Illinois Press, 1912.

———. "Taxation of Second Bank of the United States by Ohio." *American Historical Review* 17 (1912): 312–31.

Bohmer, David A. "The Maryland Electorate and the Concept of a Party System in the Early National Period." In Silbey, Bogue, and Flanigan, eds., *The History of American Electoral Behavior*, 146–73.

Bond, Beverley W. *The Civilization of the Old Northwest: A Study of Political, Social and Economic Development, 1788–1812*. New York: Macmillan, 1934.

———. *The Foundations of Ohio*. Vol. 1 of Wittke, ed., *History of the State of Ohio* (1941).

———, ed. "Memoirs of Benjamin Van Cleve." *Quarterly Publications of the Historical and Philosophical Society of Ohio* 17 (1922): 1–71.

———, ed. *The Correspondence of John Cleves Symmes, Founder of the Miami Purchase*. New York: Macmillan, 1926.

———, ed. *The Intimate Letters of John Cleves Symmes and His Family*. Cincinnati: Historical and Philosophical Society of Ohio, 1956.

A Brief Sketch of the Life and Public Services of Gen'l Samuel Herrick, from 1805 to 1831 Inclusive. Zanesville, 1849. Copy at OHS.

Brigham, Clarence S. *History and Bibliography of American Newspapers, 1690–1820*. 2 vols. Worcester, Mass.: American Antiquarian Society, 1947.

Broussard, James H. *The Southern Federalists, 1800–1816*. Baton Rouge: Louisiana State University Press, 1978.

Brown, Jeffrey P. "Frontier Politics: The Evolution of a Political Society in Ohio, 1788–1814." Ph.D. dissertation, University of Illinois, Urbana-Champaign, 1979.

———. "Samuel Huntington: A Connecticut Aristocrat on the Ohio Frontier." *Ohio History* 89 (1980): 420–38.

———. "Timothy Pickering and the Northwest Territory." Northwest *Ohio Quarterly* 53 (1981): 118–32.

———. "The Ohio Federalists, 1803–1815." *Journal of the Early Republic* 2 (1982): 261–82.

———. "William McMillan and the Conservative Cincinnati Jeffersonians." *Old Northwest* 12 (1986): 117–35.

———. "Chillicothe's Elite: Leadership in a Frontier Community." *Ohio History* 96 (1987): 101–23.

———. "Arthur St. Clair and the Northwest Territory." *Northwest Ohio Quarterly* 59 (1987): 75–90.

———. "The Political Culture of Early Ohio." In Brown and Cayton, eds., *The Pursuit of Public Power*, 1–14.

Brown, Jeffrey P., and Andrew R. L. Cayton, eds. *The Pursuit of Public Power: Political Culture in Ohio, 1787–1861*. Kent, Ohio: Kent State University Press, 1994.

Brown, Roger H. *The Republic in Peril: 1812*. New York: Columbia University Press, 1964.

Brown, Samuel R. *The Western Gazetteer; or, Emigrant's Directory, Containing a Geographical Description of the Western States and Territories*. Auburn, N.Y.: H. C. Southwick, 1820.

Buel, Richard Jr. *Securing the Revolution: Ideology in American Politics, 1789–1815*. Ithaca, N.Y.: Cornell University Press, 1972.

Buell, Rowena, ed. *The Memoirs of Rufus Putnam and Certain Official Papers and Correspondence*. Boston: Houghton Mifflin, 1903.

Buley, R. Carlyle. *The Old Northwest: Pioneer Period, 1815–1840.* 2 vols. Bloomington: Indiana Historical Society, 1950–51.

Bullock, Steven C. *Revolutionary Brotherhood: Freemasonry and the Transformation of the American Social Order.* Chapel Hill: University of North Carolina Press, 1996.

Burke, James L., and Donald E. Bensch. "Mount Pleasant and the Early Quakers of Ohio." *Ohio History* 83 (1974): 220–54.

Burnet, Jacob. "Letters Relating to the Early Settlement of the North-Western Territory, Contained in a Series Addressed to J. Delafield, Esq., during the Years 1837–38." *Transactions of the Historical and Philosophical Society of Ohio* 1 (1839), pt. 2: 9–180.

———. *Notes on the Early Settlement of the North-Western Territory.* Cincinnati: Derby, Bradley, 1847.

Bushnell, Henry. *The History of Granville, Licking County, Ohio.* Columbus: Hann and Adair, 1889.

Cady, John F. "Western Opinion and the War of 1812." *Ohio Archaeological and Historical Publications* 33 (1924): 427–76.

Caldwell, John Alexander. *History of Belmont and Jefferson Counties, Ohio.* Wheeling, Va.: Historical, 1880.

Campbell, John W. *Biographical Sketches; with Other Literary Remains of the Late John W. Campbell.* Columbus: Scott and Gallagher, 1838.

Carter, Judge [Alfred G. W.] *The Old Court House: Reminiscences and Anecdotes of the Courts and Bar of Cincinnati.* Cincinnati: P. G. Thomson, 1880.

Carter, Clarence E., ed. *The Territorial Papers of the United States,* vols. 2 and 3: *The Territory Northwest of the Ohio River, 1787–1803.* Washington, D.C.: Government Printing Office, 1934.

Cartwright, Peter. *The Backwoods Preacher, Being the Autobiography of Peter Cartwright.* London: Charles H. Kelly, [1856?].

Case, Leonard. "Early Settlement of Warren, Trumbull County, Ohio." *Western Reserve and Northern Ohio Historical Society Tract* 30 (1876): 1–14.

Cayton, Andrew R. L. " 'A Quiet Independence': The Western Vision of the Ohio Company." *Ohio History* 90 (1981): 9–32.

———. *The Frontier Republic: Ideology and Politics in the Ohio Country.* Kent, Ohio: Kent State University Press, 1986.

———. "The Failure of Michael Baldwin: A Case Study in the Origins of Middle-Class Culture on the Trans-Appalachian Frontier." *Ohio History* 95 (1986): 34–48.

———. "The Contours of Power in a Frontier Town: Marietta, Ohio, 1788–1803." *Journal of the Early Republic* 6 (1986): 103–26.

———. "Land, Power, and Reputation: The Cultural Dimension of Politics in the Ohio Country." *William and Mary Quarterly* 47 (1990): 266–86.

———. " 'Language Gives Way to Feelings': Rhetoric, Republicanism, and Religion in Jeffersonian Ohio." In Brown and Cayton, eds., *The Pursuit of Public Power,* 31–48.

Cayton, Andrew R. L., and Peter S. Onuf. *The Midwest and the Nation: Rethinking the History of an American Region.* Bloomington: Indiana University Press, 1990.

Chaddock, R. E. *Ohio before 1850: A Study of the Early Influence of Pennsylvania and Southern Populations in Ohio.* New York: Columbia University Press, 1908.

Chambers, William N. *Political Parties in a New Nation: The American Experience, 1776–1809.* New York: Oxford University Press, 1963.

Chambers, William N., and Walter D. Burnham, eds. *American Party Systems: Stages of Political Development.* New York: Oxford University Press, 1967.

Chase, Samuel P., ed. *The Statutes of Ohio and of the Northwestern Territory.* 3 vols. Cincinnati: Corey and Fairbank, 1833–35.

Church, Elijah Hart. *Early History of Zanesville by E.H.C.: Elijah Hart Church Stories from the* Zanesville Courier, *1874–1880.* Edited by Jeff Carskadden. Zanesville: Muskingum Valley Archaeological Survey, 1986.

Cleaves, Freeman. *Old Tippecanoe: William Henry Harrison and His Time.* New York: Scribner, 1939; reprint, Port Washington, N.Y.: Kennikat Press, 1969.

Commager, Henry Steele, ed. *Documents of American History.* New York: Appleton-Century-Crofts, 1963.

Conlin, Mary Lou. *Simon Perkins of the Western Reserve.* Cleveland: Western Reserve Historical Society, 1968.

Connor, Elizabeth. *Methodist Trail Blazer: Philip Gatch, 1751–1834: His Life in Maryland, Virginia, and Ohio.* Cincinnati: Creative, 1970.

Corry, William M. *Eulogy on William M'Millan, Esq., . . . October 28, 1837.* Cincinnati, 1838.

Cotton, John, M.D. "From Rhode Island to Ohio in 1815." *Journal of American History* 16 (1922): 36–49, 249–60.

Coward, Joan Wells. *Kentucky in the New Republic: The Process of Constitution Making.* Lexington: University Press of Kentucky, 1979.

Cox, Isaac Joslin, ed. "Selections from the Torrence Papers." *Quarterly Publications of the Historical and Philosophical Society of Ohio* 1 (1906): 63–96; 2 (1907): 5–36, 93–120; 3 (1908): 65–102; 6 (1911): 1–44; 13 (1918): 79–130.

Cramer, Clarence H. "The Career of Duncan McArthur." Ph.D. dissertation, Ohio State University, 1931.

Crary, Christopher G. *Pioneer and Personal Reminiscences.* Marshalltown, Iowa: Marshall Printing, 1893.

Cuming, Fortescue. *Sketches of a Tour to the Western Country, through the States of Ohio and Kentucky, 1807–1809.* Pittsburgh: Cramer, Spear, and Eichbaum, 1810. Also in Thwaites, *Early Western Travels, 1748–1846,* vol. 4. Cleveland: Arthur H. Clark, 1904–7.

Cummings, Abbot Lowell. "Ohio's Capitols at Columbus, 1810–1861." M.A. thesis, Ohio State University, 1948.

Cunningham, Noble E. Jr. *The Jeffersonian Republicans: The Formation of Party Organization, 1789–1801.* Chapel Hill: University of North Carolina Press, 1957.

———. *The Jeffersonian Republicans in Power, 1801–1809.* Chapel Hill: University of North Carolina, 1963.

[Cutler, Jervis]. *A Topographical Description of the State of Ohio, Indiana Territory, and Louisiana, . . . by a Late Officer in the U.S. Army.* Boston: Charles Williams, 1812.

Cutler, Julia Perkins, ed. *Life and Times of Ephraim Cutler, Prepared from His Journals and Correspondence.* Cincinnati: R. Clarke, 1890.

Cutler, William P., and Julia P. Cutler, eds. *Life, Journals, and Correspondence of Rev. Manasseh Cutler, Ll.D.* 2 vols. Cincinnati: R. Clarke, 1888.

Dauer, Manning J. *The Adams Federalists.* Baltimore: Johns Hopkins University Press, 1953.

De Chambrun, Clara Longworth. *Cincinnati: Story of the Queen City.* New York: Scribner, 1939.

Dickoré, Marie Paula, ed. *General Joseph Kerr, of Chillicothe, Ohio, "Ohio's Lost Senator."* Oxford, Ohio: Oxford Press, 1941.

Dillon, Merton L. *Benjamin Lundy and the Struggle for Negro Freedom.* Urbana: University of Illinois Press, 1966.

Downes, Randolph C. "Thomas Jefferson and the Removal of Governor St. Clair in 1802." *Ohio Archaeological and Historical Publications* 36 (1927): 62–77.

——. "The Statehood Contest in Ohio." *Mississippi Valley Historical Review* 18 (1931–32): 155–71.

——. "Ohio's Squatter Governor: William Hogland of Hoglandstown." *Ohio Archaeological and Historical Quarterly* 43 (1934): 273–82.

——. *Frontier Ohio, 1788–1803.* Columbus: Ohio State Archaeological and Historical Society, 1935.

——. *The Evolution of Ohio County Boundaries.* Columbus: Ohio Historical Society, 1970. Originally published in *Ohio Archaeological and Historical Publications* 36 (1927): 340–477.

Drake, Daniel. *Notices concerning Cincinnati.* Cincinnati, 1810. Reprinted in *Quarterly Publications of the Historical and Philosophical Society of Ohio* 3 (1908): 1–60.

——. *Natural and Statistical View; or, Picture of Cincinnati and the Miami Country.* Cincinnati, 1815.

Dunaway, Wayland F. "Pennsylvania as an Early Distributing Center of Population." *Pennsylvania Magazine of History and Biography* 55 (1931): 134–64.

Dunlevy, Anthony Howard. *History of the Miami Baptist Association; . . . 1797 to 1836.* Cincinnati: G. S. Blanchard, 1869.

Dwight, Margaret Van Horne. *A Journey to Ohio in 1810.* New Haven: Yale University Press, 1920.

Eblen, Jack F. *The First and Second United States Empires: Governors and Territorial Government, 1784–1912.* Pittsburgh: University of Pittsburgh, 1968.

Elkins, Stanley M., and Eric L. McKitrick. "A Meaning for Turner's Frontier: Democracy in the Old Northwest." *Political Science Quarterly* 69 (1954): 321–53.

——. *The Age of Federalism: The Early American Republic, 1788–1800.* New York: Oxford University Press, 1993.

Ellis, Richard E. *The Jeffersonian Crisis: Courts and Politics in the Young Republic.* New York, 1971.

Esarey, Logan, ed. *Messages and Papers of William Henry Harrison.* Vol. 9 of *Indiana Historical Collections,* in 2 vols. Indianapolis, 1922; reprint, New York: Arno Press, 1975.

Espy, Josiah M. "Memorandums of a Tour Made by Josiah Espy in the States of Ohio and Kentucky and Indiana Territory in 1805." *Ohio Valley Historical Series* 7, "Miscellanies," no. 1. Cincinnati: Robert Clarke, 1871.

Este, D[avid] K. *Discourse on the Life and Public Services of the Late Jacob Burnet.* Cincinnati: Cincinnati Gazette, 1853.

Etcheson, Nicole. "Public Interest and Private Good: Upland Southerners and Antebellum Midwestern Political Cultures." In Brown and Cayton, eds., *The Pursuit of Public Power,* 83–98.

———. "Manliness and the Political Culture of the Old Northwest." *Journal of the Early Republic* 15 (1995): 59–78.

———. *The Emerging Midwest: Upland Southerners and the Political Culture of the Old Northwest, 1787–1861.* Bloomington: Indiana University Press, 1996.

Evans, Nelson W. *History of Scioto County, Ohio.* Portsmouth, Ohio: N. W. Evans, 1903.

Evans, Nelson W., and Emmons B. Stivers. *A History of Adams County, Ohio, from the Earliest Settlement to the Present Time.* West Union: E. B. Stivers, 1900.

Everhart, J. F. *History of Muskingum County, Ohio.* Columbus: J. F. Everhart, 1882.

Faragher, John Mack. *Sugar Creek: Life on the Illinois Prairie.* New Haven: Yale University Press, 1986.

Farrell, Richard T. "Cincinnati in the Early Jackson Era, 1816–1834: An Economic and Political Study." Ph.D. dissertation, Indiana University, 1967.

Feller, Daniel. *The Public Lands in Jacksonian Politics.* Madison: University of Wisconsin Press, 1984.

———. "Benjamin Tappan: The Making of a Democrat." In Brown and Cayton, eds., *The Pursuit of Public Power,* 69–82.

Finley, James B. *Autobiography of James B. Finley; or, Pioneer Life in the West.* Edited by W. P. Strickland. Cincinnati: Methodist Book Concern, 1854.

———. *Sketches of Western Methodism: Biographical, Historical, and Miscellaneous, Illustrative of Pioneer Life.* Edited by W. P. Strickland. Cincinnati: Methodist Book Concern, 1854.

Fischer, David Hackett. *The Revolution of American Conservatism: The Federalist Party in the Era of Jeffersonian Democracy.* New York: Harper and Row, 1965.

Fisk, William L. "John Bailhache: A British Editor in Early Ohio." *Ohio Historical Quarterly* 67 (1958): 141–47.

Fitch, Raymond E., ed. *Breaking with Burr: Harman Blennerhassett's Journal, 1807.* Athens: Ohio University Press, 1988.

Flack, Irwin F. "Who Governed Cincinnati? A Comparative Analysis of Government and Social Structure in a Nineteenth-Century River City, 1819–1860." Ph.D. dissertation, University of Pittsburgh, 1977.

Flint, James. *Letters from America, Containing Observations on the Climate and Agriculture of the Western States, the Manners of the People, the Prospects of the Emigrants, etc., etc., 1818–20.* Edinburgh: W. and C. Tait, 1822. Also in Thwaites, *Early Western Travels, 1748–1846,* vol. 9.

Flint, Timothy. *Recollections of the Last Ten Years, Passed in Occasional Residences and*

Journeyings in the Valley of the Mississippi, from Pittsburgh and the Missouri to the Gulf of Mexico, and from Florida to the Spanish Frontier. Boston: Cummings, Hilliard, 1826.

———. *A Condensed Geography and History of the Western States, or the Mississippi Valley.* 2 vols. Cincinnati: E. H. Flint, 1828.

Foner, Philip S., ed. *The Democratic-Republican Societies, 1790–1800: A Documentary Sourcebook.* Westport, Conn.: Greenwood Press, 1976.

Formisano, Ronald P. "Deferential-Participant Politics: The Early Republic's Political Culture." *American Political Science Review* 68 (1974): 473–87.

———. "Federalists and Republicans: Parties, Yes—System, No." In Kleppner et al., *Evolution of American Electoral Systems,* 33–76.

———. *The Transformation of Political Culture: Massachusetts Parties, 1790s-1840s.* New York: Oxford University Press, 1983.

Fox, Stephen C. "The Group Bases of Ohio Political Behavior, 1803–1848." Ph.D. dissertation, University of Cincinnati, 1973. Reprinted, with some minor changes, as *The Group Bases of Ohio Political Behavior, 1803–1848.* New York: Garland, 1989.

———. "The Bank Wars, the Idea of 'Party,' and the Division of the Electorate in Jacksonian Ohio." *Ohio History* 88 (1979): 253–76.

Gallagher, John S., and Alan H. Patera. *The Post Offices of Ohio.* Burtonsville, Md., 1979.

Gilkey, Elliot Howard. *The Ohio Hundred Year Book: A Hand-Book of the Public Men and Public Institutions of Ohio, 1787–1901.* Columbus: Fred J. Heer, 1901.

Gilmore, William Edward. *Life of Edward Tiffin, First Governor of Ohio.* Chillicothe: Horney and Son, 1897.

Goebel, Dorothy Burne. *William Henry Harrison: A Political Biography.* Indianapolis: Historical Bureau of the Indiana Library and Historical Department, 1926.

Goodman, Paul. *The Democratic Republicans of Massachusetts: Politics in a Young Republic.* Cambridge: Harvard University Press, 1964.

———. "The First Party System." In Chambers and Burnham, eds., *American Party Systems,* 56–89.

Goodwin, Frank P. "The Development of the Miami Country." *Ohio Archaeological and Historical Society Publications* 18 (1909): 484–503.

Greve, Charles Theodore. *Centennial History of Cincinnati and Representative Citizens.* Chicago: Biographical, 1904.

Grupenhoff, John T. "Politics and the Rise of Political Parties in the Northwest Territory and Early Ohio to 1812, with Emphasis on Cincinnati and Hamilton County." Ph.D. dissertation, University of Texas, Austin, 1962.

Gutgesell, Stephen, ed. *Guide to Ohio Newspapers, 1793–1973: Union Bibliography of Ohio Newspapers Available in Ohio Libraries.* Columbus: Ohio Historical Society, 1976.

Hamlin, L. B., ed. "Selections from the Hatch Papers." *Quarterly Publications of the Historical and Philosophical Society of Ohio* 14 (1919): nos. 2 and 3.

———. "Selections from the Gano Papers." 7 parts. *Quarterly Publications of the Historical and Philosophical Society of Ohio* 15 (1920): 1–76, 77–105; 16 (1921): 21–50, 51–80; 17 (1922): 73–104; 18 (1923): 1–36; 19 (1924): 39–86.

Harlow, Alvin F. *The Serene Cincinnatians.* New York: Dutton, 1950.

Harris, Thaddeus Mason. *The Journal of a Tour into the Territory Northwest of the Alleghany Mountains; Made in the Spring of the Year 1803, with a Geographical and Historical Account of the State of Ohio.* Boston: Manning and Loring, 1805. Also in Thwaites, *Early Western Travels, 1748–1846,* vol. 3.

Harte, Brian. "Land in the Old Northwest: A Study of Speculation, Sales, and Settlement on the Connecticut Western Reserve." *Ohio History* 101 (1992): 114–39.

Hatcher, Harlan. *The Western Reserve: The Story of New Connecticut in Ohio.* Indianapolis: Bobbs-Merrill, 1949.

Heald, Edward Thornton. *Bezaleel Wells: Founder of Canton and Steubenville, Ohio.* Canton: Stark County Historical Society, [1942].

Heale, Michael J. *The Making of American Politics, 1750–1850.* London: Longman, 1977.

——. *The Presidential Quest: Candidates and Images in American Political Culture, 1787–1852.* London: Longman, 1982.

Henderson, H. James. "The First Party System." In *Perspectives on Early American History: Essays in Honor of Richard B. Morris,* edited by Alden T. Vaughan and George A. Billias, 325–71. New York: Harper and Row, 1973.

Henshaw, Leslie. "The Aaron Burr Conspiracy in the Ohio Valley." *Ohio Archaeological and Historical Society Publications* 24 (1915): 121–37.

Hickey, Donald R. "Federalist Party Unity and the War of 1812." *Journal of American Studies* 12 (1978): 23–40.

——. "The Federalists and the Coming of the War, 1811–1812." *Indiana Magazine of History* 75 (1979): 70–88.

Hildreth, Samuel P. "History of a Voyage from Marietta to New Orleans in 1805." in *Original Contributions to the American Pioneer by Dr. Samuel Prescott Hildreth.* Cincinnati: John S. Williams, 1844.

——. *Pioneer History: Being an Account of the First Examinations of the Ohio Valley, and the Early Settlement of the Northwest Territory.* Cincinnati and New York: H. W. Derby, 1848.

——. *Biographical and Historical Memoirs of the Early Pioneer Settlers of Ohio, with Narratives of Incidents and Occurrences in 1775.* Cincinnati: H. W. Derby, 1852.

——. *Genealogical and Biographical Sketches of the Hildreth Family, 1652–1840.* [Marietta?, c. 1911].

The History of Brown County, Ohio. Chicago: W. H. Beers, 1883.

A History and Biographical Cyclopaedia of Butler County, Ohio. Cincinnati: Western Biographical, 1882.

History of Clermont County, Ohio. Philadelphia: Louis H. Evarts, 1880.

History of the Fire Lands, Comprising Huron and Erie Counties, Ohio. Cleveland: [W. W. Williams], 1879.

History of Geauga and Lake Counties, Ohio. Philadelphia: Williams Brothers, 1878.

History of Ross and Highland Counties. Cleveland, 1880.

Hoadley, John F. *Origins of American Political Parties, 1789–1803.* Lexington: University Press of Kentucky, 1986.

Hockett, Homer C. *Western Influences on Political Parties: An Essay in Historical Inter-pretation.* No. 4 of *Ohio State University Studies, Contributions in History and Political Science.* Columbus: Ohio State University, 1917.

Hofstadter, Richard. *The Idea of a Party System: The Rise of Legitimate Opposition in the United States, 1780–1840.* Berkeley: University of California Press, 1969.

Hooper, Osman Castle. *History of Ohio Journalism, 1793–1933.* Columbus: Spahr and Glenn, 1933.

Hopkins, James F., and Mary W. M. Hargreaves, eds. *The Papers of Henry Clay.* 8 vols. Lexington: University Press of Kentucky, 1959–84.

Horsman, Reginald. "Western War Aims, 1811–1812." *Indiana Magazine of History* 53 (1957): 1–18.

Howe, Eber D. *Autobiography and Recollections of a Pioneer Printer* [Painesville: Tele-graph Steam Printing House, 1878].

Howe, Henry. *Historical Collections of Ohio.* 1st ed. Cincinnati: Derby, Bradley, 1847.

———. *Historical Collections of Ohio.* Ohio Centennial edition. 2 vols. Norwalk: Laning Printing, 1896, and Cincinnati: C. J. Krehbiel, 1900.

Howe, John R. Jr. "Republican Thought and the Political Violence of the 1790s." *American Quarterly* 19 (1967): 147–65.

Howells, William C. *Recollections of the Life in Ohio, 1813–1840.* Cincinnati: Robert Clarke, 1895.

Howson, Embury. "The German Element in Ohio, 1803–30." Research paper, 1950. At OHS.

Hudson, John C. "North American Origins of Middlewestern Populations." *Annals of the Association of American Geographers* 78 (1988): 395–413.

Hulbert, Archer B. *The Cumberland Road.* Cleveland, 1904.

———. "Western Ship-Building." *American Historical Review* 21 (1916): 725–33.

Hunter, W. H. "The Pathfinders of Jefferson County." *Ohio Archaeological and Historical Society Publications* 6 (1900): 95–313, 384–406.

Huntington, Charles C. *A History of Banking and Currency in Ohio before the Civil War.* Columbus: Ohio Archaeological and Historical Publications, 1915. Reprinted from *Ohio Archaeological and Historical Quarterly* 24 (1915): no. 3.

Hutchinson, William Thomas. "The Bounty Lands of the American Revolution in Ohio." Ph.D. dissertation, University of Chicago, 1927.

Isaac, Rhys. *The Transformation of Virginia, 1740–1790.* Chapel Hill: University of North Carolina Press, 1982.

John, Richard R. *Spreading the News: The American Postal System from Franklin to Morse.* Cambridge: Harvard University Press, 1995.

[Jones, Emma, ed.] *A State in the Making: Correspondence of James Kilbourne.* Columbus, 1913.

Jordan, Philip D. *The National Road.* Indianapolis: Bobbs-Merrill, 1948.

Journal of the House of Representatives of the State of Ohio, 1803–30.

Journal of the Senate of the State of Ohio, 1803–30.

Joyner, Fred B. "William Cortenus Schenck, Pioneer and Statesman of Ohio." *Ohio Archaeological and Historical Quarterly* 40 (1938): 363–71.

Kantzer, Kenneth Sealer. "The Municipal Legislation in Ohio to 1851." M.A. thesis, Ohio State University, 1939.

Katzenberger, George A. "Major David Ziegler." *Ohio Archaeological and Historical Society Quarterly* 21 (1912): 127–74.

Kelley, Robert. *The Cultural Pattern in American Politics: The First Century.* New York: Alfred A. Knopf, 1979.

Kennedy, William S. *The Plan of Union; or, A History of the Presbyterian and Congregational Churches of the Western Reserve.* Hudson: Pentagon Steam Press, 1856.

Ketcham, Ralph. *Presidents above Party: The First American Presidency, 1789–1829.* Chapel Hill: University of North Carolina Press, 1984.

Ketring [Nuermberger], Ruth Anna. *Charles Osborn in the Anti-Slavery Movement.* No. 7 of *Ohio Historical Collections.* Columbus: Ohio Archaeological and Historical Society, 1937.

Kilbourn, John. *A Geography of Ohio, Designed for Common Schools.* Columbus: E. Glover, 1830.

———. *The Ohio Gazetteer; or, Topographical Dictionary.* 6th ed., improved. Columbus: J. Kilbourn, 1819.

———. *The Ohio Gazetteer; or, Topographical Dictionary, Being a Continuation of the Work Compiled by the Late John Kilbourn.* 11th ed., revised and enlarged. Columbus: Scott and Wright, 1833.

Kilbourne, James. Various items, including his "Autobiography" and "Congressional Career." *Old Northwest Genealogical Quarterly* 6 (1903): 111–46.

Klein, Rachel N. *Unification of a Slave State: The Rise of the Planter Class in South Carolina.* Chapel Hill: University of North Carolina Press, 1990.

Kleppner, Paul. *The Third Electoral System, 1853–1892: Parties, Voters, and Political Cultures.* Chapel Hill: University of North Carolina Press, 1979.

Kleppner, Paul et al. *The Evolution of American Electoral Systems.* Westport, Conn.: Greenwood Press, 1981.

Klingaman, David, C., and Richard K. Vedder. *Essays in Nineteenth Century Economic History: The Old Northwest.* Athens: Ohio University Press, 1975.

Knabenshue, S. S. "Indian Land Cessions in Ohio." *Ohio State Archaeological and Historical Quarterly* 9 (1903): 249–55.

Knopf, Richard C., ed. *Document Transcriptions of the War of 1812 in the Northwest,* vols. 2 and 3. Columbus: Ohio Historical Society, 1957.

Leavitt, Humphrey Howe. *Autobiography of the Hon. Humphrey Howe Leavitt, Written for His Family.* New York, 1893.

Link, Eugene Perry. *Democratic-Republican Societies, 1790–1800.* New York: Columbia University Press, 1942.

Lipson, Dorothy A. *Freemasonry in Federalist Connecticut, 1789–1835.* Princeton: Princeton University Press, 1978.

Livermore, Shaw. *The Twilight of Federalism, 1815–1830.* Princeton: Princeton University Press, 1967.

Lloyd, W. A., J. I. Falconer, and C. E. Thorne. *The Agriculture of Ohio.* Bulletin 326 of the Ohio Agricultural Experimentation Center. Wooster, 1918.

McBride, James. *Pioneer Biography: Sketches of the Lives of Some of the Early Settlers of Butler County, Ohio*. 2 vols. Cincinnati: Robert Clarke, 1869.

McCormick, Richard P. *The Second American Party System: Party Formation in the Jacksonian Era*. Chapel Hill: University of North Carolina Press, 1966.

———. "Political Development and the Second Party System." In Chambers and Burnham, eds., *American Party Systems*, 91–116.

McDonald, John. *Biographical Sketches of General Nathaniel Massie, General Duncan McArthur, Capt. William Wells, and General Simon Kenton, Who Were Early Settlers in the Western Country*. Cincinnati: E. Morgan, 1838.

Mansfield, Edward Deering. *Memoirs of the Life and Services of Daniel Drake, M.D., Physician, Professor, and Author; with Notices of the Early Settlement of Cincinnati and Some of Its Pioneer Citizens*. Cincinnati: Applegate, 1855.

———. *Personal Memories, Social, Political, and Literary, 1803–1843*. Cincinnati: R. Clarke, 1879.

Marsh, Roswell. *The Life of Charles Hammond, of Cincinnati, Ohio*. Steubenville, 1863.

Marshall, Lynn L. "The Strange Stillbirth of the Whig Party." *American Historical Review* 72 (1967): 425–44.

Martin, William T. *History of Franklin County, Ohio*. Columbus: Follett, Foster, 1858.

Martzolff, Clement L., ed. "Reminiscences of a Pioneer [Thomas Rogers Sr.]." *Ohio Archaeological and Historical Society Publications* 19 (1910): 190–227.

———, ed. "The Autobiography of Thomas Ewing." *Ohio Archaeological and Historical Society Publications* 22 (1913): 126–204.

———, ed. "Rev. Paul Henkel's Journal: His Missionary Journey to the State of Ohio in 1806." *Ohio Archaeological and Historical Society Publications* 23 (1914): 162–218.

Massie, David Meade. *Nathaniel Massie, a Pioneer of Ohio: A Sketch of His Life and Selections from His Correspondence*. Cincinnati, 1896.

[Mathews, Alfred, et al.]. *History of Washington County, Ohio*. Cleveland: H. Z. Williams and Bros., 1881.

Michaux, François André. *Travels to the West of the Alleghany Mountains, in the States of Ohio, Kentucky and Tennessee, and Back to Charleston, . . . in the Year 1802*. London, 1805. Also in Thwaites, *Early Western Travels, 1748–1846*, vol. 3.

Miller, James M. *The Genesis of Western Culture, 1800–1825: The Upper Ohio Valley, 1800–1825*. No. 9 of *Ohio Historical Collections*. Columbus: Ohio Archaeological and Historical Society, 1938.

Miller, Randall M. "The Union Humane Society: A Quaker-Gradualist Antislavery Society in Early Ohio." *Quaker History* 61 (1972): 91–106.

Millett, Stephen M. "Bellicose Nationalism in Ohio: An Origin of the War of 1812." *Canadian Review of Studies in Nationalism* 1 (1974): 221–40.

Moore, Glover. *The Missouri Controversy, 1819–1821*. Lexington: University Press of Kentucky, 1953.

Morris, B[enjamin] F. *The Life of Thomas Morris*. Cincinnati: Moore, Wilstach, Keep, and Overend, 1856.

Morrow, Josiah, ed. *Life and Speeches of Thomas Corwin, Orator, Lawyer, and Statesman*. Cincinnati: W. H. Anderson, 1896.

Nichols, Roy F. *The Invention of the American Political Parties: A Study of Political Improvisation.* New York: Macmillan, 1967.

Noyes, Mrs. Charles P. [Gilman, Emily Hoffman]. *A Family History in Letters and Documents, 1667–1837.* 2 vols. St. Paul, Minn.: Privately printed, 1919.

O'Dell, Richard Frederick. "The Early Anti-Slavery Movement in Ohio." Ph.D. dissertation, University of Michigan, 1948.

"Old Marietta Newspapers," *Marietta Register,* June 1863-January 1864.

Onuf, Peter S. "From Constitution to Higher Law: The Reinterpretation of the Northwest Ordinance." *Ohio History* 94 (1985): 5–33.

———. "Liberty, Development, and Union: Visions of the West in the 1780s." *William and Mary Quarterly* 43 (1986): 179–213.

———. *Statehood and Union: A History of the Northwest Ordinance.* Bloomington: Indiana University Press, 1987.

Owens, Kenneth N. "Pattern and Structure in Western Territorial Politics." In John Porter Bloom, ed., *American Territorial System,* 161–79.

Parish, John C. *Robert Lucas.* Iowa City: State Historical Society of Iowa, 1907.

[Peter, Sarah Worthington King]. *A Private Memoir of Thomas Worthington, of Adena, Ross County, Ohio.* Cincinnati: Robert Clarke, 1882.

Petty, Gerald M., comp. *Ohio 1810 Tax Duplicate, Arranged in a Statewide Alphabetical List of Names of Taxpayers.* Columbus: G. M. Petty, 1976.

Phillips, Kim T. "William Duane, Philadelphia's Democratic Republicans, and the Origins of Modern Politics." *Pennsylvania Magazine of History and Biography* 101 (1977): 365–87.

Pitcher, M. Avis. "John Smith, First Senator from Ohio and His Connections with Aaron Burr." *Ohio Archaeological and Historical Quarterly* 45 (1936): 68–88.

Pocock, Emil. "Evangelical Frontier: Dayton, Ohio, 1796–1830." Ph.D. dissertation, Indiana University, 1984.

———. "Popular Roots of Jacksonian Democracy: The Case of Dayton, Ohio, 1815–30." *Journal of the Early Republic* 9 (1989): 489–515.

———. "A Candidate I'll Surely Be: Election Practices in Early Ohio, 1798–1825." In Brown and Cayton, eds., *The Pursuit of Public Power,* 49–68.

Power, Richard Lyle. *Planting Corn Belt Culture: The Impress of the Upland Southerner and Yankee in the Old Northwest.* Indianapolis: Indiana Historical Society, 1953.

Prince, Carl. *New Jersey's Jeffersonian Republicans: The Genesis of an Early Party Machine, 1789–1817.* Chapel Hill: University of North Carolina Press, 1967.

Ratcliffe, Donald J. "Captain James Riley and Antislavery Sentiment in Ohio, 1819–1824." *Ohio History* 81 (1972): 76–94.

———. "The Role of Voters and Issues in Party Formation: Ohio, 1824." *Journal of American History* 59 (1973): 847–70.

———. "The Experience of Revolution and the Beginnings of Party Politics in Ohio, 1776–1816." *Ohio History* 85 (1976): 186–230.

———, ed. "The Autobiography of Benjamin Tappan." *Ohio History* 85 (1976): 109–57.

———. "Politics in Jacksonian Ohio: Reflections on the Ethnocultural Interpretation." *Ohio History* 88 (1979): 5–36.

———. "Voter Turnout in Early Ohio." *Journal of American History* 7 (1987): 223–52.

———. "The Mystery of Ohio's Missing Presidential Election Returns, 1804–1848." *Archival Issues* 17 (1992): 137–44.

Reemelin, Charles. "Reminiscences of Moses Dawson." In *Cincinnati Commercial,* 29 December 1869–14 March 1870.

Riddle, Albert G. "The Rise of the Antislavery Sentiment on the Western Reserve." *Magazine of Western History* 6 (1887): 145–56.

Risjord, Norman K. "1812: Conservatives, War Hawks, and the Nation's Honor." *William and Mary Quarterly* 18 (1961): 196–210.

———. "The Virginia Federalists." *Journal of Southern History* 33 (1967).

Rohrbough, Malcolm J. *The Land Office Business: The Settlement and Administration of American Public Lands, 1789–1837.* New York: Oxford University Press, 1968.

———. *The Trans-Appalachian Frontier: People, Societies, and Institutions, 1775–1850.* New York: Oxford University Press, 1978.

Rohrer, James Russell. "Battling the Master Vice: The Evangelical War against Intemperance in Ohio, 1800–1832." M.A. thesis, Ohio State University, 1985.

Rose, Albert H. *Ohio Government, State and Local.* Dayton, 1948.

Rothbard, Murray N. *The Panic of 1819: Reactions and Policies.* New York: Columbia University Press, 1962.

Ruggles, Benjamin. *An Oration Delivered at the New Meeting House in Marietta . . . on the Fourth of July, 1809.* Marietta: Samuel Fairlamb, 1809.

Ryan, Daniel J. "Nullification in Ohio." *Ohio Archaeological and Historical Society Publications* 2 (1888): 413–22.

———, ed. "From Charter to Constitution." *Ohio Archaeological and Historical Society Publications* 5 (1897): 1–164.

Scheiber, Harry S. "Entrepreneurship and Western Development: The Case of Micajah T. Williams." *Business History Review* 37 (1963): 344–68.

Schneider, Norris F. *Y-Bridge City: The Story of Zanesville.* Cleveland: World, 1950.

Sears, Alfred B. "The Political Philosophy of Arthur St. Clair." *Ohio Archaeological and Historical Quarterly* 49 (1940): 41–57.

———. *Thomas Worthington: Father of Ohio Statehood.* Columbus: Ohio State University Press, 1958.

Shannon, Timothy J. "The Ohio Company and the Meaning of Opportunity in the American West, 1786–1795." *New England Quarterly* 64 (1991): 393–413.

———. "This Unpleasant Business: The Transformation of Land Speculation in the Ohio Country, 1787–1820." In Brown and Cayton, eds., *The Pursuit of Public Power,* 15–30.

Sharp, James Roger. *American Politics in the Early Republic: The New Nation in Crisis.* New Haven: Yale University Press, 1993.

Shepard, Claude L. "The Connecticut Land Company: A Study in the Beginnings of Colonization of the Western Reserve." *Western Reserve Historical Society Tract* 96 (1916): 65–96.

Silbey, Joel H. *The American Political Nation, 1838–1893.* Stanford, Calif.: Stanford University Press, 1991.

———. "Beyond Realignment and Realignment Theory: American Political Eras, 1789–

1989." In *The End of Realignment? Interpreting American Electoral Eras,* edited by Byron E. Schafer, 2–23. Madison: University of Wisconsin Press, 1991.

Silbey, Joel H., Allan G. Bogue, and William H. Flanigan. *The History of American Electoral Behavior.* Princeton: Princeton University Press, 1978.

Skeen, C. Edward. "Vox Populi, Vox Dei: The Compensation Act of 1816 and the Rise of Popular Politics." *Journal of the Early Republic* 6 (1986): 253–74.

Slaughter, Thomas P. *The Whiskey Rebellion: Frontier Epilogue to the American Revolution.* New York: Oxford University Press, 1986.

Smelser, Marshall. "The Federalist Period as an Age of Passion." *American Quarterly* 10 (1958): 391–419.

———. "The Jacobin Phrenzy: The Menace of Monarchy, Plutocracy, and Anglophobia, 1789–1798." *Review of Politics* 21 (1959): 239–58.

Smith, Dwight L., ed. "Nine Letters of Nathaniel Dike on the Western Country, 1816–1818." *Ohio Historical Quarterly* 67 (1958): 189–220.

Smith, H. E. "The Quakers, Their Migration to the Upper Ohio, Their Customs and Discipline." *Ohio Archaeological and Historical Society Publications* 37 (1928): 35–85.

Smith, William Henry, ed. *The St. Clair Papers: The Life and Public Services of Arthur St. Clair.* 2 vols. Cincinnati: Robert Clarke, 1882.

———. *Charles Hammond and His Relations to Henry Clay and John Quincy Adams; or, Constitutional Limitations and the Contest for Freedom of Speech and the Press.* Chicago: Chicago Historical Society, 1885.

———. "A Familiar Talk about Monarchists and Jacobins." *Ohio Archaeological and Historical Quarterly* 2 (1888): 187–205.

Soltow, Lee. "Inequality amidst Abundance: Land Ownership in Early Nineteenth-Century Ohio." *Ohio History* 88 (1979): 133–51.

———. "Progress and Mobility among Ohio Propertyholders, 1810–1825." *Social Science Quarterly* 7 (1983): 405–26.

———. "Tocqueville's View of the Northwest in 1835: Ohio a Generation after Settlement." In *Essays on the Economy of the Old Northwest,* edited by D. C. Klingaman and Richard K. Vedder, 131–55. Athens: Ohio University Press, 1987.

Stagg, J. C. A. *Mr. Madison's War: Politics, Diplomacy, and Warfare in the Early American Republic, 1783–1830.* Princeton: Princeton University Press, 1983.

Stevens, Harry R. "Bank Enterprisers in a Western Town, 1815–1822." *Business History Review* 29 (1955): 139–56.

———. *The Early Jackson Party in Ohio.* Durham, N.C.: Duke University Press, 1957.

———. "Samuel Watts Davies and the Industrial Revolution in Cincinnati." *Ohio Historical Quarterly* 70 (1961): 95–127.

Stewart, Donald H. *The Opposition Press of the Federalist Period.* Albany: State University of New York Press, 1969.

Still, John S. "The Life of Ethan Allen Brown, Governor of Ohio." Ph.D. dissertation, Ohio State University, 1951.

Stuckey, James Herbert. "The Formation of Leadership Groups in a Frontier Town: Canton, Ohio, 1805–1855." Ph.D. dissertation, Case Western Reserve University, 1976.

Swierenga, Robert P. "The Settlement of the Old Northwest: Ethnic Pluralism in a Featureless Plain." *Journal of the Early Republic* 9 (1989): 73–105.

Taylor, Alan. *Liberty Men and Great Proprietors: The Revolutionary Settlement on the Maine Frontier, 1760–1820.* Chapel Hill: University of North Carolina Press, 1990.

———. *William Cooper's Town: Power and Persuasion on the Frontier of the Early American Frontier.* New York: Alfred A. Knopf, 1995.

Taylor, George R. "Agrarian Discontent in the Mississippi Valley preceding the War of 1812." *Journal of Political Economy* 39 (1931): 471–505.

———. "Prices in the Mississippi Valley preceding the War of 1812." *Journal of Economic and Business History* 3 (1930–31): 148–63.

Thurston, Helen M. "The 1802 Constitutional Convention and the Status of the Negro." *Ohio History* 81 (1972): 15–37.

Thwaites, Reuben Gold. *Early Western Travels, 1748–1846.* 32 vols. Cleveland: Arthur H. Clark, 1904–7.

Tinkcom, Harry M. *The Republicans and Federalists in Pennsylvania, 1791–1801: A Study in National Stimulus and Local Response.* Harrisburg: Pennsylvania Historical and Museum Commission, 1950.

Trimble, Allen. *Autobiography and Correspondence of Allen Trimble, Governor of Ohio.* [Edited by Mary M. Tuttle and Henry B. Thompson]. N.p.: The "Old Northwest" Genealogical Society, 1909. Reprinted from *Old Northwest Genealogical Quarterly* 10 (1907): 259–74, 301–42; 11 (1908): 14–37, 130–51.

Tuttle, Mary M. "William Allen Trimble, United States Senator from Ohio." *Ohio Archaeological and Historical Publications* 14 (1905): 225–47.

United States Census. *Second Census of the United States: Return of the Whole Number of Persons within the Several Districts of the United States . . . 1800.* Washington, D.C., 1801.

———. *Aggregate Amount of Persons within the United States in the Year 1810.* Washington, D.C., 1811.

———. *Census for 1820.* Washington, D.C., 1821.

Utter, William T. "Judicial Review in Early Ohio." *Mississippi Valley Historical Review* 14 (1927): 3–24.

———. "Saint Tammany in Ohio: A Study in Frontier Politics." *Mississippi Valley Historical Review* 15 (1928): 321–40.

———. "Ohio and the English Common Law." *Mississippi Valley Historical Review* 16 (1929): 321–33.

———. "Ohio Politics and Politicians, 1812–1815." Ph.D. dissertation, University of Chicago, 1929.

———. *The Frontier State, 1803–1825.* Vol. 2 of Wittke, ed., *History of the State of Ohio* (1942).

———. *Granville: The Story of an Ohio Village.* Granville, Ohio: Denison University, 1956.

Van Cleve, John W. "A Brief History of the Settlement of the Town of Dayton." *Journal of the Historical and Philosophical Society of Ohio,* 1832. Reprinted as *Transactions of the Historical and Philosophical Society of Ohio:* 1 (1872): pt. 1.

Wade, Richard C. *The Urban Frontier: The Rise of Western Cities, 1790–1830*. Cambridge: Harvard University Press, 1959.

Wallace, Michael. "Changing Concepts of Party in the United States: New York, 1815–1828." *American Historical Review* 79 (1968): 453–91.

Webster, Homer J. "History of the Democratic Party Organization in the Northwest, 1824–1840." *Ohio Archaeological and Historical Society Publications* 24 (1915): 1–120.

Weisenburger, Francis P. "Charles Hammond, the First Great Journalist of the Old Northwest." *Ohio Archaeological and Historical Publications* 43 (1934): 340–427.

———. *The Life of John McLean, a Politician on the United States Supreme Court*. Columbus: Ohio State University Press, 1937; reprint, New York: Da Capo Press, 1971.

———. "The Middle Western Antecedents of Woodrow Wilson." *Mississippi Valley Historical Review* 23 (1936): 375–90.

White, Lonnie J. *Politics on the Southwestern Frontier: Arkansas Territory, 1819–1836*. Memphis: Memphis State University Press, 1964.

Whittlesey, Charles. *Early History of Cleveland, Ohio*. Cleveland: Fairbanks, Benedict, 1867.

Wilgus, James Alva. "Evolution of Township Government in Ohio." *Annual Report* of the American Historical Association, 403–12. Washington, D.C., 1894.

Wilkeson, S. "Early Recollections of the West." In John Williams, ed., *American Pioneer*, 2:139–43, 158–64, 203–17, 269–73, 368–71.

[Williams, Charles]. "Auto-Sketch of Charles Williams." *Ohio Archaeological and Historical Publications* 18 (1909): 372–82.

Williams, John S., ed. *The American Pioneer: A Monthly Periodical Devoted to the Objects of the Logan Historical Society*. 2 vols. Cincinnati: John S. Williams, 1842–43.

Williams, Samuel W. *Pictures of Early Methodism in Ohio*, Cincinnati: Jennings and Graham, 1909.

———. "The Tammany Society in Ohio." *Ohio Archaeological and Historical Publications* 22 (1913): 349–70.

Williamson, Chilton. *American Suffrage from Property to Democracy, 1760–1860*. Princeton: Princeton University Press, 1960.

Wing, George Clary, ed. *Early Years on the Western Reserve, with Extracts from Letters of Ephraim Brown and Family, 1805–1845*. Cleveland: Arthur H. Clarke, [1916].

Winkle, Kenneth J. *The Politics of Community: Migration and Politics in Antebellum Ohio*. New York: Cambridge University Press, 1988.

———. "Ohio's Informal Polling Place: Nineteenth-Century Suffrage in Theory and Practice." In Brown and Cayton, eds., *The Pursuit of Public Power*, 169–84.

Wittke, Carl, ed. *A History of the State of Ohio*. 6 vols. Columbus: Ohio State Archaeological and Historical Society, 1941–44.

Wolfe, William G. *Stories of Guernsey County, Ohio*. Cambridge, Ohio: W. G. Wolfe, 1943.

Wood, Gordon S. *The Creation of the American Republic, 1776–1787*. Chapel Hill: University of North Carolina Press, 1969.

———. *The Radicalism of the American Revolution*. New York: Alfred A. Knopf, 1992.

Work Projects Administration (WPA) in Ohio. *Annals of Cleveland, 1818–1935: A Digest and Index of the Newspaper Record of Events and Opinions.* Cleveland: WPA, 1937–38.

Worth, Gorham A. *Recollections of Cincinnati, from a Residence of Five Years, 1817–1821.* Albany, N.Y.: Charles Van Benthuysen, 1851. Reprinted in *Quarterly Publications of the Historical and Philosophical Society of Ohio* 11 (1916): nos. 2 and 3.

Yeager, Helen F. "The Rise, Spread, and Influence of Religion in Ohio, 1783–1815." M.A. thesis, University of Cincinnati, 1942.

Young, Alfred. "The Mechanics and the Jeffersonians: New York, 1789–1801." *Labor History* 5 (1964): 247–76.

———. *Democratic Republicans of New York: The Origins, 1763–1797.* Chapel Hill: University of North Carolina Press, 1967.

Young, James Sterling. *The Washington Community, 1800–1828.* New York: Columbia University Press, 1966.

INDEX

Where appropriate, subentries are in chronological or logical order, rather than alphabetical order.